THE VIEW FROM THE BRIDGE:

AN INDUSTRIAL JOURNEY

Sir John Parker

Edited by Andrew Lorenz

First published in 2018 by Sir John Parker

This hardback edition published in 2018
by Sir John Parker

ISBN 978-1-911445-79-1

Typeset using Atomik ePublisher from Easypress Technologies

Printed and bound in Great Britain by
Clays Ltd, Elcograf S.p.A.

**This book is dedicated to my grandsons
– the emerging generation:**

Jack Parker Curry
Charlie Edward Curry
Alfie George Curry
Arthur Thomas Parker

May they derive similar levels of fulfilment in their work,
friendships, recreation and family as I have been privileged to do.

To: Andrew

All good wishes

John

CONTENTS

FOREWORD

There are many textbooks on management and leadership. This is not intended to be another one. Instead it records real corporate life experiences, crises and lessons learned, including many on leadership, during a lengthy industrial journey.

My hope is that aspiring business leaders may find some inspiration and value from the experiences on this particular journey.

My leadership style has been forged from the rich experiences gleaned alongside other human beings engaged in the common endeavour of leading company boardrooms in a range of industries, learned institutions and in voluntary work.

It all started on my father's farm in the Slievenaman Valley in Co. Down, Northern Ireland where many behavioural values were embedded. As I grew up, I learned the importance of hard work, integrity, respect for others, managing your time and focussing on priorities. These have served me well on the journey.

It's a journey that's been filled with the unexpected and some amazing coincidences, opportunities and challenges.

It could not have been accomplished without the support, advice, companionship and team work of so many great people in my life.

I acknowledge them all with gratitude.

Sir John Parker,
August 2018.

1. THE CHALLENGE OF LEADERSHIP IN CORPORATE LIFE

The axiom "Change is constant" was coined by the British Prime Minister Benjamin Disraeli. For businesses today, in the 21st century, that truth is even more relevant than when Disraeli articulated it at the height of the Victorian era.

Yet few established companies or organisations embrace the full meaning of the expression. As I reflect on the leadership challenges I have faced in my own industrial and corporate career of well over 50 years, there is only one constant: the need to lead and adapt to continuous change, wherever the need for change comes from – to adapt your business to changes in customer demands, market changes, changes in economic conditions, changes due to competitors' actions, regulatory changes, and other factors. Today's status quo is never an option for tomorrow.

Leading change requires you to develop and communicate a clear intent. You as a leader must have the courage to make change in the interest of the successful longevity of the company. The higher up the tree you go, the more responsibility falls on you: you must accept that. To adapt the company to this dynamic world, you need to embed in its culture the flexibility to change. If you deal with change in the right way, that is an exciting challenge.

At its heart, leadership is an art, not a science. A leader has to

understand human nature. For most people, companies and organisations embracing the full meaning of the inevitability of change is
challenging. We are creatures of habit and so are our organisations –
so change can feel like a threat. That's hardly surprising when change
now comes at us from so many places and at a pace and on a scale
never encountered before.

I think too of very dramatic change and the leadership needed in
corporate turnaround situations where radical, even revolutionary
action is needed to save a company on the verge of collapse or bankruptcy. I've gone into four such grave situations in my life, Harland &
Wolff, the Belfast shipbuilder, during the Northern Ireland Troubles
of the 1980s; the engineering group Babcock International in the
1990s; RMC, the cement and aggregates producer, in the early 2000s;
and leading the Board of Anglo American, the mining company,
first during the mining industry crisis and takeover threat of 2009
and, second, in the commodities price depression of 2014–2016. I
learned many valuable lessons on leadership in all of these situations.

Turnarounds are tough and often emotionally draining work. You
generally need to act very quickly to replace ineffective directors
and managers. A lot of energy also has to go into communicating
with employees, shareholders and banks. The demands on your
time are massive.

I've learned that, where a company is bleeding and suffering, one
ingredient is generally present: weak leadership at the top or in large
sections of the boardroom. Leadership that has failed to ensure that
the company adapted in the face of changing market circumstances,
or has foolishly overpaid for an acquisition and even more foolishly
over-stretched its balance sheet.

Of all the lessons I learned with these turnarounds, one stood out:
in such a situation, changing the leadership is often the key ingredient. The Chairman or the CEO is often the first and a very good
place to start, with the FD/CFO often not far behind – although he
or she may on occasions be the victim of weak Executive colleagues,
supported by a weak CEO! It is said that the fish rots from the head:

if the corporate leadership isn't right and hasn't got the right experience, knowledge, energy or will to bring about necessary change, then a turnaround will not happen.

Also pivotal is the role of the Non-Executive Directors (NXDs). In a turnaround, I always start with an X-ray of their effectiveness: have they been spectators as the company has declined, or were they concerned participants but ignored by management? The latter is not a continuing excuse that an NXD should rely on for very long in securing their lifespan on a Board! Great NXDs are invaluable and can support the transformation of a troubled company; if they have just been spectators and not engaged influencers, then they must go.

A cornerstone of leadership is mastery of your subject. When you are thrown into a big job that you have never done before, you have quickly to work out ways to cope. The great thing is absolutely to get on top of your subject; if you are, then you will be respected and your judgment will be trusted. I have been fortunate to have served in a range of roles in different industries; in each one, I needed to have a good and proper understanding of the business that I was in, its challenges and my role in identifying the priorities.

Looking back on life, I have never joined a Board where my inherent discipline of Engineering was not flowing in the bloodstream of the company. Sticking to your core domain skill set is an important discipline in corporate life. As a result, I was positioned to understand the fundamentals of the businesses and relatively quickly win respect as the Leader – while remembering that true leadership is also a matter of how you respect and treat people.

The word "leader" does not have a Latin or Greek root. The *Arcade Dictionary of Word Origins* describes one root that leads back to prehistoric West and North Germanic "laithjan" – derived from "laitho" meaning a way or journey. As someone with my roots in the maritime world I like the image of a ship, on a journey, steering a course which must be kept in both calm and rough seas.

So the Leader takes his or her organisation on a journey focussing on its people to drive corporate success. We select our teams, we coach, we develop, increase responsibilities and inspire them. In that process we continuously discover our own potential and strengths and weaknesses and that of the whole team. We will keep adapting to our customers and market conditions as we go. The Leader taking the organisation on the journey contrasts with management of the status quo.

A hunger to learn is an absolute prerequisite: do all in your power to develop yourself, make the most of your development opportunities. I learned a lot, too, on management and leadership from excellent books, for example the works of Peter Drucker and John Adair. Focus on progressing to be increasingly aligned with the characteristics of the good leader. Many of their memorable quotes and sound advice have found their way into my thinking and words on leadership. Use all the inputs to support your alignment with the characteristics of the good leader.

All of us as Leaders need to be reminded just how unique each of us human beings are. Medical science reveals that the chances of someone else having your biological make-up are more than 1 in 50 billion. You will be aware that none of us have the same fingerprints or indeed toe and ear prints! This uniqueness for me underlines the great opportunity for every leader and each team member to achieve their full potential. Yet how many Leaders set out to achieve these aims for themselves and their teams.

Leadership means giving people the opportunity to develop themselves. As a chairman, I take that very much as part of my responsibility: people must be stretched to the maximum of their capabilities, because that's the way you really learn and develop. One of the things of which I'm most proud is the way I've seen some people, with whom I've worked, grow into much more senior leadership roles than they ever imagined they could, and get to a place they never expected to be. I cannot stress enough the importance of developing your people.

From my early days in Management, I was taught to believe in "deeds not words"'. I was also taught that in each leadership role I performed I should endeavour to "leave things better than I found them". Excel at solving challenging problems. We the leaders must take ownership of everything we do – with the responsibility and authority that this implies. "Responsibility" and "authority" must be coterminous. This is particularly important at the beginning of your career, because it will single you out as key leadership material and open many doors for you. But it applies throughout your working life.

It's a great privilege to be given the opportunity to lead. To lead confidently with integrity and honesty – because these qualities are in every sense the only sustainable way. You must communicate clearly your expectations and the unambiguous goals you want everybody to aim for, whilst avoiding over-intensity because that will turn people off and alienate them. In your early years, demonstrate great horizontal communication and working, so that you are highly regarded by your peers as a real team player.

You as the leader must also have some fun, and communicate that to the team. Having balance in your life is important. Never neglect the power of good humour and never underestimate the importance of how you make people feel. You are always going to be delivering through your people, so ensure that they feel respected and appreciated. Humour is a great asset. Of course, work is a serious business – but a little warmth and enjoyment go a long way.

You must always recognise the things you can really influence and not worry about those you can't. And remember to leave your ego at home, since it will be more successfully managed there by your spouse or partner than if you bring it to work. Few companies or Boards can benefit from arrogance.

Learn, too the difference between being liked and being respected. When you have leadership responsibility, you may have to make some of the very toughest decisions, such as a major downsizing of your team. What I have learned is that you have to do that professionally. Act in the interest of the majority of employees and communicate intensively with your people throughout the process.

You have to be almost clinical since you need to get such an event over with as quickly as possible; if you have to make a lot of people redundant, do it quickly in the interest both of those remaining and those leaving. You must remove uncertainty as soon as you can. Of course this kind of painful action won't endear you to people – but if your people understand the reasons and the necessity for your actions and see that you have implemented them in a fair and responsible way, then you will be respected for biting the bullet. You must always treat people leaving with as much dignity as if they were joining – particularly if they have contributed well and must leave through no fault of their own.

Leadership can be a lonely place where you can feel isolated and solitary. If you are faced with a very tough situation, especially one that has arisen without any warning, you must demonstrate calmness – not fear. You must exude a quiet confidence that you can find the way through the crisis – because the team will respond to that, and without the team's support, you will not resolve the problems. Business needs leaders, but it also demands team effort.

Personally, I've been in some pretty tough industrial and political crises. In particular, running the Harland & Wolff shipyard in Northern Ireland in the 1980s, surrounded by terrorist bombings and shootings. It's in complex environments like these where you have to take charge and lead calmly, even though the right course of action isn't always obvious.

Always get your sleep! I came to the conclusion in my early days in management that you must never lie awake at night, because there is no point wrestling with a difficult issue for 24 hours in the day. You can't solve much in the middle of the night and if you don't get your sleep, you'll not be fit to handle tomorrow's difficulties. It was the former Labour Chancellor of the Exchequer and Deputy Leader Denis Healey who said: "When you are in a hole, the first thing you have to learn is to stop digging". Making and executing the decision to break out of a downward spiral requires mental agility, which in turn comes from being fresh and alert.

But a crisis can also present an opportunity. To quote Sir Winston Churchill: "never waste a good crisis"! That is when you can really grab people's attention. The most important thing is to have a very clear strategy to recover from a disaster. You cannot just be an observer – you have to be the person to take ultimate responsibility. Having a great Board with the right people and skill sets is critically important at these times.

Dealing with major change is never easy and puts an absolute premium on effective communication. Communication is the sister of leadership. You have to spell out what must change and that means communicate, communicate, communicate. You simply cannot over-communicate on change.

Given the constant pressures that you face as a leader, you have to learn to relax, set work aside and get time for mental refreshment. Spend time on something quite different such as charitable work or voluntary work or recreational activities – and I don't necessarily mean that frustrating game of golf! For me, mental refreshment has come from sailing or walking, in the countryside or along a cliff path adjacent to the ocean, or from helping others through charitable work. Everyone will find their own preferred means.

Taking time out does not mean that you are less than 100% committed to your role; it is because of that commitment that you must regularly recharge your batteries in order to remain mentally and physically alert. In the midst of tough challenges, you can be sure you will get a new perspective from resting the mind and giving it something entirely different to think about. All work and no play – or no renewal of the soul – is not good for us human beings. To be an effective leader, you need to be able at all times to focus positive energy on the task in hand.

Coincidentally, I have found sailing to be a great help in other respects. Empowering someone in a team to execute a plan under your general oversight – an important facet of leadership – is very much like sailing. I recall being appointed Chairman of a large FTSE 100 company with a new CEO taking on his first public company role. He needed some convincing about how the roles of Chairman and CEO would dovetail, so I invited him to come sailing with me.

The conditions that day were good – the weather was kind and the sea slight – but I could sense that my colleague was somewhat apprehensive. Understandably – he had never sailed a 40-footer before and here he was stuck in unfamiliar surroundings with someone he didn't know all that well. I'm not sure what he thought when the sails and the course were about set and I said to him: "You must take the wheel, you must steer, you are the CEO. The strategy is settled, we have agreed the general direction we want to go in and these are your guiding principles. But, given that the wind, the tide and the currents can change, you might need some advice. I'll not be far away, but I won't intervene unless you are heading for trouble. I'm your Chairman and now I'm going down below to boil the kettle." And I left him at the wheel.

My little homily might sound simplistic, but it was highly effective. This able young man not only did an excellent job of steering the boat, but our trip brought home to him just how the Chairman and CEO relationship works. We had no further debate about our respective roles and formed a successful partnership.

Quality leadership at all levels is critical to the success of any organisation. As a company Chairman, my leadership challenge is in the boardroom, which sets the drumbeat of expectations of how the management should behave, act and live out our values. We are responsible for the long-term success of the business – we set the tone from the top for all that a company stands for and all that it aims to do for its shareholders, its employees and the communities in which it operates. No organisation can expect to be bestowed with a sound reputation if the governance at its heart is unsound.

Leadership for the CEO and each Executive Director means releasing the day-to-day energy and direction into the business, ensuring that the Board decisions, not only on Strategy but also on major Policy, are implemented. Together with their management teams, they lead the organisation on the "journey" to be the best – to be at the forefront of their industry.

Some of you will be familiar with the Japanese word 'kaizen'. It captures the philosophy of constant improvement. Leaders need to be "restless" in seeking out ways for us to do things better tomorrow than we did them today. The journey of constant improvement, leaving things better than we found them, has to be at the heart of leadership thinking.

As time goes on, the characteristics and habits of good leadership become embedded in your nature. When you are facing a particularly difficult situation – like the potential corporate disasters that have confronted me – the learning process intensifies and accelerates; in such situations, you are constantly changing and adapting your leadership style. When I reflect on those experiences, I realise how much I learned in a very compressed period of time.

We all need to seize the opportunity to discover our full leadership potential. Every so often, you will see an exceptional opportunity – it might be something to expand your business, or to do with a career development chance. In this context, a cartoon caption which I encountered early in my management life contains an eternal truth: "The opportunity of a lifetime must be seized during the lifetime of the opportunity."

I believe this applies to our personal development, whatever leadership position you hold and whatever age you are. In your early career, for instance, one of the critical things is to get noticed for doing a job exceptionally well. Whatever task you do, you need to do a little extra in order to demonstrate that you are more innovative, focussed and committed than the next person. Take a lead and put your back into it; there is no short cut around hard work. You have to add more value than is expected of you – and then you will be noticed. People will have confidence in you. This marks you out as a person with more emotional intelligence than your colleagues. If you get noticed, you will get bigger and bigger jobs to do – you will have created opportunities for yourself to move ahead.

While business today is becoming ever more global and competitive, and the pace of change is ever-quickening, several of the barriers to effective leadership that existed in the past have been swept away.

There is more focus today on effective management and developing leaders. Managers are more qualified now, particularly in engineering, than they were a decade or two ago. Many people recognise the gaps in their own leadership capabilities and are happy to be coached – that wasn't generally the case in the past. It is also much easier to communicate. New systems have added a lot of value – you can speak to people anywhere in the world from your office, your boat or the top of a mountain. Technology has changed everything and will continue to change everything.

Reflecting on all aspects of my own experience, I would identify eight essential attributes of a good leader:

Integrity: a leader must always act with total integrity – lack of integrity, together with arrogance, are the single worst qualities in any leader.

Communication: The ability effectively to communicate your vision and strategy is critical because communication, it is said, is the sister of leadership. The leader must at all times secure the commitment of the management team and their people through layers of continuous communication which gain and retain their attention. Human beings like to know where they stand. Effective communication is a reflection of the respect in which you hold your people.

Inspiration: The ability to inspire and build the team to believe in the corporate strategy and its priorities, and to be confident about its execution. The leader must be credible, respected and visible; must let people make some mistakes, but step in to give direction, guidance and support when required. Never underestimate the importance of how you make people feel. You are going to be delivering through your people, so you must make people feel warm and confident and part of a great team and Company.

Empowerment: A good leader empowers his or her people, gives them clear authority with well-defined responsibilities. Great human talent is what makes great companies: the leader must ensure that his key people are developed to the maximum of their potential. A big part of the thrill of leadership is to see others, either as individuals or as a team, grow and master something they have not achieved before. The good leader firmly but fairly holds them accountable for delivery – and rewards and celebrates their success with them.

Listening: A good leader will listen and learn. There are two types of people in life: those who talk and listen; and those who talk and can't wait to talk. Listening to colleagues and others with great care – and learning from the listening – is more than valuable: it is vital. It is how you ensure that the ship is on course, pick up where things are not going right and learn from the great ideas coming from your team. A good leader should have his/her ear close to the ground.

Decisiveness: Good leaders need to be decisive: "Paralysis through analysis" can be a disastrous trait. Yes, we need to scrutinise, analyse risk and debate the pros and cons with great care – but leaders need to act decisively and give clear guidance to their teams.

Courage: As a good leader, you often need to act courageously and, in certain situations, rely on instinct. Sometimes as leaders you are confronted with the totally unexpected and have no time to study options – you are faced with making a very instant decision and have to rely on innate good judgement and on your gut feel for what is right. Courage is about operating under extreme pressure; its critical handmaidens are resilience and calmness. You might be at your wits' end but you must take charge and lead calmly, even when the right course of action might not be obvious.

Authenticity and Consistency: good leaders establish themselves as role models by being authentic and consistent in their behaviour – they live out their words. As our American cousins say, "they walk the talk". Do not as a leader sign up to behavioural codes or value statements if you are not going to be consistent. I can think of no higher risks to a leader's credibility than, first, not being a role model for the company's values and, second, sending out mixed messages to the team. Remember that your behaviour as leaders is very visible to all your people.

You will have noticed that I do not include Intelligence as a key attribute. Of course, intelligence is important in a leader. But never confuse high IQ with high inter-personal skills, which are even more important. Always be conscious that intellectual ability is not enough without being accompanied by attention to honing your emotional intelligence. Some people have a very high IQ and are also gifted with a good emotional quotient, and they are the most natural leaders. They know how to communicate well with, and inspire their people. They sense out the atmospherics and listen. There are others who have high IQ but low emotional intelligence – and that can be a major flaw in a leader. Such people need to be made aware of this gap and hopefully be encouraged, through coaching and mentoring, to address this critical defect.

I have recently read the book *Legacy* by James Kerr, which is about how the New Zealand All Blacks rugby team have consistently achieved success despite the inevitable changes in their squad over the years. For those picked for the All Blacks, capability and character go hand in hand: while constantly improving their skills, they remain committed to the highest achievements in the world of Rugby Union.

Their example translates well to business. A highly intelligent executive whose personal character lacks integrity, humility and tenacity will struggle to be a broad-based leader. As business leaders, one of our jobs is to watch out for those who will "kiss up" but "kick down". In considering the selection of senior executives, you may not at first see their whole character, but through modern assessment techniques and 360 degree referencing from those who have worked for them, you can build quite a reliable profile on behaviours and so on before making that final hire or promotion.

The leader must shape the character and culture of the company. Any business, particularly a public or consumer facing one must have a culture that is customer- and market research-focussed and with a character that is responsive to serving its customers. In turn the customers must have confidence in the values that are evident through its interface with the leadership and employees. The company must understand what consumers want – not what engineering or designers want to give them. This is not to minimise the crucial role of engineering and design but rather to underscore that dialogue with customers is critical. It is also important, in growing a business, to have leaders in the company who will take the risk of pursuing innovative design solutions and indeed explore new frontiers in design and innovative engineering that can excite customers and create new demand.

I've always been taken by the old Chinese proverb: "When the best leader's work is done, the people say: 'We did it ourselves'." If you analyse the maxim, it is clear that this means:

- The people must have known what they had to do.
- The leader must, therefore, have clearly communicated their vision, strategy and plan.
- The people must have felt empowered and had the authority to execute the leader's plan.
- The leader must have been visible and inspired the people to believe that they could collectively achieve the plan.
- The people acted as a team.
- The leader did not have an ego that wanted to take all the credit.

In other words, fulfilment of this proverb means you must have attained the key attributes of leadership.

As the leader, you must also ensure that your company conducts its business as a responsible corporate citizen. Safety is for me the number one priority. I have always been convinced that your employees who come to work each day deserve to go home safe and well to their families each evening, as do all those people affected by any of your company's products or operations. Weave safety into the fabric of everything the company does and strive for zero lost-time injuries. Train and trust your employees to work responsibly, safeguarding themselves, their colleagues and the public. Indeed, safety management is often the catalyst in driving shop-floor efficiency, through good housekeeping and a tidy and ordered environment.

The reputation of businesses today is under severe challenge by society. As Warren Buffett has remarked: "Reputation is a fragile thing – it takes 20 years to build a reputation and five minutes to ruin it"; and in this age of social media, reputational meltdown can be even quicker than that.

Sections of business have let society down, and displayed greed reflected in unsustainably high rewards. As company leaders, we must seek to participate in society to make it a safer and better place. We need to demonstrate that we are responsible corporate citizens with the commitment to work with all our stakeholders to contribute to making our societies much better places because we are present.

We have to get used to moving beyond our comfort zone and beyond compliance, recognising that we will be exposed to wider and more subjective assessments than before. Look at the public reputation hit that Starbucks and Google took when they stood accused of avoiding UK tax, even though they were apparently not acting outside any formal law.

During my time at Babcock in the 1990s we had a very heavy loss making, high-risk business designing, manufacturing and installing across the world huge power station boilers. We got the business turned around and disposed of it to Mitsui Corporation of Japan. I became very friendly with the-then CEO of Mitsui, Hoshino-san. I invited him to my home for dinner one evening with a number of other friends from industry. A typically Japanese reserved start to the evening was soon dealt with after he had some Bushmills and a few glasses of wine. Suddenly he pointed at me across the table and said: "Parker-san – do you have NATO in your company?" I looked puzzled and he explained the acronym N A T O: "No Action, Talking Only!" Discussion of any issue is pointless unless it is followed by decisive action. That demands true leadership.

2. BEGINNINGS

Mine was a privileged childhood – not in a wealthy material sense, but in the truly rich sense that I had loving parents who taught me by their example Christian principles and values – based around the good book's mandate, which I have endeavoured to live by: 'Do justice, love kindness and walk humbly with your God' - they unstintingly encouraged me in all my studies, interests and endeavours.

I was born in 1942 into a family which had farmed in the Slievenaman Valley in County Down, Northern Ireland for several generations, and who grazed their herds of sheep on the beautiful Mourne Mountains – an idyllic place for myself and my only sister Mina, a year younger than me, to grow up.

The Mournes and the famous scenic Hares Gap lay directly across the Shimna River valley from the happy farmhouse that was my home until I left in my 17th year to study Naval Architecture and Mechanical Engineering as a sponsored Student Apprentice in the world famous Harland & Wolff, Queen's Island Ship Yard in Belfast.

Tragedy struck our home just over a year before I left for Harland & Wolff and my Belfast studies at the College of Technology and Queens University. My father, who had been unwell with lung problems ever since a bout of rheumatic fever left his lungs weakened as a younger man, died on 19 May, 1957. To make matters worse, my mother at that very time was undergoing a major operation in hospital and was unable to be with us for the funeral. My sister and I survived that incredibly tragic event with the unforgettable help of aunts and uncles, particularly my Aunt Edie – my mother's younger sister – my Uncle Tommy Turner, and our local rector – Reverend Harold Lowry.

Dad was a great and devoted father whom we always loved to be with and from whom I learned many lessons for life. Always a ready smile and an optimistic outlook, he was devoted to my mother and us. He worked all hours on the mixed farm where he had cattle, pigs, cows and a great sheep flock along with his sheep dogs which were his pride and joy.

He was considered an exceptionally able judge of Mourne Black-Faced Sheep and often I'd accompany him on visits to farms and farmers around the Mournes to buy numbers of sheep on behalf of many other farmers from across County Down who valued his opinion.

My mother also worked amazing hours and there was no let-up for either of them seven days a week. She bought hundreds of young chicks each year, and as children we would be captivated by these day-old chicks delivered in cardboard boxes of 100. They were then placed into sheltered hoovers with an oil lamp to keep them warm. Given the very large number of hens we had on the farm there were always eggs to collect, wash and pack for sale.

In addition to attending her hens, mother would bake fresh bread almost every day while pancakes freshly 'off the griddle' were a special treat. Then there were the cows to milk – by hand in those days. When Dad would be away ploughing in one of our out-farms, often until late at night with his horses, mum would milk all the cows by herself – until I was old enough to help. She had a wonderful singing voice and sang as she milked, claiming that the cows, who did seem very engaged, would give up their milk more freely. The cats that were always around the farm would queue up at the cow byre at milking time hoping to get a supply of fresh hot milk. Mother was a great cook and we always enjoyed wholesome meals. We would get special treats of sponge and fruit cakes and others delicious sweet things when local farmers and relations were to visit in the evening or at the weekend (which was thankfully often!).

My mother and father did have help around the farm. I recall with great fondness Caroline Morrison who was then an unmarried lady from a neighbouring farm who took care of us little ones. She was an incredibly kind and gentle lady and spoilt us with treats as children. I recall that in those days, probably when I was around four or five, in order to get me to eat my porridge, I'd demand to eat it in one of the farm's fields! So I'd walk Caroline, who had to carry my bowl of porridge, until I found the field and the selected place I wanted to eat at – a characteristic determined streak of 'not giving up easily' was already emerging!

Mina and I were enlisted to work around the farm and one of our chores as children, which we did not delight in, was churning day. Each week mother would make her own butter and we had to turn the handle of the churn, during a one hour-long operation, until the butter gathered on top of the milk. This was drained off to make buttermilk – a critical ingredient for Ulster soda or wheaten bread. So our home was virtually self-sufficient for food supply – milk, home-baked bread, home-made jam, potatoes, fresh vegetables, chicken, pork, ham and lamb.

The lambing season, with the first arrivals due around St Patrick's Day, was a particularly busy time, day and night, for my father and the sheep dogs. Often each spring we would end up with about three 'pet' lambs that my sister and I had to feed from a baby bottle. For some years thereafter if they remained in the flock, they would separate from the other sheep and come running to meet you as you entered their field – still hoping you had supplies!

Our home was often the place where many local farmers would drop in for a chat and a cup of tea to accompany my mother's good baking. Father was a great raconteur and my mother a superb mimic. They could entertain around the fireside without the benefit of TV but BBC Radio was a regular feature, especially around news time in our home. Dad took a very keen interest in what was happening around the world and he had a daily newspaper delivered. He also was a man whom the local farmers would come to for advice or if they needed some form of helping hand. His knowledge of the family relationships in the farms around the area was often sought out by his great solicitor friend 'W G' (George) McSpadden, who was a regular visitor to the farm. W G, followed by his son Dermot, served as my solicitor for many years until Dermot's retirement from the family firm in the 1980s.

A feature of farm life was each local farmer helping out each other, for example at threshing time when uncles and other neighbours would gather to fork the sheaves from the hay and corn stacks on to the threshing machine – which as children we were not allowed to approach because of the machinery, moving belts and all the activity. We loved to watch as the farmers neared the bottom of a corn or hay stack and we saw rats and mice, whose winter home it had been, run out to seek refuge elsewhere. Many were often intercepted by the sheep dogs gathered by the stack! On one occasion I recall a mouse running up my trouser leg and me screaming in alarm as my Uncle Tommy Turner urgently grabbed my trouser leg trying to catch the beast – only to watch it run down the other leg. One local wag of a farmer, Sammy Morrison, sitting at the tea table in the farmhouse later, said it was good job the mouse didn't stop at the junction and do permanent damage!

After the day's work they would all gather around the farmhouse table for a good and well-deserved meal. As children we loved to listen in on the story-telling.

One of the farm hands who worked part-time for my Uncle Tommy at his farm in Bryansford and who would be around the supper table at harvest threshing time was a great character called James. He told the story of how he decided to apply for unemployment benefit and turned up at the Bureau Office (pronounced "Buroo" in Ulster) to find a long queue. He got very frustrated and after an hour or so shouted up the queue: "Mr Buroo Man, can you get a move on, don't you realise I've my work to go to!"

The nearest house and our nearest neighbour was Miss Duncan who lived in Garden Cottage, a mere 200 yards along the road to our farm. She kept an exquisite cottage garden. Miss Duncan was a former nurse from Co. Meath, who along with her schoolteacher cousin, Miss Blakney, had come north to be the teacher at Slievenaman School. When as children we first got to know Miss Duncan she must have been in her late seventies. She would come and collect her milk, potatoes and other food stuffs daily from the farm. Later, as she got more frail, my sister or I would deliver the provisions to the cottage and we would always have to stay for a chat.

She was meticulous about payment and added so much value to our lives. She had a great collection of books including many of the classics, and she would read chapters to us and introduce us to many new books. On one occasion over a series of weeks she read us the abridged version of John Bunyan's *Pilgrims Progress*. She also gave us a raft of questions on the wide range of books she read to us. She certainly not only extended our knowledge but instilled in us the love of good literature which has remained with me throughout my life.

Grandparents

Only two of my grandparents were alive at my birth. Grandma Parker and Grandpa Bell, my mother's father. Grandma had lived with my father until he married my mother in 1941 and she then went to live with Uncle Willie's family across the Shimna River valley in Clanawillen, until she died when I was probably around nine. I have only faint memories of her sitting, neatly dressed, beside the open fire – a very kind and gentle old lady.

Grandpa Bell lived well into his eighties and sadly died the day before I started my studies in Belfast. I was very fond of him and used to cycle the six miles regularly from home in Slievenaman to his Drumlee farm near Ballyward to see him. He had a large moustache and was a gentle and caring character, who showed much interest in all I was doing as a young boy. He also had a great supply of mint imperials and would often give me a little extra pocket money on those visits!

My sister and I used to go and stay for some days with him each summer which took us closer to our cousins, Aunt Edie's family. She and Uncle Andy had five wonderful daughters who visited us regularly in Slievenaman, as did my mum's oldest sister, Aunt Minnie, and her family of three daughters. They lived in Belfast and Aunt Minnie kept a good eye on me when I went there to study!

My mother's brother Uncle Robbie and my Aunt Aggie, who had five children, lived close by Grandpa and took great care of him. Our holiday visits were great fun in the carefree days of no school and escaping from our chores around the farm.

School

Our first school at Slievenaman, a half-mile walk from our farmhouse, had 12 pupils and a single teacher – Mrs Fails. Of the 12 pupils, seven were Parkers: Mina and I and our five cousins who lived in Uncle Willie's farm on the mountain side of the valley in Clanawhillan.

Mrs Fails was an American lady with a great love of travel – very unusual back then in the late 1940s. She would spend most of her holidays in the USA. She was keen on photography, as was her son Ronnie, and we experienced wonderful cine films which she shot during these holidays – introducing us to cities such as New York and many US scenic sights. With so few pupils we experienced 1:1 tuition across the widest possible curriculum and on a range of topics few other children could have experienced elsewhere, until the age of about nine.

We also had great fun at school – football, marbles and rounders were all popular games. We were confined to the large field which was our playground over the lunch break before the school hand-bell was rung by Mrs Fails to call us in. On one particular day I can recall being challenged to scale the boundary fence and climb to the top of a large haystack in the adjacent farm. I foolishly climbed the stack and was just clambering back across the boundary fence when Mrs Fails rang the bell! Rather than return late to the classroom and be chastised, I took off down the road leading for home – as if I'd have received a warm reception there! It wasn't long until I looked over my shoulder to see Mrs Fails and the whole school chasing me! I didn't make it very far before the tallest boy in the class, Norman Rooney, caught up with me. He returned me to Mrs Fails who beat me round my legs with a wooden ruler until we reached the school. Always face up to the consequences of your mistakes.

The school closed around 1950 and we then travelled by bus the six miles to Donard View School in Newcastle by the Sea, close to the famous Royal Co. Down Golf Links Championship course. But I didn't lose touch with Mrs Fails, who was transferred to Ardglass School and who very kindly every summer invited me to spend a few days' holiday with the family. Ardglass is a coastal fishing village and this was my introduction to the large fishing fleet, and their work of harvesting from the sea. I was captivated by the trawlers and the hive of activity around the harbour. In particular, I used to love wandering around and observing all that was going on, and occasionally would go very early in the morning to collect fresh herring direct from the trawlers landing the catch.

I have many happy memories of both Slievenaman and Donard View schools. Apart from my studies, I took part in plays and participated in drama festivals. During those years I was a keen member of the Boys' Brigade and enjoyed sport, camping, First Aid and a raft of badgeworks. My cousin Andrew Montgomery was also in the Boys' Brigade and he lived in Bryansford, where his mum Martha (née Turner) ran the Post Office. We called her "Aunt" but she was, as all the senior Turners were, double cousins of my father since my Grandad Parker had married a Turner and a Turner had also married a Parker. We were all very close as families. I saw a lot of Andrew around the farm and at Bryansford and we established a superb Subutteo table soccer league which we played in each others homes on a Saturday evening during the winter. I always seemed to end up with Everton or Rangers!

I was extremely fortunate that, after Mrs Fails, I had a number of outstanding and very influential teachers. At Donard View we had a famous Headmaster, William Hunter, who was a well known BBC broadcaster and a talented singer and keen dramatist. We had memorable school concerts at which I recall singing solos, having had piano and singing lessons with a talented local lady, Mrs Nesbitt. Sadly I gave the piano lessons up after passing several Trinity College Music grades – a regrettable mistake – but I can still sight read music, which I greatly enjoy.

I later moved to the Technical High School in Newcastle where another outstanding Headmaster, A A Downey, led the school with great distinction. I had a wonderful science teacher, Frank Curragh, and a talented Deputy Headmaster in Mr Jefferson who was brilliant at Technical Engineering Drawing. Each of them encouraged me in my ambition to become an engineer, which was first inspired by farm machinery in general and the Ford Ferguson tractor in particular. What a great engineer the County Down-born Harry Ferguson was. His patented three-point hydraulic lift is still incorporated into all major tractor designs around the world today.

What was it about the subject of Engineering that so enthused me? I loved the triumvirate of creativity, knowledge and discipline that engineering demands. It requires clarity of thought and precision in deed, but – at its best – it also involves a readiness to experiment, to break new ground. Imagination and practicality are an inspiring combination because together they enable you to translate vision into a reality which enhances or transforms lives. As the Duke of Edinburgh – aged 95 and Senior Fellow of the Royal Academy of Engineering – said in a 2016 Radio 4 interview with Lord Browne: "Everything that was not invented by God has been invented by an engineer."

There was great drive, discipline and diversity in the High School.

It was not only a mixed gender but also a mixed religious school, Protestant and Catholic. This underscored for me, through the many friends I made there, the importance of tolerance and respect for the other person's point of view. My parents had instilled that conviction in me through the years in the mixed community where I grew up, and Newcastle further embedded it as a cornerstone principle in my life.

Student apprenticeship – Naval Architecture

An opportunity to advance my engineering ambitions arose when I learned that Harland & Wolff, in common with a number of leading UK employers, held an annual competitive written examination and interviews for a student apprenticeship in Naval Architecture and Engineering. About 20 places were available each year. They attracted very many applications and, from them, about 80 students across Northern Ireland were downselected to sit the final exam. We all took the examinations on a Saturday in the famous glass-domed drawing offices, sitting on high stools at flat drawing-boards. Those offices are now being restored as part of the Titanic Quarter on Queen's Island, Belfast

I was ultimately fortunate to make the shortlist for interviews. I still have a copy of my marks in that examination, where apparently I gained 1st place. I was given this 15 years later by H&W's Chief Naval Architect, Malcolm McKenzie, who had marked the exam papers, when I left H&W to join Austin & Pickersgill Shipbuilders in Sunderland – my first Managing Director role.

Winning that student apprenticeship focussed me on my studies of Naval Architecture within the great, broad discipline of engineering. The more I learned of the maritime world, the more enthused I became and the more fascinated I was to learn more and read accordingly. We live in a world where more than two-thirds of the earth's surface is covered by sea, in which more than 90% of the world's transported goods and commodities are carried by sea, and where some 30% of global oil and gas production is located offshore. So I never had any doubts about the relevance and value of my chosen profession. It also embraced so many engineering design disciplines – mechanical, electrical, structural, propulsion, etc – not to mention the manufacturing and construction work involved in shipbuilding.

Indeed, as my career progressed and my knowledge of ships and shipbuilding increased, the characteristics of ship design evolution and the response required to service this changing maritime scene often seem to me to replicate the very characteristics of the sea itself. There are times when the period of "calm" signifies a time for consolidation, times when there is evolutionary change like a regular "swell" – and times when dynamic step-change suddenly emerges like the onset of a Force 8 gale.

The getting of that wisdom lay ahead as I pursued my college and university studies. I was fortunate to have inspiring lecturers and academic leaders. D H Alexander, a Cambridge engineer and Whitworth Scholar, was the Principal of the College of Technology, and Bernard Crosland, the all time great Professor of Mechanical Engineering at Queen's University Belfast (QUB), were outstanding academic leaders of their day. Professor Jimmy Williamson and Ronnie Patterson, superb lecturers in Naval Architecture, along with George McBratney who lectured in Thermodynamics, Don McCloy in Fluid Mechanics, and Norman Morrison in Mathematics all added immense value.

My work comprised part-time day study and up to three evenings per week along with six-month modules of training in the various technical offices and Ship Production Operations over a five-year period. Our final year of full-time study, followed by another part-time year of Advanced Ship Design and Mechanical Engineering, equipped me to become a Chartered Engineer and an Associate Member of the Royal Institution of Naval Architects (RINA). I never imagined when I was admitted to this prestigious professional institution – founded in 1861 at the zenith of the Industrial Revolution – that more than 30 years later I would become its President.

H&W paid all our college and university fees, along with a modest weekly sum starting at £2-19 shillings and sixpence and rising each year. As a student, I also had the privilege of staying in the Presbyterian Hostel in Howard Street, Belfast with its 120 students, with full board at £2. 17 shillings and sixpence a week. It was a narrow positive margin, but Mr Micawber would have been satisfied! The students were all up from various parts of the country to study in Belfast. There were five floors of students including three floors of girls!

Given the tightness of cash flow and to save on my outgoings, I would cycle the 32 miles home to the farm and back to Belfast most weekends. I felt very committed to support my mother, who was still operating the farm. She generously provided me with additional funding for textbooks and other expenses.

We had superb fun in this very disciplined hostel environment under the eagle eye of the Warden, "Pop" Rainey. He stood at the hostel entrance each evening with his pocket watch visibly held in his hand. The gates closed at 11pm sharp and he observed and noted carefully which girl you were out with! Some of the girls were exceptionally bright students and many were very attractive, which did not go unnoticed by many of us boys!

Among them was Emma Blair, a student of Latin and Psychology at Queen's. She was and still is a brilliant pianist. I dated her only after my three-year stay!

I left that great band of students to live again with my mother, who had sold the farm and come to live in Belfast, since my sister Mina had already entered the Northern Ireland Civil Service. Happily, I did not lose touch with Emma. In fact, our relationship blossomed. We had a long courtship, given that her parents thought us too young to marry as "under 25s"! I was very fond of them both until they died well in to their 90s.

Harland & Wolff as part of my post-Naval Architecture studies arranged for me to have research secondments at Lloyds Register of Shipping in London, on Structural Design of Ships, and at the National Physical Laboratory in Teddington on Hydrodynamics and

Ship Model Testing. This took me away from Emma for about a year and we finally married in July 1967. I owe her so much for the support and loyalty to me over these 50 years and for our two wonderful and talented children: Graham born in 1970 and Fiona (Fee) in 1972. Whatever one might achieve in life, there can be no greater personal legacy to the world, if you have been fortunate to be granted them, than your children. They are both wonderful friends and I truly enjoy being in their company.

Both are now married. Graham, an English and Drama graduate of Manchester University, is a writer and sports journalist, married to Ina, a former publisher, now living in New Hope, Philadelphia, USA. Arthur, their fine boy born in 2012 has the physique to be a great athlete! Fee, who graduated from QUB and Trinity College Dublin in Environmental Science and Statistics, is married to Nigel, a very successful engineer and businessman whom I admire. He is also a good friend and an excellent sailor. Nigel's father, Brian, was also an engineer at Westland Helicopters. Fortunately, we all get on well together. Brian and his wife Jean join us on some of our cruise holidays, and Brian has often sailed with me.

Nigel and Fee have three talented, sports-orientated boys, Jack, Charlie and Alfie, born in 2003, 2005 and 2011.

All our grandsons have given us immense pleasure as we talk with them and track their successes at school and in their sports. Jack, at 15, is currently participating in the Rugby Academy of Exeter Chiefs and Charlie, at 13, is competing to enter.

Fee also had a great sporting career as a rowing cox of the men's eight at both Queen's University Belfast and Trinity College Dublin, and was finally the Irish Universities cox when they won the Four Nations' men's eight championship in 1997.

On completion of my six years of studies, I was ready and enthusiastic for full-time employment. These years of working, studying and later lecturing part-time in Naval Architecture had immersed me in the world of ships – their design and construction. It had become my ambition as I had advanced in my practical and academic work to join Harland & Wolff's Ship Design Team, and I was thrilled to be accepted in 1964 to join this 'front-end' design unit, which created all the conceptual designs in response to shipowners' enquiries for new ships. For me, it was truly the 'opportunity of a lifetime'.

3. HARLAND & WOLFF

I was fortunate in the timing of my recruitment into the H&W Ship Design team, because the late 1960s and early 1970s were in many respects the last hurrah for the British shipbuilding industry as a leading force in the world industry. We were already being challenged by the Japanese, as were other long-established British industries such as car-making and machine tools, and we had yet to face the later full onslaught from South Korea. The UK shipowners too were beginning to feel the pressure of overseas competition as the 1970s progressed.

Among the famous names in the UK industry, Harland & Wolff had established a special place. In the 1950s we were the largest shipyard in the world, having produced for the Second World War effort an average of 49 ships a year which included aircraft carriers, frigates, destroyers and minesweepers, plus a wide range of merchant ships.

At the time I arrived, the variety of ship types we designed was exceptionally wide, and our facilities were exceptionally large – we had 18 slipways on which to fulfil the orders we won. We also built for a great variety of ship owners: BP, Shell and the US company Texaco came to us for a range of tankers; cargo and refrigerated vessels were ordered by Furness Withy, Blue Star Line, Bank Line, P&O and others, particularly Norwegian shipowners. In my first five years, no less than nine naval ships were also under construction: two frigates, an assault ship and a replenishment vessel for the Royal Navy;

a Whitby class frigate and the aircraft carrier Vikrant for the Indian Navy; two Ton-class minesweepers for the South African Navy and a Leander class frigate for the Royal New Zealand Navy.

H&W was therefore the ideal place for me to pursue what had become my vocation. Unlike most other branches of engineering, the dynamics of the sea and its corrosive powers single out Naval Architecture as a particularly demanding discipline. My first text book on the subject, *Applied Naval Architecture* by the Belfast naval engineer WJ Lovett, was published in 1920 and contained the memorable observation that "Naval Architecture in its application is not an exact science."

In the early 1960s, the marine designer was heavily reliant on empirical formulae and on executing masses of long-hand calculations which determined the ship's structural strength, the horsepower of its engines, its stability and capacity, and so on. Such calculations were undertaken by slide rule or the "Fuller" barrel – equivalent to a 83-foot long slide rule – and later by the mechanical calculating machine. Since then, with the aid of modern computing techniques including mathematical modelling of sea states and 3D finite element structural analysis, the whole engineering profession has moved a long way towards becoming a more exact science.

These toolkits have also injected confidence into the extrapolation of ship size and structures to an unprecedented scale, leading to significant growth in the scale of, for example, cruise ships, tankers and Liquefied Natural Gas (LNG) carriers. However, the designer's judgement and experience remain important ingredients in the overall success of a vessel's design, especially when that vessel is a unique, first-of-its-kind project.

My enduring fascination with ship design and innovation in design was kindled during my student days, given that I had the good fortune to witness in that period the construction at H&W of such a wide variety of merchant and naval ships, including the simultaneous construction of five passenger ships.

These included the *Southern Cross*, the first passenger ship in the world to have its engine room located aft, instead of the traditional position of midship. This innovation made possible greater, more suitable and higher volume space for passengers and shorter runs of shafting from the main engines etc. This established a new approach to passenger ship design which pertains today.

The *Southern Cross* was followed by P&O's famous *Canberra*, the first ship to have an all-aluminium superstructure, which significantly reduced top weight. Canberra was designed for the UK-Australia passenger service which was highly popular in those days before intercontinental flights became routine and widely affordable, but she was ultimately adapted for dedicated cruising. We delivered her in May 1961 and when she retired in 1997 after 36 years of resoundingly successful service, she had carried one million passengers more than three million miles. She also played an important role during the 1982 Falklands War as a vital Royal Navy troopship, when she was affectionately known in the Navy as the "Great White Whale".

At 45,000 GRT, *Canberra* was the largest passenger liner to be built in the UK since the *Queen Elizabeth*. I became very attached to her, since I was given a modest technical role in her construction. This involved preparing and constantly updating the deck-covering plan for the complete vessel. The plan specified the materials laid on the decks for every space, from the many varieties of terrazzo tile in galleys, bathrooms and pantries to the highest grade of Axminster carpets and associated underlay in the first class lounges and cabins. To check that work was progressing as specified, I used to go regularly on board *Canberra* during her final outfitting. I got to know every compartment in that ship exceptionally well, and the whole experience was absolutely formative for me, giving me a superb opportunity to view almost every aspect of a passenger ship fitting-out. Much later in my working life, I also came to know *Canberra's* owner P&O extremely well too.

The Ship Design team that I joined at H&W comprised a small group of highly qualified naval architects led by the famous Dr Rupert Cameron as Chief Naval Architect and Technical Director.

Dr Cameron was a god-like figure to most of us young aspiring naval architects. He had written many technical papers and had overseen the design of major ships of all types. His team would produce the conceptual design in response to each enquiry received from a shipowner. We would define its key technical characteristics and specification plus estimated weights of steel, piping, size of engines and so on, in order for the sales and cost-estimating department to come up with cost and price. It was during my early years in this design team that I published my first Technical Paper to the Institution of Engineers and Shipbuilders in Scotland (IESS), entitled 'First Approximations to the Dimensions of Large Oil Tankers'. Other papers were to follow.

Dr Cameron's Design Chief was Harry Campbell, one of the most gifted yet low-key people I have ever met, then or since. With the aid of a little data book which contained key particulars (steel weight/power-speed/dimensions/dead weight/cargo capacity etc) for all recent ships built, Harry could draft out all the main parameters needed by the cost estimating department on an A5 sheet of paper.

It would then take a team of two or three of us over the next two weeks to confirm in detail the dimensions, steel weight, horse power, cargo capacity, dead weight and so forth, as we developed an outline design and specification to go with the tender price and contract package. The frustrating thing for us was that Harry's estimate was always within a very low percentage tolerance from each item of our detailed assessment.

He had that extraordinary feel for his subject which is born out of years of experience, together with a unique ability to combine artistic and scientific skills.

One instance exemplified Harry's exceptional talent. We were quoting for a new 90,000 TDW oil tanker for Texaco (New York) and we went through the usual processes, developing the plans and specifications to accompany the estimated price being submitted.

We were keen to win the business and our Chairman at that time was C.H. Bailey, who was based in our London office. From all I heard about him, he was rather punctilious and slightly pompous.

On this occasion, he telephoned Harry Campbell and asked Harry to accompany him to New York, as he had just managed to secure an appointment there with the President of Texaco Marine, J V C Malcolmson.

Mr Bailey also advised Harry just how important this visit was, and that he, the Chairman, would do the talking. Harry was only to be there to ensure technical questions were answered. I understand that this message was once more reinforced on the plane!

However, and entirely unknown to the Chairman, when they were starting their careers Malcolmson and Harry Campbell had been fellow student naval architects working together in Workman Clarke, another Belfast yard later absorbed into H&W. Harry did not disclose his hand but on arrival in the outer room of the President's massive office, Malcolmson came out to meet them, ignored the Chairman and threw his arms around Harry Campbell.

The next hour was largely taken up by Malcolmson getting up to speed with what happened to all of their former friends and girlfriends. Mr Bailey was clearly taken aback and after an hour or so asked the President when could they discuss business. The Texaco chief replied: "We'll do that over dinner, but I wouldn't mind having Harry spend an hour with me now going through your technical proposal and we'll see you at dinner, Chairman"! Needless to say, Harry had all the details at his fingertips. He knew that, while old acquaintance counted for a lot because it guaranteed trust – the essential prerequisite for any negotiation – it would only deliver a successful outcome if it was combined with total professionalism. At the end of dinner, the technical details and price for the 90k tanker were duly agreed, subject to finalising the contract.

The power of understatement was only one of the many characteristics that I learned from the unflappable but amazingly competent and talented Harry Campbell. That incident and others also taught me how full knowledge of your subject and thorough preparation are the prerequisites to a successful major contract negotiation.

I learned never to go into such discussion with shipowners, major customers or any corporate transaction without diligent preparation –"never wing it"! Harry was mighty well prepared for discussing every aspect of that design and tender – even though he knew Malcolmson well. As the senior man or woman, you must know the strengths of your team and what they do or don't know about the customer: they may have experience of previous transactions either with that customer or from similar situations. If they don't, you need to fill in the gaps in the team's collective knowledge as far as you can. Do your homework on the likes and dislikes of your opposite number as a person and as a leader. I love the practical wisdom of the Chinese proverb: 'First make friends and then do business'.

Harry Campbell had a highly capable assistant in Malcolm McKenzie who specialised in hydrodynamics and had overall responsibility for the Technical Sea Trials of each new ship – something I was also to be involved with for a number of years and which gave me enormous satisfaction. What more could a young naval architect want than to be involved from conceptual design to going on the sea trials to test out the actual performance of a completed ship. I learned much about ship operations and navigation in the many months I accumulated on the sea trials.

The other Assistant to Harry Campbell was an excellent all-round naval architect, Billy Harrison. Some years later, in about 1971, Malcolm McKenzie succeeded Dr Cameron as Chief Naval Architect, Billy Harrison became Chief Ship Designer and I unexpectedly became the Production Drawing Office Manager. I was therefore in charge of producing all of the working drawings and production information required for the total manufacturing and production process. I was 29 and had responsibility for about 120 draughtsmen and engineers in our technical offices. Many of the chief draughtsmen and section leaders reporting to me were my previous bosses and had taught me much of what I knew about my new area of responsibility.

H&W had a large Ship Repair and Conversion business located in Belfast and Southampton. One day whilst working in the Ship Design office, I was sent for by Dr Cameron. He was very interested and quite an authority on propeller design. As part of his research, he was preparing some complex design charts. At the moment I entered his office he was using a draughting pen to ink curves in colour along a plastic batten, weighted down along a range of data points.

Without looking up from his task, he said: "John, I wonder if you would take yourself down to the Thompson dry dock as it appears that the bow section of the *Araleun* has capsized as they were towing it out of the dock!"

I was totally shocked at what I'd just heard – this was a genuine crisis. At the same moment, I was extremely impressed – not for the last time – at Dr Cameron's unflappable approach. I should explain that the *Araleun* was a 13,000-ton cargo vessel that was undergoing a ship lengthening operation via the insertion of a new mid-body section. The first stage was to cut the ship in two and move the fore end out of the dry dock, then move in the new mid-section before joining all three sections up again. Instead, the fore section had overturned.

To prepare for the ship to be cut in two, a temporary bulkhead had been built at the aft end of the bow section. Regrettably it had not been built high enough to accommodate any significant degree of heeling during the tow out of the dock section. As the bow section was being towed out, a blast of wind heeled it, allowing a large amount of water to flood in, causing an immediate free surface and loss of stability. Rapid heeling ensued, leading to the partial capsize of the fore end of the ship.

By the time I arrived at the dock, a number of very wet and cold workmen had been rescued from the icy water and were being placed in the many waiting ambulances. They had been on the forecastle deck of the bow section and landed in the water as it went through about 50 degrees. Fortunately, no one was seriously injured and thankfully she did not capsize completely, given that the cross tree from her foremast buried itself in the side of the dock. This at least stopped a complete overturn!

It was a right mess, with part of the bow now partially across the dock entrance so the dock gate could not be closed. A hasty discussion took place with Billy Baxter, the 'go-getting' General Manager of Ship Repair, and Bert Young, the Project Manager. We decided that the forward end of the bow section must be cropped back urgently to allow the dock gate to close. This would ensure control of the water level within the dock and avoid the after end of the ship from lifting and lowering with the tide.

Even in the midst of disaster there was the inevitable shipyard humour – certainly with this workforce. Bert Young's managerial style did not naturally capture the hearts and minds of all his workforce – so after this incident they took to describing him as the "Harland & Wolff manager who had achieved the biggest turnover of the year"!

I reported back to Dr Cameron and he suggested I have a scale model built of the dock and the bow section of the vessel. Salvage advisors for insurance purposes were also called in. Bobby Dodds, the highly-creative H&W model maker, and his small team did a brilliant job. We placed lead weights in the ship model fore end to replicate the weight distribution of the actual ship both vertically and longitudinally. Using a further series of lead weights placed in the centre of gravity of each double bottom tank, we determined a sequence of tank-filling combined with varying the levels of water in the dock to produce a potential programme to return the vessel to the vertical.

To avoid media attention, Ship Repair management decided that we should attempt the righting operation on a Friday night at around 7pm, by when darkness had fallen. The timing did also mean that most of our workforce had been in the pubs for a few hours. As they walked in for the start of their extraordinary night shift, the clinking of beer bottles in their plastic carrier bags could be heard in the stillness of the night air. But they all got going with enthusiasm to get the programmed levels of water in the dry dock, whilst flooding up double bottom tanks in the sequence we planned.

The readings from the sizeable inclinometer we had fitted to the section gave remarkable correlation with the model predictions until we were about 20 degrees off the vertical. But then there was no further movement, because some of the temporary pig iron ballast used to weigh down the bow section for towing was discovered to be in a different position than we had assumed. Some physical shifting of the ballast took place but that still left us 15 degrees or so off the vertical. A further inspection revealed that a significant wedge of water was located between the shelter deck and the outer shell. The line of the shelter deck was fortunately clear of the water line at this stage.

A few skilled repair men suspended in large steel cages from the dock cranes then burned three large drain holes just above the shelter deck. Through these drain holes, the water poured out and the bow section completely righted itself. A massive cheer broke out from the workforce – it was certainly "a night to remember"! Next morning. The righted bow section was towed out and the new mid-section floated in to be joined later by that forward end that had created all the drama.

Helping to deal with such a crisis was character-forming for me. But it also taught me an important technical lesson. The physical models we built to study the righting of the *Araleun* bow section taught me the value of modelling to solve big structural-related challenges. Remember, these were the days before the availability of the massive computing power in today's mathematical modelling world. Today these powerful tools would have allowed us to examine so many more alternatives and provided greater accuracy of prediction. But physical models did have some advantages: they allowed you to feel and sense out the risks in a visible way which might not always be shown up by the more clinical computer output.

As a result of this successful problem-solving project with Ship Repair, over the next few years I had a number of other assignments working alongside the colourful group of characters in this part of the business. They got some challenging jobs done.

One amazing episode, which captured for me the humour of the Repair men, occurred during the conversion of the passenger ship *Rina del* Mar to a cruise ship. She was being modified and re-outfitted whilst moored at the deep water Thompson Wharf. During a night shift, an unexpected violent storm arose in the early hours of the morning and the ship broke her moorings. She drifted into the middle of Belfast Lough with about 300 night-shift workers aboard.

Shore power was inevitably disconnected, so that the ship was plunged into complete darkness and a number of workmen were trapped in the main passenger lift. Their mates, aware of this event, headed up the spiral staircase surrounding the lift shaft, collecting fire water buckets as they went. On reaching the top they discharged the water buckets down the shaft on their fellow workmen, singing in Titanic style: "Nearer my God to Thee." Even in a crisis, you have to recognize the remarkable humour and resilience of a workforce!

A story did the rounds about a Belfast Ship Repair employee being interviewed for a job with an inward investment company. First question: "Did you go to 'Queen's University'?" – "No I went to 'Queen's Island' – that great university of life!"

The shipyard humour created many nicknames for managers, foremen and other workforce members. One of our managers was called "Sammy No More" and I asked a colleague one day about this unusual name. He laughed and explained: "It's a nickname – his real name is Sammy Kinnear. He's been called Sammy No More ever since he was promoted to be a Foreman…"

In those days, I learned, you were told on a Friday night that you'd become a Foreman on the following Monday morning – that was the extent of management development then! Sammy had been a fitter at Harland's for 20-odd years when, one Friday, he was given the good news of his promotion. So on the Saturday, he went down into Belfast to buy a new bowler hat, symbol of his new rank which entitled him to be referred to as "Mr Kinnear". Early on Monday, he caught his usual No.51 bus, which stopped outside the Harland Fitters shop. As he entered the shop, with his new bowler tucked under his arm in a brown paper bag, he saw his long-term helper Tommy sitting on a stool, as usual, reading the *Daily Mirror*. Without looking up, Tommy said: "Morning, Sammy." Sammy stopped, took the hat out of the bag, put it on and said: "Call me Sammy no more" – which the Yard workforce did for the next 30 years.

Apart from my forays into the special world of Ship Repair, I learned much about practical ship design from H&W's great naval architects. I worked hard and with real commitment since I loved what I was doing. I had the opportunity to be involved in the concept design for a wide range of ships – many being first-offs.

One of these, in 1965, was the first super tanker to be ordered in Europe and built in the UK – the 190,000-ton *Myrina*, forerunner of the Very Large Crude Carriers (VLCCs). It was originally ordered as a 140,000-ton tanker by a Norwegian owner who subsequently cancelled it, whereupon the contract was taken over by Deutsche Shell, the German arm of the oil and gas giant which wanted a much larger ship.

We produced a rapid re-design which demonstrated that a substantial increase in length was needed to achieve the desired tonnage. However, even our largest slipway was too short to accommodate this length, so the slipway would have to be extended. Having determined on the slipway extension, the new contract with Shell was confirmed and the erection of the after-portion of the ship got under way on the slipway.

At this juncture, we ran into an unforeseen problem: our Managing Director Alan Watt refused to authorise the slipway extension on the basis both of its additional cost and the fact that it required the demolition of part of H&W's manufacturing facilities. He told the design team to find another solution to the length problem.

The only alternative was, to put it mildly, somewhat imaginative and certainly unprecedented. We had to "launch" the half-completed vessel down the slipway, then stop it part of the way down and build the forward end of the ship on the newly-vacated section of the slipway. This presented a major technical challenge since roughly 17,000 tons of ship were already built and sitting on the slipway.

To retain the after-end structure in place and under control, we attached a series of "drag chain" piles, located on the slipway causeways, to the hull with traditional wire cables. The "catenary slack" was taken up in the cables by lowering the structure, step by step, down the slipway via a series of hydraulic jacks located beneath the hull. When the catenary slack was fully taken up, the frictional resistance of the drag chain piles held the vessel in position. Then, to move it progressively towards the water, the berth cranes were used through a series of block-and-tackle systems located beneath the ship to produce the desired rate of movement down the slipway. The whole operation worked very well, with *Myrina* being fully constructed, successfully completed and fully launched.

I subsequently went on her sea trials and dry docking in the River Elbe in Germany – a memorable trip, with some 50 Belfast shipyard workers on board, most of whom had never been out of Northern Ireland before, roaming the streets of Hamburg in general and the Reeperbahn in particular. On rounding them up at night, we would find some of them conducting the band in the Zillertal or propping up a wall rather unsteadily following their substantial intake of German beer. We finally got them all safely home.

Our innovative work on the *Myrina* construction and launch exemplified H&W's pioneering spirit – a fearless willingness to take calculated risks which was fundamental to its enduring corporate culture. It made H&W an inspiring place for me to learn and develop in my profession. The leadership placed huge confidence in the creativity of its engineers and naval architects to solve problems and to overcome what sometimes appeared to be challenges without an obvious solution.

In similar vein, we also played an important part in the development of Liquified Natural Gas (LNG) transportation, whose evolution began in the mid-1950s when the British Gas Council became very interested in importing LNG by sea from Lake Charles in the Gulf of Mexico to the North Thames Gas Board's Canvey Island terminal on the Thames.

The Gas Council helped to fund conversion in the US of a freighter to carry an experimental 5,000 tons of LNG in free-standing aluminium tanks to the UK. Then, on 20 February 1959, the first full LNG cargo was delivered to the UK from the US – modest forerunner of the fully-fledged British gas storage and supply industry that preceded the development of the North Sea.

In parallel with these first shipments, British Gas negotiated a long-term contract to ship LNG from Algeria to Canvey Island, and commissioned the design and construction of two commercial LNG tankers for the purpose. These were jointly-built, with Vickers Shipbuilding in Barrow producing the first vessel, *Methane Princess*, and H&W constructing the second, the *Methane Progress*. Designing for LNG, which is principally methane, was exacting. Methane has a specific gravity of 0.45-0.5 and its volume is approximately 1/600th of its gaseous state. It is carried at atmospheric pressure or slightly above, at its boiling point of minus 162 degrees centigrade. Any contact of the liquid at that temperature with steel would lead to catastrophic brittle fracture.

Methane Progress was delivered in May 1964, ahead of the Vickers ship, and I sailed with her on my first of many sea trial trips. Looking back, it was quite something to be in at the birth of a significant new sector of the marine industry. It took some 34 years from the first commercial shipments of LNG in *Methane Progress* and *Princess* for the LNG tanker fleet to reach 100 vessels. However, by June 2017 the 500th LNG carrier was delivered. The largest LNG vessel is the *Qatar Qmax* at 266,000 cubic meters – some 12 times the capacity of *Methane Progress*.

Through this project, my career for the first time intersected with that of a high-flying North Thames Gas Board engineer who had progressed to being Chief Development Engineer of the Gas Council: Denis (later Sir Denis) Rooke. As with P&O, this was very far from being my final relationship with either Denis or British Gas ...

H&W was also in at the birth of North Sea discovery. We built and, in July 1966, delivered the first-ever submersible Oil Drilling Rig – the 15,000-ton *Sea Quest* for BP and the North Sea. This was truly a world breakthrough, because no shipyard on the planet was prepared at that time to launch such a vast structure, straddling three adjacent slipways. Remember that this was before the era of the building dock and well before computer-aided structural design programmes were invented.

The scale of our challenge was such that the apparently all-conquering Japanese yards thought what we intended to do was impossible. They claimed that such a large structure could not be launched from three slipways simultaneously and accordingly had refused to tender for the contract.

Where the Japanese had baulked at the launch challenge, H&W had no such qualms – characteristically of our "can-do" spirit at the time, the rig was half constructed when a small technical team was assembled to figure out in detail how it was to be safely launched! I was one of those included, and was given special responsibility for physical modelling of the launch. Consequently, I had one of the most challenging and stimulating technical roles that I could have imagined.

H&W had just recruited a new production director, Derek Kimber, who arrived one week before the launch of *Sea Quest*. Derek was a highly-qualified Engineer and former Management Consultant who had come to us from a similar role at Fairfield Shipbuilders on the Clyde in Scotland.

Derek had established a formidable reputation at Fairfield. He and Jim Lenaghan, his Managing Director who had trained at H&W, introduced a range of modernisation projects and initiatives there. He had also formed a good relationship with the Clyde workforce after they tested his strength of character.

A ship was due for launching at Fairfield. The evening before the launch, the staging at the bow remained in position late into the night shift – as was customary, in order to freshen up the paint work, the ship's name and the owner's crest.

The staging was due to be dismantled first thing on launch day. But on this occasion, the stagers at Fairfield had some grievance and were determined to test their new Production Director's character, by refusing to remove the staging – thereby forcing Derek to postpone the launch. Undaunted, Kimber ordered his startled management to launch the ship through the staging! He of course advised the Sponsor of the ship and its owners of his decision. The Sponsor duly named the ship and pulled the lever to release the launch triggers that held the ship in place until that last second. The ship took off through the staging, carrying large parts of it still attached to the hull, as she entered the waters of the Clyde!

Derek was never held to ransom again by his workforce. In fact, from then on he would never accept an excuse as to why a ship launch might need to be postponed, which gave me many a headache years later as his Managing Director at Austin & Pickersgill when high winds meant that it really would be safer to delay a launch! He drove a bright red Ford Zephyr car which sat outside the main offices until he took himself off home, which was late most evenings. He burned the midnight oil from his very start at H&W, because he could not have arrived at a much more critical time. The *Sea Quest* launch was only seven days away and as the new Production Director, this was now Derek's primary responsibility.

As a member of the launch team, I was one of the first people Derek called on at H&W. I had been asked to set up a physical model office to study the likely forces that would be transmitted during *Sea Quest's* launch. We had built a scale model of the rig and the three slipways it was straddling, in order to help us study the critical launching issues. Derek came to see the model, and to cross-examine me.

He asked some penetrating questions about the various risks involved in the launch. I knew his reputation – he didn't suffer fools gladly and was not everyone's cup of tea – so this was a testing meeting. At the end, he told me to carry on, so I must have coped reasonably well. I did not realise the impact, or should I say the propelling power, that this highly qualified, intelligent and experienced engineer would have on my career.

That first encounter was the start of what for me was a very important and rewarding relationship. Derek was to become a major influence on the future direction of my career and a life-long friend until his untimely death from asbestosis in 1995. I gave the address at his memorial service in the City, which was one of the toughest speaking challenges I have ever encountered because of our special relationship and the need to do full justice to his life, which was so rich in qualities and achievements.

Launching *Sea Quest* was a very big challenge for him. Nothing like it had been built before in a British yard. It was an awesome sight: a triangular-shaped rig constructed straddling three slipways – each of its three legs with a huge "elephant foot" was located on one of them – while its drilling deck only just cleared the overhead cranes.

To avoid the rig "tipping" during launch, which would have been a catastrophe, a temporary barge attached to the rig was built on the middle slipway to provide greater buoyancy and uplift as the rig entered the water. The calculated loads on the barge were enormous and we estimated that we had little margin, particularly if the tide was not as high as predicted on launch day, which would have reduced the buoyancy uplift on the rig structure. The physical modelling work indicated that special attention should be paid to its longitudinal structural integrity and not just on load-bearing. Subsequently, we modified the structural design accordingly.

Public interest in the launch was immense and intense. The tide on the day was indeed somewhat lower than predicted, due to wind direction, but Alan Watt, our Managing Director, made the typically courageous leadership decision to "let her go in", despite the inevitable risks.

As the rig launched on a reduced and falling tide, loads on the barge were significantly higher than predicted and, in full view of the assembled crowd, the barge started to buckle, as did my knees. For some worrying moments, I was sure a promising career in Naval Architecture was about to go out of the door. But the H&W team's audacity was vindicated: the rig was safely launched and we had achieved another landmark in the industry's development.

The media of course saw things differently and promptly crowded around my boss Dr Cameron, declaring "the launch has obviously been a disaster – can we have a comment?" Rupert, calmly smoking his pipe and wearing his trilby hat, responded: "Gentlemen, the barge was designed to be expendable!"

Thanks to his adept handling of the journalists' questions, the *Sea Quest* experience – which had taught me so much about offshore design and technology – also brought home to me a very important lesson in how to deal with the media: you should always remain cool, calm and collected – never let them see you in a panic! I have adopted this approach throughout my career, and it has served me extremely well in numerous high-pressure situations.

Relatively soon after starting to explore in the North Sea, *Sea Quest* made the first discovery, in about 350 feet of water, of what became the giant Forties field. Ultimately, this led to BP's famous announcement of the Forties find at 8.30 pm UK time on 10 October, 1970. The announcement was timed for immediately after the New York Stock Exchange – where BP shares were quoted – had closed for the day. The next day, newspapers in both Britain and America trumpeted the strike and the financial markets went wild.

This early experience of the North Sea taught me much about energy and natural resources markets, invaluable education later supplemented by my experiences at Babcock International, British Coal, British Gas and Anglo American. In such major industries, you learn in the boardroom the vital importance of careful investment decisions in such long-cycle industries and the need for the best possible Engineering, Risk and Project management expertise, coupled with leading safety management processes.

During this extraordinary period, H&W also worked on a conceptual design and bid to replace the *Queen Elizabeth* with a liner to be known as *QE2*, but we lost the tender to the John Brown yard on the Clyde. Happily, I was able to view the *QE2* and her replacement, the latest *Queen Elizabeth* and Cunard's unique transatlantic liner, the *Queen Mary 2*, at very close quarters three decades later, but that story can wait a while. Suffice for the moment to say that there have been many strange coincidences in my life which have added to the richness of my industrial journey.

We also produced the design for the world's first 100,000-ton bulk carrier, for the Norwegian Bulk Carrier Group, and later a highly successful 119,000 TDW series inspired by the same group of owners (Rudd Peterson; Skaugen alongside Ropner of the UK).

For me, the very wide design experience I garnered as a result of H&W's pre-eminence was further enriched by research secondments arranged by the company to accelerate my development as a naval architect.

The first of these was a six-month secondment to the UK's National Physical Laboratory, where some of the leading ship model research in the world was executed in its long established towing tanks at Teddington and in its then-new facility at Feltham which included world class manoeuvring basins. There, I learned much about hydrodynamics and the development of the shape of ship hull forms and their interaction with propellers under the leadership of great names such as Bob Clements, Jim Dawson and Alex Silverleaf.

About a year later, when the industry began to contemplate building ultra-large crude carriers (tankers) of the unprecedented size of more than 300,000 tons – what became known as ULCCs – I was seconded to Lloyd's Register of Shipping – Structural Research department in Fenchurch Street.

This opportunity largely resulted from the Department of Trade and Industry (today's Department of Business, Energy and Industrial Strategy) having placed feasibility development contracts with H&W for a 400,000 TDW tanker and with Tyneside's Swan Hunter for a 1,000,000 TDW vessel. At the Lloyd's Research department, we were to ascertain the technological and structural design challenges involved via these feasibility studies.

I had a wonderful experience working under the late Alan Kershaw, then Head of Research at Lloyd's Register, and a youthful Naval Architect, Dr David Aldwinkle, on these unique projects. We were applying new approaches to structural design using computer based framework analysis programmes – a precursor to today's advanced modern finite element techniques.

4. GOLIATH, ONASSIS AND ME

Our next major project after *Sea Quest*, led by Derek Kimber as Production Director, was the extensive modernisation of the shipyard.

The centrepiece of this work entailed constructing what was then the largest building dock in the world, capable of accommodating a 1.2m TDW vessel. The dock was equipped with an 800-ton KRUPP crane, which was manufactured in Belfast and erected by KRUPP engineers in 1969 and named Goliath. Goliath at 315 feet high has changed the Belfast skyline to this day; in 1974, it was joined by Sampson, another 800-tonner but even taller than Goliath. Large fabrication shops to construct huge pre-outfitted blocks were also built. This new infrastructure ushered in the age of modular pre-outfit construction and brought about a step change in productivity and reducing the build cycle time.

To help define the scale of these new shops, their cranage and other issues, I was given the job in the Design Team of producing structural designs for conceptual 500,000-ton and one million-ton tankers. This brought me into further contact with Derek, with whom I studied optimum block sizes to reduce work content in the building dock.

Even Goliath was dwarfed in significance by the next phase of modernisation, because this involved nothing less than the transformation of our approach to production.

New computer numerical controlled (CNC) burning machines

were to be installed. The new technology enabled steel plates to be automatically burned by the NC machines, eliminating the traditional mould loft work of building full-scale templates in wood to define the shape of the myriad of different piece parts. These templates had until now been created by skilled joiners and were scribbed around to transfer the shape of each piece part on to pre-ordered steel plates which were then burned by hand.

Because the new technology rendered this time-honoured technique obsolete, it created the basis for a productivity step-change, massively reducing the manpower requirement and ensuring highly accurate piece parts for each subsequent stage of assembly. Because of its implications for manning levels, the project potentially faced major trade union issues and, above all, huge retraining challenges.

Joiner loftsmen had to learn a form of computer programming and in turn be trained to work new NC drawing machine equipment. The key shop-floor role was played by the Head Loftsman, Alfie Heaney, who I had worked under during my student days in one of my six-month practical modules in production. He was a quiet unassuming man who was gifted with 3D vision, which enabled him to devise methods to develop the surface of any complex shape. I never did see him unable to solve such complex problems.

At Derek's request, I moved out of Ship Design and into Production in order to head up this project. I had the title "Numerical Applications Manager", but even this grand title didn't really reflect the new era we were embarking upon. I was fortunate to be given a leading role in implementing a shipbuilding revolution: the start of computer-aided production.

One of the earliest decisions that had to be taken was which software and computer system to adopt. There were very few systems in the world to choose from. They were inevitably large and had to store a huge volume of numerical data that would define the complete 3D hull shape of each ship. The computer would also have vast capacity to digest the mass of punched card programming instructions, and punched paper tape output to drive the new control equipment for the NC burning machines. These machines could burn up to six plates at a time with great accuracy. The computing programmes also permitted the careful allocation of the piece parts to each plate to reduce scrap steel plate material.

We homed in on the Autokon system then operating in the AKER Stord Yard close to Bergen in Norway. There were no such systems in Asian yards. Incidentally, the Norwegian shipping magnate Fred Olsen at that time was also a major shareholder in the AKER shipbuilding group. About 20 years later, he became the leading shareholder in H&W at its privatisation.

AKER were very progressive and seeking constantly to improve productivity to counter the high wages and social costs in Norway. AKER were also in conversation with Chantiers de L'Atlantique at the St Nazaire shipyard in France about the possible sale of the system.

Derek and I visited AKER and the technical team at St Nazaire to compare notes on the implementation challenges. This was my first visit to France and St Nazaire, and I was intrigued to discover, on walking through the workshop, that the employees had a two-hour lunch break. This was halfway through lunch, and many of the workforce were sitting on the shop floor propped up against the walls asleep with an emptied bottle of wine alongside!

It was the evening visit to the local seafood restaurant that presented me with some challenges – oysters, clams and mussels were sitting around in galvanised buckets of water. I'd not seen the like before and it was here I opened my first oyster in the shell. My St Nazaire colleague helpfully explained that you can see it is alive by just touching it with your fork!

We finally recommended to the H&W Board that we buy the Autokon system and training support package from AKER. I went to be trained in Oslo for two weeks along with a few of the team leaders from the loftsmen. We were then in a position to start training joiners to do programming back in Belfast.

The joiners, helped by an excellent small team from AKER, responded exceptionally well to the training and proved amazingly adaptable. The Norwegian team in those early days seemed to particularly enjoy their social evenings out on the town and spoke rather warmly about the attractiveness of the Belfast girls!

I also recognised the need to have our own dedicated Software Support Engineer and I had the good fortune to hire Malachy O'Neill to maintain and adapt the system. He was a key person in this significant transformation from wood template to paper tape.

During my time as Numerical Applications Manager, I had a heavy day job training the loftsmen (who made the wooden templates) into Numerical Control Coders for the Autokon system, and overseeing the installation of the new NC draughting and burning machines.

The only major computing system in Ireland big enough to process the software was the large ICL 1907 at QUB which I was able to hire, but only between 1 a.m. and 3 a.m. During the testing and commissioning phase for the new burning machines, I would take the punched cards prepared from the loftsmen programming, return home for a very short evening with Emma and then go to the university for 1 a.m. with my block of punched cards.

I'd collect the output of paper tape after the computer run and return to the Loft Office on the H&W nightshift with the material. We tested them for accuracy on the newly installed numerical controlled drawing machine before going to test on the new burning machines. In the commissioning stage, instead of burning, we would scribe the shapes on to a steel plate checking for dimensional accuracy before getting the burning machine torches lit up for cutting. As a result of these nocturnal activities, I had not many hours' sleep each night for some months.

Inevitably, we'd collect a great audience of night shift steel workers to watch the magic of these huge machines cutting shapes directed by a paper tape. The workforce adaptability was tremendous. They recognised that this transformation was key to our future and we encountered no serious industrial relations problems during implementation.

We moved swiftly to spread NC cutting to lift productivity especially through the new accuracy of the piece parts and their subsequent ease of fit-up. This was an exciting time: to be in on the ground floor of a new technology which was transforming production methods. One could look ahead and see the day, not all that far ahead, when production drawings and manufacturing information would be prepared via computer screen which would displace the traditional draughting table – just as punched paper tape replaced wooden template. Within a few years, CAD-CAM technology with drawings compiled on a computer screen became the norm and ushered in another advance in this new era.

As I was seeing through this dramatic change in our way of working, my personal life also underwent a transformation. Early one morning on 31st July, 1970 when the phone rang at 6 a.m. to tell me that Emma had given birth to a son, whom we called Graham, at the Royal Victoria Hospital. I went to see them a few hours later. These were times when there were no scans to give you advance warning about the baby's sex and fathers were not expected in delivery rooms! When Graham came home he slept little and was a very colicky baby – including projectile vomiting for his first six weeks! I'd come home from these day shift/night shift hours to find an exhausted wife carrying Graham around and I'd have to take over! How we got through those early weeks was a miracle.

Graham brought great joy to our lives and grew up loving school, literature, drama and the Arts, played the bassoon and was a very good all-round student. He crashed his mum's car a few times before going off to study Drama at Manchester University, where he gained a First. He later went to New York for a two-year scholarship to the Whitney Museum of Art. It was during this period that he met his wife Ina.

Ina, a very talented lady, was in publishing and Graham, after writing his first book on Art, found his niche in sports journalism where he specialises in soccer reporting and interviews with the world stars who are joining the growing sport in the US. He also covers tennis and golf and recently his articles made the front page of The New York Times. I guess this all started when he was about five years old and I was running Austin & Pickersgill shipbuilders on Wearside. We went regularly to watch Sunderland play at Roker Park and at his early age, I used to lift him over the entrance turnstiles. He became highly knowledgeable about football and is a supporter of Sunderland to this day. Our Roker visits also had a business benefit for me: they allowed me to meet informally with shop stewards and foremen from the yard – very valuable people time.

Fiona, or Fee as we now know her, was born almost two years later on 1st June 1972. I can still recall so clearly sitting at my desk in H&W and taking the telephone call from the delivery Doctor, Dr Roger Cromey – a friend who had been at school with Emma – to say we had a baby daughter. I rushed to the hospital to see this dark-haired little beauty with a very happy mum. That very afternoon I had to leave for Greece to lead a Sales and Marketing effort planned for some time. Fee still teases me today for abandoning her!

Just over a week later after Fee's birth, vigilante groups had formed in various parts of the country as the Northern Ireland 'troubles' increased in intensity. Emma decided to go with the new baby and Graham (nearly two) to stay over with her parents, about twenty miles away in North Antrim. With a few miles to go she encourntered a makeshift road block manned by hooded young men with guns. They ordered her out of the car and she refused. She asked them "why are you doing this" and they responded "we are protecting civil liberties" Emma replied "not from where I am sitting you are not and I am not leaving a new born baby and another infant alone in the car. If they wake and see your hooded faces they will be terrified". After some further delay and consultation they partially opened the road block and she arrived rather shaken at her parents home. Fortunately a lot has changed for the better in Northern Ireland since these and other inexplicable sad events occurred.

Fee was always an independent child and full of fun and curiosity. She had to be left to do things by herself including, memorably, taking the stabilisers off her first bike after I'd claimed it was too early to do so! She grew up loving animals and children. She was and still is a good horsewoman and persuaded me over many months in her early teens that she must have a horse. I finally agreed, subject to it keeping her away from the boys. This first horse was followed by the building of a stable, then a horse box and a Jeep so she generally achieved her goal.

She was a good all-rounder at school and set her heart on being a children's nurse. But after a year's nursing she decided to go to University and study Food Science. She gained a 2:1 and followed this by a Masters in Environmental Science with Distinction, plus a Diploma in Statistics thrown in. All the while she coxed the men's eight at Queen's and at Trinity College Dublin. She then spent a year in Australia, rescuing fruit bats in the rain forests and doing other environmental work, gained a deep sea diving certificate and worked in game parks. It was in one of the game parks that she had the unique experience of witnessing the birth of a baby giraffe. Following the birth, the mother giraffe, with whom she'd stayed for many hours, lowered her head until it was within an inch of Fee's face as if to say thank you. She said it was one of the most moving moments of her life.

My time as Numerical Application Manager drew to a close as we successfully launched the computerisation project. I was certainly noticed afresh by the company's top management, who brought many visitors and shipbuilding customers to see our computer-based production technology. The automatic drawing machine attracted the crowds and we were now well ahead of our competitors across the world.

About now, Derek Kimber decided on a career change and left to become Director General of the Chemical Industry Association in London. I didn't think our paths would cross professionally again. Life can be full of surprises …

Derek was succeeded at H&W by Amos Sutcliff, from the DTI's Shipbuilding division. Amos had been trained at Harland & Wolff and later had a period as CEO of the Dundee yard Robb Caledon. He was very knowledgeable about the industry and progressive in his thinking.

I worked happily with Amos and his able General Manager, Stuart

Tennant. Alan Watt, our MD, continued to give me enormous support in my different roles and indeed throughout my training and development. Alan was a shrewd judge of people and knew how to stretch a few of us by his particular form of talent management – which consisted largely of dropping you in at the deep end and seeing if you sank or swam.

A great friend of Alan's and a regular visitor to the yard at this time was Robbie Robinson, the Director of Shell International Marine. He had just placed orders for four 315,000-ton deadweight oil tankers. I struck up a great relationship with Robbie, who remained a lifelong friend and later wrote me wonderful letters of advice from his retirement home in Cornwall.

Regrettably, I subsequently lost his address during one of our house moves. However, I recalled it was in St Mawes and ultimately went there to search for him. I called the local estate agent and found that Robbie's daughter was working part-time in their office. She directed me to his home, and Robbie and his wife received us warmly. We had wonderful discussions about the industry: he truly was the pioneer of the VLCC and ULCC oil tankers and led much change in the tanker industry. I visited him many times over the years until he passed away in the late 1990s. On my last visit a year earlier, he was still very lucid and had great recall. He explained to me with some humour and in Ship Repair terms that his personal ballast and fuel systems were in need of replacement. Robbie was an industrial giant and I learned so much from him.

At about the time I completed the Numerical Application assignment, the Manager of the Production Drawing Offices, Noel Coulter, died very unexpectedly. I was approached by Amos Sutcliff to ask if I'd be prepared to take this sizeable management role, involving management of some 120 draughtsmen and engineers.

I was still only 29 years old and I was now being invited to manage Chief Draughtsmen and many Section Leaders who had been involved in my training just a few years earlier. I was very uncertain about such a move but Alan Watt got hold of me and said: "You can do it – just go for it. There is a lot to do, and one day this operation will also be computerised and you understand that!"

So I went for it, but with a great sense of humility and gratitude that my bosses had more confidence in me than I had in myself.

The Production drawing offices were responsible for delivering to Production all manufacturing and construction information, and to Procurement for providing all data needed for purchasing and sub-contracting. The particular challenge was that generally they lagged behind schedule with this vital information, and inflicted delays in production.

We set about establishing with the Chief Draughtsmen a proper planning, scheduling and monitoring process. This was much needed for our whole operation, but in particular, it was very relevant to one specific and major problem contract which presented me with an immediate managerial challenge.

Production was being impeded on two 250,000 TDW oil super-tankers (VLCCs) for the Onassis Group – *Olympic Brilliance* and *Olympic Banner*. The delays were partly due to Onassis's own repetitive plan approval cycle at their Monaco office and partly to poor planning and organisation on our side. On our side, the Drawing Office programme and hence the manufacturing information for Production was running behind schedule. On theirs, their technical teams insisted that plan approval kept rotating, which meant that every modification involved several resubmissions until it was finally accepted by them as approved.

Onassis's Technical Director was Dr Andrew Spyrou – a Greek national with a degree in Naval Architecture from Glasgow University. Fortunately, he and I hit it off and between us, we solved a lot of the scheduling problems between Belfast and Monaco.

In a spirit of cooperation, I approached Andrew for a new way of working the Plan Approval cycle – and he responded in a similarly constructive way. Together, we boiled down the multiple times that plans were being resubmitted to a one-time submission cycle, incorporating an undertaking that changes requested would be accepted except those we notified them by Telex. Any outstanding disagreements would be dealt with by us in 1:1 meetings – face to face technical discussions to resolve the requests that were deemed unacceptable by one party or the other. Because of our good working relationship, this new system worked extremely well, removing the bottlenecks and enabling us to recover some of the schedule.

Andrew was a gentleman and a true professional, and I learned from this challenge that open dialogue with your client is always critical. It takes two to tango! It should be done in an open and transparent way because that is the only way to achieve cooperation, and usually leads to a common sense approach. Never let a situation fester that is damaging your business. Regardless of the apparent mountain to climb – seek a solution and crack the problem. That is Management in the real sense – adding value by resolving problem areas, clearing the way and creating success.

As it happened, that was not the end of the problems with the Onassis contract – but this further trouble had nothing to do with Andrew and my harmonious working relationship. I will comment on it later.

I had just got to grips with overcoming some of the reform challenges of the Drawing Office management role when I was promoted, following the arrival of a new Managing Director, Ivor Hoppe, from Denmark. I was given a completely new commercial role as General Manager for Ship Sales and Marketing (including Cost Estimating, Contracts and Market Research). Ivor, a distinguished Danish lawyer, had been with the A P Moller shipping group in Denmark for some years and had been very close to Captain Moller, the founder of Maersk.

Ivor had been Managing Director of Moller's Odense Shipyard but had fallen out of favour with Captain Moller's son and heir, the-then young Mr Maersk McKinney Moller. His appointment at H&W caused great commotion in our management ranks as he brought with him more than 14 Danish, Swedish and Norwegian managers to Belfast.

Enrichment of the Belfast management was necessary but this was such a revolution that the morale of some good local managers crashed. It brought home to me that, when managerial change is necessary, as it quite often is if you are to change the performance culture, it still has to be handled carefully. Otherwise, the effect can be counter-productive – you can cause more problems than you resolve. And the greater the change, the more sensitive your touch has to be.

Ivor was certainly a brilliant maritime lawyer and, on reading the Onassis contract, he discovered that Onassis had inserted a clause dealing with renegotiation of the price if the vessels were delayed. We had managed to make up some of the delay but not all of it, and Ivor believed that this could be turned to our advantage.

These VLCCs had been contracted probably at around £10 million each and were now, because oil tanker freight rates were soaring, worth around £25 million each. Such was, and is, the volatility in the shipping market where many fortunes are won and lost. Hoppe decided we must send a notice to Onassis advising them that the delivery of the first vessel would be held up until the price renegotiation under this clause took place.

The balloon went up immediately – Bob Crawford, then the leading maritime lawyer in London with Ince and Co, called me in an absolute rage: what kind of way was this to treat Aristotle Onassis, who by the way owned 15% of H&W, etc, etc . It was indeed true that Onassis and Jackie had enjoyed the equivalent of a state visit to the yard in Belfast only months earlier.

It was agreed that an early meeting with Onassis personally had to be arranged. We were due to meet him in London, but then a message came through that it had to be in Greece, with no exact destination confirmed. He would send his Learjet to London for Hoppe, David Alexander, a maritime lawyer from Norton Rose, and myself. The Learjet duly landed at an air force base in Western Greece and a helicopter whisked us off for the yet unknown location which turned out to be the island of Scorpios, Onassis's private island on the Ionian Sea on the West Coast of Greece.

He was there, at the top of the island at a dusty landing pad, personally to meet us in a Mini Moke. He drove it down from the top of the island and we stopped at the little chapel to pay our respects to the tomb of Alexander, his son, who had been killed so tragically in a helicopter crash. This was also the chapel where the wedding ceremony with Jackie Kennedy had taken place. David Alexander was directed to one of the houses on the island and Ivor Hoppe and I were taken on board the *Christina*, Onassis's very large and opulent private yacht. It was lavishly appointed with gilt gold tap fittings in the bathrooms and bar stools said to be made out of whales' scrotums. We were on board for two nights but caught no sight of Jackie, although he told us she was aboard with some American guests.

Our meetings were conducted by day in one of the large houses on the island. At night, we had dinner with our host on the terrace where he personally peeled peaches and other fruits and placed them on your plate with a happy and smiling countenance, telling many stories about his business adventures.

He was truly a Jekyll and Hyde character: on one hand the most gracious and charming host you could imagine; on the other the most aggressive negotiator that I have ever come across. His language (including a rich description of us collectively implying that we didn't know our parents) would have shocked most shipyard men.

All in all it was a memorable experience, but we made no progress whatsoever and after two days, Hoppe sent me home to ensure our building dock gates were secured to avoid any likelihood of both ships, now afloat, being towed out by Onassis at night! A most unlikely scenario perhaps, but I did what I was told. We passed the matter into the hands of the lawyers with a view to arbitration, but Onassis kept resisting and frustrating the process. Hoppe and I had one further meeting with him without a glimmer of progress, in his stunning Paris home in Avenue Foch where we were introduced to his daughter Christina.

I travelled the world with Ivor Hoppe and we had considerable order book success including the series of 119,000 TDW bulk carriers to the NBC consortium in Norway. Some of these were sold with the help of a great character, the fun-loving Harold Jacklyn, the very experienced Managing Director of the Oslo shipbroker Fearnly & Egger.

We developed a new generation of product carriers at 60,000-ton DW for Furness Withy of London, where the able Brian (later Sir Brian) Shaw was Deputy Chairman and later Chairman and the Chief Naval Architect was the outstanding Walter Cairns. Walter was assisted by Charles Arkinstall, who later became the Technical Director of P&O Princess Cruises and later was appointed to the same position at Carnival. He served both companies with great distinction and has retired close to our home in Newton Ferrers in Devon. The largest ships we sold were 333,000 TDW ultra large crude carriers to Maritime Fruit Carriers in Haifa, Israel.

I learned a great deal about international commercial and contractual negotiation from Ivor, who was a brilliant negotiator and maritime lawyer. He had a superb network of shipowning contacts in London, Europe and the USA – especially in the US Oil Companies – and together we visited most of them. He had also developed a compelling expansion vision for H&W resulting in a second phase of our modernisation programme, which we called "P200". The new programme was designed to increase annual steel throughput capacity from 120,000 to 200,000 tons.

H&W undoubtedly emerged from its major investments as one of the world's best-equipped shipbuilders of the 1970s. But this is where the massive influx of new management from Scandinavia under Ivor Hoppe worked against us. Some of the new people were excellent and some were mediocre; but their overall effect was to undermine the morale of some very dedicated Belfast managers. As a result output did not move forward at the pace the new investment should have delivered.

This drawback was exacerbated by Hoppe's uncompromising stance over working practice changes against the moderate local leader of the steelworkers' union, Sandy Scott. This led to a highly damaging 12-week strike.

I recall speaking to Sandy during this testing period, when I tried my best to explain the damage being inflicted on our ship-owning customers and in particular Harland & Wolff's reputation overseas. He said: 'I'm totally willing to be part of building the future, but there needs to be a dialogue not a diktat. This is about me being faced with the inevitable force and I have no choice but be the immovable object!'

Sad, but this was largely Ivor Hoppe's undoing. It taught me a life-long lesson to build strong bridges of communication with your workforce and union representatives – since management generally gets the union opposition or co-operation it deserves.

Some chief executives and managers whom I have encountered believed this practice reflected weakness and sent the wrong message to the shop-floor. I have always believed that is a fundamental misconception which actually reflects a lack of self-confidence by the leadership. There are always going to be occasions where you need to stand up to strong union or workforce resistance to necessary change: that is precisely when you most need really good channels of communication, because when you can explain to your people why the change you want is necessary, you are very likely to win their – possibly reluctant – agreement. That has always been my experience.

The strike had not been over long when I received an unexpected job offer. It came from none other than Derek Kimber, who had discovered after joining the Chemical Industry Association that he was still bitten by the shipbuilding bug. Derek was lured back into the industry by the Greek shipping magnate Basil Mavroleon, then Chairman of London and Overseas Freighter, to become Chairman of the Sunderland shipbuilder Austin & Pickersgill (A&P), which Basil owned. Derek had settled into his new position when, in 1973, we both attended the biannual Oslo Shipping Exhibition. Derek had a proposition for me: he asked me to join A&P as Managing Director.

This was a huge gamble on Derek's part – I was only 32 years old and, although I had experience of all facets of shipyard operation, I had never been a MD. I recognised this was an offer which I could not afford to turn down. The adage that the opportunity of a lifetime must be seized during the lifetime of the opportunity was never more true!

However, leaving H&W proved far from straightforward because, although there was no contractual notice on either side, Ivor Hoppe refused to accept or indeed acknowledge my resignation. I was forced to stay on for several months to help try to win contracts which we had under discussion with the East Asiatic Company of Copenhagen for some 60,000-ton tankers.

Such was Ivor's unwillingness to face up to my departure that we had to say goodbye in the East Asiatic boardroom in Copenhagen. This was necessary so that I could catch a flight to Dublin and drive to Belfast to get back for a farewell party which friends had organised on the Friday night – I had the Saturday to clear my office at H&W and we were moving house to Sunderland on Monday morning!

I left things tidy for my successor, Ken Ruddock, who I had recommended to Ivor Hoppe. Ken had been a student in the same Naval Architecture year as myself. He was not only very able, with wide technical experience, but he had the personality and stature to meet with the world's shipowners.

A decade later, when I returned to H&W as Chairman and CEO, he was still leading Marketing and Sales, and I had no hesitation in immediately appointing him to the Main Board as our Sales and Marketing Director. We worked very successfully together until Ken's tragic and sudden death from a form of galloping leukaemia at the all too young age of 45. He left a wife and two young sons, and we set up a memorial student prize in his memory. I lost a great professional from the Boardroom and a valued long-term friend.

I have always believed, whatever my job and however long I might be in that post, that one of my primary responsibilities is to identify a suitable successor. Of course, my immediate boss or the Board (after I became a CEO and then a Chairman) might eventually choose to appoint someone else – although this has very rarely happened to me – but I will have done my duty by the company in finding at least one highly capable candidate. I have seen so many companies, some of them exceptionally well run in almost every other respect, come to grief when the CEO moves on and they have not put in place a firm succession plan. Such an error is, to my mind, one of the worst failures of corporate governance that a Board can commit.

Ivor Hoppe did not remain in charge of H&W for very long. A matter of weeks after I joined Austin & Pickersgill, he was dismissed by Stan Orme, who had become Secretary of State for Northern Ireland. I don't think it was a total surprise, given that Orme had a strong relationship with the trade unions in general and with Sandy Scott, the senior shop steward at H&W, in particular. Sandy had no time for Ivor, and the feeling was mutual.

It was also true that Government were becoming concerned at Hoppe's high lifestyle. He would hire the odd private plane, stay in a luxury suite at the Savoy and dine there on the finest of wines. On these occasions, I would stay across the road in the somewhat less well-appointed Strand Palace hotel! It was rumoured that Hoppe had also carried out extensive modifications to his house, provided I believe by the company, without proper approvals.

So I guess it was an accumulation of events that gave grounds for a short letter of dismissal from Sir Ewart Bell, the highly-regarded Head of the N.I. Civil Service. One incidental result was that the Onassis case was scuppered, because Ivor had been its champion.

This was a very sad end to a promising new beginning for Harland & Wolff. As I've said, Ivor was a brilliant maritime lawyer and I had great respect for his visionary outlook and contract negotiating skills, learning much from him about this part of business. However, no CEO, however adept he might be in one or two aspects of business, can succeed if he has particular shortcomings in crucial areas of management – particularly the management and leadership of people.

In Ivor's case, his inability to build a trusting bridge of communication with the workforce was a fundamental weakness. The majority in his Scandinavian management invasion, on balance, did more harm than good. He was not a great listener and did not relish advice. But he had the vision to create a shipyard that at the time was the best equipped of its type and of a scale to be a world leader.

Experiencing so much of this at first hand and weighing Ivor's strengths and defects, I learned that a leader has to win the confidence of his or her management team and through them, the employees. You do that through your management style, communicating clear strategic objectives, because this empowers your managers to inspire their people to deliver. You have to demonstrate the art of building a team, and your leadership should be visible. You have to learn that none of us are as smart as all of us! I'm not a disciple of Karl Marx, but one of his maxims makes absolute sense in management: "Refuse light from no quarter" – that underlines the need to listen.

Of course, at the end of listening, ventilating, debating and analysis, democracy ends and decisions must be taken. "Paralysis through analysis" is no way to run an effective business. But if people feel their views have been given a proper hearing, they will be prepared to support your decisions as their leader. It is when your colleagues believe they are being ignored or railroaded that the rot sets in and the leader loses authority.

There was one bizarre footnote before I finally joined A&P: I received a message that Mr Onassis would like me to consider joining his shipping group. Quite apart from the commitments I had made to Derek Kimber, on the basis of my two days' experience on the island of Scorpios, that was never going to be a runner.

I look back with great affection and thankfulness for the opportunity I gained in those early H&W years. The thorough technical and research grounding I got, along with the depth of experience in Ship Design, Computer Applications in Production, Management and the Contractual and Commercial experience in ship Sales & Marketing around the world, was extraordinary and thoroughly equipped me for the future. Many managing directors and CEOs reach the top through one or perhaps two lines of work; I was fortunate to have been exposed to the workings of virtually every part of the company. As I look back now at this holistic development experience, I recognise that it is one of the main reasons why I was able to progress both in my original industry and later in others.

Above all, H&W was a great "university of life", where I experienced not just the design, engineering and construction of great ships, but where I first learned about human engineering and the management and challenges of leading teams of people.

5. AUSTIN & PICKERSGILL

A&P employed about 2,500 people in the Pickersgill and Bartram's yards in Sunderland. After I arrived, I realised that – thanks to all the experience I had gained at Harlands – I was probably better equipped than most managers, regardless of my relatively young age, to take on this huge role. However, I still had so much to learn and thankfully I've gone on learning since. In fact, I have never stopped learning; the moment you think that you know it all is the point at which you start closing your ears to fresh insights and good advice – and that is something as a business leader that you should never do.

Fortunately, my upbringing left no place for arrogance or complacency. It had taught me respect for the individual and that integrity is a critical success ingredient in management. My first Managing Director role was a daunting task but also a marvellous opportunity, and I owe it all to Derek Kimber and his faith in me. He was a valued friend, along with Gwen, his wife, and his family whom we got to know well through the 12 launch parties a year at A&P.

That's how busy the yard was at that time. Our main product was the best-selling SD 14 general cargo vessel, and we produced one every 27 working days. With this packed schedule, Derek's refusal to delay a launch – a principle he had held to ever since his days on the Clyde – did give me some testing times. In excruciating high wind situations where delay by 24 hours would have significantly reduced risk, he would not give way – so my heart was in my mouth on a few memorable high risk launch days.

As I mentioned, I gave the address at Derek's memorial service in 1995 and I can say it was one of the most challenging public addresses I have ever made. Two decades on, a number of us were still meeting annually for a memorial lunch to this remarkably gifted man. Our friendship stood the test of time and some very difficult personal challenges, particularly when I became his boss after the industry was nationalised and I went full time to the British Shipbuilders Corporation.

We had a superb management team at A&P Appledore, which delivered great commercial success to our owner, Basil Mavroleon. We were Britain's most successful and profitable merchant shipyard. Virtually all our 12 ships a year were sold on the export market. I spent many weeks negotiating in our largest market, Greece, as well as in China, Hong Kong, the Philippines, Vietnam, Norway, Finland and other countries.

SD 14 was our cornerstone product. It was a great series production success story for British merchant shipbuilding – a brilliant case of identifying a market opportunity and satisfying it through a no-frills design – equivalent to Henry Ford's approach of "any colour so long as it's black" – efficient production and effective international sales.

SD 14 was a 15,000-ton dry cargo ship designed, developed and built by A&P, which became the world's best-selling post-World War II standard vessel. The concept of the standard ship went back at least to World War I, when the speed at which vessels could be completed and put to sea to transport much-needed supplies and material to war zones took precedence over their production cost or operational economy.

The most famous standard ship in the world was the 10,000-ton Liberty cargo vessel, first built by the Kaiser Corporation in the US in the Second World War. In all, 2,580 were produced during World War II, and they continued in service worldwide for a good quarter-century after 1945. The Liberty replacement class spawned a number of such standard ships around the world, all with the common attributes – or attempted attributes – of being reliable, cargo-friendly and with low maintenance and operating costs.

SD 14 was one of this group, developed with astute timing in the 1960s – just when the Liberty ships were beginning to approach retirement. The first SD 14 was delivered in 1968 following a challenge from Basil Mavroleon to the yard management to build a Liberty replacement for £900,000 – Basil said he would buy the first one. The story of the SD 14 is brilliantly documented in a fine book by the talented former Estimating and Contracts Manager at A&P, John Lingwood. Over its lifetime, a total of 211 SD 14s were sold all over the world, including a number built under licence from A&P in Greece, Brazil and Argentina. Its biggest rival was the Freedom class built by our Japanese competitors IHI – and designed by George Campbell, a North-East naval architect who set up GTR Campbell Consulting Naval Architects operating out of Japan.

SD 14's strongest marketing feature was its highly competitive price, which for the first 1968 delivery was £915,000. It also had low fuel consumption based on a reliable slow-speed Sulzer diesel engine, and versatile cargo-carrying ability. Moreover, in keeping with the great Japanese principle of "kaizen", or constant improvement, A&P did not rest on its laurels with the first design and instead progressively updated it through a number of Series upgrades – so that by the time of the Series IV in 1976, the ship had a price tag of about £5 million. Productivity gains coupled with improved production methods ultimately enabled A&P to produce a new SD 14 every 27 working days.

Apart from the benefit it brought directly to A&P, SD 14 generated a very strong supply chain in Britain. The main Sulzer engines and much of the key equipment including windlasses, winches and rudder stocks were manufactured on the North-East coast at companies such as Hawthorn Leslie, Clark Chapman, George Clark and Northern Engineering Industries (NEI). The vast majority of equipment and material were supplied from other UK marine suppliers that were household names at that time and, sadly, with the demise of UK merchant shipbuilding, are now no more.

Virtually all the SD14s were sold in international markets and we won a series of Queen's Awards for Export. This involved much travelling by either myself and/or my Chairman to destinations in Europe, Asia and South America – shipowners in Hong Kong, India, Pakistan, the Philippines, Vietnam, Greece, Norway, Finland, China, Brazil and Argentina all wanted such ships.

We had some memorable marketing journeys – one particularly notable trip was a visit with Derek and a Standard Chartered banker, Michael Madden, to Vietnam and the battle-scarred port of Hai Phong in 1977, only two years after the end of the war. We had to sleep there in a single room, into which was squeezed three beds complete with mosquito nets, in a bombed-out hotel with most of its roof missing along with a lot of services! We had to use a bucket to flush the loo and had a stone trough in the corner for a tiny bath. Two years later I went back with the Chief Ship Designer at A&P, Frank Thompson, and we finalised a deal for four SD14s.

Derek and I knew from the outset of our partnership that we could not rely on SD 14 alone to make A&P successful, so we introduced the B26 – a 26,000-ton DW bulk carrier conceived with the same no-frills approach as for the SD 14. In order to produce both SD 14 and larger ships competitively, we needed significantly to upgrade our facilities. We wanted to create the most modern yard in the world for vessels up to 40,000 tons.

We therefore drew up plans to modernise and expand the yard, including a new covered slipway berth. A&P Appledore, an associated shipyard design house provided consultancy support. Derek, Chris Langley, our Ship Production Director, and myself formed the core project team.

The project was to cost around £30m. Of this, £10m was already earmarked from our own cash resources and £10m from a DTI-supported loan with £10m to come, during the construction phase, from profits yet to be earned from our current and future order book.

Derek was anxious to have Basil Mavroleon, our owner, aligned with such a major investment. He invited "Mr M", then around 80 years old, to visit the yard. I was given the task of accompanying him around the site, inspecting a scale model of the new facility and also viewing an additional 30 acres of land which we had already acquired to enable the expansion.

Mr M asked a number of questions and was generally interested in all that he saw and I think was enjoying his day out of London. On arrival back at the office, as he was freshening up, Derek was anxious to know whether he was positive on the way around about the project. I said he seemed more than interested but had made no committal.

Over lunch we talked of many things, including, I recall, that he explained he was having increased difficulty finding things at home. His wife was constantly moving things around. As an example he said that on visiting his loo at home he noticed a very striking small painting on the back of the door. To his surprise, as he looked closer he discovered it was a Canaletto!

When Derek finally raised the topic of the scale of the investment at £30m, Basil, quite unperturbed, went on eating his lunch and without looking up said, "Derek – it is only money. It looks good."

We were all really enthused by Basil's endorsement of what was a massive investment which would transform output and productivity. It would also concentrate all production at our Southwick yard and close the ageing Bartram facility at South Dock on the south of the River Wear's entrance.

Having acquired some 30 acres at the west end of the existing Southwick site, we needed a further five acres to the east of the site to extend our steel stockyard and automate its handling. The land was a disused British Rail embankment site which was occupied by a pig farmer who was squatting!

We agreed a deal with British Rail but the recalcitrant farmer refused to move. We then proceeded to have conversations with him and offered to relocate him to a smallholding that we identified in the area. He was still holding out for other goodies and explained that a key reason he couldn't move was that he had buried his horse on the site a few years earlier, and he wanted to know what we intended to do about the grave. This was a major obstruction but the situation then took an unexpected turn for the better – as they often do …

One Sunday, I came to the shipyard knowing we had a morning shift. Chris Langley and I often met for an hour on a Saturday or Sunday to discuss progress on the new project and any concerns about production over the coming week. On approaching the yard, I saw very dense smoke and flames coming up from the embankment. A smiling Chris Langley explained that the farmer's pigs had got swine fever and the army of agricultural officials now present had insisted on the pigs' carcases being burned on the spot without delay. The fire started to burn along the complete embankment which, we discovered, comprised a high percentage of coal fires. It burned for days and we gladly assisted with bulldozers from our site works, to move and level the embankment under the direction of the fire brigade!

The yard expansion was targeted to increase annual output by about 50% from 12 SD 14 equivalent vessels to a potential 18, reducing further the cycle time of deliveries from the current delivery of a ship every 27 working days to one ship every 18 working days.

As a result, we had the infrastructure necessary to support our international sales drive. Exporting to the world market place is often very challenging, but it can also be fun. You learn about and show respect to the many different cultures. You study negotiating styles. You build long-lasting friendships.

In China it is said: "First make friends, then do business". This is a key principle applicable in all markets, especially when selling capital-intensive projects.

Greece was undoubtedly our most prolific SD 14 market because Greek shipowners, from Onassis onwards, had prospered by buying up, post-World War II, the huge number of Liberty ships then available for sale by the US authorities and which by the 1970s, were more than 30 years old and needed replacement.

Our many long and tough negotiations with Greek owners were part and parcel of the challenges of exporting. We were greatly helped by the wide contacts that Nick Petmezas, the highly effective manager of our Greek office, built up over his period in charge for A&P and later for British Shipbuilders.

Emma and I made many ship-owning friends at A&P but few friendships stood the test of time more than that with Aristidis Alafouzos, the owner of Glafki Shipping, his wife Lena (who sadly died in 2013) and their sons Yannis and Themis. Aristidis built a number of SD14s with us and was an exemplary customer. On one of the ships, he invited Emma to be the sponsor and name it *Capitan Marcos*. Over the years when we get together, it is as if we had seen each other only yesterday.

On the subject of Greece, I recall the hours that Frank Thomson, our sales director, and myself spent negotiating the extras for three SD14s for Vassos Haj-Ioannou – an uncle of Stelios, founder of EasyJet. I first met Stelios when he was a young boy, along with his late father Loucas, who at that time was the owner of the largest tanker fleet in the world.

During these particular SD14 negotiations, Vassos insisted on getting a particular extra package of equipment at about one-third of its real price. I had no option during the two weeks of negotiations to resist this, as it was a significant amount. My only solution was to bury the potential hit in the lengthy list of other extras where he was generally accepting the prices – but of course I didn't tell Vassos I was going to do this. We held our negotiating line until Derek Kimber arrived for signature of the contracts.

Derek asked me the evening before the signing if there were any problems and I told him that I had resisted yielding on the huge discount on this particular extra. However, I told him: "I've put you in a position to give it away at the contract signing, as I've now covered for it and more." Sure enough, on the morning of the contract signing, Vassos insisted I give way and I turned it over to my Chairman who magnanimously agreed to meet the customers' wishes. At the generous celebration lunch of caviar and lobster, Vassos, who was hosting and sitting beside me, dug his elbow into my ribs and said with a huge smile – "I won." The fun of negotiations!

Sadly, the shipping market deteriorated and the contracts were cancelled after I left A&P, but the yard at least retained the customer's deposit. I enjoyed Vassos's company and since he was a keen soccer fan, we attended a number of football matches together including visits to Chelsea and of course to Sunderland at its then-stadium Roker Park.

One of the Chelsea games was against Fulham, who had signed my fellow Northern Irishman George Best late in his career. We were just taking our seats as the whistle went for kick-off, and Best promptly took off like a rocket, beating several players to put the ball in the net within the first minute. What talent you could not help but admire. After that initial run he visibly slowed down!

There were many memorable occasions during negotiations for new contracts and at the subsequent launch parties which continued at the splendid rate of one per month. They were expertly managed by Murial Jeffrey, the joint PA to myself and Derek – an exceptional manager and administrator.

Around midnight at one such party held at Newcastle's Gosforth Park Hotel, a certain Greek shipowner poked my Chairman's fairly rotund figure and said bluntly: "You are getting rather fat." Derek, enjoying his post-dinner drinks, took fierce exception and challenged the 50-year-old ship-owner to a race all the way around the Gosforth Park racetrack! He gave me instructions to have a cooked breakfast ready for their return. Much to my surprise they did make it without one or other collapsing, and I joined them for a cooked breakfast in the early hours of the morning.

The longest launch party that I knew about – although I certainly wasn't present for all of it – was for the Bergen shipowner Arne Steckmast of Wallem Shipping and his brother Karl Emil from a Paris-based firm of shipbrokers. This started, as I understand it, on a Saturday night in a London supper club hosted by the brothers'

80-year-old mother. This was prior to a "high liquidity" train journey the following day to Newcastle, where the group stayed overnight in the city's Station Hotel ahead of the launch on the Monday.

We had a small dinner party for them all that Sunday evening in Newcastle. It was a happy and lively affair, until they inevitably began to flag, given the extent of partying they had been engaged in over the weekend.

The following day's launch was successful and was followed by a champagne reception at A&P. The formal launch dinner was back at the Station Hotel in Newcastle that night. At midnight, we had to agree to pay the band extra to remain for another two hours, after which Karl Emil took over at the piano. The A&P representatives, including me, got away at around 4 a.m. with the party still going but reasonably well behaved. Subsequent stories revealed that the Chief Engineer for Steckmast, who had supervised the building of the ship, became "well the worse of wear" and decided to call it a day. He attempted to persuade his wife to let him into their room, which she had returned to hours earlier. After much knocking, she finally opened the door and immediately put out the lights. He undressed in the dark and then realised he needed to visit the loo. After locating a door handle, he opened it and walked through it – only to find himself in the corridor of the Station Hotel in the "altogether"! A very different negotiation with his wife followed, before he regained entry to the room.

The following morning I received a phone call from the manager of the hotel. He advised me of the 5 a.m. football match held apparently in one of the corridors with much singing and many annoyed hotel guests. He further advised me that our business was no longer welcome if we could not control our guests. I apologised profusely and said I fully understood his decision and was unaware of this post-launch dinner party activity. We did go elsewhere for a number of launch dinners after that, but eventually he was very happy to have our business back!

My final launch party with A&P as a private company was for the

Capitan Marcos event, which took place on 1 July 1977 – the day that the Labour Government had determined as the "Vesting Day" to nationalise the shipbuilding and aircraft industries. Emma had been invited by Aristidis Alafouzos to be the sponsor, and Graham (then aged seven) and Fiona (five) along with my mother and Emma's parents were all there to witness the ship naming, the bottle of champagne successfully breaking, and the ship graciously sliding into the River Wear. Derek Kimber was there as Chairman, the Master of Ceremonies, replete with his bowler hat which he always wore on launch days. It was a rather nostalgic occasion.

Next morning, I caught the train to London and started a period of secondment at the newly created British Shipbuilders Corporation.

6. BRITISH SHIPBUILDERS CORPORATION

I had joined Austin & Pickersgill in the same year – 1974 – as the Labour government was elected and then re-elected. There were two general elections in that year, but Labour was returned with a wafer-thin majority. As a result of this unstable situation – Labour in power but with no guarantee that it could enact its policies – a huge cloud of uncertainty hung over the shipbuilding industry for several years.

Clause Four of Labour's constitution committed the party to bring key industries into state ownership, so it was clear from the moment that the government was elected that it wanted to nationalise ship-building and the aircraft industry. By the same token, however, it was far from clear whether Labour could actually succeed in its objective.

Nothing much happened for two years and all of us in the industry therefore continued with business as usual, except for the fact that we knew the Government still wanted to nationalise. In 1976, the event appeared to move closer and gain substance because the civil servants at the DTI set up a three-man organising committee in 1976 to plan in detail for "Vesting Day" – the intended date of nationalisation. The committee members were intended to be directors-in-waiting: when nationalisation took place and the new British Shipbuilders was created, they would form the core of the corporation's Board.

The committee members were a slightly mixed group: Admiral

Sir Anthony Griffin, former Controller of the Navy, who was to be Chairman; Graham Day, a Canadian lawyer who had been a successful CEO of Cammell Laird shipbuilders in Birkenhead and who was to be the Group CEO; and Ken Griffen, a former senior official of the Electricians' Union in South Wales, who was to be Deputy Chairman. They were to prepare for nationalisation and produce a Corporate Plan, an organisation structure, and everything else that the new entity would need to get up-and-running.

A nationalisation bill was drafted – it was combined with the plan to nationalise the aerospace industry, creating the forerunner of today's BAE Systems – and brought before the House of Commons. The Bill set 1st July 1977 as the intended Vesting Date for Nationalisation.

However, it remained totally unclear whether the Bill would win a majority, and this uncertainly increased as the day of the crucial vote neared. The Opposition Conservative party fought a protracted rear-guard action against the Bill and the resistance was such that, by the time the night of the vote arrived, very few people expected the Bill to pass.

Because of the Bill's tortuous passage through Parliament and the serious doubts about whether it would ever become law, the organising committee had broken up a few months before the actual vote took place. Graham Day returned to Canada to become head of Dome Petroleum, the Alberta-based oil and gas company.

Then, much to everyone's surprise, both politicians and industrialists, the Bill did pass – by one vote, and that was an accident: the decisive vote was cast, it was said, by a Northern Irish nationalist MP, a pub-owner from County Fermanagh, who was attending the House of Commons for the first time and apparently found himself in the wrong voting lobby!

For the industry, it would have been hard to imagine a less auspicious start to our new era of ownership. Shipbuilding was a very important part of the British economy. British Shipbuilders employed 86,000 people directly and tens of thousands more in support or related supply chain activities. It encompassed a swathe of marine operations – large-scale naval and merchant shipbuilding including so-called "mixed" yards which did both; Small shipbuilding yards, Ship Repair, Diesel Engine building, General Engineering and (the newest and fastest-growth segment) offshore equipment. It sustained hundreds of communities throughout the UK and generated vital exports, making an important contribution to Britain's balance of payments.

Yet British Shipbuilders at nationalisation had no Corporate Plan, no corporate organisation and no shadow financial controls in place. Indeed, no-one knew for many weeks what the true financial state of the industry actually was.

Within 24 hours of Nationalisation, I was asked to help plug these yawning gaps. My involvement was triggered by a request from Admiral Griffin to Derek Kimber for A&P to second me for two or three days a week to British Shipbuilders' London head office. My assignment was to set up a centralised marketing and sales organisation. Derek agreed reluctantly to release me – he was convinced that once the Corporation got me in, they would strive to keep me on a full-time basis. As usual, his instincts proved uncannily accurate.

I could not get to BS immediately because we were having the important SD 14 launch at Sunderland for Aristides Alafouzos of Glafki Shipping. Having taken the train the next day, I arrived at the rather cramped offices of the National Enterprise Board (NEB) in Grosvenor Gardens, near Victoria station, where British Shipbuilders had secured temporary occupation of one floor. The NEB had been created by the Government to own all the industries that were already or had just been nationalised.

It was here that I first met with Dick (later Sir Richard) Morris, who was Deputy Chairman of the NEB. Dick was a brilliant engineer and later a Fellow at the Royal Academy of Engineering. Our relationship continued for the best part of 30 years – he later became chairman of the American engineering group Brown & Root. We ended up as competitors on naval refits after we in Babcock International in the 1990s bought the Rosyth Dockyard in Scotland and Brown & Root bought majority control of the Devonport Dockyard in Plymouth.

Among Dick's qualities was a great sense of humour, which despite him not being involved in British Shipbuilders, proved an asset in our somewhat stressed atmosphere. The new management team, both full-timers and seconders, had its hands full – to put it mildly.

Like the Board, the executive team was an odd mixture – hardly surprising, given the lack of detailed strategic planning which had accompanied the birth of British Shipbuilders. Sir Anthony, a former Controller of the Navy, was a gentleman but by his own admission not a commercial businessman. The first CEO following Graham Day's departure was the Civil Servant, Michael Casey, who had handled the Nationalisation Bill at the DTI and set up the original Organising Committee. He was parachuted in on us at the last minute! Graham Day, a very competent lawyer-turned-industrialist, did return to BS six years later as Chairman and CEO, shortly after I had been invited to return to Belfast to turn round Harland & Wolff. Michael was highly intelligent and affable, but, like the chairman, had no industrial operational experience.

We used to joke that on Day One we had an Admiral, no CEO (Michael Casey had not yet arrived) a few secondees from the Civil Service and the shipyards, Michael Haines (formerly of the accountants McClintock) acting as Finance Director, myself and a box of paper clips!

Because there was no Corporate Plan left by the Organising Committee, we had it all to do. On top of this, the creation of BS coincided with one of the worst shipping recessions of the century.

For some weeks, we hadn't a clue whether we were making or losing money. We ultimately discovered that collectively the industry was losing well over £100 million a year. Under the Nationalisation Act, the Government had of course to pay compensation to the previous owners of all the businesses, so long as they were going concerns. Some troubled yards had limbo-danced their way under the bar of bankruptcy across the line of Vesting Day. They thereby avoided what would otherwise have been inevitable bankruptcy and, under the compensation agreement, therefore did better for their shareholders than otherwise may have been the case.

Meanwhile some of the profitable yards, particularly in naval ship-building, took claims for inadequate compensation to the European Court to contest the compensation formula, but their cases were not upheld.

Derek Kimber's forecast that the Government would want to hang on to me came true a few months later, when he was approached by Gerald Kaufman, the minister at DTI responsible for British Shipbuilders, to release me to join the Board of the Corporation as full-time Board Member for Shipbuilding. Initially, this responsibility included not only all of the merchant yards, but also all of the naval yards. Later, thankfully, a Naval Division was established under Jack Daniel, Head of the Royal Corps of Naval Constructors, who was recruited from the MOD. Jack was a man of great intellect and knowledge about the Royal Navy and its requirements.

Derek was upset, as indeed was I, that I was to leave him less than five years after joining him at A&P. It was also unfortunate timing, given that the new shipyard we had worked on together was now under construction, including a unique, covered 1½ berth slipway.

My new full-time task was quite an undertaking for a 35 year old: I was told that I was the youngest-ever Board member of a Nationalised industry. Iain Vallance of the Post Office (who later became chairman of British Telecommunications) was slightly younger, but he was not yet a member of the P.O. Board. I didn't have much time to reflect on these statistics!

We spent the initial months wrestling with the development of a realistic Corporate Plan in our small, single-floor office at the NEB. The office was open plan and I was given a "pig pen" adjacent to Michael Hanes. Michael and I worked closely together over the coming months to try to get some grip of an industry faced with the deteriorating global shipping market, with yards all over Europe being forced to close. The lower cost labour yards of Asia (Japan and Korea) were presenting ever-fiercer competition for every order going.

We gradually built a team from some of the management that had been earmarked by the Organising Committee. Dr Ken Chapman, with a fine naval architect brain from the North-East, and Dr Peter Milue, an experienced MD from Swan Hunter, provided the operational overview and monitoring of Contracts and Operations. This gave us a vital line of sight as to what was happening in the shipyards.

Richard Heyhoe, Private Secretary to Sir Peter Carey, the DTI Permanent Secretary, was seconded in and I later put him in charge of Far East Marketing where he did a superb job. He subsequently had a long and very successful career with ANZ Bank.

Richard and a few other Civil Servants seconded from the DTI provided the backbone of an Administration system. This included establishing a central system of enquiries for new ships required by ship owners from around the world.

Later we got another excellent official in Alistair McDonald, who managed a great deal of the administration interface, including the Intervention Fund under which financial support was made available from the DTI and the European Commission in Brussels. About a year after we started work, the team was greatly strengthened by the addition of a very talented lawyer, Bob Ayling, whose advice and wise counsel I valued highly. He was also a delightful professional to work with. He went on to be the General Counsel at British Airways and later its CEO.

Gradually, we also built a Marketing team. Chile Chambers, a London shipbroker, was recruited to handle the UK shipowners he knew well. The team was well-strengthened in around 1981 by the arrival of Michael Robinson, an experienced shipbroker from Egger Forrester. Richard Heyhoe accompanied me on our first of many Far East marketing trips and we subsequently opened a sales office in Hong Kong. We also took over A&P's office in Greece which was headed by the very able Nick Petmzas – who remains a good friend to this day.

The days were very long and we had little free time as we strove to get to grips with the continuing global market collapse and the consequent crisis in the industry. For me, this was truly sink or swim. I had never been in an organisation of this scale before, let alone in a Nationalised industry, or ever faced such a market crisis – few executives would have experienced such a combination at any age. I likened it at the time to a wave breaking on every operational rock on the shore of the Corporation.

Inevitably, I got caught up in operational issues as well as setting up Central marketing, particularly with the arrival of Michael Casey as CEO. Michael brought attributes, despite his lack of business experience. With his legal training, he did tease out issues and in the early days was happy to take advice to get the organisation shaped up in an orderly and effective way. However, his attention span was often short and he certainly enjoyed long lunches and the social side of the CEO role! His relationship with Admiral Griffin was not wonderful.

The Admiral may never have run a large corporation, but as Controller of the Navy he knew the naval yards well and understood their business. He was meticulous in his time-keeping which suited me. My father used to say: "If you can't manage your time, you can't manage anything". Always turn up on time – try never to keep anyone waiting who has fixed an appointment with you.

Admiral Griffin in his second week at BS got a new driver who was to collect him at his flat at 07.45 a.m. The Admiral was waiting outside from 07.40 and the car failed to turn up on time. So he planted a yellow sticker on the lamp post by his gate. The sticker said: "It is now 07.44 and I have started walking, given that you are late." It never happened again!

To emphasise the time-keeping, he had a clipboard with his day mapped out to the minute. Shortly after Vesting Day, we were due for the first time to meet the Confederation of Shipbuilding and Engineering Unions (CSEU), the group of industry unions which was led by John Chalmers of the powerful Boilermakers' Union. John was also appointed to the Board of the Corporation in line with the original nationalisation plan laid down by Tony Benn, the then DTI Secretary of State who believed fervently in worker participation on company boards. This original blueprint also included a dictate that our head office would be located in Newcastle-upon-Tyne, which the unions liked – the Boilermakers' head office was on Tyneside, for a start.

The commitment to regionalisation was all very well – it was true that the North-East had a great shipbuilding heritage – but it was hardly the most practical proposition given that Government, civil servants, shipowners, the financial sector, shipbrokers and maritime lawyers were all located in and focussed on London.

Save us from well-intentioned politicians who have no industrial or business experience and seem to take no relevant advice in arriving at key political decisions. They ultimately add no value and indeed position themselves well to destroy value. Happily, that was not the case with many of the union leaders. Alex Ferry, the CSEU General Secretary, accompanied John Chalmers to our first meeting along with representatives of all key unions in the industry – about 15 people in total. Alex was an outstanding man who never lost his cool – always full of common sense and focussed on seeking a solution. When I later returned to Harland & Wolff, I proposed him for our Board, much to the consternation of the N.I. civil servants. But Alex was to prove his worth as a highly-effective NXD and was later admired for his Board contribution by Fred Olsen, when he became the Norwegian majority-owner of Harland & Wolff.

At this crucial first meeting, we had the Admiral in the Chair, Ken Griffin, Peter Milne and myself. We had appointed an HR Director, Dick Whalley, but he had not yet arrived at BS. I was sitting beside the Admiral and was intrigued to see that his clipboard had the timing of the Agenda very visibly set out:

Item 1: Welcome by AG (Admiral Griffin) 14.00–14.02
Item 2: Invite John Chalmers to say a few words 14.02–14.07
Item 3: State of the Industry order books 14.07–14.15 – John Parker

We got to Item 2 and John Chalmers went into full flow. He obviously saw this as a (pardon the terrible pun) watershed moment, and his speech was full of rhetoric along the lines of: "Our time as the trade union movement has come. We now are masters of this industry. You will have to get an agreement as management on all major policy and strategic issues etc etc etc."

After about five minutes of this – the allotted clipboard time – John was just getting into his stride. His team were enjoying it all and looking forward to our reactions and the Admiral was realising that his Agenda timings were now seriously at risk. He took out his pipe, cleaned it, constantly looking at his watch, tapping his pipe on his signet ring and clearly showing some exasperation as John went on for a good 15 minutes. Half way through this performance, Ken Griffin who had a great sense of humour, passed me a note: "I think the Admiral has gone to submarine depth!!"

We all wondered, given the challenges and gauntlets John had thrown down, how the Admiral would respond. As John's major speech came to a close, the Admiral said: 'Thank you very much John, let's move on to Agenda Item 3'. John was so shocked at this unexpected response that his jaw just dropped and, yes, we moved on.

To his credit, the Admiral did not allow the shredding of his clipboard timetable to deter him from discourse with the unions. Indeed, I can't recall a meeting with the CSEU when the Admiral did not turn up. Indeed, our open communications with the unions about the challenges we faced, the importance of improving our competitiveness, the need to target certain orders to maintain yards as "going concerns" created a very valuable forum. We had reasoned debate and the building of trust that enabled us to make much progress on restructuring and productivity deals without serious industrial strife over the next few years.

The Polish Project

I had had a fair amount of experience dealing with the unions at both H&W and A&P. By contrast, one significant area where I had very limited knowledge – and which was quite an eye-opener for me – were my regular dealings with Whitehall. I had met Sir Peter Carey, Permanent Secretary at the DTI, and some of his officials when they visited A&P, but that was about the limit of my acquaintance with the machinery of government.

To underline my naivety in this area, I was advised by the Admiral that the DTI wanted to revive a dialogue, which Graham Day had started in his period as Shadow CEO, with the Polish National Shipping Company PZM

I asked one of the young civil servants, David Asprey who in later life had a senior role in the Chamber of Shipping, to accompany me to my first meeting on what was known as the "Polish Project", and for any previous notes of these PZM meetings. He produced a slim file with not a great deal of information, other than that the Poles had a requirement to buy 20-odd cargo vessels and that they would seek attractive export credit terms. The Export Credit Guarantee Department (ECGD) was part of the DTI and its job was to structure financial loan packages for large export orders from foreign customers.

We went off to the DTI meeting room to discover a team of about 15 civil servants across the table, drawn from a range of Government departments, opposite the two of us. Well you have to learn quickly.

The meeting was led by the then DTI Under Secretary Kit Farrow, whom I got to know exceedingly well. He had a powerful intellect and arrived at decisions in an open and logical way. His Yes was Yes and his No – No. I respected him very much and you could do business with him. Kit later left the Civil Service, and I kept in touch with him over the years. He joined the merchant bank (these days we'd call it an investment bank) Kleinwort Benson before returning to the public sector and serving in an executive role at the Bank of England.

After he retired from the Bank, Kit took on the chairmanship of Aga Food Services amongst other corporate appointments. But he still had a Bank of England role – he chaired the Staff Pension Scheme at the Bank of England – and that was where we were once more in contact, after I took on the role of chairing the Court of the Bank of England, effectively the Bank's board of directors.

That Whitehall meeting was my initiation in the complexities, political and industrial, of what I called the "Polish Project". This project was my first encounter with something I have seen many times since: the dilemmas and doubts that are raised by major Government-supported contracts or investments which hold out the prospect of great reward but come with at least equally high risk. As a rule of thumb, I have learned to avoid such situations wherever possible. My experience has taught me that, however enticing the promised benefits of the project concerned, those returns are unlikely to justify the financial exposure involved. The notorious De Lorean car factory saga in my native Northern Ireland is a classic instance.

However, hindsight is a wonderful thing and at the time there were very good reasons why the Government should be so interested in the prospective Polish deal. We were now in early 1978 and a general election was due, at the latest, in 1979. The Government was not in good shape and its chances of winning against a Conservative party revived by Margaret Thatcher looked slim. Moreover, it was obvious from the deterioration in the global shipping market that substantial streamlining was needed to put the shipbuilding industry on a sustainable and profitable footing. That would involve the removal of thousands of jobs.

Unsurprisingly, Gerald Kaufman and his boss Eric Varley (later Lord Varley), DTI Secretary of State, were not too keen on the massive surgery that was required. So the opportunity to save many jobs in the industry through signing a massive order was too good to pass up.

Recognising this fairly obvious fact, I followed up on the discussion at the DTI by requesting a meeting with Varley and Kaufman. Eric was a gentleman with a style of laying issues on the table and hearing your views. We discussed the severity of the world markets, overall employment challenges and the survival prospects of various yards. I truly came to admire his honesty, his approachability and his clarity of expression. I trusted him – not something I can say about every politician I have met!

Gerald was keen to know how they as ministers could assist. He was a clever operator with whom I got on well, but you always felt he had hidden cards up his sleeve. He demonstrated in the run-up to the 1979 general election his ability to squeeze orders out of the Ministry of Defence and any other quasi-Government body he could get his hands on!

The Polish order, whatever its shortcomings, did provide the potential for some degree of stability amid very turbulent market conditions and the chance of mitigating some of the unprecedented major restructuring that had to take place. The idea was to share the order around the industry in yards such as Govan and Scott Lithgow on the Clyde, Swan Hunter (Tyneside), Sunderland Shipbuilders (Wearside) and Smiths Docks at Middlesbrough – which all needed new orders.

The complexity of the whole deal was compounded by huge political opposition from the British shipowners. They saw our efforts to secure the contract as tantamount to helping Poland compete against them, and were not too friendly to us for many a year. I had much bridge-building to do with their Director-General, Patrick Shovelton (a former Deputy Secretary in the Department of Transport), their President Sir Ronnie Swaine of Overseas Containers and, later, with his successor, the outstanding business leader Sir Adrian Swire.

Patrick and I had a number of grown-up discussions about the project. My understanding was that the Department of Transport had briefed the British owners of the transaction and that few owners competed directly with PZM – although some, such as Bank Line, would inevitably in their global tramping operations run up against PZM in some markets.

Sir Adrian as the new President, succeeding Sir Ronnie Swaine of Chamber of Shipping, was constructive in our discussions, including ultimately a dinner at his London home when Robert Atkinson became Chairman. There are few industrialists whom I admire more than him. Along with his brother Sir John and their offspring, he built up the mighty Hong Kong-based Swire Group in private company style. I always valued a conversation with Adrian and I have been fortunate to meet him occasionally as he is a long-serving Elder Brother of Trinity House.

The bulk of my efforts was, however, directed to negotiating the actual order. It was a huge personal burden for me, both dealing with the industry's massive problems and travelling to Poland sometimes twice or three times a month for negotiations with Richard Karger, the Chairman of PZM. Don't believe that everyone in the Communist system lacked business nous: Richard was apparently a Polish communist, but in all my dealings he had one of the sharpest commercial minds and knowledge of shipping that I'd ever met up to that point. He was every ounce a capitalist. He knew we weren't in a strong negotiating position and intended to drive the hardest possible bargain.

So started a series of meetings in Szczecin with Karger and his team. These continued for many months until we finally reached agreement on design and specification for two sizes of General Cargo vessels – 22 ships plus two crane barges.

Often these journeys were made by colleagues from marketing – Anthony Harvey handled much of the administration and financing packages along with Michael Barry and Frank Noah. I steered the project and led on face-to-face price and contractual negotiations. This being the Cold War, the journey to Poland was not easy: fly to Copenhagen; ferry to Swinoujscie and, finally, car to Szczecin. Once I was persuaded to try an alternative route, and flew to Berlin along with Michael Barry. From there, a car took us to Checkpoint Charlie so that we could pass through "the wall". Coming through the checkpoint was a humiliating and disturbing experience – Alsatian dogs barking in the background, your baggage searched with guns at the ready by the unsmiling East German guards who appeared soulless and robotic. Once in East Germany, we were driven through the country up to the Polish border, where we were collected by a PZM Car.

The outward journey worked, but on the return our PZM car was stopped at the East German border and was not permitted to make the transit through to Berlin, as the car's paper work was not in order. Of course, our Polish visas had been cancelled as we left the country, so we could not return with the car to Poland. We were now literally in no-man's-land with no information about how we would get back to the West. This experience was similar to going through Checkpoint Charlie: dogs and guards everywhere.

The Polish car driver stayed on with us and we were allowed to sit in the car for what was around three hours. Darkness had fallen when a tourist bus containing Polish citizens who lived in West Germany arrived, was stopped and was searched. They had been visiting their relatives in Poland and were returning to Hamburg. There were two free seats on the bus and we were granted passage after money changed hands with the driver! We were mightily relieved that something positive was happening.

We travelled for many hours through the night along the northern coast of East Germany where a further East German border experience awaited us. The border crossing was close to Lubeck, where I had conducted negotiations with the German shipowner Egon Olderdorff to sell SD14s from A&P. This crossing too had all the hallmarks of Checkpoint Charlie – but now it was night, bitterly cold and considerably more eerie.

At least a mile from the checkpoint we could see the mass of flood-lights along the wall and along the approach road to the waiting guards. A quarter mile off the border you could hear the whining and barking of the Alsatians. All passports were collected by the guards – all of us taken off the bus and our luggage searched at gun point in the freezing cold. Questions were asked: "Why are two Britons on this bus amongst you Poles and Germans?" Fortunately, the bus driver knew how to handle the situation, and he got a further well-deserved tip on our safe arrival in the morning, as dawn was breaking over Hamburg. It's not my favourite of all European cities but we were certainly delighted to see it. We made undue haste to catch a taxi to the airport and get the first available flight back to London. After that endurance test – of mind and body – I took the Copenhagen route to Poland every time – and there were a lot more meetings with Karger.

Eventually, we reached a point where contract closure was looking possible. I went back to Poland with Ron Dearing, the exceptionally able Deputy Secretary at DTI (later Lord Dearing and chairman of the Post Office) to finalise with Karger all outstanding points from their side .

Ron and I ultimately went to the British Embassy in Warsaw and, along with our Ambassador, Keith Morris (later Sir Keith), descended into the secure transmission room at the embassy to discuss with London where we had finally got to in the negotiations and what was still outstanding in order to close the deal. Our subsequent meeting with Karger went okay but still left a few points unresolved.

So two weeks later, I returned to finalise these outstanding issues, which included negotiating delivery and speed penalties in the contracts. Karger was particularly inflexible on his demands and I finally said: "Well, I can't accept this, so I'd better return home – no deal." At this point, Karger broke into the most generous of smiles and said: "Well, I need to tell you, John, it seems acceptable to your PM, as he has just announced the deal at the Labour Party Conference!" Top that for cutting your negotiating legs off below your knees!

The drama didn't end there, because the proposed initial distribution of the 22-ship order included a number of the larger vessels being allocated to Swan Hunter. But the workforce at Swan's was in dispute with the management and there was no way that we, the management of British Shipbuilders, were going to jeopardise such a vital order by putting work into a strike-bound yard.

This was made clear to the Swan Hunter shop stewards not just by us, but by the regional and national union officials including the courageous and moderate Gavin Laird (later Sir Gavin), head of the Amalgamated Engineering Union (AUEW), who personally addressed the workforce. But the stewards refused to budge. So we did exactly what we had said we would do if the dispute wasn't sorted out: we moved the orders elsewhere.

Swan Hunter's loss benefited Smiths Docks at Middlesbrough and Govan Shipbuilders on the Clyde, after we and the unions agreed that there would be no "blacklisting" of the transferred work. We ensured such an undertaking was in place at both yards before we transferred the work. It's vitally important in such situations to be fair and firm. We gave the local unions time to consider and explained clearly what the consequences would be if there was no positive decision to embrace the valuable orders. I guess they thought it was an empty threat.

How absurd it was that Tyneside turned down vital work over trivial local issues which ultimately led to quite unnecessary redundancies, but that unfortunately was part of the labour relations climate in Britain at the time. Many industries – the car industry was one of the main victims – were undermined by wildcat (unofficial) strikes led by local shop stewards against the advice of their national leadership. Management was not guiltless – in many cases weak management created the vacuum that allowed union militancy to thrive. But the whole country suffered as a result of these disputes because foreign rivals took the business that we forfeited. And no-one was harder hit than the workforce themselves because many of them ultimately lost their jobs, and jobs for their children, as a result of the disruption.

Throughout 1978, we had been working on the long-term Corporate Plan, but its detailed finalisation was postponed while we concentrated on fire-fighting the global industry slump and winning as many orders as we could to mitigate the impact of the downturn and our overcapacity. We had reasonable success – not just with the Polish order – and this bought us some time by temporarily stabilising the industry whilst we worked out its likely future shape and scale.

It was crystal clear that we could not survive on our original scale in a declining market where the competitive pressures were being intensified by the onslaught from Asia. We also needed substantial investment and changes in working practices to improve efficiency and the adoption of innovative new technologies. In the run-up to the 1979 general election, we drew up a Corporate Plan that incorporated these ingredients, along with substantial reductions in numbers of yards that could be retained through the crises.

The Plan also examined global market prospects, and by now

I had hired the excellent Dr Martin Stopford to head up our Market Research and support Michael Barry in his Strategic Planning work. Over subsequent years, Martin has established himself as the world's leading global shipping analyst in his role as Director of Research at Clarkson, the shipbrokers.

We concluded that we were in for a number of years of low demand before supply and demand in the global market would get into balance. In the event, this equilibrium took longer to occur than even our downside scenarios projected.

To put the industry on a sustainable footing in these adverse conditions, we planned radically to cut capacity: we would close 11 shipyards and cut engine-building capacity. The overall impact would be a reduction of about 13,000 jobs in shipbuilding and marine engine building.

The sterling effort by Gerald Kaufman and our global marketing efforts, including the Polish deal, postponed the day of radical industry restructuring to after the election. As soon as Mrs Thatcher arrived as PM, our Corporate Plan therefore had to be discussed with DTI officials and with the new ministerial team. The new Secretary of State for Trade and Industry appointment was awaited with baited breath and we certainly weren't prepared for it being Sir Keith Joseph.

7. MRS THATCHER AND BRITISH SHIPBUILDERS

Sir Keith Joseph had a great intellect and was a close Policy Advisor to Mrs Thatcher. But he was ill-fitted for this demanding DTI role leading, which required day-to-day decision-making to deliver on the strategic priorities, not just for the shipbuilding industry but for the whole national industrial base.

In our various meetings, he seemed ill at ease, nervous and distracted. His head never seemed to get engaged in Industrial activity or its place in the future of Britain's economy. He seemed to believe that the free market would look after everything. He was more than inclined to the view that our future economic wealth and health could be generated and secured via the services sector. He, like many others in Government, did not seem at that time to recognise that a large percentage of a developed economy's service base leverages off its research, technology, engineering and industrial capability, be it manufacturing consultancy or the after-sales servicing of high tech equipment.

This was the start of several decades in which ideas such as "Manufacturing doesn't matter" and "All we need is the knowledge economy" (whatever that really meant) held sway. There was ever greater Government emphasis on promoting service industry, particularly financial services. This de-emphasis of engineering and technology at the expense of financial services culminated in the financial crisis of 2008.

Below Sir Keith Joseph, Adam Butler, son of the great Lord Rab Butler – Deputy PM to Harold Macmillan and Chancellor to Churchill – was appointed DTI Minister of State. Adam was an honest and very decent man, quietly spoken with great sincerity and politeness. After DTI, he went to Northern Ireland shortly after I returned to Harland & Wolff, and our respectful good relationship continued. I believe we shared a trusting view of each other which was borne out of our past honest dealings through the exceptionally tough times at British Shipbuilders, followed by those in Northern Ireland.

At one of the early meetings that I attended with Sir Keith, he said he must visit a shipyard. I told him we would be delighted to arrange it and discussed where he would like to go. I suggested Govan Shipbuilders in Glasgow.

Govan was one of our largest yards and had an interesting recent history. It also had a new Managing Director, Eric Mackie, who had run BS's Ship Repair business. Eric was a no-nonsense Ulsterman who knew how to build ships and lead men.

On Eric's appointment, we went up to introduce him to the management and to the shop stewards, who were led by the redoubtable Sammy Gilmour. Govan had been part of Upper Clyde Shipbuilders (UCS) and Sammy had been one of the three articulate leaders of the famous Upper Clyde sit-in under the previous Conservative government of Ted Heath. His former sit-in colleagues were Jimmy Airlie, who had gone off to head the AUEW, and Jimmy Reed, who became a freelance journalist and Rector of the University of Glasgow in 1972.

Rather oddly, Govan as part of UCS had previously had a Chairman and CEO who came, respectively, from Polly Peck, the ladies' tights manufacturer, and from the Singer sewing-machine company. Mackie duly met the stewards and was asked by Gilmour: "Do you come from a ladies underwear factory or did you just sew panties up?" Mackie decided to strike back. He retorted: "Sammy, if I ever hear that rubbish from you again, I'll put my boot right up your a—!"

Gilmour promptly turned to his colleagues and said: "Do you know what – we might just have a shipbuilder here at long last."

Sammy Gilmour, Jimmy Airlie, Jimmy Reid – these three and their shop stewards were all talented and articulate men from the shop-floor. I have met many of them in my industrial life. Had they had the educational opportunities, they would have been PhD material. The chance to attend university did not exist in their school days, and often their family circumstances did not permit either.

Some self-educated shop stewards have been supported in their advancement through the trade union programmes at Ruskin College, Oxford University, which has made a significant contribution in this area of personal development. Many such men and women take up union leadership positions out of frustration that their leadership qualities are not recognised by their employers. For some, particularly in the days when there was often significant conflict between management and unions, it was culturally unacceptable to be seen to join the "management".

On the other side, companies often were concerned at promoting shop stewards into supervisory or ultimately management roles. It never bothered me – my only question was whether the individual had the required talent and innate leadership capability to do the job. That's what matters.

Back to my suggestion that Sir Keith visit Govan. "Fine," Sir Keith said. "I'll fly up the night before as I want to arrive at the same time as the workforce". We planned a tour of the workshops and a visit on board one of the Panamax Bulk Carriers that Govan was building for the CH Tung group of Hong Kong. This was to be followed by an opportunity to meet Sammy Gilmour and the rest of the shop stewards.

On the morning of the visit, Sir Keith was fitted out with his safety gear. As we walked through yard, the manufacturing shops were a hive of activity. The message from the MD about a VIP visit had obviously got down the line. We duly toured the Panamax Bulk Carriers under construction and Sir Keith was clearly interested in how the ships were all being brought together – an operation he'd not witnessed before. We then gathered in the boardroom to meet the stewards. I introduced the Secretary of State to Sammy Gilmour, who always sat close to the table with several of his colleagues half a chair's distance out from the table.

The Secretary of State addressed them nervously for several minutes and they listened to him in a very respectful way. Then I invited Sammy to respond. Oozing charm, Sammy said: 'I want to give you a warm welcome, Sir Keith, on your first visit to Govan as we don't often get the chance to talk directly to such an important man."

Sir Keith, for no reason, promptly interrupted to say he had meant to mention another point in his initial remarks. He did, and then Sammy respectfully said: "I'd like to continue". But Sir Keith then interrupted him twice more. By this time, Sammy had had enough: 'Secretary of State," he said pointedly, "I didn't interrupt you once and you've now interrupted me for the third time. If you do it again, I'll believe all I read about you in the newspapers'. Sir Keith was somewhat taken aback – he didn't get this reaction when he interrupted his civil servants. But he had the good grace to allow Sammy to finish, and he departed Govan having had his eyes opened in more ways than the one he had anticipated.

Shortly after this visit, we went into lengthy discussions with DTI civil servants and sometimes involving Sir Keith and Adam Butler for the Government, about the very significant restructuring that our plan entailed and the social hardship for communities around the country that this would inflict. There were big political as well as industrial ramifications. The plan affected yards covering most industrial centres around the shipbuilding rivers of the UK and therefore also impacted a raft of Members of Parliament.

Moreover, the plan was predicated on our winning 45 new ship orders over the next 12 months in order to keep the remaining yards not earmarked for closure as going concerns. If we fell short of that target, even more yards and jobs would have to go.

We agreed with the CSEU that we would have a "private briefing" on the Corporate Plan at our Newcastle offices and then make a decision about the process of consultation that would be necessary before going public.

We had discussed with Sir Keith about the redundancy numbers, the timetable involved, and so on. He felt it was all very difficult – yards closing; 13,000 redundancies. He needed to go away and think about it. "Come back in a week's time," he said. We did and he looked much happier. "I've found the answer," he told us: "It is an enhanced redundancy scheme".

For the CSEU briefing in Newcastle, most Executive Board members turned up including Mike Casey, our CEO. The Admiral was in the chair. Keith McDowall, our new and highly-experienced Communications Director, also attended. I had the burden of describing the Shipbuilding closure plan and with the aid of capacity charts, demonstrating the volume of work we had to win if we were to secure the future of the unaffected yards. The unions were understandably aghast. My presentation was followed by my Engine Building Board colleague Leo Curran who detailed their proposed structuring.

Finally, our HR Director Dick Whalley presented a way forward on consultation, including the enhanced redundancy scheme. The meeting broke up and John Chalmers immediately went out to a waiting press gathering, including TV cameras, and made public the plan's contents from what was a private consultation! This was explosive. He called it "blowing the gaff".

There followed much noise in the press in the affected areas and much traffic with local MPs. This was a feature of the politics endemic in nationalised industry, in that some MPs felt you had to devote as much time to them as they needed of you – regardless of the demands of the day job. However, through it all I built great friendships with many MPs, some of whom subsequently ended up in the Cabinet or House of Lords.

We agreed with the unions that, immediately after the Labour Party Conference in Blackpool that October, at least three days would be set aside for the CSEU members and the shop stewards from the impacted yards to meet with us in small groups comprising two to three yards. John Chalmers referred to this process as the "Blackpool Conference". The union leaders would then have all of the detailed presentations we made in Newcastle. We all prepared thoroughly for what we knew would be some stormy sessions.

At our Executive Committee the week prior to the "Conference", both Mike Casey and Maurice Elderfield, the Group's relatively new Finance Director, were both aggressively firm as to how the Blackpool event was to be handled – both being in the camp of "no surrender" and no watering down of objectives, etc etc .

I told the committee: "Well, we will all be there and we must stand together." However, on the opening day the Group CEO did not appear – nor did he turn up for any of the three days thereafter (not surprisingly, the meetings needed a fourth day). The Group FD, after witnessing the first session of shop stewards collectively from three of the impacted yards having a "real go" at us, went off home that evening and did not return.

I personally felt very let down that Board colleagues who should have been alongside us, especially when they had been rather vocal on the issues, did not participate. The experience cemented my very firm and enduring view that Management and Board teams hang in together, regardless of whatever gale is blowing – as one certainly did for all those concerned over those four tough days in Blackpool. It's not enough to "talk the talk" – you as a group have to "walk the talk" as well. As I learned later from the President of Mitsui, the Japanese expression for this kind of failure to follow through is "N A T O" – "No Action, Talking Only".

Despite the absence of my Board colleagues, we all survived these sessions which went well into the wee small hours. I recall we ended that first session about 3 a.m. Ken Griffin, our Deputy Chairman, said to me: "Don't go to bed. I'll take a table in the bar with the Sunderland shop stewards, if you will take the Govan lads and Dick Whalley the Scots of Greenock ones. I replied: "Ken, I'm whacked and I need sleep." So he said: "You are winning them over, give it a go".

I agreed and proceeded to pay for their beer whilst I stayed on water to try and keep a clear head in this very heady atmosphere. The Govan boys really worked me over. In particular, they wanted to know how confident I was about winning the target orders for two 35K Bulk Carriers, which we had pencilled in amongst the 45-ship industry target in order to keep Govan alive. I told them I was in serious talks with a shipowner, but equally until we had signed on a contract there was no steel to cut. But I was 60:40 hopeful of delivering and they had my word that we wanted to see Govan survive. I assured Sammy and the team of stewards that I would personally leave no stone unturned. They could assist by continuing responsible behaviour and keeping in touch with their MP. Finally, around 4.30 a.m., I announced that I had to get some sleep. Sammy Gilmour said: "Well, we have now worked with you for a while and I believe you're an honest bugger. Now you may be going to close the Scotstoun yard, but din'y close your wallet – buy us all another drink!"

We eventually secured the two target orders for 35,000 TDW bulk carriers and Govan stayed open. It is still open today, almost 40 years on, as a naval yard under the ownership of BAE Systems. For the remaining years that I spent in British Shipbuilders I visited Govan often and had many talks with the remarkable and highly intelligent Sammy Gilmour.

Under the ownership of BAE, Govan has done proud service as the builder of the latest series of Royal Navy T45 destroyers. It has also constructed some of the massive blocks – one that was of the order of 13,000 tons – for the Navy's giant new aircraft carriers. Govan is now named as the yard to build the Navy's eight new Type 26 frigates for delivery through to the early 2030s.

Govan-Barrow coincidences

Coincidences and curious crossroads in life never cease to amaze me. At the "Plate Cutting Ceremony" of the first plates at Govan for the new aircraft carriers, Queen Elizabeth and Prince of Wales,

I was present along with the First Sea Lord, Jonathon Band, and the senior management of BVT, the joint venture between BAE Systems and VT Group that I was chairing in the lead up to the construction of the carriers.

As I stood in that same shed that we'd walked Sir Keith Joseph through all those years earlier, I inevitably thought back to the battles down the years for Govan's survival. I was just sorry that Sammy Gilmour was no longer with us so I could shake his hand.

One of the triggers for Govan's transfer into BAE's ownership in 1999 came when Gus (now Lord) McDonald, then the Minster for Scotland and later a DTI minister, asked Sir Gavin Laird to study the future options for Govan, whose workload in the late Nineties was again running low.

Gavin came to see me and I suggested he ought to talk with BAE as they had taken on too much Naval and Royal Fleet Auxiliary ship work alongside the Nuclear Submarine programme at their Barrow facility, formerly Vickers Shipbuilding and Engineering Limited (VSEL). BAE had acquired Barrow when they bought the Marconi defence subsidiary of GEC, which had previously taken over VSEL. The Yarrow yard based at Scotstoun was also part of Marconi, so BAE now owned that as well. I suggested to Gavin that some of the surface ship work be transferred to Govan under new BAE owner-ship. This was undoubtedly the right thing to happen commercially and Govan got a new lease of life.

Some years earlier, John Lippitt, a Deputy Secretary in the DTI who had an unusually flamboyant management style, had left the Department to join GEC. GEC had not long acquired VSEL and had just appointed a new CEO in Brian George, who John asked me to meet and give him some shipbuilding advice.

Brian George was from the nuclear industry where he was a very professional, competent and successful project director. On joining VSEL, he developed an early ambition for winning orders for a significant volume of naval and RFA surface ships alongside nuclear submarine building.

I explained to him that this wasn't a good idea: the two businesses were very different, required their own separate cost structures and involved completely different approaches to regulation. A nuclear submarine design and build facility has so many necessary specialist engineering functions compared to that required for a naval or fleet support vessel. As a result, nuclear submarine's cost structure is inevitably so much more expensive. The result is that you can't achieve competitive build costs for the somewhat lower-technology surface ships in such an operation. This duly turned out to be the case at VSEL, so it was right that the work found its way to Govan under Sir Gavin Laird's Plan.

New Chairman – British Shipbuilders

Overseeing the consultation process for the Corporate Plan was the last major task for the Admiral and the CEO, Mike Casey. Both were due to step down in 1980.

It's extremely unusual in the private sector to have both the Chairman and CEO leave within a few months of each other, but this was the very different world of nationalised industries.

At the same time, top management change was also in the offing at another state-owned corporation – the media was rife with speculation that Sir Charles Villiers, Chairman of the British Steel Corporation (BSC), was to be replaced following a crippling steel strike which had lasted 14 weeks.

Time slipped by with no announcement at BSC, and Robert Atkinson – then Chairman of Aurora, a Sheffield-based Forgings and Castings business (later bought by Firth Rixson which I chaired in the early 2000s) sought a meeting with Sir Peter Carey, Permanent Secretary at the DTI, at Peter's office in Victoria Street.

I had heard numerous rumours to this effect at the time. But I only got the full story about Robert's approach to Sir Peter years later, when along with Richard Heyhoe, we took Peter to lunch at the Ritz to celebrate his 80th birthday. It was a tremendously happy occasion and allowed the two of us to pay our tributes to one of the outstanding civil servants of his generation. Peter's memory was crystal clear and he told Richard and me the full story of his meeting with Robert Atkinson.

Robert requested the meeting in order to set out his credentials to be Chairman of British Steel, and launched into the presentation of his case. Peter gently intervened to explain that the timing of the meeting was rather unfortunate, given that the DTI Secretary of State would that afternoon be announcing to Parliament a new Chairman for BSC. This turned out to be Ian MacGregor, the Scottish-born US industrialist, who was then working for the investment bank Goldman Sachs in America. Goldmans had agreed to release him in return for a significant consulting fee!

Robert was naturally very disappointed to hear this news, but Peter went on to explain that it was rather challenging to find experienced chairmen to take on nationalised industry leadership roles. He pulled out a drawer in his desk and ran his finger down a list of vacancies. He soon alighted on one in particular.

"What about British Shipbuilders, where Admiral Griffin is stepping down as Chairman and the CEO Michael Casey has already done so?" Peter asked Robert. "You too were in the Navy and you mentioned that you had built marine diesel engines at Doxfords in Sunderland. If you are positive, Robert, I'll get you an appointment with the Secretary of State this afternoon." Robert was indeed positive, so the appointment took place and Robert in due course was appointed Executive Chairman of British Shipbuilders – effectively combining the two roles of Chairman and CEO.

In the few months between Michael Casey leaving and the new Executive Chairman being appointed, I was made acting CEO and worked with Admiral Griffin. However, at the tender industrial age of 38 I knew that I was not in the running for the CEO role. Once Robert's appointment was announced, I visited him in his Sheffield home to get to know him, to brief him on the state of the Corporation and to hand over a range of documents. His friendly wife Hazel cooked us an excellent dinner and drove me back to my hotel in their splendid Rolls Royce.

After working in a very supportive way with Robert, he appointed me Deputy CEO of the Corporation some 18 months later. Although he was new to a Corporation of the scale of British Shipbuilders – close to 70,000 employees after the first major wave of restructuring – Robert brought a great deal of much-needed corporate discipline, and a business-focussed approach. He established a divisional organisation structure with clear lines of accountability and responsibility. We had openly discussed this together and it all aligned well with my own thinking.

I learned a great deal, particularly about sound administration, from Robert. We had the Shipbuilding Division, which I headed, and within it Small Ships, chaired by Dr Jim Venus, Medium Yards, chaired by Derek Kimber and mixed yards (naval and merchant) chaired by John Steele. Robert set up separate divisions for Offshore, headed by Cameron Parker, and Naval Yards headed by Jack Daniels.

Robert chaired each of the divisions. He was particularly strong in holding management accountable. He could also be quite bruising in these encounters. I recall one day when a cost over-run had emerged in our Small Ships division, he turned fairly aggressively on Jim Venus, who was an industry stalwart. The exchange went as follows:

Atkinson: "When did you learn of this?"

Venus: "Just last week, Chairman, when I returned to work."

"Where were you when it actually happened?

"Chairman, it happened on the day my heart was lying out beside me on the operating table of Exeter Hospital during open heart surgery!"

Robert had a good sense of humour and he joined in the laughter that followed. He did have some strange but very fixed ideas, which we had to work around. For instance, he made it clear that he did not like men sporting a beard. That wasn't a problem for me, as I have never contemplated growing one. But bearded executives were not exactly unknown in the shipbuilding industry and we had our share.

Nor did Robert like female staff wearing slacks or trousers to the office, so that caused recurrent issues. Trivial things could irritate him unnecessarily, and the only row I ever had with him was when he vented his fury about the large size of my highly-efficient Secretary Doreen Wright's left-handed signature, when she pp'd a letter on my behalf while I was travelling. These idiosyncrasies all took a little management!

As someone who had spent his working life in the private sector, Robert also faced a big learning curve in getting up to speed in dealing with ministers and civil servants on the scale you encountered in a nationalised industry. We ensured that as far as possible he was well supported and accompanied during these meetings, particularly in his early days. This was – and is – a prudent step for all to take when they are interfacing with Government ministers and officials.

The wisdom of this policy was highlighted in 1980 by one particularly testing episode for the Corporation in general and me in particular. It centred on Norman (later Lord) Tebbit, who after Mrs Thatcher's 1979 election victory had been appointed a minister at the Department of Trade.

At the time, I was consistently on and off planes along with some of the central marketing team and executives from the yards, in a constant endeavour to meet our target of selling around 45 ships a year to keep open the yards that were not impacted by our major closure and redundancy plans.

One of those was Smith's Dock in Middlesbrough, which was in desperate need for a new two-ship order. I agreed with Derek Kimber that we should try to sell two SD14s in Hong Kong, to be licensed by Smith's from A&P. Before I left for Hong Kong, the new Chairman and I had a discussion to the effect that – given that our corporate plan was still under debate in Government – he would be advised not to enter discussions with ministers until I returned, when we could review success of the planned sales trip.

My trip to HK, accompanied by Richard Heyhoe, was successful;

we signed a letter of intent for the two SD14s with the then well known Hong Kong entrepreneur, George Tan, and faxed a copy of the letter back to London. But by the time I got back, the balloon had gone up.

Robert had been invited around to see Norman Tebbit while I was away, and had been persuaded that Smiths Dock should be added to the list of yards designated for closure – something quite contrary to our corporate plan and previous announcements.

A nervous Robert confronted me with this news when I returned: Norman Tebbit and the Trade Department wished me to cancel the HK orders for the two ships. I point blank refused on the grounds that: critically, if we had cancelled an agreed deal on this basis, my word and that of the Corporation would no longer be our bond in the extremely important Hong Kong market; if that occurred, the Corporation need not show up there again! Furthermore, we had sold the heavy restructuring plans to the unions and had given our word to employee representatives that we would fight to win the orders necessary to keep the remainder of the industry intact.

Norman Tebbit did not take prisoners. It was conveyed to me how enraged the minister was to hear my refusal to accept his edict, and that my role as a Board member was now under threat. However, things eventually calmed down and we submitted the HK deal for the agreed European intervention support. It was finally approved and the construction of the ships got underway in Middlesbrough. The employment position at that time in Teesside and Middlesbrough was grim.

Mrs Thatcher then sent Tebbit to Teesside on a high-profile visit to examine what might be done for the area's economy. That evening, he was challenged on local TV about the industrial devastation that he must have seen on his visit. He masterfully brushed talk of devastation aside by citing the fact that he had just visited Smiths Dock, which he said was booming with two ships for export to HK now under construction. Moreover, said the minister, these orders had been won in competition from right under the noses of the Japanese shipbuilders!

Many years later at Lord King's retirement dinner, Lord Tebbit and I had a very friendly, one-to-one conversation. I asked him if he recalled threatening to sack me for refusing to cancel the Smith's Dock orders – and remarked how lucky it was for him, during his visit to Teesside, that he had those very same ship orders to fall back on! "That's politics," he replied. We both laughed.

I have always liked dealing with strong ministers and Secretaries of State – they could get things done! Norman was certainly one of them.

In Robert Atkinson's early days as Chairman, it was also crucial for him to get to know the international shipping market and its big characters – the individual shipowners from Norway, Asia, Greece and so on whose business we needed. I accompanied Robert to make the introductions to these markets and the owners. He enjoyed these encounters.

Overall, we worked well as a team and at the end of his second year – about five years after I had started at British Shipbuilders – the Corporation got back to about break-even. This was quite an achievement, considering that it took place in the teeth of the worst shipping crisis since the 1930s and from a corporate loss on formation of more than £100m. He deserved much credit for his leadership, and I was delighted that he was knighted for Services to Shipbuilding in 1983.

Whatever your frustrations as an Executive – and nationalised industry had many – two of your priority stakeholder groups were exactly the same as in any private sector business: your customers and your employees. Of course, in the private sector the shareholders are equally important.

Without customers, no business, whatever its ownership, can survive – let alone prosper. Too much of management's time can be expended in internal politics, which I cannot stand. Let the energy be channelled where you are paid to direct it – by adding value and not eroding it. That was one of the biggest drawbacks of nationalised industries: the Politics had a capital "P" because you were owned by the Government of the day. In these circumstances, it was much harder to take the tough decisions or to focus on the customer, since so much consultation was inevitable with such pressure being applied by ministers, who in turn were pressurised by constituency MPs.

British Shipbuilders and British Steel

We were huge customers of British Steel, not only for steel plates and sections but special forging, castings and special steels. So it was very much in our interest that BSC was well-run and responsive to our needs.

Ian MacGregor was a very outgoing and customer-focussed leader. He invited the Chairman, our Group Head of Procurement John Steele and myself around for dinner with his team to their head-quarters in Grosvenor Place, up the road from our first office in the NEB building.

Robert always seemed somewhat cool in his relationship with MacGregor – and who knows: he might well have felt more at home and had more to contribute to Steel than in shipbuilding. He asked us in advance of the meeting to discuss with him a list of major "demands" for new products that we could make of BSC to help us improve our performance.

Quite a long list emerged, including:
- wider steel plates to reduce the number of weld seams;
- large one-piece forgings for large diesel engine crankshafts;
- large diameter anchor chain;
- other items.

So when Ian MacGregor opened proceedings with: "Well, Robert, we are here to serve you", and added: "Just let us know what you need us to do" – Robert weighed in. He went through our whole list in a clinical way, while MacGregor interjected from time to time: "Robert, are these crank shaft forgings similar to what Allis Chalmers requires (they were an American medium-sized diesel engine company)?"

Atkinson replied firmly: "No – we build large cathedral-like diesel engines, so no comparison with Allis Chalmers."

"Okay, Robert – we'll get on to that," said MacGregor. "We should be able to modify our Dalzel works to do that". Jimmy McKenzie, British Steel's very experienced Technical Director was sitting at the end of the table and was requested by McGregor to take a note to get working on this.

"On the wider plates, I see your logic, Robert. Jimmy, we can get these done at Scunthorpe." McKenzie was getting concerned about these commitments:

"But Chairman," he protested, "We would have to virtually build a new plate mill."

Ian MacGregor was still serving the customer: "Jimmy just take a note," he said: "We are going to have to get this going for Robert and don't forget the large diameter anchor chains that he mentioned earlier." By now, Jimmy is in a state of shock at the potential capital investment bill that is being racked up as his Chairman responds to my Chairman's demands!

I had many occasions to meet with Ian (later Sir Ian) over the next few years – culminating in an interview with him during the Miners' Strike in 1984/5 to join the Board of British Coal as a Non-Executive Director. I'd been proposed by Sir Robert Haslam, the incoming Chairman. But that British Shipbuilders dinner was one of our more amusing encounters.

Replacing *Atlantic Conveyor*/1980s Industrial Policy

During the 1982 Falklands Campaign, Cunard's sophisticated roll on roll off cargo carrier *Atlantic Conveyor* which the Royal Navy was using as a major stores ship was sadly bombed by Argentine forces. Twelve British sailors lost their lives and the ship later sank.

After the war, Cunard decided to rebuild her. Cunard's tough but straight-shooting CEO Eric Parker (later Sir Eric) and I talked together about rebuilding it in Britain at one of the British Shipbuilders yards. He made it clear that there would be no favouritism shown to UK yards in the bidding for the contract, and that he would be going after the lowest global price. John Steele, as Chairman of the Mixed Yards in our Shipbuilding Division, had Swan Hunter produce a design specification and a cost estimate. It was technically accepted by Cunard but was clearly more expensive than the main rival bid, which came from South Korea.

We therefore arranged a number of meetings with civil servants at DTI – the sterling Arthur Russell was Under-Secretary and Ron Dearing was still Deputy Secretary. We were encouraged to put our case direct to ministers and a meeting was subsequently arranged with Patrick Jenkin (later Lord Jenkin), then DTI Secretary of State.

Patrick was a very polite man. He understood some of the points we were making from a public relations standpoint – about how bad it would look for the industry (and the Government) if this high-profile rebuild of a ship lost in the Falklands went to South Korea. But he gave us little encouragement that anything could be done to win the business for Britain.

This was one of my first direct encounters with the new Government's doctrine – I would call it dogma – of industrial non-interventionism. If you stood back a bit, you could understand where this concept came from – it was a Keith Joseph Thatcherite reaction against the post-war decades of interventionism and perceived industrial decline. We certainly needed reform – much of pre-1979 industry was inefficient, over-manned and uncompetitive. But this was a truly revolutionary approach – and like all revolutions, it went much too far. "Industrial strategy" became two dirty words and were banned from the policy lexicon. None of our overseas competitors, including the Americans, made this mistake. As a result, as well as eliminating industrial weaknesses, we lost a lot of important capability over the ensuing 20 years – many babies were thrown out with the non-interventionist bathwater.

Despite Patrick's reaction, I was determined to do all I could to secure the *Atlantic Conveyor* order for Britain. I called Eric Parker to say we were in dialogue with Government about improving our price and I asked him, although we could not guarantee a positive outcome, whether he would give us another week to see what we could finally achieve. He agreed to the stay of execution.

At that time we had an exceptionally creative, talented and experienced journalist in Keith McDowall as Communications Director of the Corporation. Keith knew the Government machine backwards, having worked as Willie Whitelaw's Press Secretary in Northern Ireland when he was Secretary of State in those dark days of the late 1970s.

Within a couple of days of my meeting with Secretary of State Jenkin, the *Daily Mail* ran a front page story that the *Atlantic Conveyor* replacement was to be built in South Korea. The story was followed up by all the media.

To this day, I'm not 100% certain as to whether Keith had direct involvement in the situation becoming public – was it in fact a leak out of Cunard that stimulated that front page story? Keith, now in his early 80s, still has a twinkle in his eye when I raise this question. It was not the only PR incident that occurred in my time at British Shipbuilding where his professional hand was probably, but not glaringly obviously, at work. Unfortunately, shortly after this, Keith – who always spoke his mind – fell out with Robert Atkinson, and the Corporation lost an excellent talent.

All industries need to communicate effectively within and without and particularly those with direct Government involvement – as the Government machine can be ruthless in positioning itself. Never go to a ministerial meeting without a note-taker or an agreement that a copy of the official minutes will be shared.

Within 24 hours of the *Mail* story, the Chairman and I were summoned to a 9 p.m. meeting with Prime Minister Thatcher in her room at the House of Commons. Half her Cabinet seemed to be there – not only Patrick Jenkin, but also John Nott (Defence) Lord Caulfield (European Minster), and Treasury and Trade Ministers, amongst others to whom Mrs Thatcher was handing out glasses of whisky and enjoying one herself. We politely refused the same and put our case. She then proceeded to interrogate us in a strident but professional way.

"What Productivity improvements have you assumed? Courtaulds achieved 20% improvement last year."

"Prime Minister, a process industry is not a benchmark for manufacturing but yes we have included improvements of around 15%," I managed to reply, and we moved on.

"Have you had good price reductions from your big suppliers?"

"Yes Prime Minister, we've been round several times and we are now doing a final round with revisions due to be tabled mid-day tomorrow."

"Has Ian MacGregor at British Steel contributed generously?"

I confirmed BSC had indeed given us a good reduction of around 10%.

"Not good enough," retorted the Prime Minister. "I'll call him in the morning."

"Could the vessel be utilised by the MOD again and what contribution is forthcoming from Defence?"

John Nott agreed that she could be utilised for naval exercises and for defence purposes and that a MOD contribution would be forthcoming by the morning.

By 11 o'clock next morning I had a further £1m reduction over the telephone from a brow-beaten Ian MacGregor, and a contribution from the MOD.

By mid-day, with other supplier reductions, I was in a position to be close enough to the Korean price for Eric Parker not to walk away – and so the rebuild of the *Atlantic Conveyor* went to Tyneside and Swan Hunter.

One could see that this formidable woman was capable of seeing the big picture and getting her ministers lined up. Whilst she had been tough in her questioning, she was not unacceptably aggressive or arrogant – maybe, I'd say, a touch imperious.

I met her on other subsequent occasions, but she did not have a natural alignment with industrial activity. I think she associated industry automatically with trade union activity. She also appeared to place great store on the thinking led by Sir Keith Joseph that Britain's future lay in the service sector. This emphasis on services caused GEC's Lord Weinstock famously to intervene in a House of Lords debate with a withering one-liner: "My Lords – servicing what?" Weinstock said, and sat down.

The reality was and remains that an economy like ours needs to build the future around design and product manufacturing, industrial activity and services. But there appeared to be a real gap in ministerial knowledge in the 1980s, which failed to recognise that a large part of service activity is generated from engineering- and technology-led businesses. Today, Rolls-Royce, BAE Systems, Babcock International are all great examples where engineering-led services are a significant part of their earnings and employment from a technology, engineering and industrial base.

The 1980s was a period when MPs and ministers failed to grasp the importance of building a strong science, engineering and technology base. It was then that we should have focussed on what was needed to usher in a new era in manufacturing and technology, and thus creating more industrial-based services businesses to set alongside a disciplined financial services sector.

I recall Sir Peter Carey saying to me at the time: "John – it's difficult to be optimistic about the future of industrial activity when you have a de-industrialisation debate taking hold right here at the heart of Government." How prescient he was, as the next grim years of industrial restructuring got underway with few foundations being laid for a new era of industrial growth.

Streamlining industrial businesses was one thing – as we knew at British Shipbuilders that was the key to improve our competitiveness. But what took place in those years and into the Nineties was a substantial shrinkage of our industrial capability – and, as any manager worth his salt can tell you, if you are shrinking, you can't grow.

Today, on the other side of the financial crisis, we are older and wiser as a nation, and we are gradually recovering and rebuilding our industrial base – but we have left it late to rebalance the economy. Nevertheless, I believe that realisation has dawned in many quarters that important as it is to have a strong, vibrant and disciplined financial services sector that alone cannot deliver the extent of national economic well-being required, particularly on the back of the North Sea oil and gas decline that is now far advanced. I will return to the absolutely vital subject of Industrial Policy later in the book.

Naval shipbuilding

Happily, my work to secure and enhance Britain's naval shipbuilding industry did not end in the early 1980s with my time at British Shipbuilders. Quite the reverse: it has been a recurrent thread throughout my career since then, spanning my years running Harland & Wolff in the 1980s, my chairmanship of Babcock International in the 1990s, and my involvement in the last decade leading some special projects on behalf of the British Government.

One of these was the creation in 2011 of BVT – the combination of Vosper Thornycroft Shipbuilding (part of VT Group) with BAE Systems' shipbuilding business. This represented the final consolidation of Britain's naval surface shipbuilding capability and formed the core of the Alliance that was established to build the new Royal Navy aircraft carriers, a group also including Babcock and the French group Thales.

I had earlier led a major review on behalf of the MOD, prior to the final decision to contract the carriers, "as to the readiness of the design, procurement, planning and project management to contract and what still remained to do." Given the chequered history of major defence projects in the UK, a number of which had overrun spectacularly on delivery time and budget, the MOD wanted to be as sure as it could that the aircraft carriers, one of the largest projects we had ever undertaken, would not suffer a similar fate.

I had an excellent team of specialists providing detailed input. Based on their analysis and my observations, I started to prepare my list of conclusions and recommendations with about 2½ weeks to go to meet the MOD deadline.

Then the MOD suddenly announced that it wanted the review completed almost two weeks earlier than planned. I was now really up against it and to make matters worse I was due to have a family weekend in Venice. I took work I had done on summarising recommendations to date with me, and over the weekend, stopping at various coffee and luncheon tables in Venice as we walked around, I managed to complete the findings as we boarded our EasyJet flight back on the Sunday evening.

The finalised version of my summary of recommendations was urgently typed up by my Executive Assistant, the excellent Chris Gribble, on Monday morning. The MOD civil servants arrived on the Monday afternoon to start drafting out my conclusions and to provide me with administrative support. They were quite taken by surprise to be handed a finalised version of recommendations and conclusions.

This role and other discussions with Lord (Paul) Drayson, the exceptionally able MOD Minister of State, led to my being invited to chair the BVT joint venture board of BAE and V.T. until it was 100% owned by BAE. Our Board included Paul Lester, the VT CEO, a very astute businessman whose company is not difficult to enjoy, his opposite number, the lower-key and financially astute Ian King of BAE, and Alan Johnston, who was BVT's new Chief Executive from Westland Helicopters. Under the joint venture agreement, VT had the right to exit the Company by selling its shares to BAE at an agreed price after three years – or earlier with MOD approval.

Whilst I knew all the characters involved, the differing agendas of the shareholders – VT wanted to achieve the maximum, non-eroded exit price while BAE needed to invest for the future carrier-building programme – inevitably created tension in the boardroom on cash allocation and other matters.

As a result, this was a boardroom where at times I felt more like the Secretary-General of the United Nations than a joint venture company chairman. At a relatively early stage in the three-year cycle after BVT was formed, I went to the MOD, in consultation with the BAE and VT chairmen, and advised the ministry that in my view VT should be released from the three- year wait. Too much energy was being wasted on issues that impacted VT's eventual exit that should have been channelled into the future aircraft carrier programme. The MOD agreed to waive the condition, and VT duly exited with BAE taking full control. VT got a significant amount of cash and was later taken over by my old company Babcock International. Babcock's new chairman was the former BAE Chief Executive Mike Turner, who had been a very dedicated NXD when I chaired Babcock.

Babcock has absorbed VT's facilities management business very successfully and the enlarged group has gone from strength to strength. It is rewarding to see this success under Peter Rogers, Babcock's CEO who retired in July 2016, and Mike Turner. It is a long way from the dire straits that faced my colleague Nick Salmon and me when we started rescuing and turning round Babcock in the early 1990s. Babcock has also been assembling the *Queen Elizabeth* and the *Prince of Wales* aircraft carriers at its Rosyth Dockyard, which during my time at Babcock we bought from the MOD. What goes around, comes around!

Then, in early 2016, I was asked by Michael Fallon (later Sir Michael), Defence Secretary, with the support of George Osborne, then Chancellor of the Exchequer to carry out a detailed and comprehensive investigation into Britain's naval surface warship-building practices so that the Government could establish an effective National Naval Shipbuilding Strategy.

I completed my report in November 2016 and the Government published it in full, including its 34 recommendations, with no changes requested. It identified numerous fundamental changes to Governance, including the need to "ring fence" capital budgets to avoid annual cash adjustments which in the existing process have imposed delays in placing contracts – and hence contributing significantly to late deliveries and escalating costs. I made some fairly radical recommendations to render the contract system efficient and effective.

I acknowledged at the outset of my Review that: "There are many highly competent and committed individuals in the various parts of the Ministry of Defence, but the sheer complexity of 'the system' in which they work negates their well-intentioned and individual professional efforts."

In particular, I found that the procurement of naval ships took too long from concept to delivery compared with the similar process in other complex industries. As a result, ships were being delivered too late and costing too much. There was no governance system to grip design and specification in a way which would ensure ships were contracted on time and to cost. And project responsibility and ownership was not always clear. Moreover – and this was a very long-standing problem – naval ships were not designed to be export-friendly.

The Navy was therefore trapped in a vicious cycle of cash consumption: fewer, more expensive ships than planned were being ordered too late; so old ships had to be retained in service well beyond their sell-by date, bloating costs. The fleet was therefore being depleted while unnecessary costs were inflicted on the British taxpayer.

To break this syndrome, I made a series of recommendations relating to new governance and improved project management by the Government – the MOD – but I recognised that industry also had to play an important role.

Both constituencies, Government and industry, needed to govern the design and specification of Royal Navy ships to target cost within an assured capital budget, and to inject pace to contract on time. Ships must be designed suitable for both RN and export through modular design approaches that offer options, for instance on defensive capability, both prior to contract or for retrofit post-delivery.

On industry's side was the fact that a shipbuilding renaissance had taken place in Britain's commercial yards – something I had established at first hand by visiting most of them in the course of conducting my inquiry. I found an entrepreneurial attitude, enthusiasm for change, flexible skilled labour practices and the ability to manage fluctuating workloads. Remembering everything we had worked to achieve in the industry during the difficult 1980s, this was very gratifying.

I was therefore able to recommend that these other yards could, under a lead yard or a consortium, form a Virtual Regional Shipbuilding Strategy to achieve competitive cost and reduced build cycle time.

My recommendations envisaged that, as the MOD had planned, BAE Systems would build the new series of eight high-tech Type 26 frigates which would provide workload into the early 2030s. It would also provide the continuity to drive world-class performance and enable BAE to emerge as the world's leading designer and builder of sophisticated warships.

However, Type 26 alone will not be enough to maintain RN fleet numbers over the next decade. I therefore recommended urgent and early build of the planned new general purpose light frigate, Type 31e, and said that this ship should be the Pathfinder Project for implementing the Regional Shipbuilding Strategy.

The light frigate had been conceived by the Government to arrest the decline in the frigate fleet numbers. The innovative Type 31e will however be a very different kind of ship from those built in recent decades. It will have a series of modular specification options to ensure an export friendly offering starting from a lower cost base. I added the 'e' to ensure continuing focus on the important aspect of winning export work, where the MOD and the UK naval shipbuilding industry have not done well in recent decades.

The Virtual Regional Strategy would competitively allocate large blocks of the T31e to be built in series in a number of yards, thereby continuing the productivity learning curve as we did at Austin & Pickersgill in the series build of the SD 14 all those years ago. Having fully outfitted blocks delivered to the lead yard for assembly will significantly reduce build cycle time and cost. To underpin this national effort, I called for close Government-Industry cooperation to achieve success in export markets, including Government-to-Government trade deals.

In short, as I noted in my report summary, "I am recommending a sea-change: with pace and grip from Government, investment from industry, to the benefit of the nation."

Subsequent to the publication of the Report, in February 2017 I made a one hour 55-minute appearance before the House of Commons Defence Select Committee giving sole evidence on the Report. At the hearing, I received a great number of concerned questions around the need to arrest the decline in frigate numbers by building the T31e effectively.

Sir Michael Fallon, an exceptionally able Secretary of State for Defence, and the Government accepted that my report should be implemented in full. I have been invited to review, one year post-publication of the Report, the extent that the Report's recommendations have been implemented. After all the years that I have been engaged in Britain's maritime industry and the accumulated experience, it was a privilege to undertake what was a rather challenging role. It is demanding work to lead such a review with its aim of charting a course for naval shipbuilding to thrive in the future, and for the Royal Navy to restore its frigate fleet numbers. In many respects, this was a most gratifying culmination of the vocation that I embraced all those years ago.

8. RETURN TO BELFAST

In late 1982, I had a surprise call from the head-hunting firm Spencer Stuart. They put me in touch with Sir Ewart Bell, then head of the Northern Ireland Civil Service. He in turn asked me to meet with Jim Prior (later Lord Prior), then Secretary of State for NI, who wanted me to take over the leadership at Harland & Wolff, combining the roles of Chairman and CEO. Ewart, who was a highly capable man of integrity, had many telephone calls with me about the job and the sensitive extraction process from British Shipbuilders

I had got to know Jim Prior as he was the constituency MP for Lowestoft in East Anglia, where the Brooke Marine Shipyard – part of British Shipbuilders – was located, and he had come to see me on several occasion at BS. I liked his straightforward style immensely.

H&W was in a bad way. It was losing over £40m a year and fast running out of work in a global merchant shipping market that was in its deepest recession since the 1930s. At the same time, Northern Ireland was in the grip of the terrorist campaign, and the Bobby Sands hunger strike had created massive community tension. Bombs were going off and ordinary citizens were being killed and security forces shot on a daily basis.

It was hardly a 'dream ticket' of a job – it was by no means as big a job as the one I was doing at BS. Nor was it the only opportunity I had, given approaches I had received from shipowners and companies in other industries to join them. However, I felt that I had to continue to give my time to shipbuilding. Confronted by the pleas of Jim Prior and Ken Bloomfield, the Permanent Secretary of the N.I. Department of Economic Affairs, to return to H&W and help it through its crisis, I was faced with a very difficult personal and family choice.

I wrestled with the decision for some days and talked only to the family and a few close friends. Finally, I decided to go, giving up my Deputy CEO role at BS, much to the consternation of the Chairman, Sir Robert Atkinson. Robert, who brought much-needed discipline to BS's corporate operations and a proper accountability structure, told Margaret Thatcher that if she approved my going to Belfast, she would have to revise upwards the cash limits under which the Corporation was working. He explained that BS would win fewer orders without me. I'm not sure that Robert intended, in all the circumstances, to flatter me in this way! He delayed my departure to Belfast by at least two months and insisted that I worked to the very last possible minute on my last day.

History was repeating itself – I was returning to H&W amid the kind of last-minute rush with which I had departed almost a decade earlier! I had to leave the BS office in London at the end of my last working day and fly direct to Belfast that evening to start the following morning in H&W. There was little preparation time.

Given that I was doing a much bigger job as Deputy Chief Executive of British Shipbuilders, I also agreed with Jim Prior and Sir Ewart Bell that I would want the freedom to have at least one Non-Executive Director roles to keep me in touch with other boardrooms and industrial activity in mainland UK.

However, Ken Bloomfield arranged for me to meet the new Chairman of the Industrial Development Board of Northern Ireland, Sir Desmond Lorimer. Desmond was an outstanding businessman who had a very successful career as CEO of the Ulster Carpet and Weavers Company. He had also undertaken a series of public appointments including Chair of the Northern Ireland Housing Executive.

Desmond invited me to join as a Director of the Industrial

Development Board (IDB) whose chief role was to promote Northern Ireland around the world and attract inward investment, something the Province so badly needed. The Board comprised some excellent members, including Sir Eric McDowell, a distinguished accountant who later succeeded Sir Desmond at the end of his first term in office.

The new CEO of the Board was Saxon Tate of the Tate & Lyle family, but I sensed that he did not find the major challenge of running an organisation so closely linked with Government, coupled with local politics, an easy ride. He was not entirely comfortable with that interface. The Northern Ireland Civil Service kept a very tight grip on this new Board given the harsh experience of the De Lorean car plant collapse and with it the dreams of many, especially in West Belfast, who had secured elusive employment on the project and then lost those jobs.

I recall Sir Kenneth Cork of Coopers & Lybrand coming to address the Board on the De Lorean collapse. Kenneth was perhaps the most famous liquidator at that time. He had a wonderful sense of humour and described himself as a "liquidiser". He said he had been engaged by HMG to track where some of "De Lorean's funding had gone walkabout!" It is now astonishing to see the prices paid for the 'winged De Lorean' car, made famous by the *Back To The Future* films, when any of these unique vehicles come up for auction.

Later, a major project came before the Board to build a composite fuselage in Belfast for a new generation of the Learjet. Sir Kenneth Bloomfield as Head of the Department of Economic Development and the Accounting Officer for the IDB decided he needed to know more about the Lear Company, since the founder, old Mr Lear, had recently passed on and his widow had taken on the leadership of the company.

Ken went out to visit the Lear HQ and factory in Texas. After being greeted by Madam Lear, he was put in the hands of Hank (Mr Lear's first test pilot) to be shown around the factory. After touring part of the plant, they stepped into the canteen for a coffee. Sir Kenneth asked Hank: "Well, what sort of man was Mr Lear?"

"Gee, Sir Ken, he was some man," replied Hank. "I recall the first test flight we were about to make and he was looking over my shoulder in the cockpit as I worked through my check list. I was doing this rather carefully given I would be flying a new plane and alone.

"I came to the parachute check and there was no parachute. I hesitated and Mr Lear, he says: 'What's wrong, Hank' – and I says 'There's no parachute, Mr Lear!' Mr Lear, he says: 'Hank if you don't fly this plane correctly I don't want to see you anymore!'"

Harland & Wolff was a turnaround job to end all turnaround challenges! There were so many uncertainties, starting with the question of how were we to attract new shipbuilding orders to Belfast, and – as we were acutely aware at the IDB – inward investment to Northern Ireland, in the midst of the horrific terrorist chaos that was transmitted daily around the TV screens and newspapers of the world. I told Jim Prior I would sign up for a maximum of three years and would be prepared to leave earlier if I could not see progress.

But life is full of surprises: in the event, I was to stay for almost 10 years.

In the course of this journey, I strengthened the Executive Management by the recruitment of Eric Helstrom, one of the effective Swedish executives who Ivor Hoppe had brought in and who had subsequently returned to Sweden. He took over as Production Director. Ultimately we recruited Per Neilson, who had a successful track record in Production at the Danish shipyard of Alborg, and he succeeded me as CEO in 1993, on my move to Babcock International.

I was lucky in the sense that I knew the environment, but even having been brought up there, I hadn't experienced the full reality of the terrorism because it was a heightened development since I left. Outside our world of shipbuilding, we had that on one side of the fence and the political parties on the other. And both these forces were constantly encroaching – both figuratively and sometimes literally – on the space where we were conducting the normal processes of doing business.

At the yard, there were no serious internal problems. The H&W

workforce was predominantly Protestant with a few Catholics. Not many Catholics were in senior management, although over time we gradually changed that. One of the key appointments I made was the highly competent Dr Maria Moloney as Head of Public Relations and later General Manager of Marketing. This appointment was followed by that of Joe Stewart as Human Resources Director. These moves raised no issue at all: the Trades Union representatives in particular just wanted competent professionals in place.

However, there was no question that in recent history, the workforce had been used by some of the political parties as a form of cannon-fodder, in terms of marches and taking them out of the yard on protests. All this was threatening the employees' livelihoods. I decided that, since I was their boss, I had a degree of responsibility to them and if that meant that I had to get into opposition with politicians or change some of the things from the past, then I had to do it – however risky that might be.

We had to normalise things as far as we possibly could, and get people to understand that this was a business: it might be Government-owned, but at the end of the day it was a business which had to fight for its survival in international markets. The central issue with Government-owned industries was that, because of their ownership, politics was always threatening to intrude into management. In the case of H&W, because of the extraordinary political backdrop, that threat was unusually prominent and persistent. All of this drove me to try to get people to forget that H&W was State-owned: the bottom line was that, regardless of ownership, we had to earn our way in the world. It was a competitive place of work and had to be treated as such.

That meant getting the shop stewards and full-time union officials on board. As the workforce representatives in the yard, and therefore the people that the politicians worked through, it was vital that they understood where we were coming from and how great was the effort that we had to make to fight for our survival. This put an absolute premium on effective communication. The first day I was there,

I addressed them and said: "I'll always tell you things as they are. I'll tell you the good news and the bad, and not hide anything from you. Transparency in our relationship is very important. We are fighting for survival and I'm on your side."

This openness was a guiding principle: you had to use your gut instinct so often – you had to be courageous and not just accept the status quo. Whilst we certainly had our ups and downs at times, as you will see, we never had a major strike in the whole 10 years that I was there. The shop stewards and full-time officials were very supportive – their response taught me once and for all that management gets the trade unions that it deserves.

If you are authentic, honest, consistent, transparent – if you don't bob and weave as a leader – you will win respect. Communication is vital – not just what you communicate, but the way you communicate it. To some extent, you have to be able to sell sensible ideas to a workforce just as you try to sell a good product to a customer. Being able to communicate clearly what your aims are and the part that the workforce and its representatives have to play in achieving is was absolutely vital.

One instance that proved this point occurred almost immediately. In the context of the slumping market, we were clearly overmanned and I had to cut 10% of the near-8,000 workforce. I told the employees: "I don't want to cut jobs but we've got to be a productive outfit". They broadly understood what was happening in the market and accepted what we were having to do.

But I knew we could not cut our way back into long-term, sustainable profit. We had to have a convincing Strategic Plan to revive the business. This was aimed at reducing our reliance on the collapsing merchant ship market and eventually – it took four years – got the yard back into modest profit from a loss of more than £40 million. By then, despite the continuing global shipping and shipbuilding crises, Mrs Thatcher was determined to privatise the shipbuilding industry.

Our Strategic Plan centred on a new "three-legged" strategy, targeting the fast-growing offshore industry and a return to naval shipbuilding, a market from which we had been absent for some time, along with reduced reliance on merchant ships where we would only tender for sophisticated vessels. My father had always taught me that a three-legged stool would be stable, even on uneven ground. And the political and industrial ground at H&W was certainly uneven.

We desperately needed stability and I had full cooperation from Jim Prior and the two Permanent Secretaries of N.I. Government departments with whom I had most dealings: George Quigley at Finance and Ken Bloomfield at the Department of Economic Development. Both were exceptionally talented men who were later knighted, with Ken becoming Head of the N.I. Civil Service and George becoming Chairman of the Ulster Bank and serving with distinction on many other important bodies, North and South.

Our first success was actually in our traditional merchant ship business: an order for four specialist refrigerated ships for Edmund Vestey's Blue Star Group. Building these was not entirely plain sailing, because in December 1984 one of the ships, *English Star*, caught fire during commissioning, just a few weeks before the naming ceremony.

This experience highlighted a fundamental truth which has stayed with me throughout my career: that any success I've had on my industrial journey has been collectively delivered by a great range of talent at every level of accountability. In particular, all those skilled work people who make, provide services, who check and do, are the lifeblood of any organisation. And occasionally in an industrial journey, you meet a larger-than-life, truly competent and skilled character who registers with you. I have met a number and can't pay individual tribute to each of them in this book. However, I will discuss one individual who stood out as representative of all those I wish to acknowledge.

Jimmy Salmon was a shipyard fitter at Harland and Wolff. I first met him during the sea trials of a new oil tanker when I was a young naval architect – probably around the mid-1960s. He was the pump room fitter and I was conducting the pumping trials – filling and emptying cargo tanks and so on over a 24-hour period, testing pump capacity and system controls.

Jimmy had enormous energy and a brilliantly optimistic and happy outlook. His willingness to get the best possible job done shone through as he demonstrated his knowledge of every valve and control in that pump room over that test period when we would have moved 90,000 tons of water in and out of the cargo tanks. I met him on many other sea trials out in the Irish Sea. We got to know each other well on these all-day, all-night vigils. On returning to H&W in 1983, I again met Jimmy. I toured the yard and workshops and received from him an enthusiastic and encouraging welcome back.

Then came the *English Star* fire. The ship was undergoing "cooling down" trials of its cargo holds over several days, starting on a Saturday. A refrigerated ship has to be cooled down as part of the commissioning to demonstrate the refrigeration, machinery, insulation et cetera is working effectively. There were about 150 men on the ship at the commissioning stage, taking readings, doing final outfit work.

On the Sunday morning, December 16, I went to the yard to check on progress. The Ship Manager, Billy Miller, was a competent and youthful naval architect and I viewed progress around the ship with him, along with Ted Hayes, the Engineering Commissioning Manager. The engine room was a hive of activity: technicians with clipboards were recording temperatures, generator loads, compressor pressures and so on. In addition some work was being finalised on pipework/hydraulics and electrics.

The ship was to be named in three weeks' time by HRH Duchess of Kent with most of the Vestey family due to be present. Final outfitting work was also going on in the superstructure to ensure that the ship's accommodation was in a well-finished state for the Royal walk through. Everything seemed fine and, having satisfied myself about progress, I drove the 15 miles home for my Sunday lunch with the family.

But just as I was getting out of the car, Emma rushed out of the house, saying: "You've got to get back to the shipyard – a fire has broken out in the engine room of the Blue Star ship!" I have never covered 15 miles so fast in all my life. My mind was preparing itself for the worst out-turn – even perhaps my having to visit homes that night if we incurred fatalities. Engine room fires are horrific experiences – confined spaces, lots of wood staging in this case to feed the fire, and steep ladders to climb to escape. The fire had been accidentally started by a welder, without a proper "permit to work". He had been asked by a mate to weld a pipe clip and his torch set alight adjacent oily rags.

As I came on to the last mile down the main road into the site at Queen's Island, I could see heavy black smoke coming out of the ship's funnel along with the odd flame – this was indeed serious. My car came to a screaming halt on the quayside, and saw Billy Miller being stretchered into an ambulance along with others – a precaution against smoke inhalation. Fire engines and ambulances were very visible.

I ran up the gangway seeking information, and who should I meet at the top but Jimmy Salmon – his face was blackened with soot: "You needn't worry John – all the men are out of the engine room alive. I was the last man out!" What a man and what a relief – I'd had visions of visiting homes that night. I salute the loyalty and commitment of people like Jimmy Salmon who have been there in every organisation where I've worked. It is great people, at every level, who collectively create a great company.

That was demonstrated by the spirit and determination of the Harland workforce over the next few weeks, as we battled to prepare the extensively damaged ship for the naming ceremony. The super-structure was partially buckled and part of the accommodation in way of the engine casing was incinerated. The engine room was very badly burned and would have to be rebuilt. The biggest challenge would be to get the partially burned-out staging planks down from heights extremely difficult to access.

We talked to the Vestey representatives and I told them that, one way or another, we would get this ship presentable for the naming. I gathered shop stewards and management together next morning and put it to them that we couldn't let the shipowners or the Sponsor down.

At this point, an interesting thing happened with the workforce. The stagers were undoubtedly the toughest people in the yard – they put up the high-rise scaffolding for constructing a ship, and so on, and they were going to have to bring the remains of staging down in the engine room, where conditions were treacherous.

I told Dave Tinkler, then our HR Director, that we would have to give these men danger money to work in these circumstances. So he called the stewards in and said: "Look, we need the engine room made safe – to do that, we've got to get all the staging planks down and take out the damaged machinery, cables out et cetera. We'll give you danger money because this is tough stuff."

But these hard guys turned round and said: "We can't accept taking money from the company when it is under this degree of duress. We'll get the engine room staging sorted out for you." And they did.

The other trades shared that spirit. Within three weeks of the fire, the lads had rebuilt most of the accommodation inside, cut off the corridors where they had been damaged, got rid of all the smoke which had created a terrible smell, put plywood on the outside of the buckled superstructure and painted over it, so that from the quayside you couldn't see anything amiss.

On the day of the naming ceremony, I could not believe how normal the ship was presented and indeed how well-finished she was in the areas where we visited. HRH Duchess of Kent looked stunning and could not have been more gracious and interested in all aspects of her ship. It turned out to be a very happy day, with so many of the workforce proud they had been part of the rescue of what could have been a real setback to us, the postponement of a Royal naming ceremony. We were at an early stage in our turnaround of the company, and such a reverse would have been enormously damaging.

Instead, with the ceremony over and the public eye having moved on, we were out of the spotlight and able to rebuild the engine room and part of the superstructure, ensuring "as new" condition for our good customer Blue Star and the Vestey family, represented by the quietly-spoken, highly honourable Edmund as Chairman of Blue Star Shipping.

This story reveals what to my mind is a universal business truth: if you have the right relationship with your workforce, they really respond in adversity. The tremendous spirit and loyalty of the H&W workforce was to serve us extremely well as we embarked on the more demanding elements of our recovery plan. It is no exaggeration to say that without that support, we would never have succeeded – as you will soon see.

MOD re-entry and Falklands Port

As we began to implement our strategy of re-entering the naval/ defence market after many years' absence, we secured a quick win: a Ministry of Defence (MOD) contract for the building of an emergency floating port for the Falkland Islands, which had been recaptured the previous year.

This was a very fast-track job which had to be completed in 10 weeks. It involved a fabricated steel roadway ramp from the land to a series of floating barges forming wharfs which had to be complete with warehouses, their own power generation units, refrigerated stores and so on: a whole port infrastructure.

The work, because of the time scale and volume, was intended to be shared with Swan Hunter on Tyneside – but Swan's workforce was threatening strike action and we were asked to take on the whole contract within the same timescale. We had taken the time to ensure that the whole workforce was briefed on our recovery strategy. I persuaded our shop stewards that this contract was so important that they should ignore calls from their trade union brothers on Tyneside to black the MOD work. I made it clear that if we did a good job, we would establish our credentials with the MOD and create significant potential for growth in the defence/naval market. They agreed and we succeeded in delivering on the tight timescale, to the astonishment and delight of the Army and the MOD.

The workforce responded magnificently. This was best demonstrated to me when I visited the night shift shortly after work had started. A welder was changing his electrode and I stopped to speak with him. He said: "Man, Mr Parker, this is a great piece of Admiralty bread and we haven't had a bite of that for a long time, so we aren't going to let you down." That's what I mean about the importance of always communicating with your employees and their representatives. Through our regular contact, we had established a bond of mutual trust which proved stronger than the old divide between management and workforce.

We used large offshore barges that we bought from the North Sea, then built warehouses on them, assembled dolphins that would be located on the seabed so that the barges could move up and down against them with the tide. Part of the warehousing on board would also have refrigerated stores and its own generating plant, and all of this we built and outfitted in the tight timescale. We shipped the whole structure from Belfast on a heavy-lift ship that sank to receive the barges on to its decks with the roadway lowered on to its decks in our building dock.

A few years ago, we were on a cruise ship visiting the South Atlantic, and called in at the Falkland Islands. We went with a farmer in a Land Rover to tour a penguin site outside Port Stanley. I said to him: "There was a temporary port built for the Falklands to help the island get rehabilitated after the war – what happened to it?" He replied: "That's still our port!" It was a thrill to visit the port and see it still working after all those years.

As I had hoped and anticipated, our work lifted our credibility with the MOD. Peter Levene, the industrialist who had been appointed Head of Procurement at the MOD and who had introduced competitive tendering, visited Harlands after we had fulfilled the port contract and said: "This yard can compete." Peter, who later was elevated to the House of Lords, introduced important change in MOD procurement. He and his wife Wendy became good friends of ours over the subsequent years.

But first, we had to win the biggest battle of all, the political battle. Since the Troubles started in the late 1960s, business and politics in Northern Ireland had become increasingly intertwined, to the detriment of the business community as it was inevitably subject to repeated disruption. I knew that, to stand any chance of reviving Harlands, we had to keep the intense politics of Northern Ireland out of the yard. The industrial and financial challenge was formidable enough – but when you added in the extraordinary element of the political situation, the scale of the task was massively magnified.

In today's UK business environment, it is hard to imagine the nature of those times. I was of course aware of the general environment, but what it meant on the ground in terms of working life and day-to-day management was soon brought home to me in no uncertain terms.

I had only been at Harlands a few months and Christmas was coming up. Just before the holiday, a shop steward asked to come and see me. I met him on my own, which was probably a bit naive when you think about it now. It was Christmas Eve and I asked what I could do for him.

The steward said: "I'm just in to tell you that Dr Paisley will be coming in to address the workforce when we get back in the New Year." The Reverend Dr Ian Paisley was the very forceful, high-profile leader of the Democratic Ulster Unionist party, which years before had broken away from the official Ulster Unionists.

I asked: "Why would he be doing that?" He said: "Oh, it's election time." I said: "This isn't his constituency. It's a Westminster election – he's North Antrim." He replied: "But this is custom and practice during elections. He comes in here and speaks to the workforce." I said: "What time is he doing this?" He said: "Just after our morning tea break. Dr Paisley will probably start speaking at 10.20 a.m." And I said: "How long will that take?" "Probably about 20 minutes," came the reply. So I asked: "Well, you'll have to get back to your work, so does that mean you'll be taking an hour off work – is he paying you?"

He said: "What do you mean, Mr Parker?"

I said: "Well, I won't. I'll give you an easy solution: I haven't had much time to think about this, but the easy solution is just to tell him that we are fighting for our life. Any electioneering has to be done outside the gates at 5.30 when you fellows get out of work."

"I don't believe what I'm hearing," he said. Then the old threat stuff comes out: "This is going to go down very badly for you, Mr Parker".

At that moment I told him: "Listen here: I'm fighting for your jobs. Politicians don't put any money in your pay packet on Friday night. That's my job. So you tell Dr Paisley what I've told you, but will you also tell him that my door is always open if he ever has an issue."

Immediately after the shop steward conversation, I telephoned Sir Philip Foreman, Chairman and CEO of Shorts, the other big Belfast employer. I said: "Philip – there's been a bit of instant policy-making around here this morning." I told him of my shop steward conversation – no electioneering in the workplace. He said: "Thank God somebody around there has taken the decision to do this." I said: "Phil – I hear what you say, but are you going to align yourself with me? Because that's the purpose of the call." He said he most definitely would – and that's how we kept politicians out of electioneering in the two workforces.

I heard nothing more about all this until I was on the plane in early January, going to London, and Dr Paisley was there too – he always sat in the front of the plane. I was further back. He boomed down the plane: "Morning John – a very happy New Year to you and I hope you are looking after that great shipyard of ours." I said: "Ian, Happy New Year to you, and with your help I will." From then on, he was very, very helpful to us.

Nevertheless, the political situation reared its head periodically. The most difficult period of all came when the Anglo-Irish Agreement was being negotiated by the British and Irish Governments, and I'll come to that shortly.

In the meantime, a second naval opportunity emerged in early 1984, when the MOD sought competitive tenders for the conversion of a container-type ship into a versatile Aviation Training Ship

(ATS), suitable for carrying troops, for training Sea King helicopter pilots and for transporting Harrier jump jet fighters. She was to be called RFA (Royal Fleet Auxiliary) *Argus*.

This was the largest naval conversion ever carried out in the UK from a merchant ship. Moreover, the MOD was determined to minimise the cost and compress the delivery time – delivery had to be in less than half the timescale that a new, purpose-built vessel would have required. The responsibility for selecting a suitable second-hand ship, its subsequent purchase and the design proposed for its conversion were all part of the competing shipyards' responsibility. The winning yard was also to take overall responsibility for procuring, installing and activating the weapon system – the first time that the MOD had made the shipbuilder responsible for this. The whole process from Invitation to Tender to Contract Award was a mere eight weeks.

We secured the £50m fixed price contract for *Argus*, and selected the Sea Container-owned *Contender Bezant*, which was around 10 years old, for the conversion. We contracted to buy her from Sea Containers while it was sailing from the Gulf of Mexico to Northern Europe, thus enabling us to meet the MOD's tight timescale.

The task of gutting the ship and removing its major systems while developing the detailed engineering information for the rebuild and conversion was an enormous challenge to our designers, planners, project management teams and production people. We met those challenges and completed the project on schedule in March 1988. As a naval vessel, it provided exceptional value for money – because it was originally a Ro-Ro container ship, it had massive deck space and could therefore fulfil its dual-mission requirement as both a troop transporter and a helicopter or Harrier carrier, with an integrated control and communication system.

Argus subsequently saw extensive service overseas in a variety of roles, demonstrating the flexibility delivered by this remarkable conversion. The ship was still in service some 30 years later in 2018, after fulfilling many roles including taking on refugees fleeing the turmoil in the Middle East.

We were mid-way through the *Argus* contract when an even bigger Naval opportunity arose. But this one coincided with the most difficult period politically that I experienced during my time at Harlands: the mid-1980s, when the hugely controversial and potentially explosive (I use the word advisedly) Anglo-Irish Agreement was being negotiated.

The naval contract involved the first "design and build" competition that the ministry had ever run for a major vessel – previously, shipyards had always tendered for new build contracts based on designs prepared by the MOD.

Moreover, this ship – ultimately named the *Fort Victoria* – was the first of a new class of highly-sophisticated fleet support vessels designated AOR (Auxiliary Oiler Replenishment) ship. Not only was *Fort Victoria* to have the capability to supply all the requirements of the Royal Navy's frigate fleet at sea – provisions, oil fuel, aviation fuel, stores, ammunition, weapons and spares – and to provide extensive helicopter maintenance and service facilities on board, but she was also to be completely "self-defended" – needing no frigate escort. She was therefore to be equipped with a weapon system similar to that of a modern frigate, including vertically-launched Sea Wolf missiles. And her survivability in the event of underwater damage was to be of an exceptionally high standard. On top of all that, she was required to reach a maximum speed of 20 knots.

Under the new "design and build" regime, the MOD mandated the contract competitors to achieve all these operational requirements and to incorporate the sophisticated weapons and communication system. How the bidders designed the ship to fulfil all these requirements was up to them. This created a massive design and costing challenge over the 18-month duration of the competition, a challenge which extended to the "Build Strategy" because this would profoundly influence the cost of *Victoria*'s construction.

We were up against Swan Hunter. If we won, we would have secured the cornerstone for our return to the naval market, thereby fulfilling one of the key objectives of our recovery plan.

But the atmosphere in Belfast was becoming intense. There was trouble in the air and much talk of getting the Harland workers out on the streets in protest at what was being discussed. Peter Robinson, Ian Paisley's deputy, was the local MP. When the Anglo-Irish agreement was signed, the blood was running very hot, especially amongst the Paisley party.

By then, I had our boys – the shop stewards – really wired up because of the *Victoria* competition. I'd taken them to Westminster to lobby; I had them really involved in every move we were making to try to win it. I had told them: "There's a lot of heat from around this Anglo-Irish Agreement and stuff; do not go out on the streets – if you go out on the streets, our cranes will be the first images on television; Mrs Thatcher will put her pen through any possibility that we win this contract. But if you show responsibility, I will be able to use that with the politicians in Westminster."

There was a vast working men's night club in East Belfast where many of the workforce went with their partners. On New Year's Eve 1985, with all sorts of trouble and attempted protests still brewing over the Agreement, I decided to go there. So although the family was all gathered round at home, I got up from my chair, put on my coat, and explained that I was going into the city hopefully to meet with a number of our shop stewards, who would be at the club – as would their wives and sweethearts. So it was my best chance of talking to them all and sowing more seeds to dissuade them from getting involved in disruptive action that could jeopardise our chances of winning the naval order, which was so crucial to our recovery. I was very anxious not to miss such an opportunity.

The club was down a dark alleyway and when I got there just before midnight, this huge bouncer came to the door. He opened it about two inches and looked down at me. "Who are you and what do you want?" he asked – rather menacingly, as bouncers do. "I'm looking for Geordie Rose," I said. Geordie was the senior shop steward at Harlands. "Who will I tell him is looking for him?" the bouncer asked. "I said, 'John'."

The door closed and eventually reopened, a bit further than

before – Geordie Rose was standing there. "What on earth are you doing here?" he asked me. So I told him: "I am worried and so I've come to see you and your mates." And he let me in and led me up the stairs into the club.

It's now close to midnight. The place had about seven bars and held, I believe, well over 1,000 people. Geordie Rose took me into the main room where most of the stewards were. They urged me to have a drink, but I politely declined, told them I was driving and got a Diet Coke. I said: "I'm here because I'm so afraid of what you guys might walk into – and anyway, I wanted to wish you all a Happy New Year."

They said: "Here's the microphone – get out on to the floor and say what you want to say."

After a short introduction from Geordie, I took a deep breath and addressed the audience: "I'm here to wish you all a very Happy New Year. Our happiness to a large extent is tied up with whether we can secure employment. That's my objective and to do that, our aim is to win this major naval order. But I can't do that without your full support. The shop stewards have been brilliant in supporting me at Westminster and I want us to win this – if we do, it will bring us three years' work."

They were listening to me carefully and I went on: "By the way, the politicians will put great pressure on you men to come out and protest. I say to you, and to you ladies and sweethearts, that I have the responsibility to put the wages in the pay packets every Friday night, so I need your support."

I got the most incredible standing ovation and off I went.

Not long after that came the Anglo-Irish Agreement. I was sitting at lunch in Harlands with my director colleagues the day it was signed. Our security boss came in to see me and he was truly ashen-faced – his face was as white as a piece of paper. This guy was a very tough fellow – he was the former deputy chief constable – so I knew something very serious was up.

He said: "I don't know how it's happened, but we have a major breach of security. Peter Robinson (of the Democratic Unionists) and Harold McCusker (an Official Unionist MP) are inside the yard and attempting to round up the workforce for a mass meeting." They were the most unlikely political bedfellows and it was clear what was going on. I said: "You don't need to tell me the rest – they want to take them out on a protest march."

"What do I do?" asked our very shaken head of security. I had to think quickly and go with my gut instinct; there was no time to consult with my colleagues. I said: "Go out with your Land Rover and three of your best men, and persuade them that I need to see them urgently. It's clear that they have been smuggled in. Try to persuade them that I want to see them in the boardroom. If they refuse, arrest them and bring them to the boardroom anyway – whether or not they come voluntarily or involuntarily, I need them there. When they are in there, lock the door and come and give me the key."

Most of my colleagues were very alarmed and said: "What on earth do you think you are up to? You can't do this. You'll get a bullet through your head!" So our lunch took on a rather icy tone.

I said: "Look guys: We are the directors of this company – are we in charge or are Peter Robinson and the other politicians in charge? I'm paid to be the Chairman and the Chief Executive here. This is my decision – you have to decide whether you are for me or against me. No more discussion about it. We'll see what happens." I added: "I'll want one of you to come with me if we get these MPs into the boardroom." Fifteen minutes later, the security chief came back, told me they were in the boardroom and handed me the key. I then took a further 10 minutes or so to finish my lunch, while my colleagues became increasingly agitated. Years later, when I recalled this incident, a close friend remarked that, whilst he wouldn't draw a direct comparison with Sir Francis Drake completing his game of bowls after the Spanish Armada had been sighted, he nevertheless got the picture.

I knew the MPs couldn't contact anyone outside – there were no phones in the boardroom and fortunately it was before the days of mobile phones. I also knew they couldn't get out. The security chief said that for good measure, he had put a guard outside the heavy mahogany door. I said: "Good man – I may need him when I open that door!"

When I got up to go to the boardroom, I took one of my unhappy colleagues with me and told him: "Get a notebook, and be seen to write down every word during the uproar that we will likely encounter – but don't say anything. I'll do the talking."

In we went and the two MPs were like two caged tigers. They were standing up, shouting and threatening, but I ignored them and sat down at the top of the table, while my colleague sat halfway down the table, put his notebook down and started scribbling away. The MPs were ranting and roaring about me being disloyal and a friend of Dublin, et cetera. All this kind of abuse. When they calmed down a bit, I said: "Take a seat – I have only one question for you guys: why are you trespassing?"

They were not prepared for this line of questioning. They said: "Your office knew about it." I said: "Hardly – you got smuggled in." They said: "Well, we got permission." I said: "You got permission to be smuggled in? I don't believe a word of it. You are trespassing and what's more, you are trespassing on an MOD secure site" – I was pushing the boat out a bit – "that means I have to make a judgment whether to turn you over to the MOD police." It was only at that moment that the penny dropped and I got their attention.

They then said: "There must be a serious mistake between our offices." I said: "No mistake. There was no call to my office, no nothing. Only when I give permission can politicians come in; it's a standing rule here."

They said: "Well we have to apologise to you because there is some mistake." I said: "I'll accept your apology but only on the basis that you give me an undertaking that you will never attempt to do this again. Furthermore, I still don't know why you came in." They said: "Oh, we just came in to calm the workforce down because of the Agreement." I said: "Look, we are managing this place. If we need any help we'll send for it, but right now we don't."

The moment they left, I called a meeting of all the shop stewards. I told them exactly what I had done and why I did it, and again underlined the importance of the workforce staying at work. The stewards didn't call a walk out and stop work – which was amazing in the circumstances.

Having ensured that the demarcation lines between business and politics were respected by all involved, we were able to build on that stability. Dr Maria Moloney as our Marketing General Manager was a very professional communications executive, and she formed a great working relationship with all political parties at Westminster, plus building solid links with the Archbishops and other civic leaders on both sides of the community. Robert Eames, the Church of Ireland Archbishop for the whole of Ireland, was one of the great statesmen during the Troubles, reaching across the so-called "religious divide". He became a great personal friend and someone to whom you could turn for unbiased advice.

Maria managed to persuade the leaders of all three Northern Ireland political parties (John Hume of the Social Democratic and Labour Party as well as the UUP's James Molyneaux and the DUP's Dr Ian Paisley) to go to see Mrs Thatcher and lobby for the *Victoria* contract to come to Belfast. The PM was so impressed – it was the first time the N.I. political leaders had ever been to see her together about anything. She was very encouraged by that.

Lord (Gerry) Fitt of the SDLP and Ken (later Lord) Maginiss, the Ulster Unionist MP for Fermanagh and South Tyrone also worked very closely with Maria and were both very helpful throughout my tenure. I saw Gerry regularly at the House of Lords after he was ennobled. He told me the most amusing stories – and the deadly serious ones. He and his family had lived in a two-up, two-down in Dock Street in the city, before moving to a larger house on the Antrim Road. One night, the IRA broke down the front door when all the family was in bed, and attempted to come up the stairs, and Gerry had to defend the family with a revolver in order to survive. After that incident, the family had to leave Belfast and move to London.

The outcome of all this was that we won the contract for *Fort Victoria*, and delivered a quality ship to the MOD in early 1993 – despite the fact that an IRA bomb was planted and detonated in her engine room just before her completion. This created huge challenges, because the engine room was flooded and the equipment severely damaged. I will cover this dramatic and sad event later.

Our build strategy for *Victoria* was critical. H&W had heavy lift capability with its two, 840-tonne Goliath building dock cranes, so we assembled *Victoria* through very large "pre-outfitted" blocks, including an 800-tonne superstructure block. We had to make and install 23,560 individual pipes and purchase and install 716,600 metres of electrical and control cable. The engine room computer control system had some 6,700 communication channels.

Our success in winning this further major naval contract did wonders for morale at the yard, which had been at its nadir when I returned to run the business. By the time the Duchess of York, Sarah Ferguson – "Fergie", then married to Prince Andrew – came to name *Fort Victoria*, the yard was humming.

Given the Northern Ireland security situation, there was naturally a tremendous concern about security around the naming ceremony. Early on the morning of every naming, I always walked around the ship with the Production Director to see that all was in order. For *Fort Victoria*, I was going to walk Fergie through a few selected officers' cabins. But when I was doing my tour at 8 a.m. with Per Neilson there was an almighty stench in the cabin area.

The foreman in the area greeted us with: "That bloody dog!" Army sniffer dogs had been on board and one had jumped up on to a fine bedspread in the cabin and relieved itself – the full works. The foreman said he had sent one of his men up to Boots to clear the store out of air fresheners. I said: "Well, if necessary we'll just close the cabin." But he said: "Don't worry, I will get it ready". And that's what he did.

The workforce were in great spirits as they turned out to watch the ceremony. The first sign of their upbeat mood came when Fergie's helicopter was sighted. The H&W shipbuilding workforce had green overalls and each of their names on the pocket. Stuart Hunter, who headed our Ship Repair division, had put all his workforce in red overalls; as Fergie's red helicopter flew in, one worker shouted out: "The Sponsor must be from Ship Repair!"

As we came off the naming platform after the ceremony, we had a whole school of disabled children in wheelchairs close to the stairway. My intention was to introduce Fergie to the teacher and one or two of the children in the front row, but she went round and spoke to every single child and was really tremendous. The crowds were continuously cheering her, with the workforce being quite a bit back behind the security guard rails.

Then as I went to walk her towards the ship's gangway. She said: "I'd like to go over and shake hands with some of the workforce". There were whistles and cheering galore as she approached, but just as she was coming down the line, I noticed this guy who was virtually up on the security railing and as she came past, he put his arm round her and kissed her full on the lips. The boys went wild. The security men rushed in, I took her to Fort Victoria's gangway, but she turned to me as we went up and said: "Will you ensure that that man doesn't get punished?"

The workforce thought she was great. She waved to them from the gangway. They were shouting and cheering. I accompanied her to the Belfast Harbour Commisioner's office for the celebration lunch and she asked me: "Do you think I did okay?" I said: "You did brilliantly." She said: "I'm getting pretty bad press at the moment so I hope this will do something to correct it." I said: "You've done a marvellous job – we are all very happy and grateful."

Offshore market

Breaking into the Offshore market presented a different strategic challenge. H&W had been successful with *Sea Quest* in the frontier days of the North Sea, but by now – two decades on – many yards were scrambling to get a share of the booming North Sea structures market, and we had to differentiate ourselves if were to establish Harlands as a sector leader and create a long-term, sustainable business.

We did build some service barges for the North Sea, but that was pretty standard work. Then we learned that BP, one of the largest players in the North Sea and a customer from *Sea Quest* days, had come up with a concept for a revolutionary new type of oil recovery vessel which would enable it to tap oil and gas from the fields in the North Sea where the scale of the reservoirs did not justify a fixed platform. These were the really marginal fields.

They called it the Single Well Oil Production System – SWOPS. And it was real pioneering stuff: its role was to recover the oil, process it, store it and transport it to a discharge port. On completion of this cycle, it would return either to the same field or a different one.

As conceived by BP, SWOPS was a 76,000-tonne ship but, because of the need to move from marginal field to marginal field, it was not fixed in position but had to hover over the fields and be held on station not by anchors, but by seven huge azimuth thrusters controlled by a computer system linked to satellite GPS navigation.

At its centre, it had a large "Moon Pool" – a huge dome within the ship's hull where the oil and gas could be brought up through the umbilical, an inflexible solid pipeline connected to a hub already embedded on the sea floor. Flexible riser systems did not then exist.

BP wanted SWOPS to operate in up to 600 feet of water, and for positioning of the riser (the vertical pipe from the oil reserve), it could only have plus or minus 1/1.5 degrees of movement before breaking out and disconnecting from the seabed. So the ship would rotate – but could only move 10-15 feet either side at the surface (10 foot equals 1 degree). The ship would be moved into station first by GPS, then by transducers located on the seabed hub and finally by lowering a camera through the pipeline umbilical which enabled the operators to view the final location of the riser with the hub. With a joystick, you would move the ship until the hub was located and riser umbilical locked in. It had to be able to stay on station in winds up to Force 7/8 in North Sea conditions.

As the oil and gas came on board, there was a massive process plant which separated the water and sand from it. The oil went into the cargo tanks, the gas went to fuel the turbines to drive the whole power plant for the needs of the total structure and its process plant.

It was regarded as the world's most sophisticated ship. BP called it *Seillean*, which is Gaelic for "honey bee" and was inspired by the idea of hovering to collect the oil and gas, just as a bee collects pollen. But while BP had the concept, the yard that built SWOPS had to take on the responsibility for designing and engineering it – for transforming the innovative thought into practical, working reality. In the immortal phrase coined by the first American astronauts on the Mercury programme, this was "pushing the outside of the envelope".

We told BP that we wanted to undertake the project, and started negotiations on the contract terms – including, of course, the price.

These discussions proved far from straightforward. The BP executive I dealt with on SWOPS was Basil Butler, who ran Exploration & Production. I became very fond of Basil, who was a decent, honourable and professional man. But he was also a very tough negotiator. At the outset of our discussions, I said to Jim Prior, the Northern Ireland Secretary of State: "We really want to win this contract – this is going to put Belfast on the map."

We started with the dual advantage that BP had a long history of building at H&W and also had confidence in our engineering capability. Basil and I met on a number of occasions and progress was slow. It was clear that he was going to drive a very hard bargain. Eventually, I said to Jim Prior: "It's important that you speak to BP's executive chairman, Sir Peter Walters, to let him know that I'll be meeting Basil Butler in the hope that we can finalise this deal I need you as a backstop. I want you to be able to phone Peter Walters and get some commitment that you'll be able to keep in touch with him towards the end of negotiations. This is our safety valve." Basil Butler and my colleagues didn't know about this plan.

Eventually, we reached the crunch point, we put in a final price and were shortly to have a final meeting with Basil. We had agreed there would be a joint project management team, drawn from BP and H&W, which was a real breakthrough: their people would be sitting with ours and we would have a neutral project director who we brought in from Matthew Hall, the oil and gas consultant engineering firm. This was unique – unprecedented in the industry.

But when I went to see Basil with our Sales Director Ken Ruddock and our experienced FD, Douglas Cooper, Basil said: "Your price is not acceptable." I said: "We are taking on huge risks, we are now taking full design risk, and you want a fixed price for something that can't be delivered for three years, the most sophisticated ship in the world." He said: "Well, I want £5m off the price" (we were talking about an all-up price of about £65m).

I said: "Sorry Basil, that's not on." So he said: "It's either that or you don't get the business." I said: "Okay, if that's the line you want to take." And I just folded my papers and put them in my briefcase. I said: "We've spent a huge amount of time on this with you and your team, thank you for that, but if that's the commercial out-turn I don't want to take it – we are just going to lose money." I think he was quite shocked because, with that, I stood up and walked out.

The others were furious with me. They said: "Couldn't you have negotiated?" They were unaware of my line to Jim Prior. I phoned Jim the next morning – he was on his combine harvester on his farm in Suffolk. I almost pleaded with him to get off the combine and phone Peter Walters. I said: "Basil is just driving such a hard bargain. There is a bit of money to give, but there's no way I'm giving him £5m – that's most of our profit if we can manage all the risks."

Jim came back to me a bit later and said: "I've been on the phone to Peter and I think there will be communication with you shortly." A few hours later, Basil came on the phone and his tone had changed for the better. He said: "With a bit of trimming here and there, I'm sure we are going to be able to do this. If you give me something, I think we can do the deal." I gave him half a million and we closed the deal.

Many challenges were inevitably encountered in developing and constructing such a pioneering design, and in managing the interface with 563 major equipment suppliers. However, at the outset of the contract we drew up a joint venture management agreement, formally creating the joint project team which was chaired by me for Harlands and Mark Wooldridge, a top engineer, for BP. We met monthly, with the chairmanship alternating between the two of us.

The joint team enabled us to resolve quickly many of the crucial engineering and commercial decisions which had to be taken day by day. The team conducted extensive ship model tests which provided critical input on vital aspects such as determination of the final power requirements and station-keeping qualities.

It was a staggering project – 962 kilometres of cable were installed with 185,000 terminations connecting the cables to all of the specialist equipment. More than 250 acres of the structure had to be painted and more than 22,000 pipes installed. About 15,240 drawings were prepared to support the whole design, build and commissioning process.

Yet, despite the fact that we were working at the leading-edge of offshore design and engineering, we only hit one big stumbling-block – and that wasn't our fault or that of BP. GEC, the supplier of the switchboards to distribute power within the vessel, was nine months late providing them. As a result, we had to leave a massive hole in the side of the ship's engine room while we waited for the boards to turn up. Finally, I had to go to Lord (Arnold) Weinstock, managing director of GEC, who had pestered us and BP in the first place to get the order.

Peter Walters had had a written undertaking from Arnold that heaven and earth would be moved to ensure no delays with the supply of the equipment. But of course there were repeated delays. We kept notifying them about the delays. Eventually, I spoke to Peter and said: "I think you will have to send Arnold a tough letter and say that you've requested that I go and see him."

So he did and I arranged to meet Weinstock, although I didn't say exactly why. By this time, Jim Prior had left government and become chairman of GEC. I had a very close relationship and high regard for him. Before the meeting with Weinstock, I went to see Jim to brief him on the situation. Jim said: "Let him have it."

My meeting with Arnold was over lunch at GEC's office in Stanhope Gate, just off Park Lane in Mayfair. Two of his Board were there – Sara Morrison and Malcolm Bates, his number two, along with Jim Prior.

Over lunch, Arnold started toying with me. Apparently it was part of his lunchtime entertainment to have a bit of fun with his guests. He had just bought Yarrow shipbuilders on the Clyde. I said: "I never thought you would want to get into shipbuilding – I understood you were always opposed to buying a shipyard and yet you have now bought Yarrow." He said: "It's run by Scotsmen – it should probably be run by a Ukrainian. Of course, I could always buy Harland & Wolff in cruzeiros." Then he said: "Are you doing anything interesting over there?"

I said: "Yes we are. We've got a good order book at the moment. In fact, I have brought a photo of one of the ships we are building." And I showed him the picture of the SWOPS vessel.

Then he fell into my little trap: "What's this big black hole in the structure?" He asked. I said: "Lord Weinstock, that hole is where your switchboards, which are now nine months late, are going to have to be shipped through. Until they are there, we can't put any power on this ship to commission it. This is the world's most sophisticated ship and we can't complete it because of your delays." "We are late?" he said, rather astonished. I said: "Yes we are. Your customer, Sir Peter Walters, I understand has been in touch with you as the MD of GEC and that's why I'm here. This has got to be sorted out; it's a serious situation and we'll need compensation."

He said: "I'll sort it." His parting words were: "I'll call you tomorrow morning." He did, and he said to me: "I've sorted that – I've sacked the MD." I said: "I didn't ask you to sack the MD – I asked for delivery of the switchboards – when am I going to get them?" He said: "There's an accelerated programme: you're going to get them without any further delay. I'll have my new man contact you in the next few days." I said: "It's not much of a solution."

He then said: "I understand you've got an order for a new naval ship – can I do a deal with you on the phone now to supply the cables?" I said: "I don't buy cables, Lord Weinstock – I have a purchasing department who buy the cables and if you want to put in a very good price, I'm sure they will be interested in your quotation."

That was Arnold Weinstock. He ran GEC for decades with an extraordinarily personal imprint and great success for such a large group. The stories about him are legion – and some of them reveal a lot about his approach. One of his chief lieutenants was Bob Davidson (later Sir Bob), who ran the Power business. Bob visited Harlands and he and I became very friendly.

By this time, in the early 1990s, GEC had amassed a huge cash pile which was mounting up and it was unclear what Arnold planned to use it for, or indeed if he planned to invest it at all – GEC's direction was unclear. Bob's colleagues running the other businesses – he was the elder statesman among them – said to him: "Can't you convince Arnold to have a proper strategy meeting with us – where is GEC going? What are we going to do?"

So Bob approached Arnold and said: "There's a lot of pressure building up: the guys want to have a proper strategic debate with you as to where we should go and where we should put our capital." Arnold replied: "Okay, I'll organise a strategy dinner."

So there were a dozen or so top GEC managers round the table, they had just sat down and Arnold suddenly picked on one and said:"I've just been going through your monthly accounts and your electricity expenditure seems to have gone haywire this month, and your overheads are trending up – what's going on?" The guy defended himself, and then Arnold started going round the table targeting them one by one – turning the whole thing into a monthly budget review meeting. Forget strategy!

Later, during a proper budget review meeting for the Power division, Bob noticed that Arnold kept staring at his tie and shirt. At the end of the meeting, Arnold said: "I'd like you to stay behind." When the others had all gone, he asked: "That tie – surely that's not a Hermes tie?" So Bob had a look at it and it was Hermes. Arnold said: "Where do you get the money to buy a Hermes tie? I must be paying you too much!" Bob said: "I couldn't have told you what make it was – my wife bought it for me at Christmas. But right now when I look at it, it's not a bad tie!"

Arnold was an extraordinarily able man, and despite the disappointing delivery performance on SWOPS, I liked and admired him. He was incredibly cost-conscious – that's not a bad habit but it can be taken too far, to the long-term detriment of the business. For instance, I was told that he really squeezed R&D investment at budget time. And he never visited any of GEC's facilities – he believed that if he arranged a visit, the MD would spend money painting the premises and freshening up the lines on the shop floor.

Eventually, we did get the GEC switchboards and the SWOPS vessel was completed. We handed it over to BP in 1989. For the naming, the multi-talented John Browne (later Lord Browne) attended with his mother. John was later BP's CEO and put BP on the road to significant growth via his big US oil company acquisitions, Amoco and ARCO.

Many years later, in 2007, he was to become President of the Royal Academy of Engineering, and I later succeeded him. We have always had a good relationship and I worked closely with him during his presidency, as Chairman of the RAE's Development Board to raise the funds to enable us to move premises and refurbish our new home in Carlton House Terrace, off Pall Mall. We subsequently named it Prince Philip House, in recognition of the great contribution made by Prince Philip to both the Academy and to engineering in general.

For me, there was also a personal postscript: after we went to live in Devon in 2000, we discovered that BP's great Offshore Engineering leader Basil Butler, now retired, lived in the next village. I still see him from time to time as he is also a highly-regarded Fellow of the Royal Academy of Engineering. Recalling the SWOPS project, he always says: "You and me and our ship."

Technically, it was a very successful vessel and won industry-wide recognition as a world first, really establishing Harlands in the forefront of offshore oil and gas technology. Eight years after *Seillean*, and following my move to Babcock, that pre-eminence was highlighted when H&W undertook another major project with BP, for a Floating Platform (FPSO) to operate in the company's Schiehallion field west of Shetland, in some of the most extreme marine conditions in the world. Today, the yard still specialises in repair, offshore wind projects and oil rig conversions and maintenance – expertise which was developed with the turnaround plan and the SWOPS order.

We had great engineers and naval architects, led by our very experienced Technical Director Stuart Tennant and his Chief Engineering Designer, Robin Cameron, who was a world-class engineer. This team was amongst the most innovative I have ever worked with. I wasn't afraid to take this kind of pioneering work on – it saved the yard and helped to pull us back to profit. Over four years, from 1983 to 1987, we turned the company round. At the start, we were losing more than £40 million. By 1987, we were just into the black.

9. PRIVATISATION

At this stage, we added one further element to our strategy: we saw an opportunity to enter the nascent market for giant cruise liners. No other British yard was eyeing this market, but a number of our European competitors in Scandinavia, Germany, France and Italy certainly were. We did a lot of market research which convinced us that this would be a high-growth and profitable sector. Moreover, we had an enthusiastic prospective shipowner, who thought the same. This was Ravi Tikkoo, an extremely innovative Indian-American shipping entrepreneur who had been the first operator to build 400,000-tonne oil tankers.

Ravi's concept was for a cruise ship carrying 3,500 passengers, all of whom would have an outside cabin and balcony. At that time, only a couple of these new and much smaller cruise ships, with around 1,450 passengers each, had been built in the world – by Aalborg in Denmark for Ted Arison, founder of the American cruise line Carnival. The largest cruise ship today carries over 6,000 passengers, which demonstrates the growth in scale of modern cruise ships.

I had recruited Per Neilson as our Shipbuilding Director, who had held a similar position at Aalborg and therefore was familiar with the construction of the first two new cruise ships for Ted Arison. We assembled a good project design team in Belfast, which worked with an equally strong consulting team from Denmark. By now, we had all the necessary credentials; with SWOPS we had proven our capability to design and build innovative vessels. And we had a lot of history building passenger ships.

In 1988, with Ravi, we designed the *Ultimate Dream* – a 3,450-passenger, 140,000 gross tonnes cruise ship. Our design was revolutionary in scale and style, with a zig-zag type of superstructure which enabled all passengers to have outside cabins with private balconies above the main deck. All major public areas – dining, lounges, shopping – were sited below the main deck.

But we weren't financially strong enough yet to do the project without the Thatcher Government's financial support through its Shipbuilding Intervention Fund, which was used selectively to support the industry. So both Ravi and I met with the N.I. Secretary of State Tom King's officials to explain our keen interest in building this ship and the opportunity that we believed it presented for the UK industry. Our efforts proved fruitless: the Government was not convinced about our market research and thought the whole thing was too risky. They turned us down.

The result was that, while we in Britain looked on, the cruise market went from strength to strength – from a handful of new-builds in the second half of the 1980s to a world fleet of more than 300 ships today, and still growing. As I have sat at the boardroom table of Carnival Corporation, which alone has 103 cruise ships today, discussing the placing of orders in other countries for new and ever-larger vessels, I have sometimes considered what might have been had I done a more convincing job with the British Government.

In today's policy environment, with our belated conversion to rebalancing the economy and recognising the need for a modern industrial strategy, things would probably have been different. But at the time, Britain was in a de-industrialisation mindset and certainly had no coherent modern industrial strategy against which to benchmark the logic of entering any new market, let alone the high-tech cruise ship market. But for me, that is cold comfort for a massive lost opportunity.

This remains one of the biggest disappointments and failures in my career. Not just because of what success in the cruise liner market could have done to boost Harlands and Northern Ireland companies, but because of what it would have meant for the UK shipbuilding industry and, beyond that, for the supply chain of British manufacturing and engineering overall. So many companies around the UK would have benefited from skilled and well-founded jobs. The skills that young people could have attained would have benefited the wider society and allowed them to grow up with the dignity of work.

We have retreated from so many sectors over the past 30 years – here was a great chance to get in at the birth of a new one, rich in potential. Like our mainland European counterparts, UK shipbuilders could not compete in mass markets such as bulk carriers and tankers with the low-cost economies of scale developed by first the Japanese, later the South Koreans and today the Chinese. To maintain a strong merchant industry, we had to move up the shipbuilding value chain – and cruise liners met that need.

In terms of the financial support we needed, we were essentially looking for the kind of launch aid that the Government subsequently granted British Aerospace and Rolls-Royce to build key parts of Airbus passenger jets, which has generated big long-term benefits for the UK. Instead, our merchant industry diminished while the continental Europeans – including State-owned yards in France and Italy and other Government-supported yards in countries such as Finland – moved up-market and built a world-leading business in what has proved to be a growth segment of the industry over the past 30 years.

Today's cruise ships dwarf the size of vessel we envisaged with Ravi – *Ultimate Dream* was 140,000 tonnes whereas the largest ones now are around 230,000 gross tonnes. In 2018, Carnival Corporation was the largest cruise ship operator in the world with a fleet of 103 ships with a further 20 ships on order, and a market share of more than 50%. What an opportunity the UK missed.

A fundamental problem was the ideology of the Government, which effectively banned the phrase "Industrial Strategy" and harped on about those who advocated an attempt to "pick winners". My simple answer to the proponents of a hands-off approach is that I would even risk backing winners on occasions than be left as a loser on the international stage.

My more extensive response is that all of our major competitors, from the US through France and Germany to Asia, nourish, value and support key industries. And, of course, the UK picked winners too. The Thatcher government ultimately backed our aerospace companies and also gave heavy support to the Japanese carmakers Nissan and Toyota to persuade them to build factories in Britain.

Shipbuilding has similar characteristics to the auto and aircraft industries, towing a huge supply chain behind it. About 65%-75% of a ship is sourced from outside the shipyard gate. These large design and assembly businesses are huge traction engines in any economy. This is one of the reasons why governments around the world seek to support the "traction engine", given its importance to a much broader industrial infrastructure, the wider range of employment in Small and Medium-Sized Enterprises (SMEs) that it creates, and the social cohesion that it supports.

I have no doubt that if Britain had had a modern industrial strategy in the 1980s, some of the more efficient merchant shipyards, including A&P, Sunderland Shipbuilders, H&W, and Govan would have been capable of competing with the best. This would have required frontier design and production technology of the kind that we progressed at H&W, together with more radical working practices and, importantly, support from Government to see through modernisation of design and production methods that would have been increasingly focussed on high-tech ships for specialist markets.

This was how we would have withstood the intense competition from the likes of Japan and Korea, and now China, with their mass production of high-volume, commodity vessels. Italy's state-owned shipbuilding industry did precisely this, and as a result it now commands a leading role in the global cruise shipbuilding industry. Finland, Germany and France also moved up-market in this way and thereby sustained vibrant cruise and ferry shipbuilding industries.

I had a close-quarters view of how other European yards evolved during my long association with the Association of West European Shipbuilders (AWES), whose Board I joined after returning to H&W. Through AWES I got to know all the leading shipbuilders in Europe and visited many of their facilities. This role also opened my eyes to the power and influence of the European Community – particularly of the EC's Competition and Industry Commissioners.

Unexpectedly, I was invited to take over the chairmanship of AWES from the delightful and highly competent Juan Saez, Chairman of Astilleros Espanoles, Spain's state-owned shipbuilder. He was based in Cadiz, where I visited him on a number of occasions and where the lunches were long and leisurely! The AWES Chairman vacancy was triggered in 1993 when Juan was suddenly switched by the Spanish Government to take over the running of Iberia, the state-owned airline that had hit a rather bleak patch. As he remarked to me at the time: "Out of the frying pan of shipbuilding into the fire of an airline".

We had rather lively meetings at AWES – they verged on what I would describe as heated! One of our most difficult and important tasks was to negotiate the annual EC-approved Shipbuilding Intervention Fund percentage – the percentage of a ship's cost that the EC Fund would contribute.

This was meant to ensure that European yards, over a range of vessel types, could compete with the suspected dumping prices from some Asian yards – which often at that time meant equivalent to a European yard's cost of materials! As part of the process of determining the annual amount to be ultimately approved by the Competition Commissioner, all yards were required to produce a cost estimate for a range of ship types. These cost estimates were examined and debated by the AWES Board before submission to the Commissioner for further interrogation. In addition, a third party consultant would table Far East price bands for the range of ship types.

The Danish shipbuilder Odense (owned by the AP Moller Group) always tabled exceptionally low estimates of costs, effectively arguing for a low or zero amount of Intervention Funding.

This didn't go down very well with other countries, who wanted to propose a much larger level of EC Funding. Frank Gadd, the Odense Commercial Director, was generally quite mischievous in his style – ducking and weaving under challenge and questioning from other members of the Board. Kurt Anderson, the Odense CEO, who had worked with me in Belfast back in the early 1970s, was much more of a statesman and tried to be as constructive as possible in the often tense discussion.

On examining the cost structure for a particular Odense ship estimate, Juan Saez one day exclaimed in a very Latin way – emotional and demonstrative – "It is clear that the Odense ship doesn't have an engine!" Whilst I could never quite fathom the Danish positioning, I think it had much to do with the fact that almost 100% of Odense ship orders came from the parent company, AP Moller Shipping. This vertically-integrated owner – shipyard relationship, along with valuable Danish Capital tax allowances which were available, created a unique and insulated position for Odense. Therefore the survival of a European shipbuilding industry was not a key objective of Odense.

When all the interrogation of estimates and prices was completed, the final decision on the annual Intervention Fund percentage was made by the Competition Commissioner, who at that time was Karel Van Miert. He was a very capable and pragmatic Dutch professional – quite a reserved and measured individual whom I came to respect. After leaving the Commission, he took up various Board roles including, in 2002, a Non-Executive Director role at Anglo American. This was prior to me joining as Chairman in August 2009.

Very sadly, we never got to work together in the Anglo boardroom as he had a fatal accident falling from a ladder at his home. Aiming to avoid serious accidents around the home remains a real challenge for most countries and societies. Karel was particularly well served by his Director-General for Competition Affairs, Asker Peterson. He was a very hard-working and pragmatic Dane with whom you could do business. He handled most of our face-to-face Intervention Fund negotiations.

The other Commissioner we met from time to time was the man with the Industry portfolio, Martin Bangemann, he of the famous EC Passport 'Bangemann wave' – a gregarious and large German with a propensity for long and high-quality lunches. He had a very sharp mind and therefore the lunches were generally very productive.

I recall a particularly worthwhile meal we had along with the then-Chairman of the European Shipowners, Lord (Jeffrey) Sterling, Chairman of P&O Group. It was held in one of the best restaurants in Brussels. In this very informal setting with the Commissioner enjoying superb food and good wine, we were able to raise a few of the big issues impacting both our industries. On all of them, Bangemann either gave a clear response or undertook to follow through – which he did. Coming from Germany, with its long history of close relations between politicians and industry, he of course had a level of business understanding that so many British politicians unfortunately still lack.

I also had the pleasure of dealing with Karel Van Miert's successor, the highly intellectual but remarkably approachable Sir Leon Brittan. By all accounts, he did a fine job as Competition Commissioner. One thing that did strike me about dealing with the Commission was the relative ease of access to Commissioners, particularly if you built a relationship within their DG and key support staff. This is not something that generally happened in the UK, unless you as an industrialist happened to know senior officials well.

My successor at AWES was Corrado Antonini, Chairman of the Italian state-owned shipbuilder Fincantieri. He retired as Chairman from Fincantieri at, I believe, the ripe old age of 80! His shipyards have had a remarkable long run of success in cruise shipbuilding. That of course could also have been Harland's destiny, had we been able to enter the market when it was in its infancy as Corrado and his company did.

Happily, since joining the Boards first of P&O Princess Cruises and then of the Carnival Group, I have been able to keep in contact at naming ceremonies with Fincantieri, which has built some [80]% of Carnival's 100-plus cruise ship fleet. I truly admire Corrado's staying-power as Europe's longest-serving shipbuilder. He achieved his success through his sheer ability as a fine naval architect with superb knowledge of his business. He also has a leadership style focussed on his customer and somehow, despite the elusiveness of consistent profitability in the shipbuilding industry, he provided confidence to his Government shareholders.

Harland's far-sighted attempt in the late 1980s to enter the cruise market was blocked off by the Thatcher Government's very different attitude to shipbuilding: far from supporting one of the UK's most technically capable companies so that it could enter a new market, the Government appeared to want the whole industry off its books and privatised – and without regard to the state of the global shipping market at that time, which was stagnant after experiencing the worst downturn since the 1930s Depression years.

So during 1988, after H&W had returned to modest profit the previous year, Mrs Thatcher ordered Tom King to sell us. Shorts, the Belfast aircraft business, was also to be privatised around the same time. By then we had recruited the former Treasurer of Westland Helicopters – Peter Swan as our Finance Director. In his meticulous way he provided valuable financial guidance on the future desired shape of our balance sheet.

I led the negotiations with the Government over our privatisation. It had to be a trade sale because we didn't yet have the profit record to float on the stock market. It was also far too early in the recovery cycle of the world shipping industry to secure anything like the full value of the business. But political priorities are very different from business ones.

For the Government, the privatisation was to be managed by a bright-eyed, bushy- tailed new Minister of Economic Development Peter Viggers – his first and subsequently his last ministerial appointment.

As Chairman, I ensured that the Board did not oppose privatisation since this was what the shareholder wanted. We did however express our concern at its timing to both Peter Viggers and Tom King.

There was of course much opposition in the media and amongst the trade unions. Viggers' naive defence on radio and TV was to criticise the company and its management, and to claim that the sell-off was an opportunity for transformation and a great future.

I was incensed the first time I heard this argument, particularly given our co-operation with the process and the fact that we had transformed the company in four years from losses of more than £40m to modest profitability.

I went to see Viggers and he assured me it would not happen again and that he realised we were both on the same side. I did make it clear to him that should it recur, I would feel duty-bound to defend the company and its management, since to do otherwise was to devalue H&W in the eyes of potential investors.

Lo and behold, within a couple of weeks, I am coming to work one morning listening to Radio Ulster and he is on the air peddling these same critical lines about management and the enterprise.

The moment I got to my office, I hand-wrote a letter and had it delivered immediately to the Secretary of State, Tom King. It spelt out how I felt about the minister devaluing in public the asset we were cooperating with Government to privatise, and that I felt I had no choice but to defend the company and its employees in public – which I did that night in a TV interview. I later had a Select Committee Hearing at Westminster on the subject.

On TV I drew the analogy, which I knew would be understood by the local population, that when my late farming father was selling sheep or cattle he would be praising their characteristics to the buyer and not talking their value down. The minister was also damaging the morale of the workforce, which I was determined he would not do because it affected the well-being of the company.

Tom King was decisive and got a message back to me to say he would be in charge of privatisation and I should work with him and the new, commercially minded and able Permanent Secretary, David (now Sir David) Fell. I had got to know David well during our time together on the Industrial Development Board, and he had just taken over Economic Development from the highly respected Sir Ken Bloomfield, who was now Head of the N.I. Civil Service.

We saw a number of bargain hunters who wanted to buy the business at a knockdown price, including a Turkish ship-owner who wanted to order 20 ships! Then I talked to our management, and particularly to Per Neilson, who was now Managing Director, about the possibility of a management and employee buyout along with an industrial partner.

The concept took shape and I visited Sir Peter Carey, the former Permanent Secretary of the DTI who was now Chairman of the merchant bank Morgan Grenfell. I asked if the Bank would advise us and Sir Peter agreed that they would take on the assignment. He put one of his top investment bankers, Mike Hildesley, on the case and we could not have had a more competent advisor for this type of complex transaction.

Together we mapped out the type of deal structure we had in mind and we had various consultations with David Fell, the trade unions and the employees themselves.

As we progressed these ideas, our focus was on finding a major shipowner willing to put in equity and place orders to secure the next few years' workload. This would have to be on a slimmer employment base with further productivity gains built in. In this process, we had private exploratory talks with the successful shipping magnate Sammy Ofer and his very competent son Eyal. These discussions also involved Jay Pritzker of the Hyatt hotel group, who was a partner with Sammy and the Wilhemsens of Norway when they bought out the other shareholders in the Royal Caribbean Cruise group. However, the instability of Northern Ireland politics was a key factor in them not proceeding.

Then, out of the blue, I got a call from John Wallace, Fred Olsen's man in London. Over coffee in a London hotel, I met with him and Fred to outline our aims and the shape of the deal we were discussing with Government. He was keen on the plan and was in the market to build either VLCC or Suez Max tankers. I encouraged him towards Suez Max, given that we could build up productivity improvements faster by a series of ships half the size of VLCCs.

I went to Oslo the following week to meet Fred's daughter Annette and their management team and we hammered out a letter of intent including the equity proposed and orders for three 140,000-tonne Suez Max tankers. On the basis of this fast progress, we reached the conclusion that Fred Olsen, the Norwegian shipowner, would be the best partner. It was of course subject to both of our Boards' approval and, very importantly, subject to my delivering an agreed deal with Government.

Many weeks of negotiation led by David Fell on behalf of the Government ensued. We also had lengthy discussions with the unions about the need to change terms and conditions from the existing company to the Newco that would be part-acquired by Fred Olsen. These ranged from redundancy pay – regrettably, there would have to be some jobs lost – to the employees' right to buy shares in the Newco.

Buyouts such as this one were not yet common in the UK, and explaining the proposed deal demanded mass communications direct with the workforce. I led these by presenting to groups of about 300-400 employees at a time with a set of slides detailing every aspect of the deal. Newco also involved further changes in working practices, including a new personal employment contract to be signed individually by those who would secure a job in the new company.

I explained how written advice on all these issues would be posted to the homes of each employee. At this point in one of these mass communication meetings, a quick-witted boilermaker rose to his feet and stated: "Mr Parker – thanks for your clear presentation and if I've got it right we will either get a thick envelope through the letter box or a thin one put under the door."

On 8th September 1989, the deal with Fred Olsen was signed along with Government, management and employee representatives. This was only after Fred and I had had a challenging conversation.

When I returned to Northern Ireland in 1983, I had told Jim Prior that I would sign up for three years maximum – and by now, 1989, I had done six. I therefore told Fred that he was now the absolute majority owner of the company, and that he should appoint a new CEO while he became Chairman. However he was very adamant: "John," he said, "you have negotiated a good deal with the Government and we are content with it and we will stick with it – but I am not going to sign it unless you agree to stay on for up to another five years as Chairman and CEO. I will join the Board with two colleagues, but you will head the Board."

There was no way I could allow the deal to collapse, so I signed up with his additional agreement that I would also be involved with his Oslo Management companies which represented his wider company interests. It was also agreed that I would continue with my Non-Executive Directorships, which comprised British Coal and later GKN.

One important issue that Fred and I discussed was the final composition of the Board, which had radically changed since 1983. I felt we should hold on to at least one of our Non-Executive Directors to be alongside the three Olsen nominees who would join. Fred agreed to one being appointed, and much to his surprise, I recommended Alex Ferry, General Secretary of the Confederation of Shipbuilding and Engineering Unions (CSEU): "But he is a trade unionist!" exclaimed Fred. I explained that he was a wise man of integrity, and greatly respected by the workforce. To his credit, Fred supported the move and probably surprised himself! It was not many months after the formation of the new Board that I was in a telephone conversation with Fred about an issue and the course of action we should take. After some probing around the issue, Fred asked: "Have you talked it over with Alex?" We were now well-aligned on the wisdom of choosing Alex.

My involvement with Fred's wide array of interests was indeed a rich experience. His operations ranged from oil rigs, oil tankers, ferries and cruise ships to stakes in airlines and newspapers, real estate in Norway and Scotland, extensive real estate on the island of Gomera in the Canary Islands, with a hotel complex there, and the fast ferries that serviced the adjacent islands in the Canaries chain. Fred's family also owned the Timex watch company, which was based in Connecticut. His father had dedicated it to the UK Government's war efforts to assist in the manufacture of components for small arms. All told, it is a mighty conglomerate which Fred had overseen in granular detail since his appointment to the Board at the young age of 26 prior to his father's untimely death. The family also owned the largest private collection of paintings by Edvard Munch, including the most famous, *The Scream*, which was sold at auction in 2012 for almost $120m by Fred's stepbrother Petter.

Fred was and remains a formidable thinker, an entrepreneur, an inventor and a unique businessman with a massive range of interests. I always enjoyed his company and his long telephone conversations including those from Connecticut, on his visits to Timex, when it was about four in the morning US time and he could not sleep. He preferred to talk to me about welding techniques and technology progress at Harland & Wolff.

Together we pursued a tie-up with Kawaski Heavy Industries (KHI) in Japan to build the new Suez Max tankers of 140,000 tons dead-weight to a Kawaski design. This was to enable us to have a close insight into the detailed production methods and scheduling techniques that could make a big contribution to closing the productivity gap between European and Japanese shipyards.

The Cooperation that we signed with KHI involved the second-ment of Japanese managers and supervisors from Japan to Belfast for six-month stints. This system was greatly enjoyed by the KHI people because it allowed their foremen and managers, who were golf zealots but could only afford to play in Japan about once a month, to go out almost every evening in summer and at weekends on one of the twenty golf courses within a 10-mile radius of Belfast.

I met with each manager and foreman as they arrived from Japan. One Monday morning, a supervisor arrived exceptionally well-kitted out in his Japanese boiler suit, safety boots and with his safety helmet tucked under his arm. He explained that he had arrived the previous morning in Belfast via Heathrow from Tokyo. I said: "I assume you must have been rather tired yesterday after that very long journey." "Not at all," he answered. "Yesterday I played two full rounds of golf well into the summer evening!"

Reciprocal visits took place. We would send teams of about 20 of our skilled workforce with two supervisors and a manager for one month to work alongside their skilled Japanese counterparts in their Kobe shipyard. The objective was for our people to understand how the Japanese organised their work and how they achieved such excellent productivity.

These exchanges also brought about rich cultural experiences with our people being taken by their Japanese work teams on various outings, including learning to drink Sake. On the day of their departure from Japan, one of our managers told me that all the Japanese work mates turned up at the railway station, with tears running down their cheeks as they said goodbye to their new-found Belfast shipyard brothers.

As a result of this co-operation, I invited Dr Obha, the very distinguished Group President of Kawasaki, to visit us. The plan was that he would see round the yard and I learned that he was also keen to address all of our management on Japan's approach to efficient production. I was very happy to agree to such a lecture, which was scheduled for the end of his tour, and looked forward to the visit from this industrial statesman.

You have to remember that throughout this period, we were working amid the ever-present threat of bombs and bullets in Belfast. On the evening before Dr Obha was due to arrive at Heathrow, I arranged to stay overnight in London and meet the KHI Senior Manager, Niomi San, for breakfast to go over the programme for the President's visit. He was coming with five supporting staff who would accompany him to Belfast.

However just before going down for breakfast, my hotel room telephone rang. It was Per Neilson from Belfast, who advised me that the Police Special Branch had received a coded warning that there was a bomb placed on board *Fort Victoria* – the sophisticated self-defended replenishment ship for the Royal Navy. She was undergoing commissioning trials afloat in the building dock. Our emergency procedures were well defined and Per assured me that all personnel had been taken off the ship and that it was being searched by bomb disposal experts with sniffer dogs.

I agreed that I would keep this all quiet from the Japanese party so as to cause no alarm, as Dr Obha and I were shortly to meet with the Northern Ireland Minister, Sir Richard Needham, in London before travelling to Heathrow for the flight to Belfast.

I always rated Richard Needham. Hailing from Northern Ireland with the family title of Lord Kilmorey – which he gave up to enter the Commons and become a minister – he was a great driver of the programme to enhance infrastructure and other investments to assist the rebuilding of Northern Ireland and to deliver it from its slow growth and an economy battered by the Troubles.

He also had a wicked sense of humour and got himself into hot water with Mrs Thatcher, via a mobile telephone conversation in 1990 which was intercepted by the IRA. Unfortunately, he had momentarily referred to her I believe, as "that cow" on a telephone call to his wife!

Later, when I was at Babcock International and he was Trade Minister at the DTI, I joined one of his many Trade Missions to Hong Kong. It was very well led in a professional way by Richard. However, some criticism reached John Major, who by then had succeeded Mrs Thatcher as PM, that Richard's behaviour had been out of order at some point in the mission.

I was unaware of this until Richard called me after we got back from London. He asked if there was anything I could suggest as he had been summoned to see the PM in two days' time. "Leave it with me, Richard," I said. "We'll think of something." Within an hour, I had a hand-written note sent around to the PM to express my appreciation of just how well the mission had been led by the minister. John Major, whose leadership was under a lot of pressure in this period, then wrote back almost by return and said he was delighted at this time to have such positive news of one of his ministers!

On the Monday morning of Dr Obha's visit, the KHI head started his meeting with Richard Needham by reading from a lengthy prepared speech, which included special greetings to Mrs Thatcher. This allowed me to leave the room and head for a fixed line telephone to find out what was happening with the search for the bomb on the ship. We did not have the luxury of a mobile pocket phones in those days – they were then the size of a brick. There was nothing further to report from Belfast and I agreed to call again on arrival at Heathrow.

Two large, black chauffeur-driven cars, which rather resembled funeral hearses, collected us at the N.I. offices and headed for Heathrow. Dr Obha turned to me as we were approaching Hyde Park Corner and said: "Parker san, we have plenty of time: I would like to have a walk in the park." It transpired that he was keen to have a smoke.

This meant more delays in getting to the next telephone I could access, at Heathrow. However, as we walked in the park and he lit a cigarette, he stopped at a very colourful flower bed. I sighed to myself, because it was labelled "Mesembryanthemum", Dr Obha then attempted to pronounce this difficult word and after many attempts and my best coaching we finally got there – but more time had passed.

At the Heathrow British Airways lounge telephone booth, I called Per Neilson and there were still no further developments about finding the bomb. Just then Niomi San came out of the adjacent booth after speaking to the Kawaski Manager in Belfast, and said: "They tell me there is a big bomb scare in the yard." I remained determinedly unruffled and said: "Yes, we get these scares from time to time – but don't tell the President because I don't want to alarm him. It will be dealt with."

On arrival at Belfast Aldergrove airport, I had arranged for someone to meet the party and collect their luggage. However, I had my car at the airport equipped with one of the early massive mobile phones. I left the party in order to bring the car around to the airport exit to pick up Dr Obha and Niomi San and personally drive them to Belfast.

I was therefore able to call Per Neilson from the car. The bomb had exploded, blowing a gaping hole in the side of *Victoria*, in the engine room. The ship was taking in a lot of water and had heeled some 40 degrees in the building dock. It was clearly in danger of capsizing or sinking. Per told me that, for the time being, the Army were refusing access to put air pumps on board – although, as we both agreed, this was an absolute necessity to save the ship and I urged him to action.

Despite the regular threats, this was the first and only bomb actually to explode in the yard during my tenure. I told Per: "I want to delay Dr Obha's tour round the yard. Can you bring forward his lecture to management from the end of the programme to the beginning – and ensure that there are masses of questions to extend the lecture time so that the trip around the yard will be at least in partial darkness."

On the way down to Belfast, I explained to Dr Obha that blue lights would be flashing in the shipyard, as we had a bomb scare. He was very relaxed and said: "We also get the same thing in Tokyo." I then gave him a tour of some of the more attractive parts of Belfast before arriving at H&W and going straight to the lecture theatre where he was to make his presentation in front of a large audience of management and supervisors. This was well clear of the building dock area. Once I had introduced him, I went to my office at full speed, held a meeting with Per Neilson and others to take stock of the situation, and answered many telephone calls from Government and the Civil Service – not to mention the raft of press questions that Maria Moloney was handling in these challenging circumstances.

By now, despite the Army's strictures, volunteer managers and workmen had lowered air pumps from a crane down into the engine room as Per and I had discussed earlier. The team had done a phenomenal job. They had almost completely righted the ship, while technicians had laser-dimensioned the size of the hole in the ship side, the fabrication shop had produced a large steel box at top speed and the welders suspended from crane buckets had successfully installed it over the hole to seal up the hull.

Inside the lecture theatre, our managers did their stuff: by the time they had exhausted their questions, it was getting dark. I collected Dr Obha, who was delighted with how the event had gone, and drove him through various large steel shops and along one side of the building dock. Blue lights were still flashing on the other side, but *Fort Victoria* was now almost upright and no obvious damage was evident.

I then drove him to his hotel so he could freshen up and had him transported to Stormont Castle, where he was being hosted at a Government dinner which Tom King (later Lord King) had laid on with Sir Kenneth Bloomfield. As I came through the door, Sir Ken and Tom King were most anxious to know how things were with the ship and, very importantly, did Dr Obha know? I told them that he was aware of a bomb scare but not the damage, and that there was no need to discuss the incident. Dr Obha departed Belfast the next day happily unaware of our emergency and with the relationship between Harlands and KHI immeasurably strengthened.

About the time Dr Obha was leaving Belfast next morning, the head of the Special Branch met with Per Neilson and myself. He advised us that they had received a coded call about a second bomb on the vessel which took us a further two weeks to find. We managed to do this before it, too, exploded. It was hidden below a generator in the main engine room, and was made safe by the brave bomb disposal specialists who saved many lives during the N.I. Troubles.

Later, when Dr Obha became President of the Japanese Institution of Naval Architects, I was invited along with the President of the US Society of Naval Architects and Marine Engineers, to speak as honoured foreign guests at the centenary celebrations of this august institution in April 1997. It was a wonderfully formal affair in front of an audience of probably 500 people. Apart from Dr Obha himself, the speakers included the Crown Prince of Japan whom I found a very gracious and intelligent man. Following our speeches, the event concluded with the traditional breaking open of the Sake barrel amidst great ceremony.

Such were the challenges of trying to keep the workplace functioning normally amid the turmoil caused by terrorism in the 1980s. In such unplanned, exceptional circumstances as we encountered, you learn the necessity of keeping your cool, focussing on the really important things and of giving clear instructions – and that there is no point creating or adding to a drama, if you can avoid it. I look back on the great team of managers that Per Neilson and I had built up to take the yard forward in production. In technical strength, we were emerging as leaders in Europe. The Kawasaki experience was a great success and contributed to significant productivity improvements on the production side.

The support of the workforce was, as I have said, absolutely crucial to our turnaround. It led to one final, unexpected meeting with Jimmy Salmon on my last day as Chairman and CEO before I joined Babcock International. As I was clearing my office on that Friday afternoon, I got a telephone call.

"Mr Parker, it is Jimmy here, I and a few of the lads want to see you to say our goodbyes. Now John, you know this yard very well but I don't think you know where our Friday afternoon Club House is! Now that you're leaving I'd love to invite you to visit us. It's located in such and such a place behind the Fabrication shop in the Musgrove Yard."

I was now curious on a lot of fronts! As I entered the wooden hut, Jimmy was seated at a table along with four of his fitter mates. A large number of bottles were on the table. I was invited to have a drink with them and I explained I was driving. With some effort they found me a coke as we settled down for quite a chat and they all expressed sadness I was leaving. Finally Jimmy stood up: "John – there are some things I need to say. For the last 10 years, you have been the only thing between us and the dole queue and we lads want to thank you and wish you all the best for the future."

I can't deny that it was a heart-wrenching moment to hear such a sentiment from these tough and proud Belfast Shipyard men. We had come a long way together from the days when the company was very much on the critical list. We had stabilised it and established a firm platform for the future.

Earlier, I singled out Jimmy as one of the highly skilled members of the workforce that I met on my industrial journey. I could have identified many other skilled and great people in the various companies where I have worked who made a unique difference. Without those people, no company can achieve the scale of change and degree of progress that is needed for an organisation to survive and prosper. Many of them were PhD material and never had the educational opportunity that some of us were fortunate to have. I salute them all through Jimmy.

There is a need and a responsibility for those of us who have the privilege to lead to bring out the best in the talent we have around us. All employees should have the opportunity to be developed to the maximum of their potential. Leaders must also communicate their expectations on all fronts.

As I said earlier, I love the old Chinese proverb which captures a key role of the leader. "When the best leader's work is done, the people said, 'we did it ourselves'".

At the end of my time at Harland & Wolff, Fred was very concerned that the workforce might interpret my departure as being a result of he and I falling out. Nothing could have been further from the truth. I explained that I would, as always, be transparent with the workforce in that I had stayed almost 10 years and well beyond the three years that I had promised Jim Prior when I started in 1983.

Fred felt the only way to avoid any unwarranted speculation was for me to stay on the Board as a NXD. This I did not want, as I could not easily raise challenges on the strategy or other policies of my successor, Per Neilson. In any event, I felt he should not be constrained by my presence.

My judgment was right and I did not enjoy my time as a NXD in a company where I had been Chairman and CEO. After a year or so, I agreed with Fred that it was safe to depart, as the workforce had got well used to me not being at the helm. This is the same governance issue as with a CEO becoming Chairman in the same company: it places a constraint on the new CEO which should not be there.

10. BRITISH COAL

I was approached in 1985 by Sir Robert Haslam – later Lord Haslam – the incoming Chairman of British Coal, to ascertain my interest in joining the Board. Bob was about to succeed Ian MacGregor (later Sir Ian) as Chairman of British Steel in 1986 after Ian was appointed British Coal Chairman, and now he was again following Ian whose time at the state-owned Corporation was coming to an end.

The 1984/5 Miners' Strike, which lasted almost one year, was still going on when it was agreed that I should meet with Ian at Hobart House, the Corporation's London head office near Victoria, to bring myself fully up to speed about British Coal.

I had got on well with Ian MacGregor when he was at Steel. The shipbuilding industry was a huge customer of theirs and Harland & Wolff was also a supplier – it built large Cape-size, 170,000-tons bulk carriers for British Steel's ore carrier fleet. On this occasion, despite the strike, Ian was very relaxed and seated in a comfortable armchair with his feet up on a footstool. He asked me a lot of questions, mainly about the Harland & Wolff leadership task in the midst of the Troubles.

We then talked about me potentially joining the British Coal Board. He said that, in considering whether to join the Board of a company as a Non-Executive Director: "You should choose your company as carefully as if you were choosing your parents." Sage advice which I have often passed on to would-be NXDs!

I had a follow-up interview with the Energy Secretary, Peter Walker. It was sad to see the deterioration in the relationship between the Energy Secretary and Ian MacGregor as the strike came to an end.

I decided to accept the invitation and join the Board – it was my first Non-Executive Directorship outside of the N.I. Industrial Development Board. I learned much under Bob's chairmanship from which he retired in 1990, shortly after being elevated by Mrs Thatcher to the House of Lords. Bob became a great friend and trusted advisor until his passing in 2002. He had lost his wife Joyce to cancer and they had been married for 48 years. They first met as pupils at Bolton School, where Bob subsequently served as Chairman of the Governors for many years. He remarried in 1996 to Elizabeth Sieff, the widow of Marcus Sieff of the founding family of Marks & Spencer. We enjoyed many happy social times with them both. Elizabeth touchingly invited me to speak at Bob's Memorial Service, and it was a challenge to do justice to the memory of this great man.

Bob always held a dinner the evening before a Board meeting, and I began to appreciate the importance of social time together with other directors, both NXDs and executives. Furthermore, if there were major issues to debate next day, Bob would start the debate off over dinner when various views and reactions could be aired. The issue that seemed 10,000 feet high on the Board Agenda was thus reduced to one of 5,000 feet or less the next day.

I use Board dinners today and generally set two aside per year for the Non-Executives alone. One is used to talk about key issues around the management of the Board and the feedback on the CEO performance, helping me in turn to give constructive feedback to the CEO.

At one of these dinners, the CEO comes and gives us a run-down on the performance of the executive team and their individual development plans. Succession plans and next moves by executives are openly debated. Other Board dinners are open to the general management or executive committee members, and these enable the NXDs to get to know the next layer of management well. This equips the NXDs to express informed opinions to the CEO when discussing succession issues.

This process of getting to know the next layer of management is strengthened by an overseas visit to one of our key operations by the Board each year, a two-day strategy session each year at which various executives present, and regular slots in Board Agendas when the MD of a division briefs the NXDs on the operations, challenges and future prospects of his or her business, including Safety, Environmental and how risks are managed.

Bob was very keen that I should succeed him, given my experience of nationalised industry. I think I demonstrated my commitment to British Coal, visiting many mines to get up the learning curve and be able to speak at the Board with some authority.

Towards the end of Bob's tenure, I had a good conversation with the Energy Secretary John Wakeham (now Lord Wakeham) who I truly rated. But I was really on the young side for the Chairman's role, and moreover the privatisation of H&W had just been completed and I needed to remain Chairman there. So despite Bob's enthusiasm, I never felt the British Coal role at that time was for me. Neil Clarke, Chairman of Johnson Matthey, took over as Chairman in January 1991. He was a reserved and softly spoken man and I served under him until 1993, when I joined the Board of GKN under the outstanding chairmanship of Sir David Lees, with whom I learned much about sound administration and practical boardroom governance of a high order.

My period on the British Coal Board was a very challenging and harsh time for the industry and the mining communities. The culmination of the pressures that the industry was under came in 1992, when Michael Heseltine, President of the Board of Trade, announced that up to 31 out of the 50 surviving deep mines faced closure.

Since the privatisation of the electricity industry in 1990, British coal was being displaced by cheaper imports while the "dash for gas" in new gas-fired power stations was underway and supplanting coal-fired power. What remained of British Coal, centred mainly on opencast mines, was eventually privatised in 1994. The disordered way in which the coal industry ran down was symptomatic of Britain's failure to develop a proper, coherent energy policy, a failure which has persisted to this day. I will return to this subject later.

11. BABCOCK INTERNATIONAL

Over the years I was at Harland & Wolff, I was fortunate to have a number of approaches from head-hunters to return from Northern Ireland to CEO roles in England. None of these roles were of interest to me, particularly given my commitment to Fred Olsen which allowed privatisation to proceed.

Specifically, as the end of my term that I had agreed with Fred Olsen was coming into sight, I was approached by Roy Goddard (formerly the lead partner in Goddard, Kay and Rogers which was merged into Whitehead Mann some years earlier) to interest me in the CEO role at the engineering group Babcock International.

Babcock's Chairman was Lord King, a formidable figure in UK business who had also been Chairman of British Airways, where he now had the honorary position of President (but felt that he had not been well-treated considering his contribution to the company, whose privatisation he had led). He had chaired Babcock for no less than 24 years and dominated the group, but in recent times Babcock had found life increasingly turbulent.

Earlier in 1993, Lord King had parted with his CEO Oliver Whitehead, who almost immediately picked up the CEO role with the construction company McAlpine. Jeff Whalley, Babcock's Deputy Chairman, had taken on the CEO role temporarily and, as I was to discover later, managed it with a very light touch. He was also

Chairman of FKI, a smaller industrial group which had stunned the City in 1987 by boldly reversing into Babcock in an agreed deal.

The merger had not worked well and, only two years later in 1989, after the usual asset-stripping of that era, the group demerged again into separate Babcock International and FKI companies. However, Babcock was still a sprawling conglomerate with interests ranging from its historic heart, its energy business based at the giant Renfrew factory in Scotland where it made coal-fired power station boilers and other sophisticated equipment for the Nuclear Power sector, to newer activities such as a German materials handling concern.

Prior to the demerger, Babcock had taken on the UK's first Flue Gas Desulphurisation plant (FGD) contract at the huge Drax coal-fired power station in Yorkshire. This contract was at a fixed price of about £400 million with construction spanning an eight-year engineering and construction cycle – a period also of high inflation.

The one redeeming feature to this high-risk contract was a sizeable down payment from National Power, whose CEO was the very able John Baker – later Sir John. I respected John enormously and I had many constructive dealings with him over the Babcock years. This contract and the cash it put into the group's balance sheet enabled the demerger from FKI to take place. Lord King remained Chairman, with Whalley as his Deputy.

After interviews with Jeff Whalley, Lord King, Sir Frank Gibb, the Senior NED, I became interested in the role. I also asked to see Eric Porter, the Finance Director. However, I could see there were many challenges ahead, despite the fact that the company was being sold to me on a very upbeat basis with a strong cash position (due in no small part to the Drax down payment).

Subsequent events, given that many months passed before I accepted, exposed the real health – or, more accurately, the ill-health – of the business and confirmed my strong view that you never really know a company until you get inside it, regardless of the external inspections and due diligence you might conduct. This certainly applies to the culture in the boardroom and in the company as a whole.

It was decided that I should come to Babcock as Deputy Chairman as well as CEO, given that Lord King was likely to retire within the next few years and I was to be positioned as his successor. As a result, Jeff Whalley would step down from the Deputy role with the intention that he remained an NXD.

At the same time, Nick Salmon, GEC's Power Division Director, was appointed as Managing Director – effectively the Group's Chief Operating Officer. I very much welcomed Nick's management and engineering expertise. We formed a great team before he left about three years later to head the Power Division of GEC Alstom, the Franco-British engineering giant which was based in Paris.

Nick and I arrived at Babcock's head office in Amersham on the same morning, and had a coffee together. On opening the *Financial Times*, we were greeted with the headline: 'All is clean and tidy at Babcock' It wasn't difficult to see who had placed this story, as it gave great credit to Jeff for tidying the group up! In his nine months as acting CEO, a generous interpretation was that this portrayal of the situation was simply mischievous – but in reality it was a very misleading story and within a few weeks, this became all too apparent.

Twenty-four hours after arriving, Nick and I were already planning visits to operations and digging down into the numbers along with the Finance Director. The harsh financial truth was that, behind the window-dressing, cash was pouring out of the back door at a huge rate, even while profits were forecast to increase. I had always agreed with the dictum by Nick's former boss Lord (Arnold) Weinstock that profit was irrelevant if it wasn't supported by actual cash, and this was never more true than in Babcock's case. There is a famous saying, quoted by Charles Murphy, the US financial guru: "Turnover is vanity, profit is sanity, cash is reality."

We quickly discovered that a range of significant contract claims in the Engineering and Process divisions, not yet resolved by negotiation, were being credited to profit despite there being no cash inflow. There were also a number of loss-making contracts which had not been adequately assessed, including losses in South Africa arising from Babcock's entry into the platinum mining machinery segment there some years earlier. On top of that, we had a new development project in Caldwell, Texas designed to turn steel-making electric arc furnace dust into benign material and to recover metals from the scrap dust. It was not working and was eating cash. This upfront diagnosis was before evaluating the risks in completing the fixed-price Drax contract – which was a massive bet on the balance sheet.

I had seen some pretty awful situations during my shipbuilding career, but even by those standards Babcock's overall position was horrific.

As the early weeks progressed, Nick and I could see that there would be significant cash outflows over the coming months. Ultimately when finalised, losses for the year were more than £40 million rather than the projected profits. In sum without major corrective action Babcock was heading towards a breach of its banking covenants.

To avert this dire fate, we needed urgently to get cash in the door, restore the balance sheet and give new direction to a conglomerate that had lost its way. Nick and I rapidly created a recovery plan which included a number of actions:

- negotiate outstanding contractual claims urgently to bring in cash;
- sell and lease back a major office block that the Process Division occupied in Crawley;
- set up major turnround plans at the Energy Division, which was facing huge losses on the Drax FGD contract and on other coal-fired boiler contracts around the world. The division also needed to be right-sized for the new market we were now facing;
- seek some renegotiation of the Drax contract with National Power;
- last but certainly not least, it was obvious to us that, despite this range of actions, we would inevitably need ultimately to go to shareholders for a Rights Issue in order to provide the Group with a balance sheet to execute a turnround and reshape it for the future.

So within three weeks of joining and in advance of our first full Group Board meeting due the following week, I went to talk with Lord King in his President's office at British Airways. In visiting Lord King, I would often run into his successor as British Airways Chairman, Colin (later Lord) Marshall, a most agreeable man, and also see Bob Ayling, the CEO. Bob, who had worked with me in British Shipbuilders on secondment from the DTI, was a great professional with not only a good legal mind but strong commercial judgement. He gave me useful advice in dealing with Lord King, who had a fearsome reputation.

Lord King was not in a receptive mood that day, but I told him frankly about the problems we were unearthing, what had been going on and how I believed we could turn it around. But I impressed on him that urgent action was needed and that, even with that action, Babcock faced a lengthy rehabilitation.

King could be extraordinarily gruff and enjoyed the odd CEO for breakfast during his colourful corporate career. Nor was he exactly keen on bad news. However, he was very intuitive. So, after a difficult conversation, he agreed that I could explain my diagnosis of the situation and my emergency plan to the Board.

He could still put his finger on key points, and asked: "How are you going to grab management's attention to execute this plan quickly?"

Then he told me the story of a farmer trying to stable a very difficult mule. Every time the farmer tried to get the mule in the stable, it would kick him out into the middle of the farmyard. The farmer tried and tried again, always with the same result, until he was sore all over and utterly exhausted. A neighbouring farmer was passing and said he would take over the task of stabling the mule – an offer which our farmer readily accepted. The other man ignored the mule and walked around the yard until he found a plank of wood. Then he gave the mule a huge whack on the head with the plank. "What are you doing to my mule?" cried our alarmed farmer. The neighbour replied: "In situations like this, you must first grab the attention of your audience."

Lord King thought that this was a good fun story – but, as usual with his stories, it had a sharp and very valid point. When the corporate strategy and plan of action is agreed, the leader must – through intensive and impactful communication – seize the attention of the management team and the commitment of all the people.

Babcock's Board was also an issue for me, because the Non-Executive Directors' ranks clearly needed refreshment. Lord King had started this process by nominating Lord (Alexander) Hesketh, the former Trade Minister at DTI, who over the years added a great deal of pragmatism and common sense to our proceedings.

Mike Turner, then an executive at British Aerospace and later BAE's CEO, was an excellent choice and made a major contribution to Board debates while I was there over the next seven years. His Babcock connection did not end there. After stepping down from BAE in 2008, he returned as Chairman of Babcock after my successor, the late Gordon Campbell, who had done an excellent job, retired. I also recruited Dipesh Shah, a very competent executive from BP whom I had met in the early days of negotiating the BP SWOPS contract in Belfast with his then-boss, Basil Butler, BP's Head of Exploration and Production.

So Nick and I arrived at our first Board meeting. We set out our initial diagnosis, the seriousness of the company's position – the stricken balance sheet and the losses we were making – and the urgent corrective action we proposed. The Board was obviously relieved to understand what was going on, as some directors clearly recognised that all was far from well. Jeff Whalley made few comments and did not challenge our diagnosis. With the full backing of the Board, we started to execute the plan with daily meetings in my office to monitor the progress in bringing in cash.

We also had to meet with our banks and provide full disclosure of our plans and financial position. Barclays, whom the group had banked with since the turn of the century, were very unhelpful despite a pleasurable lunch which I had with their then-Chairman. He made it clear that Babcock may have banked with Barclays for the best part of 100 years, but Barclays had been around for some 400 years! So much for relationship banking.

NatWest were much more realistic and receptive to the turnaround plan, and we subsequently abandoned Barclays when the Rights Issues were executed and our cash recovery plan progressed.

Lord King had been relatively quiet during the Board meeting. But less than 24 hours later, I got a call from him to say he would like to invite me to lunch at the Savoy Grill – his favourite and regular restaurant – in a few days' time. I was suspicious as to why I was being invited, and asked my secretary to check if the table was booked for two people or three. It was for three, so I knew I was likely to be heading for an ambush with the Chairman and Deputy Chairman.

It proved to be an instructive encounter. As my father used to say, you should regularly sniff the air and sometimes you might smell sulphur.

As I approached Lord King's favourite table, I could see I was to be placed between the two of them. The welcome was chilly with King glowering at me over his glasses.

I sat down and in this unacceptable atmosphere opened the menu, at which point he said: "And what do you think you are doing?" I replied: "I thought I was here for lunch, Lord King, and I have limited time". Then he said: "Now you listen to me and you listen good. I'm your Chairman and you are the CEO and I will tell you what to do. Never mind that Board meeting the other day. You can forget the idea of a loss. I want to have profits of £X million this year." This was the projected profit before the contract losses and other costs that we had unearthed and which the Board had agreed. I said: "Well, Lord King – I hope we are going to have a good Chairman/CEO relationship and I will always listen to your advice but I'm not here to do what you tell me to do. I'm here to execute what the Board approves and empowers me to do. If you are not happy then let's call another Board and you and Jeff can explain where we are wrong and how we should do it differently." He glowered at me and thumped the table and said: "You will f****** well do what I tell you or else".

He then stood up and went to the other side of the table and rubbed both his hands together and said: "I'm off to wash my hands – both of them". The symbolic gesture that accompanied this signalled I was mincemeat!

Jeff Whalley had said nothing up to now, but engaged in chain-smoking in a rather nervous fashion (this was long before smoking in restaurants was banned). He said: "You must give the old man close to that profit figure – you can't allow this loss to happen on his watch. So why not offer him 10% less than he is asking for?"

I said: "Jeff, if I were to do that I would be deceiving myself, the Board, and the shareholders. If I do that, you will also be on standby to watch Lord King preside over a bankrupt company – is that what you want for your old friend?"

At this point, Lord King returned and said: "Look, I'll take 10% less on the profit figure I was looking for!" A staged job which I found rather comical.

"Lord King," I replied, "the answer is no. This company will ultimately go bankrupt unless we face up to reality and get the restructuring plan in place urgently and prepare for a Rights Issue. Frankly I won't be around if you are not prepared to face reality."

While all this was going on, we had managed to order and eat our starter. Now, as we started the main course, the atmosphere was rather tense. He eventually broke the silence: "You are not easily frightened, John, are you?" I said: "Lord King – no, I'm not easily bullied and I'm especially not easily frightened after nearly a decade managing during the Troubles in Northern Ireland."

I've always endeavoured to be very controlled in these situations and try to avoid saying anything unconsidered, but I don't know what prompted me to say the following: "Lord King: I don't want to see you preside over a bankrupt company towards the end of your corporate career. I've admired you as an industrialist and if I'm around at Babcock when you step down as Chairman, I will see you 'over the side' with dignity, and not the way they treated you at British Airways."

He seemed rather taken aback, but by now I had had enough. So there and then, half way through the main course, I stood up, gave my apologies and told them: "I have too much work to get on with, hopefully to save the company, so I must leave now. Please let me know if you wish another Board meeting to be called, which I am more than happy to do."

I left the Savoy, phoned Emma and told her to stop unpacking the removal boxes as we may not be staying!

I was home that evening when the phone rang. It was Lord King. He said: "You must know John that I'm 100% behind you." I thanked him and said: "I trust we are going to have a positive relationship." "Yes we will," he replied, "and by the way, did you mean what you said, that you would see me over the side with dignity when I step down at Babcock?"

"Of course, I meant what I said and you will not find me going back on my word," I told him. "Well then, we are going to be good friends," he said, and rang off. And that was indeed the case up to the last years of his life. I grew very fond of him and his roguishness which he put down to having an Irish mother. Under the brusque exterior, he was fun and had a heart of gold.

My relationship with the Chairman having been resolved, Nick and I had to get on with the rescue effort. We were greatly helped about this time by our excellent PA, Valerie O'Connell, who worked for both of us. Valerie was with me until close to my stepping down at Babcock and did a superb and efficient job. Now, after her children have grown up, she works part-time at Anglo American in support of my long-serving and exceptionally able Executive Advisor, Chris Gribble, who has been with me some 18 years, since the demerger of Transco from BG in 2000. I have been truly fortunate to have had highly efficient managers in all of my PAs, including Jennifer Matchett at Harland & Wolff, Doreen Wright at British Shipbuilders and Muriel Jeffrey at Austin & Pickersgill. They, along with Simon Cant, my driver for 19 years, played an absolutely critical role, making your diary management possible and enabling you to trust them with highly confidential information.

It was necessary, after the cash-raising and operational improvement plans were in place, to move to create a coherent Strategic Plan for Babcock. As a precursor to the Rights Issue, we hired in LEK Strategy Consultants and over subsequent years I kept my friendship with Ian Evans, the senior partner, for whom I had the utmost respect as a courageous professional. He subsequently advised us on one or two potential major strategic moves, including Babcock's approach to merge our Rosyth Dockyard with DML (Devonport Dockyard) around 1997. That eventually happened a decade later in 2007 with Babcock taking over DML, and a great success it has been. It would have been an even better long-term deal for shareholders had we been able to bring it off a decade or more earlier.

To establish the criteria that would underpin our Strategy Plan, Nick and I created an Operational Philosophy Statement which comprised seven characteristics:

Customers: constantly listen to existing customers and retain their confidence, while constantly winning new ones.

Sensing markets: drive the strategy by sensing how markets are moving and developing.

World-Class competitiveness: adopt the best practices of the best companies and regularly assess Babcock's performance against them.

Modern flexible organisations: be lean and agile, minimise operational layers, simplify decision-making, systems and processes, break down internal demarcation lines and place greater emphasis on team-working.

Employees: respect each employee's dignity and inculcate a "constant improvement" culture.

Professional management: nine behaviours which we wanted all our managers to adopt, including total integrity, open and clear communication of strategic objectives and performance targets, delegation, realism, rewarding achievement and passion for change.

The Group and its investors: contribute to the delivery of sustainable and satisfactory returns to shareholders.

As a roadmap to create a successful company, this stands the test of time and changing business environments – a manual for all corporate seasons.

The Rights Issue was a crucial part of our revival strategy. Without it, Babcock would have been too weak financially to recover. We worked hard with LEK's support to build the storyboards for our road show presentations to shareholders whose support we needed. The presentations were managed by our stockbroker Smith New Court, which was headed at that time by the City grandee Sir Michael Richardson, a good friend of Lord King who had also advised him at British Airways.

Michael knew the City and the interface with Government well. He was a mover and a shaker and we got on very well together. He was indeed very amusing company, and the most charming of name-droppers, from being Mrs Thatcher's personal financial adviser to his sometimes indiscreet repetition of conversations with important figures.

The Smith New Court analyst assigned to our task was Graham Webster, affectionately known as "Wobbly" given he was close to 20 stone at that time. He had the most amazing nose for what was happening in the engineering sector, but producing analyst's notes was not his forte. He would give the input to his juniors who would then produce a piece of research. Wobbly had some remarkable coups based on his lengthy lunch-time visits to the pub or from what he picked up watching rugby at Bath or at internationals, which he loved. He organised the legendary Smith New Court food and drink stand in the West car park at Twickenham, which gathered a great pre- and post-match crowd, and was later continued by Merrill Lynch when the American firm acquired Smith. Even the Americans – not exactly Rugby connoisseurs – appreciated its relationship-enhancing value.

Rothschild's were our banking advisors and one of their top people, Tim Hancock, was most reliable and a wise counsellor – especially during the tough periods of setbacks on timing and dealing with unexpected market downturns or other unwanted surprises that you encounter on a challenging turnaround. I've learned that your first estimate of the timescale needed to achieve a turnround should be multiplied by at least 1.5 times. Better to under-promise in the forecast and positively surprise on the delivery is a sound business principle.

Wobbly would open each roadshow meeting with the shareholders by introducing us and saying: "Well you know why we are here – we are after your money!"

The investors, while raising lots of questions, were very encouraging during the roadshows. We covered a significant number of shareholders in the first five days. On returning to Rothschild's office near the Bank of England on the Friday evening to examine progress on the Rights Issue document, Nick Salmon fell asleep at the Board table – such was the energy dissipated during this intense week of roadshows.

All seemed to be well and the following week, a Board meeting to finalise and sign off the Rights Issue documentation was fixed for 3 p.m. one afternoon at Rothschild. We arrived around 1 p.m. to check all was in order. As I was getting out of the car, the phone rang. It was Sir Michael – smooth as ever. "John, great result from the roadshows, you wanted £60m – you can easily have £70m plus. However, there is a problem in that two of the major shareholders, including one of our largest shareholders, Robert Fleming, are unwilling to put in their money unless succession to Lord King is sorted out now."

I asked him if he had been in touch with his friend Lord King. "No, John: that is for you to do."

Digesting this bombshell, I immediately got hold of Sir Frank Gibb, our Senior Non-Executive Director, and gave him the news: "Frank," I said, "you will have to talk with the NXDs and then you will have to meet with Lord King." He replied: "Okay, John. I will go and talk with them as soon as they all arrive." Which they did by about 2 p.m. Frank, previously Chairman of the construction company Taylor Woodrow, was a great professional and a very good man, but he suffered unfortunately from a slight speech impediment, which under stress was more pronounced. At about 2.30 p.m. he returned to report to me in a slightly flustered state – with some challenge in getting out the words – "None of them want to tell him and they want you to do it, John – but I'll come with you"!

So Frank and I stood outside the lifts next to the Rothschild board-room awaiting the arrival of Lord King. About 2.45 p.m. he appeared and clearly, by his appearance, had had his usual good lunch.

As ever, his antenna was remarkably well tuned. As my father would have said: "He could hear the grass growing"

He immediately asked: "Is something wrong?"

I said: "Lord King, we need to have a chat before the Board meeting", and we steered him into a small meeting room adjacent to the boardroom.

"What's the matter – aren't we going to get the money?" he asked.

"Lord King, the NEDs have asked me to talk with you – that's why Frank is here. We can get the money but it's conditional, in that two of our major shareholders want us to sort out your succession as part of the deal."

"Well, we need the money, don't we?" he replied.

"Yes, Lord King. It is essential in order to see the restructuring through and put us on a sound footing."

"All right. We will have to do it then."

"John," he said, "you know I will want to be appointed President as I am at British Airways.

I replied: "Lord King, let's agree that you and I will talk about an honorary position tomorrow, but we now need to let Frank talk with the NXDs as they have to agree who is succeeding you and so on."

That was that. The Board signed off the Prospectus and I was appointed Chairman and CEO. That was in line with the succession plan we had previously mapped out when I joined – but these were not quite the circumstances that we had envisaged for implementing it. The shareholders then voted in favour of the Rights Issue. The day we drew down the proceeds was a major milestone in Babcock's rehabilitation.

I quickly came to an agreement with Lord King about his future position. He had been very magnanimous in that rushed and unexpected handover at Rothschilds. When we met, we decided that he should become Honorary President with no remuneration.

He asked to have Board papers which I could not agree to, but I told him that if he would like to attend a Board Meeting from time to time, he could call me for agreement and he would have a set of Board papers in front of him, but not for taking away. On such occasions when he wished to come, I'd always keep a seat for him beside me. He said to me one day: "You always keep a seat beside you for me – I appreciate that since Colin at British Airways puts me at the bottom of the table." Then, with a great twinkle in his eye, he added: "Or is it because you want to keep a good eye on me?" He was perceptive!

Inevitably, Babcock's turnround did not go entirely to plan. There were setbacks on timescale and financial forecasts as some contracts, including Drax, slipped and costs increased, while unexpected market downturns in some sectors occurred or we lost some critical contracts.

But gradually, helped by the appointment of Nigel Young as our new Finance Director, we started to get a much tighter grip of the business. Nigel had great cash forecasting skills and could tell you every day what was our net Group cash situation right across the world. He was just what we needed. He governed cash with great care. If he had a downside, it was that you had to prise cash out of his hands for an acquisition or investment – it was a struggle!

Babcock had no less than seven divisions and needed to be stream-lined, both as a group and within its diverse segments. We put in place operational turnaround plans in each division, and identified which divisions were core and which we would sell – after, in some cases, fixing them.

Babcock Energy and divisional restructuring

The biggest problem was the Energy Division, which had long been seen as the heart of Babcock but whose heavy losses now posed the greatest single threat to its survival. Energy had world-leading coal-burning power station boiler technology. But, like much of British industry in the 1970s and 1980s, it had fallen behind foreign rivals as the market moved from the UK and the Commonwealth to Asia. Coal in the UK was being replaced with gas and that massive market shift was very challenging for the division's management team, which was led by a fine Babcock lifer in John H. Lace. He was very cooperative in the massive divisional restructuring that was required in the run up to his retirement.

Contracts were now highly competitive, low-margin and fixed price, and often in remote locations in countries such as China where British firms were not well placed, partly because of the tensions with the UK over the future of Hong Kong. The commercial risks in this business were significant for us.

We nevertheless got the division into profit with new management and significant change programmes. However, Nick and I realised that this would not be sufficient to ensure a profitable future for Renfrew. The world industry was consolidating and Babcock Energy would have to be involved in this or it would gradually lose ground. Realistically, given our slim resources and the better prospects for growth elsewhere in the group, we could not continue to hold the division. So we looked for a suitable buyer who we considered would treat the business and its people well. After building up a relationship with Mitsui Corporation in Japan, we eventually sold the division to them for a good price.

Viewed in the perspective of Babcock's history, this was a huge departure: the Babcock name was associated above all with the Energy business and Renfrew lay at the group's core. But when you are managing a turnround of the scale that Nick and I had undertaken, you can have no sacred cows – you have to look at everything through clear and analytical eyes. Contrary to what some modern managers maintain, I have always believed that there *is* a place for sentiment in business – if it contributes to the spirit and culture of a successful enterprise. But if it is something that weighs on the company and holds the total business back, then sentiment becomes a negative that has to be removed.

We had no doubt that selling Energy was the right move if we were to move Babcock out of the doldrums in which it had languished for some years, and get it in a position to grow again. Renfrew represented a large block of invested capital and although we had cut its losses, it was making a paltry return on that capital. By selling it, we released the potential for Babcock to become a more attractive investment. And the cash income from the sale enabled us to take a big step forward in advancing the Group restructuring.

At the same time, our negotiations of the various large contractual claims across the Group were being resolved and cash was at last flowing in the right direction from that part of the plan.

Babcock's main overseas business was in South Africa, where the company had remained throughout the very difficult years of apartheid. Now, with the release and subsequent election as president of Nelson Mandela, a wind of change and opportunity was blowing through the country. We changed too. Our platinum mining equipment operation was closed and the division refocussed on major Process and Energy power plant maintenance, the latter for the State-owned electricity utility Eskom, and asset maintenance for other oil and gas companies. New agencies for Volvo trucks and equipment were put in place for the construction and mining industries. This combination proved to be durable and profitable businesses.

Lord King was keen on making a final visit to the South African operations and we travelled out together. He was greeted like a real King by the British Airways air hostesses. On the way back he showed me a charming photo of Joan Collins with a message on the back: "To John – Thanks, love Joan!" and explained how this came about.

Joan always travelled Concorde to and from the US, and usually arrived as the doors of the aircraft were about to close. New rules had been introduced so no passengers were allowed to board within 10 minutes of scheduled gate departure. Either Joan was unaware of this or just stuck to her normal programme, but a tough lady on the desk refused her access as it was only minutes before the flight departure.

She created quite a scene and demanded that she be allowed to phone the Chairman. By the time she got in contact with Lord King, the Concorde had taken off and he could only apologise and say whatever it took he would get her on the next normal flight. He reflected on this and felt he should do something more, so he rang Sir Gordon White, Lord Hanson's partner who ran the conglomerate Hanson Trust in the US, since he felt that Gordon would know what to do to make amends to Joan. David Frost in his address at Gordon's memorial service recorded that had Gordon written a book, it would not have been entitled *In Praise of the Older Woman*! Gordon advised that he would arrange to have the largest bouquet of flowers prepared and he would deliver them personally to Joan's home in Los Angeles. The signed photo closed off the episode.

Lord King could still make his presence felt when in attendance at the Board. One such occasion involved the Caldwell plant in Texas, which was exhausting my patience. Significant investment in money and expertise had been put in to get it to work. The aim was to treat the arc furnaces' contaminated dust, then recover both the metals we could sell and the tolling fee from the electric arc furnace owners to enable us safely to bury the dust, which was now benign after treatment. But just as the plant began to work reasonably satisfactorily, there was a rumour that the environmental rules in the US were likely to change to permit the untreated dust to be mixed into aggregates for road surfacing. This would make our business plan unviable.

It was the last straw as far as I was concerned, and we wanted to shut down the plant without delay. However, the Board decided that before we closed it, we ought to obtain an independent external view of the business and confirmation of the US Environmental Agency's position.

We hired a Texan-based environmental consultant who came to present to the Board in London at a specially arranged afternoon meeting held at the-then Royal Academy of Engineering building in Great Peter Street, near the Houses of Parliament.

Lord King was to attend and, 15 minutes after the meeting started, he arrived and I got him safely seated. By now the Texan is presenting in a long drawn out Texan drawl. Lord King, after looking around to see who was present, focussed on the Texan and in a very loud voice said "Who is that?" I pointed to the Agenda item and he shook his head and muttered, "Not that again". Unmoved by this intervention, the Texan carried on at an incredibly slow pace. After about 10 minutes of this, Lord King – in an even louder voice – said: "Has he come to tell us to wring its neck or cut its head off?" We all rolled about in laughter. The decision to close the plant and write the investment off was taken that afternoon.

We agreed that Lord King should have a retirement dinner for the Board and about 35 of his friends at the Savoy Hotel (naturally). He worked for weeks on the guest list and ultimately the seating plan – consulting me frequently.

Lord Tebbit was his chief guest, along with the most amazing array of talent from many walks of life. I was seated between Sir Michael Richardson and Sir David Frost. Norman Tebbit told the story of recruiting a new Chairman for British Airways when he had been the Minister at Transport.

Three shortlisted candidates were to be seen by the Department of Transport panel which Norman was chairing. Two were before lunch and one – John King – at 2.30 pm; 2.30 came and went and at about 2.40, King came in with his overcoat on, having clearly had a good lunch. Without taking off the overcoat, he sat down and said: "Now tell me about this job." Norman proceeded to outline the Prime Minister's concern about the heavy losses, the disruptive power of the unions and how the airline had to be restored to profit and ultimately privatised. John asked one or two questions, then stood up and said: "It's a very tough job but I'll take it"! Norman felt he had no choice but to accede!

Thus, we saw Lord King "over the side with dignity", just I had promised in that tense but game-changing conversation at that first lunch in the Savoy Grill.

Over the years, I have been convinced that how you treat people leaving a company is every bit as important as the welcome you give them when they join. Employees at all levels observe this aspect of a company's culture. Where a harsh culture is in place and the dignity of the individual is not respected, employees inevitably conclude – I could end up being treated just as shabbily if I have to leave. Over time such cultures create fear, distrust, and undermine loyalty and morale.

Cultures in an organisation can only be changed by the leadership, the Board and Management at different levels sharing the same values and goals. Often too you need to recruit fresh blood whose values are aligned to reinforce what the company seeks to embed. Babcock was one of the numerous companies where I have worked with my leadership team to instil just such a sea-change in the corporate culture. It had been stagnating for too long so it had completely lost its way; we had to re-energise it and give it a new purpose in its corporate life.

Of the other businesses apart from Energy, the Process Division trading under the name Babcock King Wilkinson was not in bad shape but the scale of its international contracts relative to our balance sheet size, and the high-risk nature of low-margin operations in markets such as Saudi Arabia and Malaysia was capable of springing unpleasant cash and profit surprises.

The division was well advanced in concluding an acquisition of a Houston-based pipeline design and project management company Eagleton, whose American managing director and part-owner was Duain Cagle. Duain was a good professional who ran a very profitable and well-respected company and I always enjoyed my visits to Houston. We always had to go there since he wouldn't fly. Duain would constantly remind me that, because of what he had made from the sale to Babcock, he didn't have to work! But it was a good business and remained in Babcock's portfolio for a number of years.

When I finally left Babcock, he presented me with a stunning high-quality moleskin Stetson hat which I still have. I have worn it to local village hall barn dances and it sure is some statement in Newton Ferrers in Devon!

The Eagleton purchase brought us one other major asset, because during the finalisation of the contractual documents for the purchase, Nick Salmon and I had to work with the Process Division's highly competent in-house legal counsel, Helen Mahy. We were very impressed: Helen was very professional, pragmatic and – unlike many corporate lawyers – with no ifs or buts in her advice. Nick and I agreed to invite her to move to our head office as the General Counsel and Company Secretary to the Board.

At her first Board meeting she impressed Lord King, who was in attendance in his role as President. Indeed, on observing her, he said in a loud voice: "Is she from Rothschild's?" She did a superb job and later, when I became Chairman of Lattice after it was demerged from British Gas, she was selected by the Nominations Committee to be its General Counsel and Company Secretary.

After we combined with National Grid, where I became Chairman, Helen took the same role in the merged group. She won some really challenging legal cases for National Grid going all the way to the House of Lords. She was a no-nonsense professional who added much value via her commercial and administrative skills. As Company Secretary, she provided great support in my pursuit of embedding leading governance practices in the boardroom. She was also involved in a number of charitable and external voluntary bodies, and wrote a series of books in support of the Young Offenders into Work project which National Grid sponsored and I chaired. She went on to have an important range of Non-Executive Directorships and Chair roles in public companies, and was awarded a CBE.

We ultimately agreed with Tony Bramble, MD of Process, that the division needed to scale up and would therefore have a better home within a larger process engineering company. It was subsequently sold to AMEC. I closed the deal with Sir Peter Mason, AMEC's long-serving CEO whom I had always regarded as a straight shooter, and he and I have remained good friends.

In 2003, as the Senior NXD at British Aerospace, Peter had a series of meetings with me after the company had approached me to succeed Sir Dick Evans as Chairman. Unfortunately, this was just not practicable given we had completed the merger of Lattice and National Grid less than a year earlier.

To take on two FTSE 100 companies at that time was frowned upon then, as a high-level Review of corporate governance by the late Sir Derek Higgs, formerly of the investment bank UBS Warburg, stipulated that no chairman should occupy two such roles at the same time. It was, however, deemed perfectly acceptable for a FTSE 100 chairman to head at least one FTSE 250 company as well.

I had few disagreements with Derek, but this stricture never made much sense to me: if you are a committed chairman, are prepared to work the full week and have the relevant experience, then you should be quite capable of managing the Boards of two big companies simultaneously. In fact, I would rather Chair two FTSE 100 companies than two FTSE 250s, where the level of support and talent may not be at comparable levels in the boardroom and in the support system for the Chairman. Subsequently – and, in my view, very sensibly – this inflexible stricture was loosened and whilst Chairman at National Grid, I chaired in turn RMC, P&O and finally for a time Anglo American – all FTSE 100 companies for some or all of my tenure with them.

Of Babcock's other two main divisions, Materials Handling had some great brands. One was Claudius Peters, which was based in Buxtehude, Germany and served the global cement industry with coolers, handling, grinding and reclaiming equipment. Another was Siwertell, a leading port bulk unloading equipment business based in Sweden, and a third was based in Finland and the USA and produced wood chipping, process and handling equipment for the paper pulp industry.

The division's cost base was restructured under a new MD, Dr Gernot Schaffer, whom we head-hunted from Klaas, the German Combine Harvester-maker. Gernot did a splendid job, not only in restructuring but in developing new products and in devising and implementing a coherent strategy for the business. We appointed Gernot to the Group Board. He was very strategic and a very capable manager who took care of his customers and ran a disciplined operation.

The remaining division was different from all the others, in that it was first and foremost a support services business, albeit one strongly rooted in high-quality engineering. This was Facilities Management, which managed the Rosyth Dockyard near Edinburgh on behalf of the Ministry of Defence (MOD) for an annual fee arrangement. The yard refitted nuclear submarines, aircraft carriers, frigates and other Royal Navy surface ships. It was a good operation with a strong, historic dockyard heritage, but its disadvantage for Babcock was that it could not be relied on as a source of long-term earnings – because it was a management contract, it would be regularly competed for over time.

However, we then got the chance to secure the Rosyth business stream because the MOD decided to privatise the yard with a 10-year allocated and guaranteed workload.

There were two complications: first, Alan Smith, the MD of Facilities Management who had come from Babcock Energy, had done a very good job for Babcock and the MOD, but he was approaching retirement and we would need to find his successor; secondly, the MOD at Rosyth had started a significant investment programme to build a new nuclear dock and refuelling facility for the Trident nuclear submarines and their eventual successors. Some £100m-plus was sunk by the MOD in the design and subsequent construction of the dock floor which is visible to this day. However, just prior to the sale of the yard, the Conservative Government of John Major took the political decision that all nuclear submarines would in future be refitted and serviced at Devonport (DML) in Plymouth, where an extensive new facility was to be constructed some years ahead.

This rendered the Rosyth nuclear investment virtually redundant – although the MOD believed the DML capital projections for this major project would represent better value for money. Instead, the decision turned out to be very expensive for the MOD and the British taxpayer, because DML's initial estimates proved to be hugely inaccurate and unrealistic.

In truth, the decision to switch from Rosyth to Devonport was largely driven by politics, as the Liberal Democrats were gaining a significant foothold in South West England and the Conservatives needed to demonstrate their concern for Devon jobs. There were few votes for the Conservatives to gain by staying with Rosyth, where Labour's Gordon Brown was the local MP! In time, the situation was rectified by Babcock's 2007 acquisition of DML which at last united Devonport and Rosyth. We tried enthusiastically to engineer such a deal while I was at Babcock, but could not reach agreement with DML's then-owners, Brown & Root, Weir Group and Balfour Beatty.

Nevertheless, the sale of Rosyth went ahead with the guaranteed 10-year workload including a series of nuclear submarine refits. Despite the DML issue, it remained and still is an attractive business for Babcock and we were successful in buying the yard. The acquisition broke new ground, because it was one of the first major MOD privatisations and required a complicated and very complex contract which included a profit-share arrangement with the MOD. This became a model for future MOD privatisations, a number of which involved Babcock.

After the acquisition, Alan Smith retired and I recruited Murray Easton, the MD of Yarrow Shipbuilders in Scotland, which had been bought by Lord Weinstock's GEC. I had known Murray since he was a young graduate engineer at British Shipbuilders, when he held a project manager's role at Yarrow where his father Bob (Sir Robert Easton) was the Chief Executive and one of the original shipbuilding industry barons.

Bob was a great character, appointed by the highly experienced Sir Eric Yarrow, Chairman of the famous shipbuilding family. I always got along well with Eric and his charming wife Joan, who were regular attenders at the Shipwrights. He had a wonderful sense of humour, but behind it a sharp business mind, and he paid great attention to his Royal Navy customers.

Bob would push the boundaries of rules and procedures and use his sense of humour to bulldoze when necessary. He calmly rang me up when I was Deputy CEO at British Shipbuilders and said: "John, I thought you would like to know that I am about to give the go ahead to the new £20 million module building hall at Yarrow." It was way outside the capital expenditure authority of the Yarrow Board so, gently but firmly, I had to invite him to come to London to discuss the merits and returns on the investment, all of which to him was bureaucracy getting in the way!

We remained great friends during the British Shipbuilders period and subsequent years. After I had been in Belfast for some years, most of the BS yards were either privatised or finally closed. By this time, Bob Easton, John Peach of Fergusons on the Clyde along with myself were the only surviving managing directors still in a CEO/MD role and who were there in a similar position on Day One of nationalisation in 1977.

Murray succeeded his father at Yarrow as CEO, and apparently enjoyed a great relationship with Lord Weinstock, which said a lot about Murray because Weinstock was not an easy man to work for. They continued to meet from time to time after Weinstock had stepped down from GEC and had to watch its sad demise in the form of Marconi.

On the day Murray was due to start as MD at Rosyth, I arrived early at Babcock's Amersham office and much to my surprise he was sitting there, waiting for me. I said:"What are you doing here – you should be in Rosyth." He replied: "I'll be there later in the day, but I wanted a 1:1 to get personal targets settled with you." I said: "I was going to let you settle in for a week and then come and see you." "I'd like to settle them broadly now," he declared. I thought to myself, I better set some high-level ambitions to test his reaction.

Over a cup of coffee, I said: 'Murray, I'd like you to:
- reduce the overheads by about 25% – there is a lot to go for in this MOD establishment'
- reduce the cost of refitting a nuclear submarine and a surface ship by about 20%;
- build great customer relations and don't deliver anything late to the MOD.

He didn't flinch. "That should be possible," he said "Okay. How often do I report to you?" I said:" Well it's lonely here so I'd like you to call me at least once a week to tell me how things are going. If you want to share issues with me or seek my advice, phone me anytime, day or night. You will of course have to forward us a monthly report to present to the Board in person." "Why in person?" he asked. I said: "Because I am going to put you and Dr Schafer on the Board as our two core Divisional MDs." He was quite taken aback by this unexpected good news, as that was not part of the deal he had struck in taking on the role.

"Okay, I've got it straight now as to what you want," Murray then said. By now, I was beginning to think, I'd not been tough enough on the target setting! So as he was going out of the door, I said: "Murray, it's a great idea when you start in a new leadership role to create savings equal to your salary during the first three months." He turned, smiled and saluted.

That evening he called around 8 p.m. to say he had identified savings of over twice his salary by just travelling around the massive 300-acre site that afternoon. He had started to count the numbers of Ford white 30-hundredweight vans and noticed they were all taxed for the road and therefore burning expensive diesel. He got up to 28 in his count and at the office later discovered a total of 35 on the books, with only two of them on average going to the airport twice a week to collect goods. The others were allocated per department for intra-yard transport of material, equipment et cetera.

He immediately instructed that the number of vans should be reduced to 12 with only two to be taxed for the road and therefore the rest could burn inexpensive diesel. The other 23 were to be sold. However, he would make it easy by fitting all the continuing 12 with a radio along with a dispatcher located in a hut with a radio and a telephone. Everything was implemented within two weeks and worked smoothly, with significant cost reduction.

Murray continued as he had started. He did a superb job via a zero-based budgeting team and cut overhead costs well below my target.

He achieved significant production efficiencies that pleased the MOD as, under our pioneering contract with them, we handed them back unexpected savings from profits exceeding the agreed threshold.

Defence manufacturing projects were notorious for coming in late and over budget – here was a services contract which delivered more savings earlier than was anticipated. This made Rosyth a template for what followed in the 21st century when outsourcing of MOD services became a very big business, and one in which Babcock took leadership – for example, in the management of the Faslane and Plymouth naval bases.

Our investment in buying Rosyth had a fast payback – but only because of the sound foundations laid by Alan Smith and the great teamwork and action that Murray built through his charismatic leadership, his open communication with the workforce and the respect he won through his knowledge of the industry and its key customers, the MOD and Royal Navy.

Transformational leadership generally comes about by the leader being respected for his/her competence, communication style, choice of team, and his/her reputation in the sector of expertise that is relevant to the task. Most important of all is the respect for and ability to get the best out of your people. In a sense, all businesses are "people" businesses: there is no substitute for the right people management, skills and style in the leader. This can create the environment for open dialogue with management, supervision and workforce on the front line. Respect for the leader's competence and know-how – an awareness that no-one can pull the wool over his/her eyes – is a great starting point for a leader facing a major transformational task.

Following the sale of the Energy and Process Divisions, we focussed down on to the core divisions of Materials Handling and Facilities Management, the latter centred on Rosyth and the management of the New Zealand Navy Dockyard in Auckland which we won in open competition. We also had South Africa which by then was a Support Services business.

One of the financial attributes of support services is that, generally speaking, it does not involve large-scale investment and – if managed properly – is innately cash-generative. Our net cash position strengthened until we had about £110 million in my final year of 2000 and we were able to return a tidy sum to shareholders: a far cry from the crisis we faced when I started and a fitting way to reward the investors who had stood by us through the Rights Issue and Group restructuring.

We were now in a position to contemplate acquisitions beyond Rosyth and Eagleton and targeted several, utilising the energetic Alex Marsh, who we recruited from Swan Hunter to be Business Development Director, With Nigel Young, who always needed to be convinced that the returns were right, the Board ensured there was good capital discipline and that the hard won cash was not going to burn a hole in our pocket. We turned down a number of possible purchases as we searched for the right one, and as I left we were well advanced in our discussion to buy the Hunting Facilities Management Division.

Babcock was now well on its way to becoming a support services company and, even before Hunting was secured, we started the re-categorisation move to the Support Services sector in the FTSE Index – the significance of this being that, at that time, Support Services enjoyed a higher stock market multiple than Engineering, which of itself was not highly rated by the City.

Our restructuring was tough and demanding but when I stepped down seven years after starting, we had refocussed from the original seven divisions to two, accumulated more than £100 million in cash and had no debt. My successor Gordon Campbell, former Courtaulds CEO and also Chairman of British Nuclear Fuels, did a fantastic job in building on this stable foundation over the next five years by investing for growth in engineering support services. He executed a number of quality acquisitions which were continued by his excellent successor as CEO, Peter Rogers, with Mike Turner now Chairman.

As a result, Babcock was restored to the FTSE 100 from which it had been absent for many years, and is a great example of a UK-based, international support services company founded on excellent engineering expertise.

Whilst the official statistics will categorise it as a Service company given it is listed as such in the FTSE, it is an example of one of our finest engineering companies in the country and now assembling the new aircraft carriers in its dry docks at Rosyth. Its evolution reflects the growth of the UK's services economy, which of course predominates today. But in our case, it went further than that: Babcock's problems had made it an archetype of Britain's manufacturing decline: by focussing its strategy on engineering services, it contributed to an industrial regeneration. This revival remains patchy, and Britain's long decline has left many holes in our industrial base, but stories like Babcock's, and the regeneration of the car industry, give grounds for hope that the renaissance can continue.

As I stepped down from Babcock, I also rung down the curtain on some 27 years as a company MD or CEO. My aim now was to focus on my Chairmanship of the Lattice Group (including the British Gas distribution business Transco) and my Non-Executive Director roles at P&O Princess Cruises and the automotive and aerospace engineering group GKN. I'd also just been appointed Chairman of Firth Rixson plc, the Sheffield-based forgings and castings company.

Babcock gave me a great farewell party at the Ritz Hotel, inviting some of my valued friends from different industries. It was a memorable, and to some extent an emotional evening given the immense effort and commitment that all my key colleagues had put in alongside me to save the company and set it on a new strategic direction. I believe we could say that we met the standard I was taught in my early days of management: that in any new role "… you should seek to leave things better than you found them."

12. EARLY NON-EXECUTIVE POSITIONS: GKN, BRAMBLES & FIRTH RIXSON

GKN and Brambles

Joining the Board of GKN in 1993 turned out to be a wonderful learning experience that lasted almost 10 years.

This was my first time on the Board of a top FTSE 100 group. GKN at that time was a large and diversified company operating mainly in industrial services and automotive products. I was delayed joining the Board as British Coal did not want me to leave them until some of its major restructuring was completed, but I arrived at an exciting time for this historic company, whose origins date back to the early years of the Industrial Revolution.

Sir David Lees, a GKN veteran and former Finance Director, was Chairman and CEO with Sir Peter Cazalet as the Deputy Chairman to give some balance to David's combined roles. At that time, it was still fairly common for the company leader to combine both top roles. Sir Peter, a former Deputy Chairman of BP, was a wise councillor whose friendship and advice I have valued over the years, and was ideal for the GKN role.

Sir David was a stickler for good governance and sound administration with strong financial control. He had been a member of the Cadbury Committee which carried out Britain's first review of modern Corporate Governance, published in 1992. He was meticulous in planning agendas, ensuring the high quality of Board and Committee papers and in developing his Non-Executives particularly via Committee work. Most of the Non-Executives served on all Committees as the workloads then in Remuneration and Audit were not as heavy as they are now.

I was fortunate to be given my first Chair experience of Remuneration and also later that of the Audit Committee at GKN. One of the first major transactions with which I was involved was GKN's decision to bid for Westland Helicopters, where we had the benefit of Julian Cazalet advising from Cazenove. In later years (2015-2017), Julian has done a fine job chairing the White Ensign Association, the naval charity to which I have been proud to belong.

The Westland deal was hard-fought. As one would have expected, we had prepared meticulous evaluations of what was a prudent price range to pay, having just acquired the stake held by the American helicopter maker Sikorsky's parent United Technologies Corporation (UTC) which took GKN's shareholding to 45%. There was strong resistance within the Westland Board, in that their Chief Executive, Alan Jones, was about to be appointed Chairman when GKN struck.

The deal was eventually finalised and Alan Jones joined the Board of GKN and probably felt well positioned to succeed Sir David in due course as CEO. That was not ultimately to be and Alan went off to become CEO of the cable and engineering group BICC. The Board ultimately pursued a choice between David Turner, the Finance Director recruited earlier by GKN from the distribution company Booker, and the external candidate that emerged from the headhunter search, C.K. Chow of the British Oxygen Company BOC. C.K. (later Sir C.K.) was finally chosen to succeed Sir David Lees and commenced his role as CEO with Sir David remaining Chairman.

By now Sir David was to be appointed Chairman of the textile group Courtaulds, and he and I had a discussion about whether his office should be there or remain at GKN. I strongly advised David to hang his hat at Courtaulds, given that his long years of experience at

GKN would still attract a queue of executives at his door who should be at C.K.'s door! I greatly admired David and his keen sense of doing the right thing and David always listened to his NXDs.

C.K. had a very sharp mind with strong ambitions for growth. He strengthened the Executive and made further expansions into aerospace, while growing GKN's powder technology business by acquisition at a fast pace. Some of the acquisitions in this sector were too small and added to the integration challenge and control risk. Buying too many small companies and integrating them successfully is always very challenging and has the ability to destroy value. C.K. also continued the active portfolio management approach that Sir David always pursued for value creation.

Prior to C.K. departing as CEO, we sold half the Westland helicopter business to Agusta of Italy, with whom we formed a joint venture. We retained all of Westland's aerostructures operation on the Isle of Wight which became the foundation of the large aerospace business that GKN has today.

C.K's last GKN corporate move was prompted by the growth in our highly successful Chep pallets business, which needed cash to support its expansion. Chep and our waste management business Cleanaway were both healthy growth businesses and had both been operating for many years as joint ventures with Brambles of Australia, which was listed on the Sydney Stock Exchange.

We debated long and hard and finally agreed they should be demerged from GKN and merged with Brambles, with Sir C.K. as CEO and David Turner as CFO. Sir David, Roy Brown (later to succeed Sir David as GKN Chairman) and I joined the Brambles Board as Non-Executives under the Chairman, Don Argus, former Chairman of National Australia Bank and later Chairman of the mining company BHP Billiton. Don Argus was a no-nonsense Australian, who was locally referred to as DA – for 'Don't Argue' – and much more broad-brush than David. He managed Board meetings effectively and was exceedingly capable at handling what could be extremely noisy Australian AGMs, which were a very new experience for me.

The toll of travel involved in being on an Australian company board was indeed demanding. In 2000, I was invited by Lord Sterling to join the Board of P&O Princess Cruises, which was to be demerged from P&O Group. In fact, the demerger took place on the same day in October 2000 as the demerger from BG Group of Transco etc to form the Lattice Group. I ultimately had to explain to Don that I would have to step down and he was indeed very understanding. We left with our friendship intact and I was later to meet with him on a number of occasions when I was Chairman of Anglo American and he was Chair of BHP. What goes around, comes around: on joining Anglo American, I was reunited with Sir C.K., who was serving as an NXD.

Firth Rixson

One of my earlier Non-Executive Chairmanships was Firth Rixson in Sheffield. I had joined the Board at the invitation of their then-Chairman, Martin Llowarch, the former highly respected CEO of British Steel, with a view to taking over from him as his planned retirement was not far off.

They had a number of factories in the Sheffield area and in the US specialising in forgings and castings for a range of markets including aerospace, automotive and general engineering, often involving forming very complex shapes out of specialised and exotic materials. They also manufactured the massive high-precision rings on which the turbine blades of a jet engine were mounted for their key customers Rolls-Royce and Pratt & Whitney.

Their CEO David Hall had wide experience in the industry and what he didn't know about metal forming was not worth knowing. He was closing in on retirement age and I respected him hugely as the blunt Yorkshireman that he was. Neil McDonald was our very competent CFO.

The company had recently taken over the Aurora Group – whose chairman, coincidentally, was Sir Robert Atkinson who had gone on to chair British Shipbuilders during my time there. The Aurora purchase had left Firth Rixson's balance sheet stretched in an industry which at that time had entered a period of high instability: in the early 2000s, there was a very heavy downturn in the auto industry combined with great volatility in aerospace.

Banks were not all that enthusiastic about providing us with the flexibility we considered we needed to get through the downturn. We were then approached by Glen Youngkin, the UK Managing Partner of Carlyle, the US venture capital house, to see if we would sell the company. This was an interesting experience, because neither my Board colleagues nor I had previously encountered the Private Equity fraternity.

We negotiated a target price subject to due diligence – a process during which most buy-out groups are past masters at finding ways to massively discount their original negotiated price! We did limit the period over which this had to be completed. In discussion with David Hall, I advised him that his team should keep on the tail of the Carlyle teams throughout the defined timescale of the due diligence process and to understand all the issues they were probing and privately prepare our response as they went along.

After the due diligence was completed, Glen sent one of his young men to see me when I was expecting Glen himself. He calmly advised me that Glen wanted the target price to be reduced by about 30%. He got seriously short shrift as this was not the right way to do business and not the way I expected Glen to behave, as I had come to respect his transparency and openness. I made it clear that either we get our agreed price – or no deal. We had earlier set a deadline for reaching an agreement because we could not allow the uncertainty to continue indefinitely at the company, and that deadline was now days away.

They had a few legitimate reasons to reduce the price and by now I was in no mood to cave in. There was the usual stand-off for some days, and then eventually, in a last-minute phone call on a Sunday afternoon, Glen Youngkin and I reached an agreement very close to the original number.

You have to remember that Buy-Out groups allocate significant effort in due diligence and expect to more than cover those costs by reducing their purchase price. If the deal is not closed, they have a heavy cost left on their books and no business to show for it. Negotiating large transactions in such a post-due diligence situation calls for all information and arguments to be well-defined from your side in order to counter any soft spots the bidder may encounter. The message is: close down any vulnerability to the reduction of value for your shareholders.

In the case of Firth Rixson, the company remained in Sheffield and became part of a wider, consolidated group of companies owned by Carlyle in this sector of engineering. David Hall moved to a well-deserved retirement. Neil McDonald, I understand, flourished as Managing Director under Carlyle's ownership and Glen Youngkin is now No. 2 in the publicly quoted Carlyle Company based in New York.

Many years later Glen approached me about chairing Carlyle in Europe, but his people were slow off the mark in reaching any agreement so I never seriously had to judge whether it was something I really wanted to do.

Private Equity – or "venture capital", as it was originally called – with its short term focus is not the way I have lived in business. I think, that whilst many venture capital firms work to high standards of business conduct and care for the long-term health of their businesses, others are only interested in spreadsheet management and maximising cash generation whilst they own companies. This hits long-term company health as investment in new products, processes and capital spend is artificially curtailed.

13. FROM BRITISH GAS TO NATIONAL GRID AND PENNON

At the end of 1996, I was invited to join the Board of British Gas plc following its unitary privatisation. It was a huge, vertically integrated group but was now in the throes of demerging its best-known business, the British Gas retail operation, into a new company which it had decided to call Centrica. The remaining group was renamed BG plc.

Although I was new to the company, my experiences of the North Sea with Harland & Wolff had taught me much about world oil and gas markets. This knowledge had been supplemented by my work at Babcock in the power generation and process engineering industries, and of course by my seven years on the board of British Coal. Involvement with the major energy industries teaches you as a director the vital importance of careful capital allocation and investment decisions in long-cycle industries; and the requirement to have the best possible engineering, risk and project management expertise coupled with leading safety management processes.

Dick Giordano, the American ex-CEO of British Oxygen, was the new Chairman of British Gas and very much the architect of the Centrica demerger. Indeed, Dick planned to go further at a later stage and also hive off another part of BG – its UK Gas Transmission and Distribution system, Transco, which was demerged in 2000. BG thereby became a pure Resources group rather than a utility, focussing on oil and gas exploration and production with some downstream activities.

Needless to say, Sir Denis Rooke, the former British Gas Corporation Chairman who had fought and won a battle with Mrs Thatcher to achieve unitary privatisation of the industry, was not best pleased about the Centrica demerger which reversed his hard-won victory. He would make this plain to me whenever I saw him at the Royal Academy of Engineering.

I had a lot of time for, and indeed greatly admired Sir Denis for all that he achieved in building up British Gas. We were to see a lot more of each other later, when I chaired Lattice, the renamed Transco, on its spin-out from BG, and again when it merged in 2002 with National Grid. "You are not serious about merging with those electricians," he would challenge me in the run-up to that combination.

However, time has demonstrated the exceptional value creation that has been achieved from the break-up of the original British Gas. Each of the three separate companies went their own way to create significant individual value for shareholders and value for their customers and stakeholders. This process culminated in 2016, when BG was acquired by Royal Dutch Shell in a huge deal at a very substantial premium which valued BG at £36.4 billion. This price, plus National Grid's market capitalisation of almost £28bn and Centrica's of more than £8bn gave a combined equity value of these original British Gas companies of more than £72bn in June 2018. The market capitalisation of British Gas in 1997 was about £10.5bn.

Back to 1997: Centrica was to be chaired by the Senior Non-Executive on the Board of British Gas, Sir Michael Perry, formerly Chairman of Unilever. Roy Gardner, BG's Finance Director, became Centrica's first CEO. For its part, BG recruited a new and highly intelligent CEO from Shell, David Varney, with Dick Giordano remaining Non-Executive Chairman and building a new Board. The new NXDs included Sir John Coles from the Foreign and Cabinet Offices, Dame Stella Rimington, ex-Head of M16, Elwyn Ellige a senior Partner of Deloittes who was also the Audit Partner when I was on the Board of British Coal, and myself.

When I joined the Board, BG was just emerging from the infamous controversy over the large pay rise for Cedric Brown, its then-CEO, which involved his bonus being consolidated into his salary. Even with this consolidated salary, relative to the scale of the company and the professional competence Cedric displayed, his remuneration package was by no means out of line with other comparable companies. Cedric is a fine human being, a great engineer and leader. He did not deserve the grossly unfair treatment handed out to him by some sectors of the media which created the frenzy.

After Centrica's demerger, I was asked by Dick to chair BG's Remuneration Committee – a poisoned chalice if ever there was one. He made it clear that he would also be attending the committee. The summation of the challenge was obvious! Nevertheless, we formed an able group of NXDs on the Committee and, despite interesting interventions by Dick, we stayed out of trouble with shareholders and the media.

I used to tease Dick, when he would raise some out-of-line ideas on remuneration, that not only was he American, but he had also been the first CEO in the UK to earn £1m in a year. "As a result, Dick, you have forgotten where to put the decimal point in," I told him this on one occasion and he burst out laughing. He had a very good sense of humour, sometimes hidden beneath a strong hand which, despite his Chairman's role, tended on occasions to be slightly more Executive than Non-Executive.

Dick was a firm Chairman and ran a good and disciplined Board. I held him in high regard. He held dinner meetings from time to time with the Non-Executives, keeping us well appraised of his thinking and how he viewed management or some of our potential investments.

As time progressed, a degree of tension rose between him and David Varney. Dick would express rather firm views early on in some Board debates. David, who had a very high intellect, did not always absorb this well. He also started to spend a disproportionate amount of time, as it seemed to some of us Non-Executive Directors, in dealing with UK Civil Servants and Government ministers. He subsequently left to head HM Customs and Excise and was ultimately recognised for his Government services with a knighthood.

David as CEO sat directly opposite Dick across the wide boardroom table. In the eyes of the rest of the Board, this seating arrangement magnified their differences and created a sense of literal confrontation. I learned a lesson from that and have always ensured that the CEO sits adjacent to me as I chair a Board. This enables you to communicate 1:1 with a note or stage whisper without disturbing the rhythm of the meeting. It also conveys a sense of common purpose to the other directors.

At the Board, I would always be seated beside Dick with Philip Hampton, Finance Director, on my right. It was good to serve on the Board with Philip whom I had first met when he was Finance Director at British Steel. He demonstrated a powerful grip of that business and he subsequently grew further in stature and competence. Our friendship strengthened, with me at one stage taking him to the Boat Show in Southampton to give him advice on buying a quality boat that would hold its price, rather than a production line one. He ordered a Hallberg Rassy 42, followed by a splendid Oyster and, in 2017, a new, British-built Discovery 55. Philip left BG on the demerger of Transco and joined the Board of British Telecom as Chief Financial Officer (CFO), and later took that role at Lloyds Bank. He was by then without doubt the most experienced FTSE 100 CFO. He then moved into a series of demanding Chairman roles at Sainsbury, Royal Bank of Scotland and now GlaxoSmithKline.

Two very competent young executives were on the BG Board in the person of Frank Chapman, a Project Engineer recruited from Shell in Norway to run Exploration and Production, and Dr Phil Nolan, a young Queen's University, Belfast Geology graduate who had a progressive career at BP before being recruited to run Transco.

After about 18 months, David Varney let the Chairman know he would not seek to serve beyond his three-year commitment. Dick wanted to go out and hire someone immediately who could be a replacement at that level.

Some of us Non-Executive Directors debated this in a session with Dick. I subsequently wrote to Dick to say that if we were going to demerge Transco in 18 months' time, we still had adequate time to see how Frank Chapman and Phil Nolan developed and how ready they would be to become CEOs of BG and Transco respectively. If one or other was not capable of stepping up in that window of time, we would still have time to find a replacement. But to recruit a replacement CEO now might scare one or both of Frank and Phil away.

Dick wanted to think about it and then asked me to share my thoughts over dinner with Non-Executive colleagues. We all agreed and Dick was very magnanimous and supportive in seeing the merits of the plan and the united position of the NXDs.

So it was to be that in October 2000, Transco was renamed Lattice and demerged, with Phil Nolan becoming its CEO while Frank became CEO of BG.

Frank had great success in growing BG's international portfolio, scale and values. He was recognised for this and his charitable work by a knighthood toward the end of his 11-year-plus tenure. That is a very long time for a CEO of a major company and he may have gone on just a touch too long. BG hit some problems with major infrastructure investments overseas, particularly in Australia, costing significantly more with major slippages – a feature not uncommon in major oil and gas and mining projects as we too experienced at Anglo American, particularly in the Minas Rio Iron Ore project in Brazil. But there is no doubt that Frank, who was elected a Fellow of the Royal Academy of Engineering in 2013, is the type of entrepreneurial engineer that the country needs to drive our future growth.

Phil was and is a very bright man who, like Frank, was undertaking his first CEO role in a quoted FTSE 100 Company. He fitted in well with his team and got to grips with a major Ofgem Regulatory Review. This involved both of us negotiating at the 59th minute of the eleventh hour with the Chairman of Ofgem, Callum McCarthy, to head off a Competition Reference which some of the Lattice Board

Members felt was necessary in order for us to get a fair deal. Because of the uncertainty and disruption they cause, Competition references are generally to be avoided unless the Regulator is adopting a very unreasonable approach.

The big disappointment for me and, I suspect, ultimately for Phil was that he decided after a year to leave Lattice. He succumbed, as I put it to him at the time, to the potential bag of gold placed on the table by the Irish business magnate Sir Tony O'Reilly, who tempted him via private equity to return to Ireland and run the privatised Telecom Eire. In fairness, returning to Ireland with his family also had its attractions. Phil did exceptionally well in that role and accordingly was well rewarded financially. But he has, as I told him at the time, been challenged to find another suitable FTSE CEO role: one year in post in a FTSE 100 is not easy to explain away, despite the fact that Phil has great talent.

We remain very good friends, and he and his wife Josephine are a delightful couple who enjoy life in the outskirts of Dublin. Phil has a mix of private equity chairman roles and has recently become the Chairman of Affinity Water where he has and will continue to have deserved success. He has more recently been appointed Chairman of the Ports company ABP.

Demerger of Transco

The demerger of Transco and its associated businesses to form Lattice was a tough assignment, given the enormous amount of work involved in selecting a top management team and building a new Board from scratch.

One aspect of human behaviour emerges when you are engaged in demerging part of a Group into a new company. The cohesive loyalty of management in the original Group divides into two camps fairly quickly, well in advance of the actual demerger dates. The Management camps form on both sides and negotiation on people, balance sheets and a host of other issues become more challenging as the separation date approaches.

Indeed, even up to and at the final Board meeting of BG, I was still negotiating with Dick who had dug his heels in about the amount of debt Transco should take on to its balance sheet – which I was firmly resisting because I felt what he wanted was too high. The compromise I offered to Dick prior to that Board meeting was indeed the final outcome accepted by the two new Boards.

One of those amazing coincidences in life then occurred, because P&O Princess Cruises was to be demerged from P&O Group on the same day as Lattice from BG in October 2000. I was committed to join the Board of the demerged Cruise company. I was discussing this issue of two camps emerging in advance of the demerger with Lord Sterling, Chairman of the P&O Group, and he was lamenting to me about the very same demerger behaviour at P&O that I was observing at BG.

One key appointment was to select an Executive Assistant and that's when I persuaded Chris Gribble (who had been Executive Assistant to David Varney) to join me. Eighteen years later, she is still with me as one of the most competent managers and organisers I have ever had the good fortune to have. I trust her implicitly and I have only ever heard praise for her manner in dealing with people in and outside the company.

Phil was CEO and we appointed Steve Lucas, the very competent Treasurer at BG, as CFO with John Wybrew, an ex-Shell man, as the Director of Corporate Affairs including interface with Government, communications and PR. John was a diplomat and very effective in a low-key and gracious way.

The Lattice Board had to be put together quickly and this was my first experience of assembling a Board from scratch. I was determined that it should have the right mix of skills and breadth of experience to cope with a regulated industry of national importance.

I was fortunate to hire some exceptionally talented and experienced people. Three of the Non-Executives were also nominated to go forward two years later to the merged Board of National Grid Transco (NGT), as the combined National Grid and Lattice was initially called (we later dropped the "Transco").

These NXDs included the very experienced electrical engineer and utility executive Ken Harvey. Ken had spent his career in the electricity distribution business and had been CEO of Manweb, the Merseyside and North-West England utility. He subsequently became Chairman of South West Water and the Pennon Group, headquartered in Exeter. He became Senior Non-Executive Director and Chairman of our Remuneration Committee. Ken was a courageous Non-Executive who was always prepared to address the elephant in the room and supported great discipline in the Board and its Committees.

We also managed to recruit George Rose, the very experienced and competent Finance Director of BAE Systems, to come on Board as the Audit Chairman. This was George's first FTSE 100 NXD role and he continued doing an excellent job as Audit Chairman after the National Grid merger. Another NXD was Stephen Pettit, who like Phil was ex-BP and who also had a great deal of Telecoms experience – he later chaired the Risk and Responsibility Committee at National Grid. The Board was completed by Baroness Diana Warwick, CEO of University UK, and Sir David (Den) Davies, former President of the Royal Academy of Engineering and a former Chief Scientist with the MOD. Unfortunately, we could not take Diana and Den on to the National Grid Board after the merger, but Den continued with us as a valued advisor on Safety because of his deep experience in that field from the time he had spent in the rail industry, and in particular his report, following a series of train accidents, that recommended the fitting of Automatic Train Protection (ATP) devices to avoid collisions.

Gas is an explosive substance flowing 24 hours a day, 365 days a year around the country, and its safety management and practices are of paramount importance to protect public safety. This was one area we had to tackle to ensure that safety standards were where they should be.

We also had to deal early on with a strike of Emergency Gas Service employees in East London. This was a very dangerous situation and threatened our statutory duty to attend uncontrolled gas escapes within one hour to ensure safety of persons and property.

I worked to support Phil as he established the essential substitute emergency cover. Jon Butterworth, who was heading the National Emergency Service and was also one of our most energetic and imaginative leaders, was given the task of managing the substitute service, which he relished. Having worked previously in South Wales, he persuaded 40 emergency gas specialists in 20 Transco vans to come to London to effectively break the strike.

He housed them in a hotel near Russell Square and set up a dispatch centre there. It all worked as pickets couldn't assemble in time at the site of an incident, since its whereabouts would not be known for some time after the particular emergency started. About one week into the dispute, the manager of the hotel spoke to Jon and said: "You booked 40 rooms – are you aware that only 20 are being used?" It then dawned on Jon: two technicians per van, so they must have assumed they would have to share rooms. "What do you want me to do, Mr Butterworth?" asked the manager, "Cancel 20 rooms?" So effective was this operation that the strike was soon called off.

As I have generally done when becoming Chairman of a company – be it an existing enterprise or a newly formed entity – I agreed with Phil as CEO to set up a Strategy team at Lattice in order to work out how we as a FTSE 60 company might develop and grow. Were there obvious M&A candidates that we should start to monitor?

We had a very able young man, Omar Abbosh from Accenture, on secondment as Head of Strategy. He later returned to Accenture where he has had great success and I still keep in touch with him. He did a great deal of valuable analysis for us. It became apparent that a merger with National Grid was by far the best value-creating option and so we started monitoring NG, which at this time was completing its first acquisition in the US. Within two years of the formation of Lattice, the companies merged – but that's another story.

When Phil Nolan left us at the end of 2001, I had to take over as acting CEO. We had already hired an exceptionally talented manager and engineer in Colin Matthews, Technical Director at British Airways, to head up Transco. His final act at British Airways before joining us was to sign off the re-certification to allow the British Concorde to fly again following the tragic Paris airport crash of the French Concorde.

Colin did a superb job at Transco, placing special emphasis on its safety performance and getting its costs and performance in line with the new five-year Regulatory Settlement that the Board had finally accepted.

We had a number of peripheral businesses that management believed could become non-regulated growth businesses. However, following our Strategic Analysis, the Board decided to focus on being a core utility and gradually sold and exited most of the non-regulated activities. This wasn't entirely successful: at that time, we were still developing a telecoms fibre optic cable venture using our gas network pipes as its backbone, which was called 186K. The value of such a fibre-based telco, which had been started back in BG days, slumped around the time of the NG merger because of large-scale overcapacity in the industry and a decline in the value of telecoms companies. We finally sold it off after the NG merger, but had to take an unwelcome write-down hit on the way through.

However, this negative was more than outweighed by the substantial benefits of our decision to focus on our core business as a gas utility. This strategy was supported by our investors and our share price rose steadily. That brought a merger with National Grid within reach, because we were able to demonstrate that our uplifted equity value got us through a holding of 40% of the combined group, thereby justifying merger accounting. I don't believe that you can create a genuine merger unless the smaller partner accounts for at least 40% of the enlarged group by market value. Any less and it becomes a takeover by the larger party.

For every successful merger, the industrial logic must be there from Day One. That was the case with Lattice and National Grid:

it was very logical to bring gas transmission and high-voltage electrical transmission together. This was particularly relevant when you consider the preponderance of gas for new UK power stations at the time, the balance of the Grid, and indeed the role of Lattice's own gas transmission business in the heating of homes.

The other very important element in successful mergers is that the corporate cultures should be compatible. NG and Lattice were both previously state-owned companies with a strong community service ethos, and they were both engineering cultures. So we had a lot in common and that facilitated our successful integration.

National Grid faced a particular management challenge because of its large business in the north-eastern United States. You have to build quite a personal relationship in the US with local politicians and regulators and local authorities. That's why it's so important to have your business there run by a US CEO who understands the region and is fully accepted by regulators and politicians. Scottish Power made big acquisition inroads into the US but flooded the businesses they bought with UK people, which resulted in their not being well-received. We ultimately hired a US CEO – Tom King – who did a very fine job and who joined the Group Board.

One of my most important tasks as Chairman was to lead the selection process for a new CEO to succeed Grid's long-serving, cerebral, physicist-turned-engineer Roger Urwin in 2006. Steve Holliday, the man we appointed, did an excellent job over a 10-year period. We had a very rigorous appointment system when we chose him. We benchmarked against the external community. The NXDs split themselves into two groups to interview him on two occasions; the SID took one and I took the other. We also had him interviewed by an external head-hunter who did the benchmarking for us.

I asked his colleagues two confidential questions: How do you find him as a colleague? How would you view him if he was appointed CEO? This gave us very good feedback in the transparent system we ran. The NXDs had agreed that, subject to me working with him on any individual development issues, I had the authority to appoint

My father and mother's wedding day in the war years of 1941.

Our wedding day in 1967.

Sampson and Goliath 800-ton lift cranes at the Harland and Wolff shipyard in Belfast overflown by an Airbus A380.

"Sea Quest" – the first semi-submersible drilling rig in the North Sea, destined to discover the BP Forties oil field, launching from three slipways.

The passenger liner, SS Canberra, delivered to the P&O Company, London, in 1961. A stunningly beautiful ship.

With Lord King, chairman, and Nick Salmon, MD, at our first AGM of Babcock International in 1993.

The SWOPS Project – Single Well Oil Production Ship for
BP – commissioning in the H&W building dock.

RFA Argus – helicopter training ship, converted from a Roll-on
Roll-off container ship.

RFA Fort Victoria – a self-defended Replenishment ship to service the RN Frigate fleet.

The Duchess of York being introduced to supervisors and managers at the naming ceremony for Fort Victoria.

Leaving Kemendine with my daughter, Fee,
on her wedding day in 2002.

Underground visit to the British Coal Selby mining complex in
Yorkshire, as a Non-Executive Director.

Conferment of Knighthood (Knight Bachelor) by Her Majesty the
Queen at Buckingham Palace, 2001 (New Year Honours List).

My sailing companions on 'Shimna' as we depart from the Island of Rum (Scotland) accompanied by an early morning rainbow. From top to bottom, Murray Easton, former MD Babcock Rosyth; Graham Parker, my son; Sir Jonathon Band, former First Sea Lord.

With Bob Catell, CEO of Keyspan (USA), and Steve Holiday, CEO of
National Grid (NG), following acquisition by NG of Keyspan.

Meeting the President of China XI Jinping, as President of The Royal Academy of Engineering at the Great Hall of the People in Beijing during an International Engineering Symposium.

The Elder Brethren of Trinity House 2011 in the presence of The Master HRH Duke of Edinburgh (Sir John - 2nd row, 2nd from right).

Family gathering on board a Princess cruise ship in 2017 to celebrate birthdays and anniversaries as multiples of five years. Front row – myself and Emma, with our grandsons Arthur and Alfie to the right. Back row, from L to R, grandsons Charlie and Jack with parents Fee and Nige, Jean and Brian Curry (other grandparents) and Graham and Ina.

An inspiring graduate with her guide dog after receiving a Masters degree from the University of Southampton.

Knight Grand Cross (GBE) - appointed in 2012 (Birthday Honours list) – robed for the Order's service, held each five years in St Paul's Cathedral, 2017.

'251' – a 44 storey accommodation tower delivered by Laing O'Rourke,
applying their 70/60/30 modern construction philosophy.

him, so I said: "Before reaching a decision, we'll go away for a day, Steve, and talk a number of things over."

The idea was to go sailing in Devon, so I took him to my boat, but it was the day of a perfect storm so we sat on the boat and then had a decent lunch ashore. By the end of that, I had sufficient commitments from him to know that we could work together; we had a very good relationship: he was a strong CEO and created a lot of efficiency and value in the business.

One of our first M&A decisions was the $7.3 billion (£4.1 billion) acquisition of KeySpan in the US – a very big event which made Grid the second-largest utility in the US at that time.

Before KeySpan, Roger and I put Steve in as head of the former Transco Gas Distribution operations to gain experience of that business. During this period, we sold four of our eight gas distribution networks for about £5.5 billion and recycled that into the US. So we were able to pay cash for KeySpan; it was the power company for Brooklyn and other parts of New York City, and for Long Island, and was run by a very fine chairman and CEO, Bob Catell

Bob had started life in Brooklyn Gas. To get the deal done, Steve, Bob and I had dinner in London. Bob would like to have continued as CEO of the US but was aged close to 70 and I said: "Bob, why don't you become deputy chairman of NG and continue to play an important role giving us advice on the integration of KeySpan." He was a very fine man. He was brought up by a single mother, adored her and told me: "I only wish she was here to know that I had got to be Deputy Chairman of a FTSE 100 company." It was a very happy deal. I have a lovely picture taken by Brooklyn Bridge of the two of us, the night we celebrated the agreement.

John Pettigrew, who succeeded Steve in 2016, was one of the young men in the gas industry when I first visited South Wales. He was a rugby player with the famous South Wales club Pontypridd when I first met him. He is an economist and came through as a Transco graduate – he did various jobs in the gas business and then was given the opportunity to move into electricity transmission and was later sent to the US as part of his development programme to run the power distribution company there. Then he returned to the UK and eventually ran all Grid's operations here before being selected as the new Group CEO when Steve stepped down. His appointment was one more confirmation of the benefits of the original National Grid-Lattice merger and of the critical importance and value in developing your people.

The successful merger and consistently strong performance of National Grid were even more impressive because they took place against the background in Britain of increasingly dysfunctional national energy policy. In fact, I would say that there is no single area of Government and regulatory policy in recent years which has been more mishandled by successive administrations. I am no alarmist, but the result of the policy flaws is that the UK today faces a potential crisis in power supply whose magnitude is still largely unrealised by the public. There is now a genuine question whether we can continue to meet consumer demand for a secure and quality supply of electricity in the coming years.

Who will keep the lights on?

This very concerning analysis is based on my three decades of experience in the British energy industry, going back to 1986 when I joined the Board of British Coal. At that time, Lord Marshall, head of the Central Electricity Generating Board (CEGB) which was responsible for all UK electricity generation, transmission, distribution and supply, came round to join us at a Coal Board dinner and discussed his great desire for unitary privatisation of the CEGB. Those of us who knew him and the CEGB, whilst it was a very powerful, centralised planning system that certainly did take care of security of supply in the country, also recognised its propensity for somewhat over-engineering investments, causing a resultant higher cost but equally high reliability.

Lord Marshall told us that he had just come from Mrs Thatcher, who wanted to break up the CEGB and privatise it in pieces. He had immediately asked her: "Who will keep the lights on?" And the reality since the CEGB was broken up and privatised is that no-one has had the hands-on responsibility specifically within government or industry to keep the lights on.

There was something on this written into the remit of OFFER, the Electricity Regulator set up to police the industry after privatisation which was subsequently merged with the Gas industry regulator Ofgas to form Ofgem. But OFFER/Ofgem was never really the body that could possibly be responsible and deliver Security of Supply, given that they generally believed everything could be taken care of by the market itself. That was a fundamental mistake and created a structural flaw in the system which now, years later and having been compounded by other errors, has come back to haunt us.

There are very few practical operating people in Ofgem, or indeed most of the utility regulators apart from Offwat, the water industry watchdog which is headed by Jonson Cox, who has been an experienced CEO in the sector. It is a relief for me, now that I have become chairman of Pennon Group, embracing the south-west England and Bournemouth water companies, to be working with a regulator who understands the operational realities of business life much better than most.

There was a lot of intellectual horsepower in Ofgem, a lot of legal eagles and some economists. But they often went down into minutiae and lost sight of the big picture.

For instance, during my time at National Grid, we had an enormous inquiry into the competitive market for supplying gas meters. The inquiry was instigated by Ofgem and carried out under powers assigned to them from the Competition Commission, as the Competition and Markets Authority was then known.

Some years earlier, Callum McCarthy, when head of Ofgem, had come to see me before the National Grid merger in around 2001 and asked for Transco's support in making the supply of gas meters a competitive market. At that time, Transco did 100% of the supply and installation. I said: "Of course we'll co-operate, but to be honest what's it all about? Do you think Mr and Mrs Smith will sit up on a Saturday night with gas meter catalogues deciding between the brown one from M&S or the green one from Tesco with a price difference of maybe £1? What's it going to save them for something that's going to last at least 15 years, and will cost millions of pounds in software systems development alone, which will fall on the customer bills?"

There were 21 million gas meters in the UK. I told Callum: "This is not about protecting our business – our gas engineers are there in their vans 24 hours a day, seven days a week to deal with gas explosions or any leakage. They must be on site within an hour if it's an uncontrolled event, wherever they are coming from. They also install meters in their spare time. That can't be an inefficient system and what you want to head to cannot be a more efficient system."

Anyhow, in close co-operation with Ofgem we drew up this complex contract to allow it all to happen. Within two or three years of operating the new contract, some 40% of the meter market became competitive through the participation of various competing organisations. To support this, as I had predicted, we had to build the most complex and costly computer system to give everyone involved access to the necessary data, plus a ring-fenced separate Board and Organisation.

Then, well after Callum left and Sir John Mogg became Chairman, Ofgem triggered a Competition inquiry which ultimately fined us for anti-competitive behaviour despite Ofgem's close involvement in drawing up the contract to enable it all to happen. When we went to court to get an explanation of this, we found that we had to put the cost of installing the meter up about 50p, if I recall – hardly a customer-friendly act and overall a costly waste of time, money and valuable management resource.

Despite this unwelcome turn of events, I endeavoured to build a good relationship with Sir John Mogg (later Lord Mogg). He did take a huge interest in European security of supply, which I felt was directionally good, and put a lot of good work into Europe Energy Policy. Security of supply is not just about having an adequate margin between supply and demand, but about ensuring stability of electricity supply. Ofgem's Chief Executive, Alistair Buchanan, was a very bright analyst from the City. But it took him some time to recognise that the market wouldn't satisfy some of the critical equations that had to be solved. And all the time, the Security of Supply problem was drifting, and becoming more critical year by year. This is still the case.

Energy mix

If we take the five-year period (2012-2017), a significant change in Britain's Energy Mix has occurred.

The situation in 2012 was that we depended, on average across the year, on 25% of our power supply from Gas, 34% from Coal, about 16% from a reducing Nuclear base where nine out of our 10 remaining stations will potentially close over the next 10-15 years; and we had about 5% generated from Wind.

In this timescale, the fracking revolution in the US has had the huge benefit of significantly reducing the price of oil and gas, but it has also produced other unexpected consequences. It has led to low-cost gas being used in US power stations, which has displaced higher-cost mined coal. This in turn has flooded on to the international market at very low thermal coal prices, making it attractive for a period to burn coal and depress the utilisation of gas for generation.

2017

By 2017, gas had risen to 33% with coal dropping to just 5%, whilst wind increased to 15% and biomass from 3% to 7%.

2012-2017

One factor that was evident in this five-year period has been the increase in solar output to around 13% at mid-year. This, together with biomass, hydro and wind and nuclear is heading the country in the right direction towards its low-carbon targets.

2018

The output of wind is not assured every hour of every day, given that it is dependent on atmospheric pressure distribution across our wind farms. By mid-2018, during the recent extended spell of high pressure and sunny weather, wind had reduced to below 5% and in some periods of the day was down to 1-2%. This demonstrates that the range and pattern of output from wind puts significant variable standby demands on our ageing gas generation assets in particular. We also have to take into account that solar and wind alone cannot provide the constant and stable power 24 hours per day to drive our heavy users of energy, or our critical software-driven systems that demand a "quality" continuous non-interruptible energy supply. The ultimate development of battery storage at scale will enable a more continuous and stable output from both wind and solar. However, the additional capital cost will change the economics of both.

Given the phasing-out of coal and the ageing state of our nuclear assets, along with that of the ageing gas turbine fleet, the replacement cost of these depreciated assets will have a significant impact on the future cost of electricity. This might make Hinkley Point C and other nuclear prospects a more attractive and long-term, competitive, low-carbon supplier than many armchair commentators are projecting today. However, if we are to ensure the future security of supply, there is a critical urgency to rebuild these assets. The start date, given the planning and approvals lead time in the UK, is long overdue.

The US fracking impact on international coal prices (2012-2016) and the consequent displacement of gas turbine capacity has caused UK operators to mothball a number of gas-fired power plants. In some cases these mothballed plants, having become uneconomic because of cheap coal, have ended up being cannibalised for spares – and therefore these plants are no longer immediately available to come on-stream at short notice. We are getting the worst of all worlds, because as the coal-fired power stations are being rapidly phased out to meet emissions reduction targets, so we are losing both that capacity AND not replacing it with the gas-fired and nuclear plant that we badly need. The upshot has been that the margin between winter demand and available capacity has been ever more tightly squeezed in the last few winters to the point where the loss of one or two power stations to the Grid can take us into "brown-out" territory.

This increasing problem attracted the attention of the Prime Minister's advisors. As President of the Royal Academy of Engineering, I was involved in discussions about the energy security of supply issue as a member of the PM's Committee for Science and Technology, whose other members were distinguished academics, scientists with one or two industrialists. We all agreed, with some prompting from myself, that security of supply was one of the critical issues facing the nation.

We went to see the PM David Cameron and explained the growing problem of security of supply for the winter of 2014. I'm not sure he was happy with bad news – I said the RAE was prepared to do an independent study into the situation. A working group was subsequently formed, chaired by Dr John Roberts, a Fellow of the Academy and an experienced CEO from the power generation and distribution sector.

The group prepared a report with clear recommendations to have an early auction to ensure that some of the mothballed gas-powered plants were brought back on-stream and were available on standby to deal with the potential increases in demand in the 2014 winter. This report was subsequently published and was acted upon by the Department of Energy and Climate Change (DECC). It was followed by a further detailed study by the Academy on wider Energy Policy issues, which was published in 2016.

Our great concern in 2014 was the narrowing margin between supply and demand – it was down into low single digits at that point, when we were previously operating the Grid at a margin of around 15-18%. That margin ensured that there would be no threat to supply or stability of supply, even if one or two power stations failed or if gas supplies from, for example, Norway were interrupted.

The other aspect of the conundrum that is not fully appreciated is just how important is clean quality power to our daily lives – in the sense of stable power for the raft of computer systems used in the country. Today, you simply can't fall back on voltage reduction to curb power demand, except within very fine tolerances, because that would impair the raft of bank and insurance systems and the other very large systems on which we depend every second of the day.

The reality, particularly with the Government's 2015 confirmation that coal-fired stations would be completely phased out by 2025 under European directives that we signed up to some time ago, is that we desperately need to be building either nuclear or gas turbine plants to make up for the dearth of supply.

Renewable energy sources do not necessarily provide constant 24-hour power and therefore, were we to rely on them alone to replace coal and nuclear, the risk of unacceptable voltage drops would increase. Renewables in the form of photovoltaics will make a good contribution in a local sense and waste-to-energy plants will also make an important contribution. But, for example, just to run both our railway system, which is increasingly being electrified, and our underground rail systems requires new, major power plant investment.

The realisation that I'd like to believe has at last dawned on the UK – but maybe it hasn't yet fully hit us – is that our existing energy companies who are capable of investing in new capacity are in the main all overseas-owned. Both Centrica and SSE, as UK generators, given the political flak they have taken over retail power prices and the fact that they were referred by the Coalition Government to the Competition Commission, are highly unlikely to reinvest in gas-fired power stations, which are now the only reliable means of plugging the widening supply gap in the short-to-medium term, and even this is a challenge given our very long planning approval cycles.

This means that all the investment decisions relating to our current power stations are likely to be taken either in Madrid (Scottish Power/ Iberdrola), Berlin and Frankfurt (RWE and EON) or Paris (Electricite de France). We need to recognise the reality that these companies have complete 360-degree global freedom as to where to put down their capital. They are also subject to domestic pressures over which we have absolutely no control. The extraordinary saga of reaching agreement in France and the UK over EdF's new nuclear station at Hinkley has resulted in years of delay relative to the timescale originally planned.

There is a great need to have a simplification and clarification of our current energy policy, and above all politicians must learn to stop arbitrary interference given the importance of stability in the investment climate. An example of such arbitrary interference occurred in 2014 when Ed Milliband, then Labour leader, promised a Labour Government would impose a price freeze for two years. This was one of the most negative signals to send to would-be energy investors in the UK. These power plants are assets that are being put on the ground for 30-40 years. To chop and change either in regulatory policy or in the investment climate around power generation is in my view an irresponsible thing to be doing.

There is no question that we need new gas and nuclear power stations urgently. Yet the planning system is not conducive to getting them. We undoubtedly need new nuclear stations: whilst nuclear has a high capital cost, it doesn't appear to be more expensive than offshore wind, particularly when you consider the Government incentive subsidies provided and the cost of providing reliable back-up generating capacity needed for the inevitable fluctuations in the output of wind and solar generation.

Taking these factors into account, nuclear of itself will probably not be out of line in its long-term cost-competitiveness, and it contributes to low-carbon electricity generation. Nuclear delivers steady, and above all clean, 24-hour output which contributes to resolving what has become known as the "Trilemma" – the need to guarantee security of supply at future affordable cost which meets the regulatory drive on clean energy.

Wind will be much more capable of providing a long-term reliable source of power across different weather conditions if and when effective storage via new battery technology or other competitive storage systems arrive. The cost of these systems will of course have to be added to wind costs per hour in order to provide holistic comparative costing.

The decision to build new nuclear plant should have been made a decade or more ago. The reality is that we need a mix to achieve carbon targets, to achieve security of supply and not to be beholden to a particular source of power.

LNG infrastructure

The situation around gas-fired power stations is even more exasperating because, thanks to past investments, we are actually in a pretty good position to use gas – notably liquefied natural gas (LNG) – to solve our major security of supply problems. National Grid executed two very important capital projects during my period as Chairman. First, we built a brand new £800m LNG import terminal on the Isle of Grain in Kent, which at the time was Britain's first new LNG terminal since Canvey Island on the Isle of Grain back in the 1960s.

Subsequently, two other LNG terminals were built at Milford Haven in South Wales, one called South Hook for Exxon Mobil and Qatar Petroleum, and the other called Dragon for BG and Petronas of Malaysia. To connect these terminals to our main transmission system, we had to build a large, high-pressure pipeline from South Wales to Gloucestershire at a cost of £1 billion.

The construction of this pipeline was one of the most challenging of engineering tasks, partly because it had to pass through the Brecon Beacons National Park. We also had to contend with some exuberant and inventive environmental protesters. However, after we finally got the project through the unacceptably long planning approval process, we completed the pipeline ahead of its scheduled construction time.

The three LNG terminals at Isle of Grain and Milford Haven combined can take in more than 35% of the UK's gas needs. Another 15%-20% comes from the Ormerlange field in Norway for which the delivery pipeline comes ashore at Easington in County Durham, and there is still North Sea domestic supply. We also have gas pipeline interconnectors to Bacton in Norfolk from continental Europe – Zeebrugge and the Netherlands – although not significant in volume terms. Therefore, we aren't very dependent on mainland Europe and certainly not on Russia for our gas supplies.

Moreover, despite the fact that it is all imported, the LNG that comes into Milford Haven and Isle of Grain has many sources so if there is political instability in one country, such as Egypt, supply can be easily fulfilled from the likes of Brazil, Trinidad, West Africa and/ or the Middle East, so long as our sea lanes are protected by the Royal Navy. LNG is a critical component in terms of guaranteeing security and stability of supply. However long it takes for the Government to act – and let's hope the penny drops soon rather than action being triggered by power cuts starting – LNG will therefore be a very important fuel in the future mix for many years to come.

Energy supremo

We are now very vulnerable to supply disruption. There is a critical need always to have a mix in your system and, on the basis of current investment plans, that clearly is now missing. Therefore I believe that we desperately need an independent energy supremo with the right government backing to determine energy policy, to ensure that it is simplified and is made conducive to inward investment in order to address Security of Supply over the long term, something which is clearly becoming more serious day by day.

Instead, Government seems to fiddle with tiny adjustments like making, as they did in 2015, the obvious announcement that coal-fired stations are going to phase out, and then launching a debate about whether National Grid, as the system operator, should continue as the system operator running the control centres for the whole transmission network. This despite the fact that National Grid is where the specialist engineering and network knowledge resides, that it operates a secure system completely independent of the power generating companies, peopled by people who know and have years of experience of keeping the lights on.

The idea of "breaking up" National Grid looked to me like another fiasco in the making – as was rail privatisation in the 1990s by splitting rail track ownership from train operation. That separation should never have taken place: it has proved to have created a very unworkable blame culture.

If, as I hope, a single person or entity is given responsibility for ensuring Security of Supply, they must have a very close relationship with National Grid. NG's people have all the forecasting data for 24 hours ahead or a year ahead and their estimates are probably much more reliable than any other forecaster. They provide the forecasts both to the regulator, Ofgem, and to the Government. Then the civil servants and politicians can work with the forecasts. But if there is a shortage, NG has to announce it and say, "We are asking for volunteers to switch off power and to go on to interruptible contracts." Or NG has to *impose* interruptible contracts. This is not a desirable position.

But make no mistake: unless this very serious issue of security of supply is addressed urgently, and new gas and nuclear capacity built to back up the growing but intermittent supply from wind and solar, the nation will have to brace itself for brown-outs (noticeable reductions in the level of power supply) or severe power restrictions. The intermittency of wind and solar will be eased by the ultimate development of battery storage, but obviously at a cost which will impact the economics, particularly of wind. This security of supply issue will hinder our economic growth and will be a big negative for attracting inward investment. It would be an unmitigated disaster for Britain, all the more so because it was so avoidable. Critical planning lead time and getting investors to the decision point to proceed with new power stations will now be a race against time.

Pennon Group

National Grid was not to be my last company with a strong regulatory and engineering dimension. In 2015, I was approached by the Board of Pennon Group to succeed the long-serving and highly-successful Chairman, Ken Harvey. I accepted the role and was appointed Chairman at the 2015 Annual General Meeting.

Pennon comprised both South West Water (SWW) and Viridor, the waste-to-energy and recycling business. It is also the largest quoted company in South West England (in the upper half of the FTSE 250), headquartered in Exeter.

South West Water serves Devon and Cornwall and part of Somerset with fresh clean water and the treatment of storage and waste water. As I joined, it was also bidding to buy Bournemouth Water, which it successfully acquired and has integrated well.

The company supplies a combined population of 1.75 million in Devon and Cornwall, but this number dramatically increases in the summer by about 8-9 million visitors, which puts a unique strain on the resilience of its assets. It has some 15,300 kilometres of water mains and 15,600 km of waste water networks, each capable if laid end-to-end of almost reaching Australia!

Its other distinguishing feature is that some 35% of England's bathing waters are located in its area. This creates a substantial challenge of ensuring clean beaches via the control of surface water discharges from farmland, roadways and so on: in periods of very high rainfall, the risk of sewage discharge overflows inevitably arises, because the Victoria engineers designed common systems for sewage and surface water discharges.

Despite these real challenges, and with significant investment and controls by the company, the 47 beaches in the South West meet the high standards now called for by the European Union. This is a responsibility that the company and the Board take very seriously, working with many stakeholders, given the importance of clean beaches to the local tourist industry.

To provide information for all beach users and other stakeholders, South West Water has an excellent website – Beachlive – which provides continuous real-time information on bathing water quality for 47 beaches, particularly after heavy rainfall.

Viridor now has a total of eight waste-to-energy plants operating and processing some 2.1 million tons per year of household and industrial waste, and producing some 178 MW of electricity. A further four plants in 2017 were under construction, which will bring total processing capacity to 2.9m tons per year, with an estimated electricity output of 240 MW. This, together with electricity produced through landfill gas, will be sufficient to light some 400,000 homes. Viridor also handles and recycles a further 3.3m tons of material per year at plants and sites located around the UK.

Governance and company structure

Both operating companies, along with Pennon Group – the plc – had their own Boards and separate NXDs. They had a common Chairman but the operating companies had separate CEOs, Finance Directors and Company Secretaries. The Group Board had no CEO, but a Group Finance Director and Company Secretary. This somewhat unusual structure was partially driven by the need to have a separate, ring-fenced Board for South West Water, to meet the requirements of the industry regulator OFWAT.

I felt that this somewhat complex set-up could be streamlined, and had extensive discussions with Jonson Cox, the head of OFWAT. Jonson, unlike most Regulators, has actually had extensive CEO experience in the industry, and therefore has a more pragmatic – but equally tough – streak about him. Above all, he can see the practical challenges of meeting the regulatory requirements.

I was keen to appoint a Group CEO who would manage and co-ordinate the Group's activities, and have the Group's competent NXDs more involved in the decision-making of both companies. The Board and I chose Chris Loughlin, CEO of South West Water, along with Susan Davy as Group CFO. Both have been a great success, particularly in seeking out synergies and maximising common services across the Group to create shareholder value. We also appointed a

Managing Director to run each of the two operating businesses. The key executives are all members of a Group Executive Committee chaired by the Group CEO. This has brought cohesion at the top of the Group and significantly improved line of sight into the businesses for all NXDs.

The Unitary Board that I sought in my discussions with the Regulator proved a non-runner, but I finally agreed the concept of a Pennon Plenary Board session to replace the three existing Boards. This means that over the 9-10 Board meetings a year, the Plenary Board session has all three dedicated Group NXDs present, all of whom are now also directors of both South West Water and Viridor. The three NXDs dedicated to SWW are also present throughout, plus the Group CEO and CFO with myself as Chairman.

We are joined for the SWW Board by the MD and Finance Director of South West Water, who provide clear operational and financial reports on SWW. The SWW Board discussion is followed by debates on Group issues led by Chris and Susan, and the operational reports on Viridor by its MD. Replacing three Board meetings with one Plenary session, when all NXDs are present, has enriched communication and utilised the extensive talent of our Non-Executives, who are encouraged to address and challenge on all issues, in line with best boardroom practice.

14. RMC GROUP

I was virtually parachuted in to take over as Chairman at the RMC Group in 2002 – then the largest ready mixed concrete company in the world.

I had been approached by the then-Chairman, Chris Hampson, who was formerly with the chemicals giant ICI. I had known Chris ever since my British Shipbuilders days, when we were on the same "DTI Node" of industrial leaders and high-flying senior civil servants meeting for a few days at the Shell Centre in Hitchen. As a Group, we continued to meet informally year by year for the next decade.

Chris, who was on the brink of retirement, was a real gentleman and he confided to me that the RMC executive management had made it very challenging for NXDs to "get in on issues, with the tendency to keep them (the NXDs) at bay." He knew that was unacceptable to me. He arranged for me to meet with the Senior NXD, Sir Keith Stuart, former Chairman of Associated British Ports, and another NXD, Alistair Robinson, a former director of Barclays. Both were deeply concerned about the health of the company. I also met with Stuart Walker, the relatively new CEO, who on all issues I felt I could work with – subject to there being transparency: the NXDs could not be ignored.

RMC had been a stock market darling during the 1980s but got itself into serious financial difficulty by overpaying to acquire Rugby

Cement, a UK cement group which, prior to the RMC takeover, had commissioned a new cement plant which didn't work. At the same time, RMC had over-invested in the former East Germany, lured by the construction boom there after reunification. The boom turned to bust, and the market became massively over-supplied. One of these problems would have been enough to cause serious trouble; the combination subjected the balance sheet to unsustainable stress.

I joined the company as Deputy Chairman – one of six Non-Executive Directors including the Chairman – and went to my first Board meeting. Normally, I have a golden rule to listen and say nothing at my first Board meeting in a new company. However, I recall that at this Board meeting, the Finance Director explained that our debt was now over £1.8 billion, shareholders' funds were about £900m and we were close to breaking our banking covenants. Pretty startling news. No one spoke.

Finally, I thought this is too serious: it must be discussed. For effect, I said: "Chairman, I think I just heard the FD say we were close to bankruptcy," to which one very long-serving NXD said: "Certainly not: this is a sound company," so he went into the bag where ineffective NXDs go.

Reluctantly, I felt I had to pursue this critical situation so I said: "Maybe I have misinterpreted what the FD had to say, so could we hear from him again?" Now the FD spelt it out more starkly and still no one spoke. So I said: "I think I would like to know what management intends to do about this." Another NXD rather arrogantly said: "Since you have just arrived, what would you do about it?" (so he went in the bag). I said: "I'd set a target to reduce our debt to £1 billion within 12 months and urgently advise our banks of the Board's decision." Yet another NXD then rather imperiously chimed in with: "How would you propose to do that" (so he went in the bag, which was getting quite full). I replied: "I would sell non-core assets and indeed other assets if necessary to meet the reduced debt target." The fourth NXD then said: 'Oh, we don't sell assets in this company" (so he went in the bag too).

All four NXDs left as soon as I became Chairman, as they were clearly out of touch. When companies have successful runs and get cheered on by investors and the media, complacency can set in in the boardroom. When – as almost inevitably happens – the company enters tough territory, this is not noticed right away and corrective action is not taken with the urgency required.

We recruited four excellent replacements, including Philip (later Sir Philip) Hampton in what I believe was his first Non-Executive role. The new NXDs went to work and with management set the £1 billion debt target: we met it within a year, slimmed the company's areas of operation from 28 countries to about 23 and boosted the share price, which had sunk to about 330p, to almost 600p by autumn 2004.

This was achieved with extensive executive management changes, and I had the good fortune to recruit Adrian Auer as Finance Director, originally an ICI man. He had the great analytical capability that I always expect in a finance director:someone who can beat the numbers out into the open so you have clear potential for diagnosis, accountability and corrective action.

In due course following a long period in hospital, Stuart Walker, who knew his industry well, was replaced as CEO by a new recruit from the mining group BHP Billiton – David Munro. RMC had some excellent management further down the line, which David harnessed. Along with the disposals and debt reduction targets, he bolted on further organisational cost reductions and performance improvement initiatives. The Board and I thought very highly of his decisive leadership.

The investors too were pleased with the direction of travel and the response of the share price. Then, in September 2004, I was approached by Lorenzo Zambrano, Chairman and CEO of CEMEX of Mexico, a global cement and aggregates company, who requested a meeting with me.

At this time, the building materials industry was undergoing a wave of consolidation worldwide. In the UK, there had already been a number of acquisitions by overseas groups, including two big takeovers by France's Lafarge – of Redland and Blue Circle cement – and later one by Holcim of Switzerland, which acquired Aggregate Industries. I could guess why Lorenzo wanted to meet me – to discuss an offer for RMC.

We met at my office at National Grid, just off Trafalgar Square. Whilst I went through the motions of saying that the company wasn't for sale, he put a decent premium price on the table and he agreed with me that he would not go hostile. I told him that I could not recommend the figure to my Board but that I would advise them of the approach. He told me that his advisors were Goldman Sachs – his chief adviser was Simon Dingemans, now CFO at GlaxoSmithKline. In turn I advised that ours was JP Morgan Cazenove and that Nick Wiles would lead for us. I had worked with Nick in a number of M&A transactions, including the Lattice-National Grid merger and the sale of P&O Group to Dubai's DP World.

The relationship between a chairman and his lead investment bank adviser and the company's corporate broker is crucial. It can make or mar a company's success in dealing with challenging or special situations. I trusted Nick implicitly and he would always give you clear advice after listening carefully to your concerns. He had no airs or graces and no trace of arrogance which commended him to me. He has subsequently worked with me on a range of corporate activities, including working alongside Anglo's long-term advisors UBS and Goldman in removing Xstrata's tanks from Anglo's lawn after my arrival at Anglo in August 2009.

I agreed with Lorenzo that if we had anything else to say to each other, it was best to initially use our advisors but he did give me his personal contact numbers in case we needed to have a direct conversation. I agreed with Nick that there should be radio silence with Goldmans, in order to leave them to make the running. Our Board's aim was to get the offer price up before any further dialogue between Lorenzo and myself. Sure enough, some days passed before Goldman's approached JPMC again, and within a number of days we had the price lifted to a premium close to 40% from the undisturbed level.

I had agreed with the Board that there were two numbers on which we had to focus. The first was, at what number must we enter dialogue with Cemex; and the second, at what price must we recommend an offer.

For me, the "first number" is always determined by the discounted cash flow forecast of what the CEO and his/her management team believe they can deliver over the next three years. In shareholder eyes, if a bid includes a decent premium over the undisturbed share price prior to the approach, then it is derisked value relative to the uncertainties in any forward three-year forecast.

David Munro did not have to wrestle with this equation for too long as we were already sitting on a level of offer premium where our shareholders would expect us to talk and potentially move to a recommended offer – "the number you go out at."

Boards and individual directors, in bid circumstances, need to understand their fiduciary duties. If an offer is at or above the "first number", you have a duty to explore if a recommended position can be reached. You must do this after also taking account of wider stakeholder interests, including those of your employees.

At this stage of the RMC negotiations, the Board agreed that I should explore with Lorenzo Zambrano just what further increase might be possible. There are certain stages in a major transaction when secrecy even from your advisors is necessary. You as the Chairman, representing your Board and with its full support, are in the position to make the final call on price, without any further steerage. Without any discussion with the advisors – who can inadvertently alert the other set of advisors – I called Lorenzo, as he had left with me his personal contact numbers. I proposed to him that we meet without advisors present and without them being aware of the meeting. He agreed that we should meet for dinner in his flat in New York overlooking Central Park.

We had an excellent dinner and wide-ranging conversation and got to know each other much better. In the course of this discussion, we agreed a further uplift in the price, which I told him I would unconditionally recommend to our Board. The price was 845p a share, which gave us an exit premium of around 43% – a very high premium by any standards, but particularly when you considered that not long ago RMC shares had descended to 330p.

I knew that our investors would welcome this offer, and told Lorenzo I, with our Board, would support the deal at this price, and that I was fairly confident there would be little chance now of an interloper. Lorenzo was an excellent host, and at the end of the dinner had his chauffeur drive me back to my hotel. I immediately called Nick Wiles from my hotel room, waking him up at around 4 a.m. his time to tell him the outcome of a meeting which even he did not know was taking place!

There was no leakage of the deal. We moved quickly through high-level due diligence and our advisors knew our attitude to leaks. On announcement, the transaction was widely recognised as very successful by both shareholders and the financial media. Indeed, for the first time as a chairman, I received calls from a few shareholders expressing thanks for the turnround and the high exit price. They understood from me that it was down to a great team effort involving the Board, both NEDs and executives, and the line management.

There was an interesting sequel to the deal. I was called by the highly respected fund manager, Hugh Jones, the Senior Executive at Prudential and M&G which was one of the largest UK pension funds. I had built up a good rapport with Hugh during the P&O Princess merger debate and through the mergers of Lattice-National Grid. Hugh invited me to come in for lunch with himself and Michael McClintock, M&G's long-serving and successful CEO. They wanted to thank me for steering RMC through its recovery and for the value we had created through the Cemex transaction.

Over lunch, Hugh said in his canny Scots accent: "Well as RMC's Chairman, you were really the Company Doctor! We are delighted since we thought at one stage we had lost our very high double digit percentage investment. I hope, John, that you personally did well out of it." I said: "First I'm glad to say our new CEO, who was with us for a year, did very well, and made a few million pounds based on the shares he was allocated on joining and subsequently. I was very happy for him since that was his deal and he did a very good job." "And yourself?" asked Hugh. I said: "I did okay."

When I joined as Chairman, I was hired at £120,000 a year, and because of the demands of the turnround and the CEO having to be in hospital for a period, I was there a number of days every week, so the Non-Executives felt I was working rather hard and lifted my salary to £140,000. I had a one-month notice period, so I did okay in line with my contract – I got £11,666 gross before tax! Hugh and Michael were very embarrassed when they heard this. But I signed up to this conservative type of contract because that was what chairmen were then expected to take on. Governance at that time was against anything like a six or 12 months' notice period for chairmen, and certainly shares could not form part of a chairman's remuneration.

Company chairmen, especially in turnround situations, are not highly rewarded relative to the day rate implied by Executive Reward packages or those of advisors! However, I have never been motivated to chase high reward packages. If that's what you want, you should join Private Equity rather than continue on plc Boards.

Hugh and I have seen each other on many occasions since – a valuable meeting for me was during the defence of Anglo when I needed shareholder support to see off Xstrata. Anglo was not universally popular and Xstrata had strong support from one or two investors – but I got the backing I needed from Hugh and Prudential-M&G without too much debate. This is another absolutely critical aspect of the chairman's role – he/she must have a good relationship with large investors because it is vital that they trust the chairman's judgment.

A final postscript. It was with great sadness that I opened the *Financial Times* on 13th May 2014 to learn that Lorenzo Zambrano had died the previous day from a heart attack in Madrid during a business trip. He was only 70 and still very active, leading Cemex where he had been CEO since 1985. Lorenzo was a gentleman and a man of integrity.

15. MONDI

In 2007, I was approached by David Kimbell, Managing Director of Spencer Stuart and at that time the doyen of London head-hunters, to see if I could be interested in chairing Mondi – the Paper and Packaging Group that the mining group Anglo American had decided to spin out of its portfolio.

Tony Trahar was then Group CEO at Anglo. He and the Board were coming under pressure from shareholders, like many other corporates, to focus down on core activities. I also had subsequent discussions with the Chairman of Anglo, Sir Mark Moody Stuart – a man of integrity and commitment to responsible business. This was my first contact with Anglo American.

Anglo wanted to activate a Mondi quote in London and a secondary quotation in Johannesburg. On the face of it, this seemed logical as only about 20% of Mondi's operations were South African-based.

Initially I was not all that keen, but when he heard genuine hesitation, David seldom if ever accepted it as a No! "Look," he said, "meet the CEO David Hawthorn, I think you will like him."

I agreed and on meeting David, almost immediately I liked his style along with his uncomplicated approach to business. I could also see he knew the business inside out. I agreed to be Chairman and set about recruiting a Board and setting up the governance framework. There followed a great deal of negotiation with the South African

Authorities who refused to accept a listing along the lines Mondi were driving for.

We ended up with a dual-listed company – the third DLC I had experienced in my boardroom journey (GKN Brambles – London and Sydney; Carnival – London and New York, Mondi – London and Johannesburg). These structures are different legally from unitary companies, with two Boards each representing the separate listed entities, although each Board is generally comprised of the same directors. DLCs create a great deal of extra administration, compliance and accounting workload. However, once proper compliance and administration systems and key people are in place, DLCs can be almost seamless as far as the Board is concerned.

The South African Authorities demanded, despite only 20% of Mondi's activities being located in SA, that the Head Office, CEO and CFO must be located there. This led to us losing a very fine CFO in Paul Hollingworth who was not willing to transfer, but fortunately Andrew King, an Anglo finance man, took on the Finance Director role and did an excellent job.

Then at the last minute, a demand that we must have a joint South Africa Chairman was made. Some of my business friends at the time said: "Are you really going to stay with such an arrangement? This is politics not business". My response was that I had signed up and committed to do the job and I would stick with it. As it turned out, we persuaded Cyril Ramaphosa to join us as joint chairman. He was a great choice with wide-ranging knowledge of South African business and politics. He had been trained as a lawyer, was the former leader of the National Union of Miners, sat on the executive committee of the African National Congress (ANC), which he had helped to found, and was also a very successful businessman and a member of a number of Boards including SAB Miller, the brewing group that listed in London about the same time as Anglo American.

This was a new experience for both of us, and we worked together as a 'seamless team Chairman'. Just before our first Board, I asked: "Cyril, how do you think we should share out our duties?" Cyril said: "I would like to hear your ideas, John." I suggested: "What if, when we have our Board Meetings in the southern hemisphere, you chair and when we are in the northern hemisphere, I'll chair. "Done deal", said Cyril and "I think you should chair the Strategy days and manage the Board Agenda". We were fortunate on this score to have an excellent and hardworking Company Secretary in Carol Hunt, who was based in London. She reported into Mervyn Walker, the new HR and Administration Director who we had recruited from British Airways. Mervyn later moved to a similar role at Anglo American where he did a fine job.

With Mervyn's support and that of the head-hunters, we began to build a very strong Board and set up the new governance structure. David Williams – a former CFO of Bunzl and an experienced Non-Executive Director was appointed as the first NXD and accepted the invitation to become Chairman of Audit. He was a former Chairman of Audit at P&O Group when I was Chairman. Not only is he technically very competent but he has excellent business judgment. He shares similar views to myself on the critical need for a good governance culture to be embedded in the company, starting in the boardroom.

David subsequently succeeded me as joint Chairman of Mondi when I resigned to take up the chairmanship of Anglo American in the summer of 2009. He was reluctant at first to consider this, telling me frankly that he never had the ambition to be chairman of a plc. I gave him full encouragement, noting how well equipped he was for the role since he had served a long boardroom apprenticeship as a NXD, working on a range of committees including chairing several Audit Committees. Above all, I said to him: "In David Hawthorn, you've got an outstanding CEO. You have also a strong Board and good corporate governance. You will work well with Cyril Ramaphosa who is a man of great wisdom and experience". David was encouraged and took up the post. Under him, Mondi has weathered the industry's cyclical storms and has been a tremendous success, with its London-listed entity climbing the rankings well into the FTSE 100.

I wanted to have two women on the Board with international business experience of a type which would be relevant and would blend easily with the cyclical nature of Mondi's business. We were fortunate to hire Anne Quinn and Imogen Mkhize. Anne was the Global Head of BP's Gas Operations who brought from that industry not only impressive international business skills, but also a deep appreciation of industrial safety. She served as a very effective Chairman of Remuneration and made an excellent contribution to the Safety and Sustainability Committee. Imogen joined us as a resident South African Director with extensive NXD experience in a range of boardrooms, including in the USA.

We also hired Colin Matthews, who at that time was CEO of Severn Trent, the water utility, and had been CEO of Transco before the National Grid merger. He is a world class Cambridge-trained engineer and former Technical Director of British Airways. He was an ideal Chairman for the Sustainability and Safety Committee of a group with large forestry operations and huge industrial processing plants. As Chairman of the Committee, Colin took no prisoners when it came to addressing big safety risk issues.

Mondi prospered following its demerger under David Hawthorn's strong and pragmatic leadership with his excellent management team based in South Africa and at the European headquarters in Vienna.

In our very early days, we committed to expansion via two major capital investments – a new packaging plant in Poland and a major expansion of our Russian manufacturing plant in Syktyvkar. These projects meant that we needed to keep a close eye on the balance sheet, which was relatively strong but which required careful monitoring and stress-testing by the Board – something I am rather keen on, particularly in industries with volatile and cyclical earnings: paper and packaging, mining and shipping all have similar characteristics of volatility.

This was particularly apparent after the Lehman Brothers collapse in September 2008 triggered the global financial crisis, with banks cutting lending to the bone and the normal corporate funding system virtually seizing up. I recall David calling me the week after the collapse with the news that our order book intake had fallen 40% across the board. We discussed the seriousness of the situation and agreed that markets were unlikely to improve quickly as the cash squeeze on our customers was likely to persist for some time. They would inevitably continue to squeeze their inventories.

Urgent and dramatic action was therefore needed to take capacity out across our operations. We both agreed that, in particular, we should close those factories with the lowest returns on capital and which were absorbing cash. David said he would bring a plan to the next Board in three weeks' time.

This was the most precipitate and extreme downturn that I had seen in my entire business career. My advice to David therefore was: start tomorrow. I agreed I would talk with Cyril and all the other Board members about the emergency actions he was taking. I told him that as CEO, he could assume he had full air cover from the Board to act immediately without waiting for formal Board authorisation. He could report all actions taken and actions still to take at the next Board. We could not risk unnecessary cash haemorrhaging. The NXDs were fully supportive and at the next Board, David updated us fully on what further measures were necessary to protect the business.

Despite the harshness of such urgent restructuring, it was critical to act quickly in the interest of the majority of employers and stake-holders. Otherwise there could have been no business. I attended the RemCo at Anne's invitation and we discussed what award system we should put in place to focus management in a unified way on the need to preserve cash and increase competitiveness during this unprecedented downturn. I recall that we discussed the question: 'What would a good out-turn look like in these circumstances in one-two years' time'? We were unanimous that optimal performance outcome would be if we could ensure that our net debt-EBITDA ratio remained within what was our tightest banking covenant, thereby avoiding any risk of default-triggering with our banks.

All Senior Managers' bonuses were realigned to this simple net debt-EBITDA ratio objective. It focussed them on preserving cash, controlling costs and maximising profitability. About three months later, David told the Board that he had never seen working capital squeezed to the extent that it was across the business. As a result of this and other initiatives, Mondi, unlike many other paper and packaging companies, successfully managed that horrific market downturn.

In Mondi, as in all the Boards I have chaired, it was important for Board members to have social time together. This allows informal discussion with the CEO about the business and its people. It's also a great way for the Board to get to know the next layer of management, by inviting them to Board dinners. This makes subsequent management succession discussions at the Board come alive.

At Mondi, I can recall many happy evenings in London, Vienna and South Africa. In Johannesburg, we had a number of dinners at David's home. At a few of these, as we sat around the swimming pool after our meal, we enjoyed late night conversations – often myself with Cyril.

One night, I said to him: "Your country will call you one of these days to lead it." "No John, ‚no", was always Cyril's reply. I would persist, pointing out that he had retained his position on the ANC Executive Committee. He was a founding figure, a lawyer, had led a major trade union, was a successful and intellectual businessman. "South Africa needs you," I told him. "You need to be ready when the call comes." We had a wonderful email exchange, reflecting on those late night conversations, following the December 2012 ANC Conference when Cyril was proposed as Deputy President of his country.

Six years later, Cyril became South Africa's President. It was clear in our Mondi days that he has all the qualities of a great statesman. He has rich cultural knowledge, wide business experience and significant support from the people of South Africa. He is a wise counsellor, commands substantial international respect and has business and political contacts all over the world that few others can match. He will be a superb international ambassador for South Africa, particularly in attracting inward investment on the scale the country requires.

South Africa has to change and adapt on many fronts if it is to win the confidence of international investors. Exchange controls, as currently operated there, are a deterrent to many investors because they have little place in a modern economy. Consistency in policy towards business is not always uniformly practised across Government. Confidence to invest is a delicate plant that needs to be nourished and constantly cared for, and not undermined by arbitrary policy-making which introduces uncertainty.

Mark Cutifani, our CEO at Anglo American, who has lived and worked in South Africa for some six years made a major speech in August 2013 involving Government, the mining industry leaders and the trade unions. I quote a moving but critical proposition from him:

"I cannot say it enough – we need stability to prosper. And if we prosper, so does the country, so let's create a partnership." Mark went on to say that the starting point for that partnership already existed in the shape of the National Development Plan (NDP), which he called on the Government to implement.

"Let the NDP be a living document, a map for change and an engagement tool that brings us together to work for a common future," Mark said. "The mining industry will play its part, if we are given an opportunity to settle into an 'investment rhythm' that comes from a stable and predictable regulatory regime.

"We must make sure that South Africa positions itself as the economic gateway to Africa, and not continue with its current restrictions on foreign exchange, dividend withholding policies and the like – which make it more like the 'cash trap' of Africa ... All industries, labour unions and Government must work together within the context of this strategy to promote South Africa as an open, stable, transparent and investment-friendly economy."

That said, my time with Mondi, my co-chairmanship with Cyril, my first real contacts with Anglo American were all an enriching business and personal experience. It was a personal wrench to stand down and say my farewells to such excellent Mondi people when I was joining Anglo American. Cyril was very supportive that I should take on the Anglo Chairman's role. He gave me great advice and I will always be grateful to have worked with and built a strong bond of friendship with this great man. Mondi has continued to flourish and grow, and – like Babcock International after its turnround – became a highly respected FTSE 100 company which I can look back on with some pride, alongside the five FTSE 100 companies that I have been privileged to chair.

16. P&O, CARNIVAL AND DP WORLD

In October 2000, I joined the Board of P&O Princess Cruises as a Non-Executive Director and later becoming Deputy Chairman. The company was being demerged from the P&O Ports, Container Shipping and Property business. After the split, Lord Sterling, who had chaired the combined P&O Group, also became Chairman of P&O Princess Cruises. This, I understand, had led to some tensions on the P&O Group Board. The well-regarded executive Tim Harris, who was Chairman of the Cruise business at the time, left the P&O Group following Lord Sterling's appointment.

The executive team of the demerged cruise company was led by Peter Ratcliffe, a very experienced, competent and strong CEO of P&O Princess who had a finance and container shipping background, and Nick Luff, one of the ablest CFOs I have ever worked with. They were a superb combination.

Apart from Lord Sterling, we had four Non-Executive Directors: Baroness (Sarah) Hogg, the Senior Non-Executive Director and ex-McKinsey partner Peter Foy, Horst Rahe, founder of the German cruise line AIDA that P&O had just bought in to, and myself.

The demerged cruise company had an excellent reception on the stock exchange with its market worth rising to more than £2.5 billion by December 2001 when it was promoted to the FTSE 100 index.

We had the first of a new class series of ships, called the "Grand" class, already in service. This was the *Grand Princess*, built at Fincantieri. We also had two further ships on order at the St Nazaire shipyard in France, the *Coral Princess* and the *Island Princess*.

We also placed contracts for two 2,600-passenger ships – the *Diamond Princess* and the *Sapphire Princess* – with Mitsubishi in Japan. These were Mitsubishi's first major cruise line contracts for an overseas company. Unfortunately, the first ship caught fire during construction in the building dock at the Nagasaki shipyard. Half of the vessel had to be scrapped and construction restarted. The second vessel became the first to be delivered and of course was rather late, which was a major disappointment despite the liquidated damages compensation. However, they proved to be excellent, high-quality ships.

Both P&O and Princess have a long relationship with Fincantieri, which was chaired by Corrado Antonini for 12 years from 2000. I already knew Corrado from the Association of West European Shipbuilders, where he succeeded me as Chairman, and it was good to renew our friendship through P&O Princess and to continue it after we were acquired by Carnival.

As a newly demerged company in a growing global industry, the Board examined where M&A might take us. We were number three in the market, behind Royal Caribbean (RCCL) and the largest group, Carnival Corporation, which was the clear number one. NCL was behind us.

Much as we felt drawn to a merger with Carnival, the legal advice we received was that, for Competition reasons, joining with them would not be a runner.

As we examined the various options, a merger possibility was opening up with RCCL because the relative values of the two companies were within the 60-40 equity split required for a genuine merger. The Competition legal advice suggested that it was likely we would get clearance for this in the key markets of US, mainland Europe and the UK. A merger with RCCL would have created a new number one. We also knew Carnival's Chairman and CEO, Micky Arison – son of the company's founder Ted – would not be happy with that as an outcome and he would not necessarily be aware of the background that led us to pursue RCCL.

Peter Ratcliffe and Nick Luff secured an agreement with RCCL for a merger subject to shareholder approval. This included understandings on the key social issues of who would be CEO, CFO and Chairman. Peter and Nick would both join the management of the combined group and Richard Fain, RCCL's CEO, would become Chairman. The announcement of the merger created enormous interest in the media and among investors.

As we had anticipated, Micky Arison reacted by tabling a bid with a premium for the company, despite our Competition legal advice that it could not be pulled off. The complexities of proposing the RCCL merger to shareholders with a takeover bid in the wings from Carnival created huge technical and legal problems for our Board. We had to obtain detailed evaluations of the relative shareholder value that would be produced by a merger versus the value that would come from a Carnival take out bid assuming this could get through the Competition Authorities – the big technical challenge throughout for the Board, given our legal advice on competition process and forecast out-turn.

We had endless Board meetings, including one almost every Sunday morning for about six weeks at the offices of Citigroup, where we were being advised by a team led by Robert Swannell. These meetings really clocked up the hours. To lighten the atmosphere one Sunday, I remarked to Lord Sterling that, with all the hours we Non-Executives were having to put in, he could expect a claim under minimum hourly wage rate regulations from his NXDs! Major events such as mergers, acquisitions, disposals or demergers really place considerable demands on a Board and on the time that directors need to put in.

Legal and banking advice led us to submit the RCCL merger proposal to shareholders for a range of reasons, not least of which was it had much greater certainty of Competition regulation clearance. However, many shareholders believed the Carnival bid should also be given the opportunity to be put to the test with the Competition Authorities.

The resulting EGM to consider both transactions was a unique, late-night affair. First, its start was massively delayed. The Registrars were overwhelmed by the volume of paperwork. Corporate Shareholders turned up with Share Registrations for a range of their funds, while others representing Nominee Holdings had incomplete paperwork in some cases. When we did get going, it was a rowdy affair with many questions on the merits of RCCL Merger versus Carnival takeover. We had the even rarer sight of major shareholders speaking in person at an EGM. I had never before seen many of them attend an AGM, let alone speak up at such a meeting – and I haven't since!

Micky Arison requested that he and Howard Frank, Carnival's Deputy Chairman, be allowed to address the meeting, and we agreed to this. Both spoke convincingly from the platform on the merits of their bid and how it should be tested with the Competition Authorities. Micky also answered a number of questions, some of them unnecessarily barbed, from small shareholders.

The general view that emerged through shareholder speeches was that our decision should be delayed to permit the Carnival bid to be tested with the Competition Authorities. Then a poll was held and the meeting was adjourned very late in the evening while the votes were counted. Hotels had to be found overnight for shareholders who had travelled a distance. The Registrars had a massive job dealing with the voting and checking all the registration paperwork.

I took Peter Ratcliffe and Nick Luff to the Royal Thames Yacht Club on Knightsbridge for a late dinner, before we returned to the meeting place at around 11 p.m. However, the Registrars made it plain that a result could not be expected until the early hours of the morning. It was like a General Election night.

The results, when they did emerge, were indeed in favour of delaying the decision to enable the Carnival bid to be tabled with the Competition Authorities on both sides of the Atlantic. This process took months but, contrary to all our Legal Competition advice,

Carnival's offer was cleared by all the Authorities given that Carnival successfully promoted cruising as just one segment of the global tourist/holiday market.

We finally agreed that the enlarged Carnival-P&O Princess would create a dual-listed company, quoted on both the New York and London stock markets, There were very few DLCs in existence, and I was now a director of two (the other being Brambles, which after some years de-listed in London. Mondi later became my third).

As with all DLCs, Carnival's dual-listed structure inevitably creates differentials between the two share prices – on occasions, the shares are at a discount in the UK and at others at a discount in the US, so some degree of arbitrage takes place and is exploited by hedge funds and others. But this has never impaired the company's stability. Today, UK shareholders hold about 14% of the combined entity and about 46% of the UK plc.

After the takeover, Baroness Sarah Hogg and I joined the Carnival board as NXDs alongside Peter Ratcliffe. Micky Arison was very welcoming to us as were the US board members.

The presiding director – equivalent to our Senior Independent Director – was and remains Stu Subotnick, who has been there since Carnival floated in 1987 and served under Ted Arison as the founding chairman. Stu is a great example of why the UK's rule that NXDs should not serve more than nine years is both flawed and immaterial to a director's independence. He is one of the most independent voices on today's Board and I would hope that I'm alongside him in this respect. He is a man of integrity and business wisdom.

Carnival is a remarkable growth story. In 1972, Ted Arison, its founder, acquired an old, second-hand ship – the *Empress of Canada* – renamed it the *Mardi Gras* and adapted it for cruising. The Carnival Group, after the merger of the P&O Princess fleet and the then-fledgling German cruise line Aida (which comprised only two ships), probably had about 80 cruise ships involving the brands of Holland America, Carnival Cruise Lines (CCL), Cunard, the Yachts of Seabourn and Costa.

The Audit Committee which I joined was the committee under which all HESS (Health; Environment; Safety; Security) monitoring oversight took place, and with my maritime background, I inevitably got quite involved in this.

It was also evident that, with a cruise group of Carnival's scale and growth plans, HESS issues needed to be discussed in more depth than the Audit Committee could provide time for. In discussion with Micky and Stu, the Board agreed that the time had come to set up a separate HESS committee, which I was invited to chair. I considered this to be a very important development, as it was, to the best of my knowledge, the first major HESS committee of a Board in the global cruise industry and I put my energy behind it.

HESS was even more relevant because of the enlarged Carnival's expansion potential. In 2004 in discussion with Micky, I observed that at the rate we were ordering cruise ships, by 2010 my estimate was that we would have all the 10s: 100 ships, 100,000 crew at sea every day and carrying 10 million passengers a year. Micky challenged this, saying he would sell ships well in advance of reaching this point. My estimate was in the event only two years out: by 2012, we did indeed have 100 ships and were carrying close on 10 million passengers a year.

These numbers demonstrate the scale of human activity around so many vessels, and the health and safety of passengers and crew are absolutely paramount to the Board and for brand reputation. The HESS committee has grown since the early days of a couple of NXDs and one executive. Now all the CEOs of our brands throughout the world attend the committee quarterly, alongside their technical operating leaders, and the meetings will cover environmental issues, safety issues that may have occurred, the framing of corporate standards above the requirements of classification and flag state rules, to ensure that our standards are the highest in the maritime world and ensure that the passengers and crew are kept safe.

We made a major investment at Almere in Holland to create a world class training centre, now virtually a university, complete with simulators for both bridge and engine room training. All bridge teams are expected to work to the same standards, to be trained in a similar way like airline pilots, and Senior Officers are regularly recertified. This was a first for the industry of this scale to be dedicated to a single cruise group. Indeed, in 2016 a significant expansion of the Simulator Centre has taken place, and it has been renamed the Arison Centre.

I salute Micky's willingness – as the major shareholder, the Arison family interest in 2016 was 22.4% of Carnival Group – to have agreed to these major investments. Not a single recommendation from the HESS committee to invest to increase safety or environmental protection has ever been turned down by the Board.

We now have a great history of trends in safety performance and minor accidents to passengers and crew, covering any environmental violation from even the spill of a small paint can to recording any allisions etc, which happily are few and far between.

One high profile incident which profoundly shocked us all was the *Costa Concordia* accident. The tragic loss of 32 lives and the sadness brought to families resulted from the vessel striking a submerged rock and the subsequent flooding of several compartents. This occurred after the Captain decided to divert from the normal course to do a 'close in' viewing of the Island of Isola del Giglo.

This should not have occurred and was a shocking out-turn given the focus that had been placed on safety by the Board. It signalled its importance through commitment to new HESS Committee Safety policies, additional capital expenditure on extra ship safety equipment and systems and training, all well beyond compliance with international regulations. The Italian Courts subsequently sentenced the Captain to a lengty prison term.

At the request of Micky Arison and Howard Frank, the Deputy Chairman, I chaired a Review by the HESS Committee, to identify what lessons we could learn from the incident to further enhance our management of safety. Our work was fully shared with the Italian Coastguard.

As an ongoing part of HESS management, directed day by day by our highly experienced Chief Maritime Officer, Admiral Bill Burke, we continue to harvest all lessons learned from operating a fleet of over 100 cruise ships. These are incorporated into HESS policy updates and our training programs at the Arison Centre in Holland where our Officers are trained, assessed and re-certified on an agreed frequency.

Another initiative we have taken in the group is to move from a whole series of different ship management systems, required to be maintained by the different brands, to one Carnival HESS system against which all audits are carried out to satisfy the regulatory authorities and our internal corporate standards. This uniformity was fully implemented by the end of 2016.

Growth in ship size and market

It has been stimulating to sit around a Board table where growth in the business has been so evident and – from the standpoint of my origins as a naval architect and engineer – where the scale of ships has continued to increase and the associated technology has developed in leaps and bounds. In 2004, the average size ship in the fleet carried less than 750 passengers; today it's more than 1,700. The projection for 2020 is that with the 20-plus new ships we have on order, the average passenger size in new build vessels will be more than 4,300. The capital costs involved are enormous – the latest orders are close to €1 billion for each of four new mega-ships, each of 180,000 gross tons, to be delivered between 2018 and 2020.

It has been gratifying to see an increasing number of people across the world take up cruising as a holiday. I have always found it to be an amazingly attractive way to relax, and it is one which my family, especially our grandchildren, greatly enjoy: the pleasure of boarding a ship, hanging up your clothes, emptying your suitcases not to see them again for 10 or 14 days. All this time you are moving, you'll often wake up in a different port in a different country, sometimes every day – it's a wonderful way to see the world in an economical way, given that the price of a cruise is very inclusive – it covers all meals and entertainment on board. It's in sharp contrast to the cost of bed and breakfast in a European city with the task of finding a – frequently expensive – place to eat lunch or dinner, never mind entertainment.

The cruise market still has enormous growth potential. Even today, only about 3-4% of the US population has taken a cruise, while it's just in the past couple of years that the UK market has gone through 1m passengers. Germany has now overtaken the UK with the significant investment we have made in Aida, which now has 12 ships. The Italian and Spanish markets are contributing to a European growth story.

The market has grown at around 6.5% a year over the past quarter-century, and it continues to expand at this rate. Now we are seeing Asia gradually opening up, serviced partly from P&O's Australia base: we currently have eight cruise ships operating out of Australia all year round plus a further 12 ships from different group brands operating seasonally. Some of those ships are going North to Asia along with ships from Holland America, Princess and Seabourn now sailing in Chinese, Vietnamese and other Asian waters. China in particular is opening up significantly, which is another exciting development and the reason why the Group via Costa and Princess has put down an important investment to establish operating bases in China, particularly in Shanghai.

Given that the company has remained dual-listed, Micky has always endeavoured to more than tip his hat to UK corporate governance and where possible, to meet the requirement of the UK code, having regard always of course to US corporate governance practice.

In 2013, he relinquished the dual role of Chairman and CEO, and appointed one of our NXDs, Arnold Donald, to be CEO. At the same time, Howard Frank stepped down after many successful years as Chief Operating Officer and Deputy Chairman.

One of Micky's wisest decisions has been to protect the individual brands. They are operated on a decentralised basis, so that P&O, Princess Cruises and Aida have flourished under their own brands, as have the other brands within the group fleet. They are held financially accountable but once budgets and plans are agreed, operating lines are permitted to get on provided they are complying fully with the Group policies, including International Regulations and HESS corporate policies.

Over the years, as a member of the Nominations Committee under Stu Subotnick's chairmanship, we have been conscious of diversity and have increased the representation of women on the Board. Right now, we have three women which gives us comfortably a 30% representation, with our CEO Arnold Donald an ethnically-diverse candidate.

I've had the pleasure of going to see many new cruise ships named. Many of our ships are built at state-owned Fincantieri in Italy and in the privately owned German yard Meyer-Werft. I have been to see ships under construction and on occasion to invite executives from one of the yards to come and explain themselves to the HESS committee where we weren't satisfied with the quality of installation, particularly where it pertained to systems that could impinge on safety.

For me, there has been only one recurrent regret: every time we order a new cruise ship to join this fleet of over 100, I inevitably think back to my shipbuilding days and my failure to persuade the British Government to get Britain re-engaged in what has been a bonanza market. That was truly a great opportunity missed.

P&O Group

Post the sale of RMC to Cemex and following P&O Princess Cruises being merged within Carnival, I became Chairman of the P&O Group, the container ports and ferries operator, on the retirement of Lord Sterling with whom I retain valued contact. Robert Woods became CEO of the Group, and Nick Luff left P&O Princess Cruises and joined us as Finance Director. Robert was a charismatic leader, and he and Nick formed a powerful combination. Robert communicated very effectively with his teams all over the world on a regular basis – he had his finger on the pulse.

In late 2005, we were approached by DP (Dubai) World, led by its-then chairman, Sultan bin-Sulayem with a number of his Board colleagues, at a meeting in London at which he tabled a proposition to buy the company. DP World's offer did recognise a premium for the business; inevitably, one went through the usual ritual: "The company is not for sale, but I will inform my Board and I trust you can assure me that you aren't intending a hostile offer" – which he did confirm. He left me a clear letter of offer which I took to my Board and passed to our advisors.

I immediately agreed with Robert that he should focus primarily on operating the company while I would lead negotiations with the Sultan, working with Nick Luff and our advisors.

The clear division of responsibilities between Chairman and CEO is crucial in an M&A situation. Too often a CEO can get so caught up in corporate transactions that management of the company's day-to-day operations and the accountability for performance are weakened. Then, if a deal falls away, the company is inevitably and unnecessarily impacted.

The proposal was certainly pitched at a very decent first-round approach. I agreed I would meet Sultan in Switzerland two weeks later, at which point we reached an agreement on an increased level of pricing which I agreed I would put to my Board as a potential deal.

Our announcement about the DP World offer drew in the Port of Singapore Authority (PSA), which declared its interest in making a rival bid. An intense battle began and over the following weeks, we had a number of different figures posted by both sides, culminating in one day when we recommended the Port of Singapore in the morning, only to rescind that in the afternoon and recommend the sale of P&O to DP World.

The media sometimes criticise a Board for changing its original recommendation during a contested bid in favour of a rival offer. But as a Chairman and an NXD, I have never had a problem with such changes of stance. Quite the contrary: as a company director, you have a fiduciary duty to maximise value for shareholders unless you feel this isn't in the interests of other stakeholders and particularly your employees – under the law today, you have to take those into account.

In the end, DP World won the battle with a bid of £3.3 billion, and it has proved to be a good employer. Our people joined a growing business and helped it to grow further. DPW retained the P&O office in London and invested £1.5bn in an all-new UK container port, London Gateway, on the Thames. All in all, a very good out-turn.

At the time of the deal, while our major investors were very pleased with the outcome, some of our individual private shareholders did not share that view. The sale was subject to an Extraordinary General Meeting which had to be held in London's vast Olympia exhibition hall, given the crowds of people that were expected. This was a very stormy affair when I was accused of selling out Britain, and many people in the audience were wrapped in the Red Ensign. I explained that it was the Board's fiduciary duty to accept a bid of this size – a 44% premium over the undisturbed share price was an exceptional deal for shareholders and the Board had an easy fiscal decision to make.

One other significant and unexpected obstacle reared its head as we completed the transaction. Because P&O owned ports in the US, the American Government had to approve DP World as the new owner. But Hillary Clinton, who was campaigning for the Senate at the time, opposed the deal, raising the spectre of Al-Qaeda taking over US ports!

It never ceases to amaze me what a politician will do to get elected, and in the process be quite prepared to distort facts – we have seen this in spades in the Brexit referendum campaign. Dubai actually was one of the few locations in the Middle East where US aircraft carriers and warships could dock for repairs and refuelling, but this obviously was conveniently overlooked. The row became very public and gained completely unexpected momentum, to the extent that the Sultan called me one night and said: "We are quite prepared to pull out of the US and sell the container ports". And this they did – it was a great shame and a rather awful twist to what was otherwise a very clean deal.

When the acquisition was finally completed and announced to the staff of P&O, at the handover Sultan asked to speak to me privately. He said that he would like me to come to help him in Dubai to establish a board that would be properly governed in a way that would allow the merged company to be partially floated on the Dubai stock market and perhaps later in London.

I did agree to do this for a period and after a couple of these board meetings, it was clear that it would be extremely difficult to float the company given that it was an amalgam of Property, P&O Ferries, our container ports, the container ports inside the original DPW, property in Dubai and the Dubai Freezone, et cetera. In addition, the Board comprised many local advisers and professionals, which wouldn't be regarded as independent.

I therefore recommended that we should extract or demerge from this business all the container ports, which numbered 42 across 22 countries, to form a pure-play container port company. We did this and very soon after establishing independent directors on the Board, we floated 23% of the company in Dubai, raising almost $5 billion and valuing the business at $21.6 billion. Later, to gain greater flexibility to raise capital if required, we also listed in London, in 2011. We only finally delisted in London when it was obvious that most of the share trades were being done through Dubai.

Sultan persuaded me to remain on the Board as deputy chairman, after creating the new Board and governance standards. I remained there during the group's significant growth period until 2015. I had great admiration for the executive team led by Mohammed Shiraf, the highly-competent CEO, and for Sultan's entrepreneurial flair which did on occasions present some interesting challenges in the management of the Board.

Dubai has quite a high standard of corporate governance written into its corporate code and during my time on the Board, DP World has abided by that. One of the biggest decisions was to buy the Freezone World in Dubai for $3.5 billion during my last year on the

Board in 2015. This added a huge raft of tenanted businesses and office property adjacent to the port, and complemented a transit area for containers from Jebal Ali, one of the largest container ports in the world.

DPW's growth has been amazing. In 2016, it operated 77 container terminals across six continents in 40 countries; it was the world's third-largest container port company, handling about 60 million containers a year – 25 years earlier, it had handled one million a year. This expansion was driven by technological advances – innovative engineered facilities and increasingly automated handling equipment – coupled with leading international and entrepreneurial management: the classic requisites for successful growth.

In Britain after the P&O acquisition, the parent group Dubai World continues to own the P&O ferry fleet on the cross-Channel and Irish Sea routes. The single most important UK development for DP World has been the £1.5 billion London Gateway, the UK's first new port since the Second World War, at the old Shellhaven site on the River Thames. This project, which involved dredging the Thames to 14.5 metres, is adjacent to what will be Europe's largest Business Park. It is highly automated and one of the most modern container ports in the world – a great example of how engineering-led infrastructure development can fuel economic growth.

The port was conceived by P&O when Lord Sterling was Chairman, long before the DP World acquisition, but minimal progress was made for many years because of the extensive time taken by the planning authorities to approve an infrastructure project of that scale in the UK. Probably from concept design to start of building was close on 10 years. This was and is an unacceptable position for a major infra-structure investment in a developed country like the UK.

These UK timescales to attract and approve much-needed inward investment are just not internationally competitive. Yet responsible inward investors such as DPW and Carnival add enormous value to the country. While DP World has made London Gateway a reality, Carnival has invested about $5 billion by rescuing the moribund

Cunard brand with its ageing fleet to the point today where the Cunard fleet can boast three new Queens – *Mary, Elizabeth* and *Victoria* – with a further new Queen of 113,000 gross tons announced for launching in 2022. In P&O, the cruise fleet capacity has been doubled since Carnival took over.

There was one amusing footnote to the DP World transaction. During the bid battle with Singapore, Sultan stayed regularly in Duke's Hotel at the bottom of St James's Street. I'd often go to have a breakfast or a cup of tea with him during the three months that negotiations took place, and on many of these occasions, he'd express his delight at staying there, and would ask, did I think it was a nice hotel? One day, he questioned me about who owned the hotel – I found out from P&O Properties and advised him – and a week later, he called me to say he had personally bought Duke's Hotel!

This train of events was capped the morning we travelled together by car to announce the sale of P&O to Dubai World. As we passed through Trafalgar Square, Sultan announced: "Oh, Dubai World bought a building around here yesterday – it's called Grand something." I said: "Don't tell me it's Grand Buildings – first you buy my company and now you buy the office block that houses National Grid!" These were heady and over-enthusiastic investment days for Dubai World, the Government-owned holding company, and for some of its subsidiaries.

17. BANK OF ENGLAND

The Bank of England, known as "The Old Lady of Threadneedle Street" is the second oldest central bank in the world after Sweden's Riksbank. It was established in the reign of William and Mary by Royal Charter in 1694 as a Banker to the Government. Its headquarters and current imposing building, has been located in Threadneedle Street since 1734. It is one of the most famous landmarks in the City of London. It has a visitor's museum which provides those citizens and tourists with the curiosity and the opportunity to understand its history and its crucial role as a Central Bank in today's financial world. Each day thousands of UK citizens and visitors to the City pass by the famous building but few will have an understanding of what goes on behind the huge secure doorways. It is one of Britain's most trusted institutions. It was granted operational independence over Monetary Policy for Government by Gordon Brown in one of his first major decisions as the new Chancellor following the 1997 Labour Government election victory. A number of key economists and specialists working at the Bank, under the direction of the Governor and Deputy Governors, are rated as amongst the best in the world. Like most of our citizens I was not fully aware of what went on within this revered institution but the unexpected happened and I was fortunate to find out!

In 2004, I was encouraged to respond to an open advertisement seeking new Members of the Court of the Bank of England – the Bank's Board of Directors.

My initial interview was with Sir Gus O'Donnell, then Permanent Secretary of the Treasury who later became Cabinet Secretary and Head of the Civil Service. On stepping down from this role in 2012, he was appointed to the House of Lords. Gus is a man for whom I have a lot of time. He was a moderniser, he listened, he could deliver and I believe he was a true professional civil servant who had the courage to give clear advice to politicians in the Cabinet. In today's world of political spin, we need outstanding and courageous civil servants.

The interview was held in the Treasury building in Bird Cage Walk. It is similar in style to many of the other buildings of central Government, built in the late 19th – early 20th century and heavily influenced by the Victorian era. The very high ceilings, wide corridors and staircases and marble columns provide a daunting aura of grandeur. The modernisation of the building around 2002, during Gordon Brown's period as Chancellor, did much to improve the quality of working life for the staff and modernise the image. We met in the very large conference room that Gus and his senior team utilised and again in keeping with the building it was certainly on the large side. It took me back to the vast Victorian-style Chairman's office, complete with large fire place, I inherited when I returned in 1983 to Harland & Wolff in Belfast – before we moved to more modern premises.

Gus indicated to me that from the selected new Members of the Court, I might well, if deemed suitable, succeed Sir David Cooksey as Senior Non-Executive Director, chairing the monthly Court meeting – effectively the Board of the Bank. The discussion with him later led to a formal interview with the Governor, Mervyn King, the Permanent Secretary of The Treasury and an observer from the Nolan Committee, which vets all senior public appointments.

I was subsequently called by Gus to say that the Committee were in agreement to invite me to become the Senior Non-Executive Director and de facto Chair of Court. Up until the Bank gained its independence, under the 1998 Banking Act, the Court was chaired by the

Governor. It was then deemed that the role of Chair and Governor should be split by having the Senior Non-Executive assume the role of Chair. It was not until the further amendments to the Banking Act of 2009 that the role of the Chair was formalised. "The Court" might sound a bit archaic, but there is nothing antiquated about its operation or agenda. These are very relevant to the conduct and direction of the Bank of England, and therefore of considerable significance for the UK economy. And that is in normal times – my tenure as chairman included the most extraordinary period anyone, even the most senior Bank official or Court member, had ever experienced because of the 2008/9 global financial crisis.

There is a great sense of history about the Court, which was established following the creation of the Bank of England in 1694. The Court Room was designed by Sir Robert Taylor in 1768. The room is a very special example of 18th century architecture, with one feature which particularly aroused my interest: above the central arch of the Western Arcade there is a working wind dial dating back to (1805) which was used in the days of sail to forecast the likely arrival time of sailing ships. Depending on timing, their cargoes could affect commodity prices, impact cash in circulation and influence interest rates. So this mechanical wind dial, still working today, was a very early version of a 'real-time' market information system!

Those interested in antique furniture will find some splendid pieces in the Court Room and in the ante-room. Probably the most noteworthy is the Hepplewhite period writing table c1785 which once belonged to William Pitt the younger who was Prime Minister 1783–1801 and 1804–1806.

The Court meetings each month were around a great oval (ringed) table in the Court Room with each member having a microphone. It was a daunting experience for most members to sit around this Court table for the first time. For my first few meetings I was no exception to that experience. Alongside 16 Non-Executive Directors, you had the Governor and two Deputy Governors and a number of Senior Executives in attendance – who were valuable contributors when their advice was sought. Our terms of reference, and the list of functions we were expected to focus on, were laid out in the Bank of England 1998 Act.

I soon learned that the commitment required by the new post was quite demanding: a good half day-plus of Court Meetings each month, which entailed much reading and preparation. As Chair, I had to oversee the preparation of the Court Agenda with the Court Secretary each month, as well as attending Remuneration and Audit Committees. I was also involved in a range of interview committees at both the Treasury and the Bank on new appointments and promotions within the Bank and ultimately appointments to the Court.

In addition, I had a regular monthly 1½ hour working breakfast meeting with the Governor, about a fortnight ahead of each Court meeting. These were particularly valuable exchanges and I learned a great deal from the Governor about the issues involved in the economic and political interfaces with the Chancellor of the Exchequer, the Treasury and the PM, who was now Gordon Brown.

I had a few valuable months of handover with Sir David Cooksey. David has contributed much to society in a range of Government, private sector and voluntary roles. During this time, I learned the Bank's administration processes and began to comprehend some of the issues Court dealt with. I also observed the approaches and style of the Non-Executive Directors and indeed that of the two Deputy Governors and the Governor in Court. You can soon figure out who are the genuine contributors around a Board table. There are those who pose genuine questions to clarify assertions or professionally challenge assumptions made in Board papers – these are members who have studied the paperwork, considered and got to grips with the key issues. There are also those who have an ego and have not thoroughly prepared but feel they must be seen to participate. Their questions are often shallow or worse still the answers they seek are already in the paperwork! Then there are those who are comfortable to confine themselves to topics where their own domain knowledge can effectively be deployed and add real value in doing so.

This was the first appointment where I did not stick to my long-held view that I shouldn't take on a boardroom role which did not draw directly upon my inherent engineering training and experience. However, within the vaults of the Bank there is a fine multi-diesel-engine mini power station. It is kept in excellent working order and indeed the Bank has an apprentice intake in support of its maintenance programme. This power station, along with independent bore holes for self-sufficiency in water, would allow the Bank to continue operating including its critical computer systems, in the event of power strikes or any form of civil disruption. Given this impressive engineering installation I was reassured that I should be able to comment with authority on at least one of the Banks assets!

After chairing the Court for a year or two, and in discussion with the Governor, my conclusions were that Court itself was too large to be really effective. In addition, a monthly Court was placing high demands on the Bank officials. Mervyn subsequently invited me to draft a paper on Court's reform, in case the opportunity to change legislation occurred. We debated my draft together and, given his great skill-sets with the written word, he polished it. The aim was to reduce the number of Non-Executive Directors from 16 to 8, ensuring that the Bank had a full part to play in their recruitment. We also proposed reducing the frequency of meetings from 12 a year to a minimum of seven and formalising the role of the Chairman of the Court.

These and a range of other changes were debated and supported by Court and were subsequently incorporated into the 2009 Amendment to the Banking Act. The amendments also granted formal powers to the Bank to deal with a failing institution – powers which were not there, for example, at the time of the Northern Rock collapse in 2008, which was the harbinger in Britain of the global financial crisis.

As Mervyn and I got to know each other, our mutual trust and confidence increased. At our breakfast meetings we would discuss organisation, people challenges, interface with Government, policy issues – but not the Bank's Monetary Policy Committee or interest rate-setting.

I had no role in the MPC other than to conduct an annual interview with each of its members to ensure they had sufficient research support and that they, from a governance point of view, felt free to act independently. I would then provide feedback to the NEDs and the Governor with any recommendations for change. I greatly enjoyed my interface with the MPC members. Collectively, they were a highly professional group with a great depth of experience in their field.

I recall raising the question of their ability to act independently with Professor Sir Stephen Nickell, the highly respected economist who served on the MPC. He said: "You can be assured we don't do consensus – that is our great strength." As members of the Court, we were free to attend the theatre-style presentations over a morning each month to the MPC members. The members would then interrogate the officials at the Bank and you witnessed some excellent exchanges between very able people.

From time to time, an able member of the Court would throw down a tongue-in-cheek challenge to the Governor: "Couldn't monetary policy be conducted by one man and a dog?" Given the amount of research and modelling of data that the MPC Members executed, this question caused some wry amusement around the Court Room. It was particularly welcomed at times of stress! It so happened that, during my tenure, I attended a lunch organised by the Carlyle Group, where I was seated next to Alan Greenspan, who had just stepped down as the long-standing Chairman of the US Federal Reserve. He possessed a folksy and attractive sense of humour. I asked him what he thought about the "one man and a dog" question. He thought for a moment and mischievously replied: "Why the man?"

Every so often, Mervyn and I also discussed a range of modernisation issues, as he was keen to upgrade the Bank's organisation and Court processes. I read media comments from time to time claiming that Mervyn wanted no change at the Bank. This in my five-year experience was totally untrue. The appointment of a professional Finance Director was one important milestone in this reformation process. We subsequently hired Warwick Jones who did a superb job. The scope of his role increased over time to include formal Risk Management and Strategy implementation monitoring.

Strategy formulation and debate was another area that Mervyn was keen to modernise. We subsequently moved in Court annually to debate each area of the Bank's organisation and strategic priorities, funding and resource requirements. Following these debates each year, the Bank produced an excellent Strategy Communications booklet for all staff, which would have put most FTSE 100 companies in the shade for its sheer quality. We also tackled and developed a plan to phase out the Defined Benefit Pension Scheme, a controversial but necessary step in adjusting the cost profile of the Bank for future years.

The Audit Committee under the chairmanship of the diligent Amelia (now Dame) Fawcett, a Morgan Stanley banker, performed a thorough review and interrogation of the Bank's financial health biannually with the support of the new Finance Director and his team and the internal auditor. Similarly, the Remuneration Committee under the chairmanship first of Bill (now Lord) Morris, formerly head of the Transport & General Workers Union (TGWU), and later under Dr David Potter, former Chairman of the electronics group Psion, carried out necessary and excellent work.

Annual remuneration during Mervyn's Governorship was in a way very straightforward, in that he would never agree to a personal increase in excess of inflation. This was despite the fact that international bench-marking exercises, which we carried out, demonstrated that his remuneration was very low by the standards of that paid in other Central Banks. It was particularly low compared to that received by both the CEO and Chairman of the Financial Services Authority (FSA) – the body created by the Government in 1997 to take over from the Bank of England responsibility for monitoring and regulating UK banks and building societies. As for the Governor's remuneration relative to senior City Bankers – he would not even get on their radar screen of reward expectations.

In terms of the Deputy Governors, Sir Andrew Large stepped down as a Deputy Governor about half way through my term. He was a very experienced banker, knew the City well and had primary responsible for financial stability. He was replaced by Sir John Gieve, who was parachuted in from the Permanent Secretary role at the Home Office.

Neither Court nor the Governor was consulted on this appointment and had no part in the process. This was a great disservice to John by his former ministerial and civil servant colleagues. It put him at an unfair disadvantage from Day One. It was all the more unfair since he has a fine mind and is an agreeable and competent man. John finally resigned in 2009.

The second Deputy Governor was (ex-Treasury civil servant) Rachel Lomax – strong and robust in her views. She focussed on support for the MPC as one of her key roles. I got to know Rachel and enjoyed our conversations. I was happy to give her what future career advice I could, as she reached retirement age at the Bank in 2008. She subsequently served on the Board of HSBC Bank and later the Board of Serco and other appointments.

There were two outstanding internal candidates to compete for the two Deputy Governor roles: Charlie Bean – the world class economist, who had serviced the MPC for a number of years, succeeded Rachel, Paul Tucker, who was highly regarded within the City and had a deep understanding of Financial Markets, ultimately succeeded Sir John Gieve, focussing on financial stability.

Paul Tucker was the first Deputy Governor to be appointed via a formal interview panel process. It was led by the Treasury Permanent Secretary Nick MacPherson, (now Lord MacPherson), the Under Secretary at the Treasury Tom Scholar and myself as Chair of the Court – plus a Nolan independent representative. Paul Tucker was ultimately a contender for the Governor's role that went to Mark Carney in 2013 on Mervyn's completion of 10 years of rather gruelling service – particularly the latter five years.

Mervyn told me that, during his governorship, he had more than 100 appearances at the House of Commons Treasury Select Committee and attended 194 Monetary Policy Committee meetings, chairing

120 of them. I was delighted that in 2012 Mervyn was Knighted with a GBE. On his retirement in 2013, he was appointed to the House of Lords, taking the title of Lord King of Lothbury, and later was appointed as a Knight of the Garter. All these national honours were truly justified for a man who served his country so diligently and independently in the role of Governor.

Given that our appointments as Members of the Court required us each to sign the Official Secrets Act, I am clearly limited in what I can or may want to say about our meetings. The composition of Court took little account of the skill range required to create the right blend of experience around that important table. I, and others, could only assume that appointments over the years were made direct by Treasury ministers with little or no consultation with the Bank on the skill sets or experience required.

I found this unacceptable in modern governance, and after discussion and agreement with the Governor, I had a meeting with Sir Gus O'Donnell about it. I put it to him that we should endeavour to modernise the process of recruitment of Non-Executive Directors. The Governor and I proposed that as and when a vacancy occurred that:

- The Governor and myself would propose that the search be focussed on a particular skill set and experience need.
- The Bank should have an involvement in the interview process, at least after short listing of candidates by the Treasury.

Gus, who was always open to creating modern systems, agreed and I ended up joining the-then Under Secretary at the Treasury, Jon Cunliff (now Sir Jon and a Deputy Governor of the Bank), and a Nolan representative each year in interviewing and finalising a very short list for the Chancellor to select and formally approve new NXD appointments to Court. After three years of this approach, the Court gradually was moving towards a more suitable and balanced skill-set, with the recruitment of new members of the calibre of the then-chairman of Centrica Roger Carr (later Sir Roger), Dame Susan Rice,

CEO of Lloyds Bank in Scotland, and James Strachan, a very talented man and former chairman of the Audit Commission, who overcame the challenge of his deafness. Roger Carr's contributions during my time at the Bank were those of a very experienced Non-Executive Director. His wide business experience, common sense and wisdom shone through. He has remained a close business confidant and a valued personal friend. He is doing a fine job as Chair of BAE our leading defence company.

The Court, whilst having no direct role in monetary policy, had a responsibility for approving the use of the Bank's balance sheet to support financial institutions.

After the financial crises of 2008 bared its teeth, the Court established a small, six-person Intervention Committee, comprising three NXDs and the three most senior Bank officers – the Governor and his two Deputies – to deal nimbly with the crises. We met as frequently as necessary to provide the required balance sheet approvals with the Treasury being aligned. This further increased the workload and I can recall, at the height of the crises that engulfed the UK banks and building societies, that this Court Committee met three times in a single day when the Royal Bank of Scotland crisis was approaching its peak.

My Non-Executive colleagues on the committee were the chairs of our two Committees of Court, Amelia Fawcett and Dr David Potter. Both put in a great deal of effort and were impressive in raising key issues and giving wise advice to the Governor and his two Deputies on the Committee.

In the early stages of the crisis, a number of the bankers who were NXDs on the Court were largely in denial of the true nature of the solvency challenges facing their institutions, and persisted in their belief that this was only a temporary issue of liquidity. This was also very much the line constantly promoted by the FSA. It seemed that they did not or could not entertain the possibility that there might be some institutions which were facing meltdown – having over-leveraged against inflated asset values.

By contrast, to me and most of my non-banking colleagues on the Court, there seemed to be no question that leverage was at the root of the crisis and some institutions were clearly significantly over-leveraged. This denial syndrome was underscored for me by a Court member from a bank who offered to have his Risk Managers give a presentation to the Bank of England's officials to enhance their knowledge, as he was confident about the modern risk management processes in his institution. Regrettably, it was by then virtually public knowledge just how leveraged this particular institution was and, indeed, the institution itself soon had to confront the issue.

Mervyn did not buy into this view that it was just a "liquidity crisis". He was much more sceptical, believing that over-leveraging and over-lending on inflated asset values was at the heart of the crisis. This brought the wrath of many bankers down upon him via aggressive negative briefing to the media – and we suspected some in the FSA were doing their bit too. Nevertheless, Mervyn was regrettably proven right as the traumatic events sadly unfolded over the next two years.

It was about this time that Warren Buffet, with his famous dictum that "You only find out who is swimming naked when the tide goes out", commented: "The banks have brought this on themselves and they have only themselves to blame."

The crisis and the blame game that was played in certain quarters also spotlighted some less agreeable features of the Court's composition. Amongst our 16 Non-Executives, there was a range of abilities and skills with one or two who in my view fell short of the behaviour one would have expected of a Non-Executive of the Bank of England. Given NXDs were paid £6,000 a year for the workload I've outlined (and £12,000 a year for the Chairman), no one did it for the money. It was an honour to be invited to serve.

From time to time in Court, we also had mischievous questions which had been clearly constructed over previous weeks. They were generally aimed, it seemed to me, at putting the Governor in a challenged position. I suppose they were meant to demonstrate how clever was the interrogator to pose such a brilliant question! Never once did we see the Governor fail to bat away one of these time-wasting and non-added value interventions.

This helps to explain the background to a somewhat extraordinary incident which occurred one evening as the crisis was raging. I was called by Sir Nick Macpherson, the Treasury Permanent Secretary, who told me that Robert Peston, the BBC Business Editor, had just published a story on the BBC website that the Court had lost confidence in the Governor. As a former Banking Editor of the *Financial Times*, Peston was regarded by many people in Britain as the most authoritative reporter of the financial crisis. I replied: "Nonsense, Nick" and told him that I would attempt to reach all Members in the next hour before I attended a business dinner." I really respected and rated Sir Nick Macpherson, as did Mervyn King, and we worked closely together on a range of difficult issues. It was important that he understood as quickly as possible that Peston's story was erroneous.

I made all my calls, and not one single Court Member aligned with Robert's information, so I responded to Nick and advised the Governor accordingly. One was left with the question: who purveyed this nonsense to a responsible and experienced reporter such as Robert Peston? He would hardly accept such input from anyone other than someone within the Court, who must have been running a personal agenda entirely at odds with the position of the overwhelming majority of Members.

On the other side of the coin, against the flawed and irresponsible behaviour by one or two on the Court, we were blessed with a majority of Members with high ability and plentiful common sense. They also understood the importance of standing shoulder to shoulder in a crisis. I always said to individual members, when they raised concerns with me, that in order to get alignment and clarity, any uncertainties in their mind about direction or policy should be openly debated within Court or in the private NXD Meetings with the Governor. Mervyn was always willing to listen and was never evasive in dealing with genuine concerns and questions raised. He demonstrated a great deal of respect for individual Members of Court and for our committees as a whole.

One member in particular, who throughout my time was remarkably well prepared for every meeting, was Peter Jay – a distinguished economist in his own right. He had previously been the BBC's Economics Correspondent and I truly valued, as did I believe the Governor, Peter's authoritative interventions. He was all too aware, as we often discussed together, that the root of many financial crises in history involved institutions recklessly lending too much against over-inflated asset values, thus incorporating high leverage. This time around that dangerous parcel was topped off with overly light covenants.

All of us on appointment had to sign the Official Secrets Act. At one stage during the later stages of the crisis and following a newspaper leak of highly confidential information, which could only have come from a Member of Court, I requested all Members to re-sign to re-emphasise our responsibilities.

I regard myself as reasonably experienced in dealing with the media. It was, therefore, an issue of puzzlement and huge disappointment to me that any member would get involved in leaking to the media and in this case the *Financial Times* about the Deputy Governor's succession plans. How could someone appointed to such a responsible national role be so disloyal as to divulge such highly sensitive information – disclosed on a confidential basis by the Governor to the Non-Executives. I addressed all NXDs in a robust way about our individual and collective responsibilities. I also advised them we were continuing our investigation into the leak and already were accumulating valuable evidence in our Press Office. We got close to confirming the culprit and from there on there were no more such leaks!

I have gone on public record to say that our country was very fortunate to have a man of the calibre, intellect and integrity of Mervyn King as Governor for 10 years. He was someone who could not be pushed around by the media, by politicians or ministers. The same could not be said of some of those bankers most critical of him, who subsequently were exposed as "swimming naked", as their institutions and roles fell apart. Sadly, when the tide went out, it became all too clear that a number of major UK banks, along with their European and US competitors, were swimming naked and had been caught up in the hubris of the day. More than eight years later, the consequences of these errors are still unwinding.

Fortunately for our country, we had a number of highly professional chairmen of some of our larger banks, which have a critical role to play in servicing the capital needs of our businesses. I think of the strong leadership with integrity shown by Sir Win Bischoff of Lloyds and in particular by Douglas Flint (now Sir Douglas) in his role as Chairman of HSBC.

There has been some criticism, both during and after the crisis, of the Bank's role in it. As time has moved on and the "tide has gone out", I have absolutely no doubt that much of this criticism was and remains unwarranted. The unfortunate truth was that, in the early stages of the 2008/9 crisis, the Bank did not have the powers to do the job it could have done. Some of these missing powers and responsibilities were subsequently incorporated in the 2009 Amendments to the Banking Act. Court debated the Bank's proposals for many of these amendments prior to submitting final proposals to the Treasury.

Even then, this much-needed reinforcement of the Bank's powers was incomplete. For instance, one of the amendments that Court was keen to see was the ability of the Bank to formally direct the FSA to tighten its regulatory supervision of financial institutions, if and when the Bank's analyses of financial stability showed that risk was significantly heightened. Unfortunately, this approach was not supported and therefore this necessary power of direction was not incorporated into the Amendments. Lord Turner, the then-Chairman of the FSA, who sat on Court was clearly not keen to buy in to this concept and may have swung the Treasury and ministers against it.

I advised the Governor and the Treasury, well before my five-year term was up, that I would not seek re-appointment. My plc workload and Chancellor role at the University of Southampton, plus a range of voluntary work – including Young Offenders into Work – was such that I knew my Court role should not continue.

Nick Macpherson invited me to join the interview panel for my successor. We had the benefit of an open advertisement and a head-hunter search by Whitehead Mann, and interviewed a significant number of potential candidates, but did not find a convincing leader for the role in that process. Nick and I scanned the horizon for other possible candidates and we wondered if Sir David Lees, who was stepping down as Chairman of GKN, could be persuaded to throw his hat into the ring. David had the advantage of having served as a Member of Court for some eight years in an earlier period, well before I became Chairman.

Following interviews by the Head-hunters and Nick's panel he was appointed for a five year term.

Reflections

I mentioned earlier that in accepting the role, of Senior Non-Executive and de facto Chair of the Court at the Bank, I was no longer aligning my discipline of engineering with the Board and companies key activities as I had previously done in plc life.

How glad I was that I accepted what was 'the opportunity of a lifetime'.

It was also, despite real challenges to fit in all of the time demands of the Bank, a great honour to be a member of the Court and serve in this lead role. I learned a great deal about central banking and its role in a modern economy at a time of great turbulence. I got to know and learned much from so many talented people in the Bank who render unsung service to the country day by day. So many of them including the Governor and Deputies, had little if any time off for about a year or more during the crises.

My monthly working breakfasts with the Governor were great educational sessions covering many topics of global significance whilst debating and mutually agreeing practical ways forward on day-to-day management issues of the Bank.

We built a transparent relationship and I endeavour to add value where I could see the opportunity. There were a number of common yet different issues in chairing a plc to that of chairing the Court. First the common – included many of the same disciplines in financial control, balance sheet management, strategic debate, pension funding, budgeting et cetera. It also underlined for me the common need for a Board/Court to ensure strong relationships with the Executive whilst reserving the right to challenge robustly if necessary. Second the big difference was the size of the NXD team (16) compared to say the eight, compatible with a large plc – a number which we ultimately recommend and got included in the 2009 amendments to the Bank of England Act. Thirdly as a Chair you 'inherited' a group of NXDs, the majority of which were appointed without any Court consultation or process equivalent to a plc Nominations recruitment process – which would have considered their relevant and complementary skill sets, corporate experience and any previous roles as an NXD. Nevertheless I was fortunate to have this priviledged chairing experience, demanding as it was.

As I pass down Threadneedle Street today, I am now much more aware of what goes on behind the secure doorways of The Bank of England.

18. AIRBUS

Airbus (then known as EADS – the European Aeronautic, Defence and Space company) was created in July 2000 and today is one of Europe's largest and most successful companies, employing over 130,000 people mainly in France, Germany, Spain and the UK. It brought together a series of major European aerospace and defence brands and today comprises the Airbus Civil Aircraft, Helicopters, Defence and Space Systems divisions.

I was invited to join the Board in 2006 for a five-year term. This happened rather suddenly after BAE Systems sold out its 20% stake in the Airbus arm to fuel its Defence acquisition programme in the US. As a result of BAE's sale, Britain no longer had any voice at the EADS Board table, even though some 20,000 people were, and continue to be employed by EADS (now Airbus) companies in the UK – making it by far the most important civil aerospace business operating in the country.

I was advised by the DTI that transformation of Governance was taking place at EADS. It was moving from a system where it had joint German and French chairmen and joint CEOs, to a single Chairman (at the time German) and a single CEO (at the time French). The DTI also wanted me to know that, if I were to be approached by the head-hunter employed by the Board of EADS to find a new independent NXD, they would be supportive of me as a British candidate.

I told them that, given EADS was a critical and important company for mainland Europe and the UK, I would be willing to discuss my possible appointment both with the head-hunters and the Chairman, so that we could mutually explore if I were really suitable for the role. I was later approached by Spencer Stuart, who had been retained by EADS for the search, and I agreed that I would be prepared to talk to the new Chairman, Dr Rudiger Gruber. We subsequently had a telephone call which was cordial and businesslike. I assumed this approach would be followed up by a series of more formal interviews and an opportunity for me to do some due diligence, and, if offered the role, to clear my appointment with my colleagues on the Board of National Grid, and so on.

I was therefore more than embarrassed, a few weeks later, to be called by the *Financial Times* when attending a National Grid Board meeting in the US to say they were publishing an article on EADS the next day on the modernisation of the Governance and changes in the Board. The journalist, who seemed to be exceptionally well informed, laid out the facts for me which he said he was publishing the next day:

Sole Chairman – Dr Rudiger Gruber (German)
Sole Group CEO – Louis Gallois (French)
Sole CEO Airbus Civil Aircraft – Tom Enders (German)
Four new independent directors
Lakshmi Mittal – Chairman, Arcelor Mittal
Herman–Joseph Lamberti – Deputy Chairman, Deutsche Bank
Michael Pebereau – Chairman, Bank de Paris
Sir John Parker – Chairman, National Grid.

In addition, said the journalist, the Governments of France and Germany would appoint two directors each from Daimler Benz and Lagardere, the German and French companies that owned substantial stakes in EADS, and that one would be appointed by the Spanish Government, whose aero company Casa had a 4.2% EADS stake.

This was a highly premature leak because as I had received neither a verbal or written proposal from EADS, let alone discuss and clear my lines with the Board of National Grid. This resulted in some hasty footwork to explain the situation I found myself in. Ken Harvey, as the excellent Senior Non-Executive Director, then led a discussion with the National Grid NXDs which cleared the way for me to accept the appointment when, as happened soon after, it was formally offered in writing. On joining the Board I was immediately requested to chair the combined Remuneration and Nomination Committee – later to encompass Governance – a heavy lifting job it was for the next 11 years.

Louis Gallois was an excellent choice to be the first sole CEO and he and Rudiger Gruber worked well together. Rudiger and Louis were both statesmen with no personal egos or agendas. They were focussed on making this new Board work, and rose above nationality. They wanted to move the company forward and keep normalising the governance of the Board towards that of a more orthodox public listed entity.

Before the governance reform, the Governments of France and Germany, along with the Lagardere and Daimler Holdings plus the Spanish Government's 4% share, effectively controlled 49% of the votes. The new governance arrangement was a significant step in the direction towards non-Government directors, but such large share-holding blocks, directly or indirectly influenced by the Governments, reduced the free float and distanced us from being a normal quoted company. For example, we were not free to appoint Board Members other than the new group of four independents. The Governments made or approved all other appointments.

Louis Gallois observed, just before he stepped down in 2012, that the four independent NXDs during their first five years in office played an important part in modernising EADS's governance and accelerated its journey towards normality.

Progress was also due to Rudiger's work as chairman in wanting to modernise the company and its boardroom processes. Indeed, he spent some time with me in London discussing and understanding the role of the Chairman of a UK plc and how modern UK govern-ance was achieved.

In 2009, Rudiger was appointed by the German Government to be Chairman of German Railways – Deutsche Bahn. He had to hand over rather quickly to the other Daimler nominee on the Board – Bodo Ubber, Daimler's CFO. Bodo did a good job, taking over at short notice and working very hard. His previous position on the Board was taken by Wilfred Porth, Daimler's HR Director. Wilfred served with me on the combined Remuneration and Nominations Committee as a valued and professional member. Bodo remained as Chairman until Louis Gallois stepped down as CEO, when we moved to a German Group CEO in Tom Enders and a French Chairman in Arnaud Lagardere.

In my first two years I also served on the Audit Committee under the chairmanship of Herman Joseph Lamberti. He has done a magnificent job as Audit Chairman in also ensuring a strong voice for Internal Audit and for building up our Compliance organisation along with Louis Gallois and Tom Enders. The organisation was subsequently further strengthened by Tom Enders, following his appointment as CEO. He combined the roles of Head of Compliance, Legal and Company Secretary, and we appointed an external lawyer, John Harrison, from a similar role at Technip, the French international consultancy company. This combined appointment was one that I had discussed earlier with Tom Enders as being the right development, particularly given his leadership on our Compliance journey. It was this increased focus on compliance that led to the establishment of an Ethics Committee chaired by the company chairman, of which I was a member, which oversees the investigation of compliance irregularities.

As Chairman of the Remuneration and Nominations Committee, I have worked closely with the experienced HR Director, Thierry Baril, to ensure the Nominations Committee had a thorough examination of succession issues at all levels each year from the considerable pool of engineering and management talent throughout the organisation. Tom Enders and Thierry put in considerable effort on this front. The culture has moved to ensure that the most talented and experienced person is appointed to a key role regardless of nationality. In the old days, someone could be appointed because it was the turn of France or Germany (or Spain or the UK) to have their national in that particular job. However, we also seek to ensure a good nationality balance overall, particularly amongst the top executives.

There has also now been some success in moving executives from one country to another, which again had not always been the case. Moving executives from one division to another has been more challenging but has been successful where implemented.

During the first five years under the CEO team of Louis Gallois at Group and Tom Enders at the Airbus Civil Aircraft division, spectacular strides were made by Airbus in overtaking Boeing's annual output. In 1996, the Airbus consortium (the GIE, as it was known before EADS was formed) produced 123 passenger jets; 20 years later, it produced more than five times as many. In total, by March 2017 the company had delivered over 10,000 commercial aircraft and had booked over 17,000 orders – 50 times the order book of two decades ago. Now that is growth, driven by great engineering innovation, exploring the frontiers of technology and outstanding leadership.

I joined the Board when Airbus was facing challenging production and ramp-up issues with its initial A380 Superjumbos (or, as Airbus calls the aircraft, the "double-decker"). But the A380 is a great engineering success as the world's largest aircraft. It is also a delight to fly in with a distinct noise reduction for the passenger versus any other aircraft that I've flown in. A technical comparative that conveys the amazing scale of this aircraft is that the wing span of the A380 tailplane is similar to that of the main wing span of the A320!

In 2012, Louis Gallois completed his five-year contract. He had steered EADS through some very choppy waters, particularly during the impact of the 2008/9 global finance crisis. Another huge task which he had to manage was the renegotiations with the European Governments on what, 10 years earlier, had been a fixed-price contract for the design and build of the A400M military transport aircraft. This required all his considerable diplomatic experience because the aircraft was so late into production, with costs overrunning initial expectations by a considerable amount. It demonstrated once again the foolhardy approach of fixed price for a long-term contract incorporating high-technology, often unproven, plus all the design risk inherent in such a venture.

Moreover, Louis's great commercial skills were needed to realign the A400M programme with the technical challenges and commercial realities surrounding the sophisticated technology and engineering sought by the various governments – each with their own particular specialised preferences for this aircraft. I have learned over the years that "preferential engineering" is a costly disrupter of projects.

The A400M received its necessary airworthiness certificates and the first aircraft was formally handed over in 2013. During its extensive flight tests, pilots were incredibly enthusiastic about its handling and manoeuvring capability. It has all the hallmarks of being a successful and, importantly, an exportable plane for many years to come in the international defence market.

Arnaud Lagadere took over as EADS Chairman at the AGM in 2012 – although he did not turn up for the AGM! Arnaud is a very bright, intelligent and humorous man whose company one could enjoy. However, I never felt that being Chairman of this large group was his first professional love. Unlike his father, Jean-Luc, who was one of the creators of EADS, Arnaud's main interest was and remains the very successful Lagardere media group.

Tom Enders took over as Group CEO and, as we expected, set about revisiting its strategies. He also consolidated the EADS's Paris-based central organisation, which became a largely administrative office, with the Airbus corporate functions located in Toulouse, which effectively became the Group headquarters. This streamlining improved operational effectiveness and reduced cost. Thus Harold Wilhelm, the youthful Airbus Division CFO, took over the combined CFO role for Group and Airbus Division after the well regarded Group CFO Hans Peter Ring retired. Similarly Thierry Baril assumed the joint HR roles. Thierry works very closely with me in supporting the work of the Remuneration and Nominations Committee. He does it in a truly professional and highly cooperative way.

This was a busy time for the Nominations Committee as Tom built his team. I commented in a 2012 press announcement:

"It was with great satisfaction that through our succession planning process, we have found such a wealth and breadth of talents inside EADS. We seek to choose the right person for each of the open positions, to rise to the upcoming strategic challenges facing this Group, and to maintain its hard-earned leadership positions. It is regrettable that this generation of management could not yet incorporate female appointments, but I feel comforted that the next wave is showing some very promising prospective candidates for subsequent rounds of succession."

EADS was not alone in suffering from a dearth of senior female executives – the problem remains widespread in Western Europe and the sooner we solve it, the better. Diversity, including gender and ethnic diversity, is one of the keys to corporate success. I am glad to say that the Group Board now incorporates three talented professional women from France, Germany and Spain.

Shortly after Tom took over, he discussed with the Board the possibility that, based on signals he had received, he believed that BAE Systems could be willing to discuss a merger.

As a Board, we examined with our advisors the industrial and financial logic of the combination. The advisors included the Evercore Chairman Bernard Taylor whom I got to know well through the process and in subsequent deals at Anglo American. I trust and admire his creative flair in seeking solutions.

We were convinced that in a shrinking Western defence market, consolidation of two major defence businesses would throw up not only cost synergies but also growth opportunities. We could create the world's largest defence and aerospace company, resulting in the strongest combination of leading technologies in the field of global defence and security.

Scale and technology, in a shrinking home market, are key

ingredients in winning big international defence and aviation contracts. Furthermore, the key personnel were well known to each other, given that numerous EADS-BAE joint projects and joint company operations had been in existence for many years – notably the Eurofighter project and the missile company MBDA, whose partners also included Italy's Finmeccanica (now renamed "Leonardo"). The 'cultural difference' risks, which can undermine the value creation potential of many mergers and acquisitions, were therefore unlikely to be present. Furthermore, integration would be confined to the Defence and Space Divisions of EADS with Airbus Commercial Aircraft not being 'merger' impacted.

After extensive financial modelling and working with our advisors, the Board authorised discussions for a 60:40 merger. At that time, this implied a premium of 14-15% for BAE, which was the smaller company – certainly a much lower premium than a takeover would have demanded!

Regrettably, with some four-six weeks' intensive work still left to be done, and before a formal announcement describing the transaction to shareholders could be made, news of the merger leaked. This was very damaging as shareholders and the business media started speculating on all sorts of issues. Had the leak not occurred, all these issues would have been covered off in our Merger Prospectus.

What made the destructive leak so frustrating was that EADS and BAE had essentially resolved the big potential stumbling blocks to an agreement between them. As I have observed over the years, there are three main reasons why mergers don't get off the ground and cause both sides to fail to reach a deal:

1. Who is to be the CEO? Many of us can recall the first Glaxo/SmithKline Beecham pharmaceuticals merger attempt when Glaxo's Chairman Sir Richard Sykes and his opposite number had to pull the plug at midnight the day before their merger was due to be announced. In our case, this was clear and accepted – Tom Enders as Group CEO.

2. What is to be the 'Name' above the door? Again, many

will recall the Daimler-Benz/Chrysler car industry merger almost failing at the final hurdle because of disagreement over the name! I should add that in the case of that particular merger, perhaps 'failing to conclude' would have been much less value destructive for shareholders than proceeding with the deal. However, in our case this question was capable of satisfactory resolution.

3. Whose head office is it going to be? Almost always an emotional issue, but less challenging to resolve than 1) and 2). In the merger of National Grid and Transco/Lattice Group, I reached agreement up front that we should go to an entirely new office on Day One. We therefore left both our existing offices behind. This enabled those staff who were not joining the merged business to tidy up and depart in a low-profile and dignified way. That process worked well and we had a clean and successful start in a new building under a new name and logo. The combined company would have had its operational headquarters in Paris but BAE's London office would have continued to be the key location for the Defence business, particularly given the need to minimise disruption of BAE's special arrangements with the US.

As a Chairman, I would never permit merger negotiations to get under way without resolving these three issues in the first days of the cycle, before the bankers' and advisors' bills start mounting.

Mergers, however, require another sensitive task – agreeing the membership of the new joint Board. This can be an incredibly challenging negotiation to pull off. It almost always requires a marathon of meetings and debate. This one was no exception.

As Nominations Committee Chairman, I, along with my three Independent Director colleagues, had responsibility to lead the discussions on behalf of the EADS Board. We opened talks with the BAE Chairman, Dick Olver, and Lakshmi Mittal joined me for those sessions. I was indeed grateful to him, not only for being alongside but also for holding the meetings in his palatial Kensington home where confidentiality was assured.

There were many competing objectives to be discussed. For example, we needed to achieve a satisfactory geographical balance in the Board of Directors – across Germany, France, Spain, UK and USA – to reflect our combined presence on the ground in these countries. We also did not want a Board larger than about 14. In my experience, any Board with more than this number is unwieldy and ineffective, and the ideal number is 12 or less. In terms of the Executive Directors, the Group CEO was clearly going to be Tom Enders, while Ian King, CEO of BAE, was the lead candidate to head and integrate the combined Defence business. It was also important that he retain his seat on the "ring-fenced" BAE US Defence Board, which under US law had to be incorporated as a separate entity.

Normally, the Chairman is selected when the Board is formed, but in a merger of equals often (not always), goes to the side that is not getting the Group CEO role. And the CFO role often goes to the side which is not providing the CEO. Lakshmi and I had some tough discussions with the BAE Chairman Dick Olver, whom I've known and respected for many years. We had worked together on a range of topics at the Royal Academy of Engineering, so knew each other well.

At one meeting, Dick did not come across as the most flexible of chairmen and we terminated the discussions as Dick was driving down a one-way street on BAE's behalf. Lakshmi and I felt that there needed to be more joint focus on the importance of getting the balance of the entire new combined Board right. However, given our personal relationship, a few days later, Dick and I had an excellent heart-to-heart discussion over dinner when we arrived at a mutually agreeable position on the key outstanding issues. During these negotiations and later, during interviews for the Non-Executive Directors for Airbus Group (post-the BAE merger having fallen through), Lakshmi and I inevitably spent many hours together. This strengthened and deepened our friendship. I greatly admire his sharp commercial mind and his pragmatic and logical style of decision-making. He has also contributed a great deal to charitable work in the UK, including his donation of the main sculpture, The Orbit, at the 2012 London Olympic Stadium.

Suffice to say that, despite a lot of challenges, we eventually achieved alignment between the existing Boards of BAE and EADS. The Governments had to be consulted on the composition of the new combined Board, given their still sizeable shareholdings and we were ready to proceed with this part of the process.

In parallel with this Board Committee activity, management was working very long hours pursuing agreements with the French and German Governments with the aim of reducing their sharehold-ings and preparing the way for Daimler and Lagardere to exit by selling their shareholdings over an agreed timescale. Both companies wanted to focus on their core businesses, vehicles in Daimler's case and media in Lagardere's. The leaks meant that the public spotlight was on the Governments, who therefore had to contend with much media speculation and rumour.

The main obstacles were expected to emerge from France and UK. But their issues were largely resolved when we were hit by the last-minute bombshell of having the German Chancellor, Angela Merkel, pull the rug from under us. Speculation had it that the partners in her Coalition Government wheeled out their opposition as they became concerned about what a UK defence-led business would mean for German defence companies.

Very disappointingly, we had no option as a Board but to pull the deal. Had we been able to publish our Prospectus, we would have put to rest much of the press speculation and indeed shareholder concerns and premature comments regarding all sorts of matters, ranging from National Security to Dividend Policy. In my view, once a deal of this magnitude gets into the public arena and the media is off the leash, the real story of the companies' actual intentions gets distorted and increasingly built on rumour. Was Tom Enders right to push for this ambitious transaction so early in his time as CEO?

A resounding yes. The Board at its first meeting after we pulled the deal gave him a unanimous vote of confidence, led by the Chairman, Arnaud Lagardere.

I remain absolutely convinced that the merger, on the terms that we had agreed and with the Board line-up that we had settled, would have been good for the shareholders of both companies. Of course, we would have had to go on to obtain US approval, but we believed that we would have been able to achieve this, because we were not going to disturb the BAE-US axis.

Happily, we did not lose the momentum we had built up to reform EADS's corporate governance. The Board recognised all the work our management had done with the French and German Governments, and with the decision made public that Daimler and Lagardere wished to sell down their stakes, the Board agreed that all this work should not be wasted. We asked management to pursue with the Governments the continued normalisation of the company.

This led to another, very significant agreement allowing the free float of the company to rise from 49% to about 75%, with clear independent processes defined for the election of a future Board. The Nominations Committee of the three Independent Directors had to swing into action again. We appointed the head-hunter Egon Zehnder to assist us in the search for new Board members, including a new Chairman.

On paper, this should have been a straightforward journey as the Governments gave up their powerful influence to nominate and select. However, old habits die hard, at least in France! Despite the agreements, there were very pointed articles in French newspapers, which seemed to emanate from the Government, about who should be on our Board and who should be the next Chairman.

We as independent directors remained resolved to build a Board with the right skill-sets and to select an experienced Chairman who knew the industry and who would be compatible with Tom Enders as CEO. We were also determined to ensure that we acted with integrity on behalf both of existing non-Government shareholders and new investors buying in on the increased free float to ensure that our new Board was free from Government interference on appointments in line with published announcements. Tom Enders, as usual, was a tower of strength during this process, having been invited to attend our Nominations Committee. Finally, all the new Non-Executive Directors were in place including a new Chairman – Denis Ranque, the former CEO of the defence and civil electronics group Thales.

An EGM was held on March 27th 2013 when all our nominated Directors were appointed for a three-year period. The Board now comprises an excellent blend of skill-sets and relevant experienced individuals from Germany, France, USA, Spain, India and UK. I was certain that our new Chairman would prove to be a good choice, and this has been the case. We said our farewells to the Daimler-nominated Directors, Bodo Webber and Wilfred Porth, while Arnaud Lagardere stepped down as Chairman along with his CFO Dominique D'hinin. All had made their contributions in a professional way. Tempting as it must have been on occasions, I seldom witnessed them 'promote' a parochial view in the interest of their own companies. Instead, they did what they believed was right for EADS.

The new Board under Denis Ranque's Chairmanship, with Tom Enders as CEO, made a very positive start. The more I work with Tom, the more I am impressed by his leadership, the clarity in his objectives, his integrity – and his charm and toughness when they are required. One of our first actions was to confirm a new dividend policy and share buy-back of up to $3.5 billion. The increased free float and normalisation of the company, along with the continuing super-cycle in civil aircraft demand, helped drive the share price to more than five times what it had been five years earlier.

In late 2014, we announced the decision to rename EADS the Airbus Group and to consolidate into three main business streams:

1. Airbus (Defence and Space) – Military aircraft, Defence Electronics and Equipment and Space – with a turnover of some €15 billion;
2. Eurocopter, renamed Airbus Helicopter;

3. Airbus – the largest business concentrating on passenger aircraft which in 2016 had sales of more than €49 billion. This business now has great products which has led to record Group order books worth close to €1 trillion.

The decision which we took in the Board in 2012 to re-engineer the highly successful A320 family with a more fuel efficient engine and winglets, to be designated A320neo (new engine option), has built this family order book up to some 6000 aircraft by 2018.

The surprise first flight of the new A350 Composite Aircraft at the 2013 Paris Airshow demonstrated not only leading-edge engineering but significant advances in the strength and depth of Airbus Project Management, an area in which the Board has taken a keen and active interest.

This is a Board to which I feel proud to belong, and one where the scale of industrial, engineering and project management challenges is close to my experience base. As I look around the Board and see the collective depth of talent and richness of industrial experience in our NXDs, alongside the quality of our executive team led by Tom Enders, I have no doubt that we should be confident about the future.

However, as in any company the Board cannot be complacent. Aerospace history tells you that the remarkable civil aircraft supercycle will not last for ever. The success of the new Airbus Group in any market conditions will be due to the continued quality of innovative engineering, to the strength of the global teams' project, commercial and compliance management and to the focus on customers and what they require. As in any company, success is driven by the quality of leadership at every level that ensures good communication and secures constant buy-in from the highly-trained employees that are proud to belong to such a world class company. I finally stepped down from the Board of this great company at the AGM in April 2018, after serving for over 11 years.

19. ANGLO AMERICAN

I was parachuted into Anglo American at very short notice in July 2009, after the Board had failed in a process a year earlier to confirm a successor for Sir Mark Moody-Stuart, the chairman and former head of Shell, who was planning to retire. I was approached at that time and I was reasonably interested, but there were divisions on the Board and that appointment didn't take place, so Mark was asked to continue.

I was attracted to mining, partly because of having previously served on the Board of British Coal, but also since it is such a crucial industry for the world economy. Mining matters because civilisation depends on it. Or take one specific which influences countless lives today: how many people know that there are around 70 of the Periodic Table's 118 elements in an iPhone?

Look at two of the commodities of which Anglo American is a major producer: copper and platinum. Around 20 kilograms of copper goes into the average car – and it can be more than double that in a hybrid vehicle. An industrial-sized onshore turbine consumes around four tonnes of the metal, while from fridges to wiring, copper continues to be a major component in the rapid industrialisation and urbanisation of developing countries dependent on the distribution of electricity by copper. As for platinum, autocatalysts that clean up noxious gases in both petrol and diesel engines are by far the biggest market for platinum group metals, with around 95% of new vehicles fitted with them as standard.

In early 2009, the Anglo Board re-started the Chairman search process, and reappointed Spencer Stuart as head-hunter. I was approached again and this time I wasn't really interested – despite my fascination with the industry. After my earlier experience, I had pulled the blinds down on that window and was moving on in life. By now, Anglo had fallen prey to attack from a smaller but more aggressive miner, Xstrata, which had proposed a nil-premium merger of the two companies, an idea which had achieved some traction with a number of Anglo shareholders. At this point, the Board asked me, via Spencer Stuart, to reconsider, and invited me to talk to the NXDs who, I was told, were keen for me to accept. I said: "Okay, I'll talk but I'm not exactly crying out for this job."

Without a doubt, the Board had some divisions. That's always exploited by a predator who wants to take you out. Cynthia Carroll, the CEO, with whom I had a number of useful and valuable conversations, was being criticised in some circles as well, which in their eyes increased the company's vulnerability to Xstrata. Mark said to me: "We don't have many rehearsals for this kind of takeover situation at Shell, so we need to get you on board." I replied: "I don't look for corporate fights, but admittedly I've had to have a number in my life."

The NXDs met me one by one, and really convinced me that I should come across. So I agreed and in mid-July I joined the Board for appointment as Chairman from the beginning of August. Mark immediately asked me to take the chair of our Defence Committee against Xstrata. He was very welcoming and very supportive of me getting on with it.

It was clear that I had to have a major refreshment of the Board. With the divisions, there was a lot of rebuilding to do. So this restructuring became a very important objective, along with getting a strategy in place very quickly which shareholders would buy into.

I sketched out what I thought was the logical strategy to put before shareholders and our new Board after discussion with the Defence

Committee. All clear strategies should fit on an A4 sheet of paper, which we drew up. Anglo had a long tail of assets, and we needed a series of measures to reduce our debt. Getting rid of this tail of smaller and non-core assets was an important part of that. We needed to focus on the key assets.

I used my July run-up to visit a huge number of shareholders – about 35, in the UK, US and South Africa. I showed the UK and SA shareholders the one-sheet diagram I had drawn up about the group's structure and the assets. Then I took the *QM2* to New York in order to read a massive volume of paper to get me updated on the company and industry trends. On landing in New York, I met the US shareholders and took my diagram with me. Long afterwards, when I visited Anglo shareholders, they would still wheel out that one sheet of paper!

David Challen, originally from the investment bank Schroders (subsequently acquired by Citigroup) was on the Board as Chairman of the Audit Committee – he of course had a lot of M&A experience. The Board on my recommendation appointed him SID and a member of the Defence Committee, and in all three positions he did an excellent job. UBS and Goldman Sachs were the company's advisers at the time and supported us against Xstrata. I also brought Nick Wiles, who was now with Nomura, on board as an additional adviser.

South Africa was crucial, and not just because of our large shareholder base there. Of all four of the big mining companies listed in London (BHP Billiton and Rio Tinto were the other two, along with us and Xstrata), Anglo had the largest operations in SA. Different constituencies in SA had been raising issues which we needed to resolve quickly in order to secure our platform for seeing off Xstrata. So I made sure that I was in SA on my very first day as Chairman, August 1.

First, I went to see the South African Mining Minister, Susan Shabangu. She had put forward in public various South African names as possible Chairman before I arrived – none of them being mine!

This had created unnecessary speculation in the media. We had an open exchange and she indicated that the succession had not turned out as she had expected, and I said to her that I could tick most of the boxes for the role but not all of them! We laughed together and parted on good terms.

Then I turned to our senior management there. A number of them were said to be critical of Cynthia – in fact, most of the criticism being levelled at her from SA was coming from Anglo's retired ex-mining people. Very macho remarks were being made which were extremely harsh on her. I was determined to give her "air cover" and stamp this carping out.

So after seeing the minister in Pretoria, I went down to our head office in Johannesburg for a buffet lunch with the senior management. I had no speech prepared – I just spoke off the cuff. I said that I was honoured to be the new chairman of Anglo. "I'm sure a number of you are looking over your shoulders at Xstrata's tanks on our lawn," I told them. "That's not your problem – that's for the Board and me to deal with and we will."

"Secondly, your job as senior management is to devote your efforts to improving our performance – that should be your focus. But some of you don't seem to devote all of your time to that – you seem to spend part of your time criticising the CEO and undermining her. That can now stop. I am backing the CEO. There will be no change unless there is a failure to perform – which I am not contemplating." Almost immediately, the noise level died down both in the company and in the media. Numerous senior managers thanked me for clearing the air, because people like to know where they stand in situations such as this. Hence the importance of the leader grasping the nettle.

Then we really had to rally shareholder support. If you are going to drive someone's tanks of your corporate lawn, you can't do it without strong shareholder support, which we secured. Xstrata withdrew and was subsequently taken over by Glencore, the commodities trading giant that owned a large minority stake in Xstrata.

Now we were able to continue with implementing our strategy.

We had a major reorganisation that took quite a number of people out, simplified the structure somewhat. We sold non-core assets; took more cost out of the business – albeit nothing like what we had to do between 2014 and 2016.

The focus then became very much on rebuilding the Board. You never know a company until you are inside and Anglo was no exception. I attended one Board meeting before I took over, which gave me a lot of signals on behaviours. There were one or two NXDs with aggressive attitudes on display, which is not really what boardrooms should be made of. By all means, forthright debate, strong debate – but there is no place for aggressive attitudes to management. If that's the case, there is something fundamentally wrong on one side or the other. If a Board gets destabilised, and I think the Board had got destabilised, the company becomes vulnerable. That contributed to what was happening at Anglo.

Sir Mark Moody-Stuart is a very fine and honourable man; indeed, he has subsequently written a book on responsible management which is a real textbook on a crucial topic. I think that he had a few difficult NXDs. He had very much backed Cynthia and had some divisions in the ranks as a result. There were tensions in the boardroom and that was all part and parcel of the situation.

The Board had quite glaring expertise gaps. It was clear, for instance, that we needed urgently to find someone who was a miner – there was no mining engineer with extensive experience in the industry on the Board at all, either at executive or non-executive levels. Cynthia was the closest – she was a geologist with zinc mining experience. So I found Jack Thomson from the US. He had a fine record in mining, had been in the industry all his life. He has been a great success and today chairs Anglo's Sustainability committee. Then came Sir Philip Hampton, who I knew from my days at BG and, way back, from British Steel. He was probably the country's leading finance director having been at Steel, BG, BT and Lloyds Bank. Later, of course, he became chairman of Sainsbury, RBS and now GlaxoSmithKline. He is an outstanding individual with no airs or graces. He cuts to the chase and is a statesman in a crisis. He is very shockproof and has outstanding business judgment.

We also needed to have someone who had extensive experience of large projects and modern project management. I had recently go to know Ray O'Rourke, the Irish founder of the international contracting business Laing O'Rourke, having met him for the first time at an international rugby match. I discovered we had very similar views on business, project management and how to go about things.

Ray was in my view by far the most forward thinking contractor in the UK. He was heavily committed to new technology and digital engineering. He had a vision as to where to take the business to improve productivity and quality for clients. He invited me to visit his huge new factory, to manufacture off site modules, at Steetley. No other contractor in Britain , then or since , has such an advanced facility. LOR also had a strong reputation for modern project, safety and environmental management. They had provided the core project management team for the London Olympics project. However despite the strong alignment with skills and experience we needed, I had great difficulty convincing Ray to allow his name to go forward as a prospective NXD.

Then I sent Ray a copy of the Anglo annual report and said, please at least scan it as I think you will be intrigued by the industry. Next day he called me and said: "What would a Paddy from Ireland be doing amongst all those fellows with PhDs?" I said: "I'm not looking for PhDs – I'm looking for someone who has experience globally of running big construction sites with itinerant workforces in remote areas. You have that from the Middle East, Hong Kong, Australia and you've just finished Terminal 5 at Heathrow." These were huge projects and great successes in terms of delivery on time and budget. Finally, I persuaded him to have a talk with David Kimble of Spencer Stuart, following which Ray eventually agreed to meet the NXDs who all then called me and said: "You must get him".

He was an outstanding success as an NXD, bringing to the Board his wide business expertise in all aspects of modern management of major projects. Above all, as a successful international businessman, he automatically won the respect of management, and being a great and magnanimous human being, he built excellent relationships with every Board member.

Companies get into trouble when the Board and the very top management don't have a feel for the industry, for its risk profile. My father used to have a saying: "You must be capable of smelling sulphur in the air." You need to be able to sniff things out and you can only do that if you have relevant experience. For a mining group, major projects are one of the biggest sources of risk. Ray gave the Board increased capability to assess and understand all that with his frank assessments and challenges.

These first three NXD recruits created the core of change in Board performance and culture.

Over the next two years further new NXD appointments were made to address diversity, including ethnic diversity, and we built out the range of our skill sets.

At Ray's final Anglo Board dinner, when we said our farewells, one of our excellent new NXDs, Dr Anne Stevens, an engineer and the former COO of Ford Motor Company in the Americas, tabled a list of 10 things she would miss and find irreplaceable with Ray leaving the Board: "Knowledge, experience, insight, perspective, execution, oversight, only overshadowed by your caring, friendship, humour, and ability to have time to love your sport and a drink!"

At Anglo, I endeavoured to bring my philosophy of Board composition. I believe that you've got to build out a Board with a broad-based range of skill-sets and diversity –but a number of them have to have domain knowledge and experience relevant to the business itself. I always feel that you should have someone in the boardroom who can deal with almost any issue that walks through the boardroom door – that's terribly important.

Apart from the identification and sale of non-core businesses, our strategy included cost and debt reduction to strengthen both the P&L account and the balance sheet. We sought to improve management of large projects which we adjudged to be core. Importantly, we also decided to buy out minority interests in those majority-owned assets which we judged to be core with good growth potential – "Tidy the Minorities" as we termed this element. We debated this objective at the Board's strategy days in 2010 and 2011, scrutinising the long-term growth and earnings prospects of these businesses.

De Beers

The assets included the world's largest diamond company – De Beers, where Anglo owned 45% and the Oppenheimer family (Nicky's grandfather Sir Ernest Oppenheimer had founded Anglo in 1917) owned 40%.

De Beers had rarity value and growth potential. No new diamond mine of scale had been discovered for some 15 years, and China and other Asian emerging countries had the potential over time to take over from the US as the largest market for diamonds. So we decided that, if the opportunity presented itself at the right price, we would be tempted to buy out the Oppenheimer family interest.

We recognised that the obstacles were high, given the family's strong commitment to the business. However, if this could be achieved, it would take our ownership to 85% with the Government of Botswana owning the remaining 15%. The timing was also attractive given that De Beers had concluded a new 10-year supply agreement with the Government of Botswana.

In the depths of the financial crisis, post-Lehman Brothers' collapse, the diamond industry, like so many others, was under enormous commercial pressure – so much so that the Anglo Board agreed to lend De Beers $500m at the end of 2008. In the autumn of 2009, had Anglo then possessed the surplus cash firepower, we might well have been able to secure a particularly favourable deal for the Oppenheimer interest.

Towards the peak of a cycle, mining companies have loads of cash burning a hole in their pocket. This leads on occasions to their squandering the money on high-cost assets or long-dated project options. Equally, they often have inadequate liquidity at the trough of a cycle when bargains could be had. The parallels with that other great cyclical industry of shipping, which I know well, are uncanny. In autumn 2009, Anglo was closer to the cyclical trough than the peak.

However this was in any case hypothetical analysis, as the Oppenheimer family led by Nicky Oppenheimer remained a member of the Anglo Board and was very committed to diamonds. He served as Chairman of De Beers for 14 years.

I got to know Nicky initially through our fight against Xstrata. As Defence Committee Chairman, I needed to ensure alignment against the Xstrata proposal amongst our Non-Executive Directors, including Nicky. In this process, he and I had a somewhat shaky start to our relationship but I believe we both grew to have mutual respect for each other. I certainly came to have a high regard for his integrity and his commitment to De Beers.

In relation to De Beers, we satisfied ourselves as a Board on its good medium-term prospects and prospective returns. Given that a new De Beers-Botswana supply agreement had been concluded, the Board decided that we should open discussions with the Oppenheimer family. Cynthia Carroll was of the view that, since I had built a good relationship with Nicky, I should explore with him if there was a willingness to sell the family stake to Anglo American.

To maintain absolute privacy, Nicky and I met in my office at National Grid. We concluded at our first meeting that, at the right price and terms, the family might be open to a sale. We also agreed that if it was to be done, we should not work through respective advisors. Rather we should negotiate together 1:1. This we did over some six-eight weeks in complete secrecy as only the Board, Cynthia and a few executives knew our meetings were taking place.

Inevitably, there were some 'wobbles' during these weeks as this was far from an easy decision – particularly for Nicky personally given the family's long-standing involvement in De Beers, which dated back 80 years. Ultimately, we reached agreement for Anglo to buy the family's

40% interest for $5.1 billion in cash. Our business development team led by Peter Whitcutt, with the involvement of Rene Medori, Finance Director, prepared a detailed letter with me setting out the deal, which superseded an earlier proposal for a paper-and-cash acquisition, and the other matters to be dealt with. These included due diligence, Competition clearances with various Authorities and shareholder approval including, importantly, the Government of Botswana via an EGM. The Oppenheimer family formally approved the proposal at a family gathering in Ireland and we proceeded to clear the various subjects. The EGM Shareholder vote held in early 2012 was overwhelmingly in support of the transaction with 99.9% in favour.

Throughout this process, the personal relationship between Nicky and me was crucial. That Chinese proverb – "First make friends, then do business" – was never more relevant than in this situation. I trusted Nicky and I hope and believe that, having seen me in action in our boardroom and in private discussion, I gave him no reason to doubt my commitment to Anglo or my integrity.

Nicky also knew De Beers would have a natural home within Anglo, and this meant the decision for him to relinquish the stake was made at a slightly lower pain threshold than would otherwise have been the case. He is a private man and, despite his significant wealth, lives a relatively modest lifestyle amongst his peer group. He is focussed on family, including having a close and understandably special relationship with his son Jonathan.

When Nicky stepped down from the Board of Anglo at the 2011 AGM, after 35 years in various roles, we laid on a special Board farewell in a marquee with red carpet laid on the famous lawn at Vergelegen in Somerset West, which is owned by Anglo. This was only my second visit to Vergelegen – an Eco-estate situated in the Western Cape near Cape Town. The estate, with its Old Dutch Cape-style home, dates back to 1700 when it was settled by Willem Adriaan van der Stel, who worked for the Dutch East India Company and became a Governor of the Cape.

Vergelegen's history as a wine producer began in 1798, when

the estate was sold to the Theunissen family who planted extensive vineyards. The estate flourished for almost a century, until a pest infestation in the late 19th century wiped out most of the grapes. Apart from a limited and temporary revival of wine production in the mid-20th century by a later owner, Charles "Punch" Barlow, no grapes were cultivated there until Anglo American bought the estate from Barlow's son in 1987.

Anglo restored Vergelegen as a vineyard, concentrating on the production of high-quality wines. The first vintage under Anglo was harvested in 1992, and within 10 years the estate was recognised as one of South Africa's finest vineyards.

The 107-hectare estate is open to the public daily and many historical significant events have been held there. It was here that Nelson Mandela held his first ANC Caucus meeting in May 1990 after his release from Robben Island. It was on the lawn that Elton John had his major AIDS concert in January 2005. HM The Queen and Prince Philip have stayed there.

The estate is managed by the enthusiastic Don Tooth who cares deeply for its well-being. It has an excellent vineyard and a world-class wine maker in Andre Van Rensburg. The winery sits at the top of the hill within the estate and wine-making cellars are located underground. Vergelegen produces 50,000-60,000 cases per annum and is increasingly available in a number of markets including the UK. The grape varieties are Cabernet Sauvignon, Chardonnay, Sauvignon Blanc, Merlot and Cabernet Franc.

The wine maker is determined to produce the world's leading wine and has Chateau Lafitte in his sights! In a blind tasting led by the wine critic Jancis Robinson several years ago in Davos, Vergelegen's top estate blend from 2001 was tasted against some of the leading French growths, including Chateau Latour, and two Napa Valley cult wines including Screaming Eagle. Vergelegen outperformed the line-up and ended as the top-scoring wine. So who knows? Vergelegen could be a real winner within the Anglo American portfolio.

For Nicky's farewell dinner, we had many distinguished South

African guests present including Finance Minister Pravin Gordhan on my left with Mrs Oppenheimer on my right. I had not met Mrs Oppenheimer before but we engaged in memorable conversation. Nicky gave an extensive and well-crafted speech on Anglo's history and his family involvement in South Africa. A printed edition of the speech was available for each guest to take away in booklet form. It was a fitting way to mark the ending of an era in Anglo's history.

Major corporate transactions

I've been fortunate to have been involved with Board colleagues, in many varied major corporate transactions during my industrial journey - either in the lead or in a supportive role. Apart from the De Beers acquisition, these include:

As Chairman:
- Sale of Harland & Wolff majority shareholding to Fred Olsen (Norway) as the company transferred from Government to private ownership.
- Babcock International acquisitions of Rosyth Dockyard in Scotland and Eagleton Pipeline Engineering in Houston.
- Sale of Firth Rixson Group plc to Carlyle
- £3.3bn sale of P&O Group plc to Dubai World
- £2.3bn sale of RMC Group plc to CEMEX of Mexico
- £14.8bn merger of Lattice Group plc (incl TRANSCO) with National Grid plc
- £5.8bn sale of four National Grid distribution networks
- $7.3bn National Grid PLC acquisition of Keyspan Utility (US).

As Deputy Chairman:
- £3.5bn acquisition of P&O, Princess and Aida Cruises in Dual-Listed Company by Carnival Corporation

- $4.96bn DPWorld partial IPO in Dubai
- $5.3bn DP World acquisition of Freezone World.

As a Non-Executive Director:
- GKN acquisition of Westland Helicopters
- GKN merger of its industrial services business with Brambles of Australia
- GKN merger of Westland with Finmeccanica.

A number of these large transactions – like De Beers – had special features. But there are also some common principles and perhaps the most important, whether the transaction is large or small, is that building of trust as a negotiator with your counterpart, be they buyer or seller, is a criticality. That and preparing around key shareholder value issues are the basic ingredients for positive out-turns. However, having done this important groundwork, Boards have above all to be convinced of the industrial logic of a merger or a major acquisition and furthermore make important judgements on compatibility of cultures. The absence of either has the potential to massively destroy value despite what the spreadsheet output might lead you to believe.

In the case of an acquisition, key elements for success include the establishment of a talented in house composite skills team, drawn from strategy, finance and operational management, alongside a group of trusted advisers. They need rigorously to evaluate all aspects of risks and synergies around the deal and put their analysis to the Board. The Board, with a broad-based skill-set, should then be in a position to stress test the team's analysis and, in particular, the assumptions behind their valuation. I cannot over-emphasise the importance of such a thorough process: few things can undermine a company more fundamentally than a major acquisition that goes wrong; and by the same token a successful acquisition and high-quality management that may come with it can benefit a company for many years.

In a number of these corporate transactions, Alan Parker (now Sir Alan), as Chairman of Brunswick, would be on the Advisory team to give the lead on corporate communications and financial P.R. In some, Andrew Lorenz, the Editor of this book, now of FTI Consulting, would have been advising. Sir Alan has built Brunswick up from scratch to a global consultancy which is a great personal achievement.

The corporate years – building the team to compete

In my early time at Anglo, my most important day-to-day relationship was of course with Cynthia Carroll. Cynthia had many great strengths. She was excellent with Governments, she was a good communicator with her people and very respectful of them. She was the closest to a specialist mining CEO that Anglo had had in its history, in that she was a geologist and had run a zinc mining operation in Ireland. She put a huge effort into safety, which needed it. She was very courageous about that – we had big problems in one of the platinum mines in SA. She went there and shut it down for the whole day to focus the people on safety management.

Anglo wasn't the easiest company for anyone to come into from outside as CEO, and it was particularly challenging for a woman. Particularly with the macho comments and attitudes at the outset, which were completely offside and which I was not prepared to tolerate.

Cynthia, like a number of CEOs, did not get on with all the shareholders all of the time: she came under criticism from some without a doubt. But at the end of the day, you have to look at what someone is doing inside the company: a lot of very positive things were being done. From the trough of earnings in 2009 after the Lehman crisis, in 2011 we had record earnings before interest and tax (EBIT) of $11.2 billion, supported by a significant recovery in commodity prices.

As NXDs, we had also been debating succession planning because in 2012/13, Cynthia was coming up for six years as CEO. I had talked with her about the lifespan of a modern CEO. We had put a comprehensive process in place of assessing the readiness of internal management to take on the role, but we recognised through the succession planning work that it was unlikely we would have an internal successor ready to take over in the next year or two. Indeed, we had a strong reminder of the vulnerability of a CEO in that one day Cynthia fell off her horse and broke her thigh bone, but she was in work again almost right away – we could hardly believe it. She had great commitment and high energy levels.

Finally Cynthia reached a decision to leave and the time was right for the change in CEO to take place. So in October 2012 we announced that Cynthia had decided to step down, but that she would remain until her successor was appointed. On succession, when you realise that you are unlikely to have someone internally and you have to look outside, it is better to have a silent research project running with a head-hunter to identify who is out there and when they might be available, and to work out how close they would come to fit the criteria that you and the NXDs have discussed. This is what we had put in place and were able to start interviews for a shortlist right away.

The Board had a very clear focus on what we needed – that led us by January 2013 to be in a position to announce Mark Cutifani, who was CEO of the South African gold-mining group Anglo Gold Ashanti. Mark came to us in April 2013.

We were in that part of the cycle where we needed an experienced operational miner – it was clear, for instance, that the operations and engineering had to be strengthened. Mark brought massive experience in this regard – he had been in the mining industry since he was 18 having put himself through university by working in a coal mine in Australia. He was a global mining citizen – born in Woolagong of an Irish mother and an Italian father, he had experience on all six continents and had mined around 30 commodities – the only one he didn't have first-hand experience with was diamonds. He was a great fit and there was no question that he was the right person for the job, especially with the drastic drop in commodity prices starting in 2013, but reaching its full frenzy in 2015. In 2014, $2.4 billion was wiped off our Earnings Before Interest, Taxation, Depreciation and Amortisation (EBITDA) and these two digits were reversed in

2015 when $4.2 billion disappeared. We had therefore to deal with a $6.6 billion fall in EBITDA through price erosion over two years.

Mark is a very good communicator with tremendous respect from the mining community, so no-one was going to pull the wool over his eyes. On his first day, I introduced him via a conference call to all our senior people around the world. After joking to them about being brought up in Woolagong – "the intellectual capital of Australia" – he said: "I'll get around to see you all in short order, but I'd like you to send me a three-line email at the end of each week to tell me what you've done this week compared to what you were expected to do. Then we'll have the luxury of the weekend to have a conversation about it." That was a huge wake-up call. He sharpened people up very fast. Within a matter of a couple of months, we saw productivity lifting.

Mark joined us just when the tectonic plates of the industry were shifting fundamentally. China, which had been the great engine of the sector's extraordinary super-boom, had started to soften in 2012 but really began to slow down in 2013. Several of the big industries that I have experience of – shipping cement, paper and mining – are all volatile in terms of demand. Supply and demand is a fickle thing: it doesn't need to be out of balance too much to cause a very rapid rise or fall in price.

These industries are all global. So all are at the mercy of the world economy and all are at the mercy of the development of economies. Many mining commodities are very much related to infrastructure development, as is cement. Large parts of shipping are similarly influenced, because it's transporting these bulk commodities around the world. So the industrial health of the world is very linked in to all of these commodities. There are strong correlations between economic activity, global investment trends and the demand for mining commodities.

The industries are also highly capital-intensive. Of Anglo's big projects, the largest and most problematic was our multi-billion dollar iron ore development at Minas Rio in the State of Minas Geras in Brazil. Anglo had embarked on expanding its iron ore production, and on Minas Rio, for this reason: the iron ore market was booming in the mid-2000s because of China's breakneck industrial growth and Anglo's global peers – BHP, Rio Tinto and Vale of Brazil – had a much larger market presence. In fact, Anglo was a relative also-ran in iron ore. Shareholders and analysts were pressing Anglo to expand in iron ore, and the upshot was that the Board bought 49% of Minas Rio in April 2007.

A year later, Anglo took 100% control by buying out the Brazilian entrepreneur IK Batista. By then, the mine was supposed to have been largely mapped out and engineered: in reality, this proved not to be the case. Moreover, the transactions were executed at the height of the commodities boom: within six months of Anglo acquiring full ownership, the collapse of Lehman Brothers triggered the global financial crisis.

Minas Rio was a vast engineering project. So large, in fact, that I was quite keen in the very early days of my chairmanship to sell down part of the project in order to lay off some of our risk. But the Board at that time was not supportive because a number of the directors who had committed the company to the programme believed it was such a good asset, and that we therefore must retain our 100%. I used the months immediately after taking the chair to visit most of our major assets, including Minas Rio. Nothing I saw in Brazil changed my view that we might have bitten off more than we could easily digest.

Here was this massive mine with engineering, legal permitting, land acquisition and environmental challenges on a huge scale. The ore had to be pumped in slurry form via 525 kilometres of pipeline over mountains and through mountain tunnels to a brand new port that had yet to be built, where de-watering had to take place. The costs were astronomical: the company had paid a total of $5.1 billion for its 100% stake; the forecast out-turn development cost was then believed to be $3.6 billion, but the final out-turn in Q4 2014 was just over $8 billion.

Doing business in Brazil was not easy: many of the cost overruns were due to planning sanctions and permissions being delayed for months on end. Extortionate efforts were made by landowners along the length of the pipeline to extract the maximum price. There were occasions where plans and permitting were agreed and suddenly rescinded. The main power line to the site was delayed ultimately for several months by such interventions, even after it had been approved.

Costs continued to spiral through the period. The first ore-on-ship date was put back on several occasions. Eventually, in 2012, the NXDs decided to initiate an independent assessment of the project's timescale and cost following the appointment of a new CEO of Iron Ore Brazil, Paolo Costelho, who was to make a very good contribution to bringing it under control.

Ray O'Rourke lent us three key people from his project management team that had delivered the highly successful London Olympics, headed by a very able man called Barry Dye. Barry came to the Board after three weeks working in Brazil with Paolo and a number of his new management team, some of whom were brought in from the Brazilian mining group Vale. Barry presented a slide pack to the Board and without looking at a note, gave the Board a comprehensive rundown and predicted that Minas Rio was capable of delivering the first ore-on-ship in Q4 2014, which it did, and that the cost out-turn would be around $8 billion, although he recommended a contingency of $500m-$600m. This was fresh eyes and very impressive. The actual out-turn was indeed about $8.1 billion, with first ore-on-ship in October 2014.

Minas Rio was just one of Mark's many challenges as the super-upcycle turned down with a vengeance. He first restructured his team – quite a number of people left. He reduced the number of direct reports significantly, both at his level and the next level down. He moved a number of executives around and brought in Tony O'Neill as Chief Technical Officer with responsibility for engineering, safety, exploration and technical development.

I had felt for some time that we had let our engineering go somewhat. It didn't have the dominance inside the organisation that it clearly once had and we needed to get that back. Tony, who is Australian, has massive experience. He rebuilt the engineering team, hiring several top class senior people from around the world. As well as reducing the team in size from about 1,200 to 800, he uplifted the quality and streamlined the processes.

The biggest question for Anglo was to decide what core assets we should focus the future on. Mark worked hard on that strategy with many Board discussions during 2014/5. We formed a clear view at our mid-2015 Strategy Day that the core businesses were copper, diamonds, a reduced scale of platinum concentrating on higher productive assets, plus metallurgical coal, nickel, and iron ore. One of the biggest challenges we had was the platinum deep mines at Rustenburg, which were at the original historic heart of Anglo's South African operations. We decided to exit those because they were higher up the cost curve and we believed local miners should be able to operate on a more efficient basis than we could, so we sold them to Sibanye, a local gold company. That reduced our employment numbers in platinum by about 17,000 and that sale was completed in 2016.

Our core strategy was to concentrate on Tier One assets while ultimately reducing the overall numbers employed in the group, including our key contractors, from about 150,000 to 98,000. Not all were direct job cuts – some would be the result of disposals like the deep platinum mines. We also decided to shed two smaller, higher-cost copper mines in Chile.

The key criterion was that Tier One assets should all be capable of keeping a competitive position on the cost curve, enabling us ultimately to lift our gross margin by about 10% simply by exiting the lower-performing businesses.

It was also a case of managing the balance sheet extremely carefully – we reckoned that $10-12 billion of debt was probably around the level that a company transformed along core asset lines should have been able to sustain. We were helped by the fact that we had kept the balance sheet in a reasonably stable debt position at a debt level of $12.9 billion during 2014 and 2015.

The task then was to watch the developing situation closely at every single Board meeting and take a very prudent view – not allowing any hockey stick forecasts to enter the boardroom. We also took a very prudent view of spot prices.

We managed that for a period after Mark announced our Tier One strategy, but then the industry turbulence intensified to a quite remarkable and unprecedented level, particularly during 2015. In total, the slump in prices in 2014 and 2015 across our basket of commodities wiped a cumulative $6.6 billion from our EBITDA. Of that figure, close on $1.5 billion alone came in the last two months of 2015, just as the Board were about to approve the budget for 2016. However, throughout this time it was clear that we had a very good grip on the business operationally, with an excellent management team across the world starting to apply Mark's operating model more consistently.

At our December 2015 Board, we realised that we would have to yet again revisit our strategy in order to reduce debt further to counter the commodity price falls, and to create positive cash flow opportunities. We had to have this in position with full Board approval for our 2015 Full Year Results day in early February 2016.

During this period and into 2016, we began to see huge volatility in the share price. This was a reflection of massive hedge fund activity, known as "churn", as mining stocks were driven down one day and up the next. Mark and I kept in close contact with the longer-term shareholders. No-one said: "We don't agree with your strategy." In a situation like this, with fundamental change under way in the industry and the share price under pressure as a result, the first requirement is to get investors aligned with the strategy. The second is to convince them that you have the wherewithal to see it through.

To support management in making the urgent decisions they would need, the Board agreed my proposal that we form a sub-committee of three NXDs plus myself to meet every 10 days or so with Mark and his team to debate options and reach agreement. The three NXDs included Sir Philip Hampton, Jim Rutherford a very analytical former mining investor who had recently joined the Board and Byron Grote, the very seasoned and highly-competent ex-CFO of BP who had much corporate restructuring experience. We had recruited Byron back in 2012 as our Audit Committee chair, and he has contributed massively in that role and on the wider NXD issues. My role when decisions were made was to reach out to the rest of the Board to ascertain if members were supportive and aligned.

By the time of our scheduled Board in early February 2016 to approve our results presentations, the Board was totally aligned on the announcement of our new strategy and cash targets.

During the 2015 downturn, Glencore and Anglo's share price falls were the worst in the FTSE 100 index. There was much speculation that we would need a Rights Issue and the Hedge Funds were having a field day driving the price down. I cannot see the "Value Add" to society – as distinct from the value to some individuals – of this roulette short-term type of activity.

I am glad to say that, following the announcement of our new strategy, Anglo shares by the end of 2016 had risen almost 500% from their nadir in January – making us the highest performer of the year, not just in the mining sector but in the FTSE 100! I didn't shed any tears for the hedge funds that subsequently lost a great deal of money against our fast-rising share price! While it can be tempting for company leaders to think about "proudest achievements", I tend simply to focus with a Board and CEO on getting the right strategic response in place and ensuring that the CEO has the resources to get the job done. But some milestones do stand out and our recovery during 2016 is certainly one of them.

However markets react, constant care and attention by a Board in any company, especially in a cyclical industry such as mining, is an ongoing and essential discipline. Never throw your hat in the air for long when success comes your way. Equally, when things turn down, leaders cannot hang around like a rabbit caught in the headlights.

Early moves to evaluate the best course of corrective action have to be a natural way of life. In our case, Mark Cutifani as a leader, with his team, rolled up their sleeves and regardless of the bow waves breaking, didn't let go of the wheel. They decided with the Board's backing on course adjustments and, whatever the storm, have been steering the ship through it.

It's when you have a professional team working in a committed way, such as this, that success will be delivered. After many years of observing and driving through crisis actions in a number of industries, when I read some of the trite, sensationalised business media commentaries or listen to the dictates of young City analysts on what you should do, I realise that unless you have been in the furnace, you don't have much of a clue about the intensity of corporate heat or how to turn it down!

We also put an immense effort into sustaining and building our corporate reputation. As I've said earlier, Reputation is crucial to any company in any industry – and it is absolutely critical that it should be at the heart of every mining company's social licence to operate. Even in the midst of the mining crisis, the Board and Audit Committees took time out to review and revise our Code of Conduct, putting it into a communication-friendly form.

Unfortunately, the extractives industry has a poor image in many quarters. In a recent survey, covering more than 100 countries, the International Council on Mining and Metals (ICMM) found that less than one-third of stakeholders trusted the industry to act in the best interest of society, and only a quarter positively perceived the mining industry's progress towards sustainable development.

What we realised at Anglo was the importance of speaking with a consistent and aligned voice to all constituencies. We also acknowledged that we had first to influence our reputation from the inside, looking outwards. We therefore determined to move away from the top-down paternalism so characteristic of the "traditional" mining industry and engage with all our employees by really listening to their concerns – so that they would completely buy into the organisation and become our front-line advocates, living out our values.

Externally, in relation to the communities and countries where we operate, we moved away from the traditional contractual approach to one which emphasises the negotiation of our social licence to operate.

To support this fundamental change, Mark and his management both devised new, and built upon several earlier initiatives – local procurement to boost economic growth in our communities; an upgraded Socio-Economic Assessment Toolbox (SEAT) to improve our understanding and management of the social impact of our operations; FutureSmart, a forum for bringing together different stakeholders to solve major technical challenges; and "faith group" dialogue with the Roman Catholic and Methodist churches whose leaders are often at the heart of the local communities where we operate. Above all, a Corporate's reputation rests on how successfully we build trust by narrowing the gap between what we do and what we say we do.

The least-discussed plan for succession is that for the Chairman. For me, the timing for departure is driven by the need to leave well ahead of anyone on the Board considering that you should – there should be no visits from men in grey suits to tap you on the shoulder and tell you that your time is up! One over-riding factor is to ensure that you leave at a time that allows your successor to get well bedded into the company before the next CEO has to be chosen. Following this principle leads to the best-planned successions. Equally, you cannot leave if a large transaction has just been completed or if there is clearly a need for major restructuring of the company. Continuity in times like that is often critical in leading the Board.

In Anglo's case, in our revised strategy of February 2016 we had set a target for the 2016 year to bring down Net Debt to $10 billion through cost reduction, cash savings and further improvements in performance. As one of our directors put it: our net debt of $12.9 billion at the end of 2015 was about the total cost of Minas Rio. The outcome for 2016 was net debt of $8.5 billion with all cost reductions achieved. As a result, net debt was down to 1.4 times EBITDA.

Furthermore, a range of assets which we had declared ourselves willing to sell to solve the debt issue – not knowing at that time which would fetch real value – now did not need to be sold. We placed all our bulk assets – iron ore, coal and manganese – in one grouping to focus on their performance. This group was led by Seamus French, an Irish chemical engineer, who had done a great job for us in Australia. We had conquered the balance sheet stress, achieved excellent operating performance, demonstrated our resilience, established competitive cost positions across the majority of our commodities and placed the company in a secure position. We had a strong management team in place, led by Mark Cutifani with a very experienced Board.

Therefore, as we approached 2017, during which I was going to complete my eighth year as Chairman, I indicated to Sir Philip Hampton, our Senior NXD that I felt my successor should be appointed in the course of the year. The Board made a strong appeal to me to stay on. However, I felt the time was right to seek a new Chairman and I pointed out that Mark would have completed close on five years as CEO by the time the new Chairman arrived.

Sir Philip, as Senior NXD, and the Nominations Committee Chairman led the search with Julia Budd of the head-hunter Zygos, and in mid-June 2017 the Board selected Stuart Chambers, a chemical engineer and former Chairman of the packaging company Rexam and of ARM, the semi-conductor business. I wish Stuart, who has extensive boardroom and international experience, all success in leading the Anglo American Board.

The selection was achieved in a very professional and timely manner, and was noted by the market as an orderly process completed within a shorter timescale than that achieved by the other large miners, BHP and Rio. They had both made earlier announcements than Anglo of their intention to change Chairman, but had not announced successors by the time we made our decision.

During 2017 the Indian billionaire, Anil Agarwal, Chairman of Vedanta Resources, the mining group, built a c.20% stake in Anglo American through his family investment company. This was achieved via a mandatory exchangeable bond engineered by JP Morgan. It involves paying a rent to hedge funds and other investors who lend stock over a 3 year period, during which voting rights are secured by the Family investment company, but all dividends go to the hedge funds and investors.

At the end of 3 years Anil has two options: he can return the shares to the original shareholders or pay cash to own them outright.

A 20% stake in Anglo today would be worth around $5.7 billion.

As a Board we agreed that despite the unusual option structure of ownership he would be treated and communicated with as any other shareholder.

I got to know Anil a few years ago and he has lived part time in London for some 20 years and has contributed to a number of worthy causes in the UK. He has a sharp strategic mind and is quite an Anglophile. I admire him for his decision to donate a large proportion of his wealth to future charitable work in India and South Africa.

The year 2017 was also the 100th Anniversary of the founding of Anglo American by Sir Ernest Oppenheimer. The Board was keen that I should lead our celebratory dinners to mark the Centenary in September at Vergelegen, London and in Chile. I would then hand over to Stuart from 1 November.

Chairing Anglo was a tough assignment – one of the toughest I've experienced. However, it was a special privilege to serve as Chairman of such a great company with its deeply embedded values of respect and decency. It was also pleasing to leave Anglo with a strong Board and great executive leadership. Having emerged from the crisis years with a resilient balance sheet and a highly competitive portfolio of excellent assets, the company is now well-placed to build a good future for our shareholders and indeed all our stakeholders.

It was particularly pleasing to read the 2017 financial results achieved or improved on key targets we had set. EBITDA increased by a further 45% and net debt reduced by 47% relative to 2016. Net debt to EBITDA was now a very conservative 0.5. The significant improvement in operating performance that Mark Cutifani has achieved with Tony O'Neill and his management team speaks for the calibre of the leadership. From Mark's appointment in 2013, productivity across the Group has risen 80% with a 26% reduction in unit costs. Mark is a remarkable professional leader who has stamped his authority on the Group.

Laing O'Rourke – Private company journey

After I announced my intention to step down from Anglo during 2017, Ray O'Rourke approached me to ascertain if I would join Laing O'Rourke as Chairman. His brother Des, as the other shareholder, also supported the approach. Ray had re-taken over the CEO role prior to leaving the Anglo Board and wanted to have an independent Chairman. I readily agreed to chair my first privately owned company of that scale and did so on stepping down from Anglo in November 2017.

After serving on the Anglo Board, Ray had got to know me well in my role as Chairman and I had got to appreciate his integrity and his creative management and leadership style. So we didn't expect too many surprises as I embarked on my journey. The journey is now under way, meeting clients, getting to know key executives, meeting the academics at Cambridge University where Ray has established close links, as he has with the Imperial College London and Oxford University Engineering departments.

There was a range of reasons why I was attracted to join Laing O'Rourke, apart from wanting to continue an association with Ray. Without doubt, the group with their heavy investment in digital engineering and their huge module manufacturing facility in Steetley are setting the agenda for a leading 21st century construction company.

Laing O'Rourke is focussed on Ray's version of "70/60/30" where:

- 70% is the target value of a project to be factory-built, providing increased accuracy and quality. In addition, workload is displaced from, for example, a London site to the Midlands.
- 60% represents the reduction in on-site resources with all the attendant benefits of fewer people on site and reductions in parking and transport adjacent to site.
- 30% represents the overall build reduction time. A recent example where the approach has been applied is "251" – a 44-storey residential tower in Southwark, London which

was completed in 2018. This has demonstrated the reality of 70/60/30.

The digital engineering and modular construction approach is hugely attractive, given its transformational power to increase the productivity of the industry. Ray has plans to take this forward via a 95/80/60 approach by introducing greater robotics and jigging et cetera in a factory, closer to the approach being pursued by the car industry. This concept can be applied to the factory production of attractive housing and apartments, enabling a home to be erected, fully outfitted, within 24 hours on a prepared site.

As in most businesses, the key is high-quality, well-qualified people who have the ability to lead teams and departments and manage major projects. Employment in the Group's operations in the UK, Australia and the Middle East is around 15,000 people. The recruitment of high-performing graduate engineers and other disciplines enter into the company's development program known as "The Guns" with the potential to progress from the entry point of a Young Gun to a Gun after about five years. This is via internal and external further education and job experience with high-flyers later progressing to Big Guns benefitting from great leadership development programmes and well equipped to take on senior roles in the company. This development programme which far outshines many FTSE 100 companies produces outstanding professionals who remain exceptionally loyal and committed to the company.

Ray and the Board have set out a clear strategy to 2025, driving new levels of productivity and client involvement to maximise modular build capability, speed of build and quality of delivery. I am looking forward to being part of this innovative company, creating industry transformation.

20. VOLUNTARY ENGAGEMENTS

There are few more satisfying things in life than to serve your fellow man and hopefully add value to the life of an individual, organisation, a community or indeed wider society.

Young Offenders into Work

I cannot think of any role that I found more rewarding than the 10-year stint of chairing and rolling out nationally the 'Young Offenders into Work' initiative. I could not have done it without the support of the Board of National Grid and Dr Mary Harris as the scheme's Director, or the commitment of a group of managers in National Grid and a raft of CEOs from a range of companies who joined in with enthusiasm for what we were endeavouring to do.

The original pilot scheme was started in Reading prison by BG under the-then CEO, David Varney, and Mary Harris as part of BG's Community Engagements programme. As a Non-Executive Director on the Board of BG, I was very supportive of BG's community projects.

When Lattice Group was formed via the demerger of Transco from BG in 2000, this pilot scheme came with us. I was delighted because I could see its potential to get our management involved. We had a real need for recruitment as we'd just agreed a 30-year cast-iron pipeline replacement scheme for the gas industry with the Health & Safety Executive (HSE) and Ofgem, the Regulator.

We found some real champions of integrating young offenders into the workforce via such committed drivers in Jon Butterworth, then the National Operations Director for Transco, and many others – and we had Mary's enthusiastic drive and planning skill. We negotiated and set up a scheme with the Home Office and Prison Governors to enable young offenders to be screened for a specific job role whilst in jail. They would also be accessed by the potential employer for suitability for the job role, aptitude and so on. Then on selection they entered a tough period of technical and practical vocational training, leading to the required NVQ certification for the role. No young offender was selected by a future employer for all these challenges without the individual knowing that, if all pre-qualifications were achieved and skills mastered, there was a permanent job at the end of the sentence.

During work experience the participants accumulated some payment of wages with a further payment to them on their appointment to the job, in order to assist with accommodation and relocation.

A very important part of the entry to work, post-prison, was the appointment of a mentor by the employer to the young person released – sometimes a supervisor or a skilled employee. When we introduced this at National Grid in the early days of the merger with Lattice, we got the – not totally unexpected – reaction from one senior manager in Operations: "Don't you think we have enough challenges every day without you giving us jailbirds to manage?" I told him about the scheme and our commitment as a Board of Directors to contribute to a better society and bring hope to these young people. We also urgently arranged for him to spend a day in a Young Offender's Institution. He returned from that experience in a state of shock with the realisation that these young men were the same age and with many having the same interests as his own son. After that life-changing event, the manager concerned became a brilliant supporter of the scheme.

The level of support these mentors had to provide was astounding. Some lads didn't know how to register with a doctor or how to apply for a driving licence. Mary Harris told me how she was woken on her mobile at 3 a.m. by a young offender with a toothache because he did not know what to do to find relief or make an appointment with a dentist.

I had been talking to Gordon Brown about the scheme when he was Chancellor, as he challenged me about what National Grid as a larger corporate was doing in the community. Gordon and his wife Sarah have a very strong social conscience. I wish many other politicians had similar genuine social concerns. Shortly after this discussion, on Budget Day, a colleague asked me: "Have you heard the Chancellor's speech?" I hadn't. "Well, he's announced that you will roll the Young Offenders programme out nationally"!

Part of my role as Chairman of National Grid was to accelerate and promote the scheme and expand it into other YO institutions and prisons around the country. We needed to reach out to companies, including National Grid's contractors, and of course to build relationships with many potential employers and Prison Governors. To this end, Mary would organise regular dinners at National Grid, which I would chair, to involve a range of CEOs from different companies. They would be invited along with either an NG manager or one or more of our contractors who could articulate their experiences. These companies did a superb job building the success of the scheme and were very committed to it. People like Charles Morrison, CEO of Morrison Contractors, were great champions of the scheme.

By sheer dint of effort, we secured the commitment of close on 100 companies as potential employers. We were present in 20 prisons around the country. What was remarkable and satisfying was that after a few years of operation, the re-offending rate – which if you don't intervene is around a horrendous and costly 70% – was reduced to single-digit percentages. Gordon Brown, after hijacking me into the role, promised a reception at Number 11 when we achieved 1,000 into work. By the time we reached that figure, he had moved to No

10 as Prime Minister, but Alistair Darling, his successor at No 11, fulfilled the promise even though the event took place during the financial crisis. Many employers and many Young Offenders turned up, receiving their "Graduating from the Scheme to Work" certificates from the Chancellor. It was a very happy evening which meant an enormous amount to the participants.

Each year, we held a public reception at Lancaster House in London for all the young people graduating into work to receive their certificates. It was very well attended by many people, including politicians from all parties. These were wonderful occasions when those company leaders, heavily involved in supporting the programme, would not only meet Prison Governors but talk direct to these young men who were now leaving custody and going into employment with new hope and aiming for a transformation in their lives.

Often too, some Young Offenders who had graduated in earlier years and who had now won promotions to team leader roles in their organisations, would come along. They were inspirational to the young people who were starting out. Other tangible support for the scheme emerged via my long-time friend and former Deputy Chair of BP, Sir Peter Cazalet. He inspired the Tallow Chandlers City Livery Company to support the scheme with awards for the most successful Young Offender already in work. The young men and their company leaders would be invited to a superb lunch at Tallow Chandlers for the prize-giving ceremony. I never missed one of these great award occasions. In 2008 I was invited to become an Honorary Freeman of the Tallow Chandlers which I truly valued given the number of fine Liverymen of that company who were so committed to the scheme.

My last reception at Lancaster House as Chairman of Young Offenders into Work was in 2011, after 10 years in the role. I was able to announce that more than 2,200 young people were now out of prison and into work, with reoffending rates reduced from 75% when there was no intervention in their lives to below 6%.

Charities

I've been fortunate to have been able to serve on a range of other charitable Boards. For 10 years, I was a member of the Council of the Royal National Lifeboat Institution that delivers a great humanitarian service around our coast – with Lifeguards in 2016 alone helping some 32,116 people at sea and on beaches, saving 558 lives, with 8,851 lifeboat launches. All this wonderful work by brave men and women all supported entirely via voluntary funding to match annual costs of about £177m. In all, 95% of lifeboats are manned by volunteers.

In 2010, I became Deputy Chairman to Lord Boyce of the White Ensign Association (WEA). It was founded by Lord Mountbatten after World War Two to support and provide advice to Royal Navy personnel leaving the Navy and entering civilian life. The Association Association has greatly benefitted from the dedicated and unique commitment of its President, Sir Donald Gosling. Donald has been the most generous of benefactors to the Royal Navy and the WEA, Sir Donald received the unique title from Her Majesty the Queen of Vice Admiral of the United Kingdom in 2012 – how richly deserved.

Sir Donald Gosling owned the stunning yacht *Leander* for many years, before eventually selling it to the Barclay brothers: the yacht had to go to an owner committed to keeping it in the pristine condition to which it had always been accustomed. Don has a fund of great stories, naval and otherwise, to tell. On one occasion, Lord Fieldhouse when First Sea Lord was spending a few days on board *Leander*. As a courtesy to the First Sea Lord being aboard, before they set sail Sir Donald arranged for the Union Flag to fly at the cross tree of *Leander*'s mast. John Fieldhouse dressed very casually indeed on days off, with a well-worn sea captain's hat, T-Shirt, shorts and deck shoes. He had just got to the bottom of the gangway of *Leander* when a rather pompous man approached him and said: "Is the owner of this yacht aware that he can only fly the Union Flag if the First Sea Lord is on board?!". John, without stopping, responded: "He is – I am"!

The WEA has had a number of distinguished former Royal Navy

First Sea Lords as members and down the years I am happy to have known and regarded a number as my friends: Lord Fieldhouse, Lord Boyce, Sir Jock Slater and Sir Jonathon Band. Sir Jonathon took over as Chairman of the Association in 2013 for a two-year stint. He was succeeded as First Sea Lord by Sir Mark Stanhope and then Sir George Zambellas. The current First Sea Lord is Sir Philip Jones, who worked with me in a highly collaborative way on my National Shipbuilding Strategy Review in 2016.

I have been privileged to know them all as leaders of our senior service, the Royal Navy. They have led and rendered a vital range of defence and security services to our nation, both at home and overseas. As we embark on our Brexit journey, their role will become all the more important to the security of this Island Nation. The sight of the Russian Navy passing through the Straits of Dover in 2016 caused considerable concerns for many of our citizens, only ameliorated by the presence of Royal Navy ships.

Closely associated with the Royal Navy is the Royal Marines & Royal Navy Charity, and I was honoured in 2009 to become a Vice-President, and stepped down in 2018.

Voluntary work all adds to the workload and late nights, but through it all I learned more and made many friendships with great people. Moreover, you felt that you added some value to young people and hopefully inspired some along the way. I've found that what you put in, you get back in abundance.

Universities and schools

Much of my other voluntary work throughout my professional life has been associated with the hugely important worlds of youth work, schools, universities and professional bodies.

Back in my student days in Belfast, I was a member of the Boys' Brigade and eventually took over as Captain of the 7th Belfast Company situated in a tough downtown area of the City, close to the loyalist area of Sandy Row. I remained as Captain until I moved to Austin & Pickersgill in Sunderland.

The demand to speak at school prize-givings in Northern Ireland intensified when I returned as Chairman of H&W, as did invitations to speak at engineering and business dinners and educational conferences, North and South of the border. I also became Patron of the Northern Ireland Science in Schools organisation. The opportunity to attempt to inspire and encourage young people in their studies and the importance of them "dreaming their dreams" and aiming high is one that we, who have had the privilege of corporate leadership, should seize with enthusiasm. The Speakers in Schools organisation, which I fully support and with which I am involved, offers unique opportunities for business leaders to meet with and inspire young students.

I have always been grateful for the quality and inspirational style of so many of my teachers at the schools I was fortunate to attend. The same can be said of the range of dedicated and inspiring lecturers I had whilst studying Naval Architecture and Mechanical Engineering at the College of Technology and Queen's University in Belfast.

In particular, I learned the importance of passing on the valuable lessons of my own experience gleaned from two academics, who in my Belfast years both as student and as Harland and Wolff's Chairman were all-time greats as outstanding and inspirational Engineers.

D H Alexander, the former Principal of the College of Technology, was a great mentor and advisor to me as a student, and I was delighted to return a small part of the knowledge he had imparted to me by showing him round the sophisticated engineering of the BP SWOPS vessel when he was well into his eighties. "What you make of your qualifications is what really matters," he always told me. That message coming from a Cambridge Whitworth Scholar had to be cherished and recalled.

The other great was Professor Sir Bernard Crossland, Professor of Mechanical Engineering at Queen's University when I was studying there, and later Head of the School of Engineering at QUB.

The Engineering lecturers at QUB published a fine book on the history of engineering at QUB in 2013, and I was honoured to be invited by a former excellent lecturer of mine, Dr Don McCloy, to write a tribute to Bernard.

I quote: "During a long career, I have had the privilege of inter-facing with many outstanding engineers from industry and academia. Inevitably, as in any profession, there are few individuals who would be judged universally by their peers as truly 'one of the greats'. Sir Bernard Crossland was undoubtedly one.

"Bernard received many honours, including his knighthood in 1990. However, I do know how thrilled he was to be especially recognised by his peers in the Royal Academy of Engineering when they conferred on him the Academy's 'Lifetime Achievement Award' in his 86th year.

"This was just one year before he passed on from all of us who held him in such high esteem. We did so, not just because he was an 'Engineering Great', but because he was also a wonderful human being. He was a great companion at many a dinner table that I and others shared with him. His wry sense of humour, his wise counsel accompanied by strong views on a wide range of issues ensured lively debate and memories of occasions that endure. His observations and challenges to you in conversation always seemed so practical, down to earth and relevant."

I concluded: "Above all, Bernard was a man of integrity who cared passionately about engineering and the important contribution it makes to the well-being and prosperity of society. I will always recall, with considerable affection, this 'Engineering Great' and wonderful human being whom I was fortunate enough to call my friend."

In 2014, I had the honour to be invited by Queen's University and the Irish Academy of Engineering to give the Sir Bernard Crossland Memorial Lecture. This was for me an occasion not without emotion as I recalled the great man. The lecture, which I called 'Engineering for Growth', was held in front of a very large audience representing a broad cross section of Northern Ireland society.

I told the amusing story, which some in the audience may have known in much more detail than me, about the particular occasion which took place around the mid 1980s. Bernard had arranged for a number of professors and other specialists interested in explosive welding to meet in Belfast for a few days.

As part of the programme, a dinner and overnight stay was arranged at the Glasdrummond Lodge near Annalong in the Mourne Mountains, where you could enjoy good food and excellent wine. Unknown to Bernard, the wine steward, James Barlow, worked for Harland & Wolff as a well-qualified metallurgist. James had a huge interest in good wine and he worked at weekends at the Lodge.

At dinner, Bernard and his colleagues were in rather heated debate about the failure of a particular explosive welding test carried out that afternoon in the Quarry in North West Belfast that Bernard used for his experiments. James heard most of the discussion as he hovered at the table, dispensing wine. The debate went on and finally James, tea cloth over his arm, walked over and said "Excuse me gentlemen, I couldn't help but hear about the failure you were describing. I suspect you are using a steel with too low a niobium content and too high in nickel". Silence ensued and the whole table of guests were agog. James was about to slip off quietly, when Bernard addressed him: "That's the first time in my life I've had metallurgical advice from a wine waiter." He then proceeded to enquire from James about his background. Bernard, who was very amused, related the story to me later.

Both DH Alexander and Bernard remained mentors and valued friends until close to their deaths. Both of them visited me at Harland & Wolff and showed great interest especially in the advanced computer and leading CAD systems we were installing to promote modular construction methods in order to drive new levels of productivity.

Lecturing in Naval Architecture

The inspiration from great academic leaders also led me to lecture in Naval Architecture at evening classes at the College of Technology. I sought to instil enthusiasm for engineering and naval architecture in a new generation of students. Some subsequently achieved high office – I think for example of Tom Allen, who progressed to be the Senior Ship Surveyor at the Department of Transport and was later involved in chairing committees of the International Maritime Organisation (IMO).

During both my periods at Harland & Wolff, I worked closely with the new Ulster Polytechnic, later to become the University of Ulster, where one of my previous lecturers, the talented Professor Jimmy Williamson, was now Head of Department. Indeed, in 1972, during the week that the Ulster Polytechnic held opening lectures, I had to step in at very short notice and give the opening guest lecture, when my then-MD, Ivor Hoppe, cried off at very short notice. My co-guest lecturer was Sir Vic (later Lord) Feather, the famous General Secretary of the Trades Union Congress.

Shortly after returning to Belfast in 1983, I joined a small advisory board called QUBIS that was established to fund and encourage the spin-out of early-stage companies leveraging off Queen's University research. This was amongst the early start-up boards established by UK universities and I greatly enjoyed the contact with the academics and young researchers.

Just a few years ago, around 2008, I joined the QUB Development Board and was able to put something back into this great institution which added so much to my life and that of Emma's as a Latin and Psychology graduate. As a Board, we helped to steer and raise the funding for a significant expansion including a world-class library. I was particularly pleased during my time chairing the Court of the Bank of England to arrange a dinner at the Bank to assist the University and its funding ambitions.

University of Southampton – Chancellor

I had served for a few years on the Council of the University of Southampton prior to the retirement of Lord (John) Selborne as

Chancellor in 2006. I was serving also on the Nominations Committee and we were asked to suggest names for the next Chancellor by the Vice Chancellor Bill Wakeham (later Sir William). I came up with a number of names and no other Committee member appeared to have submitted any.

I was then asked by the Committee to approach the first three on my list – the first being Lord (Eddie) George, the retired Governor of the Bank of England. Eddie was just too busy, as were the next two eminent candidates. I reported back to the Committee accordingly, requesting authority to approach the next two potential candidates on my list in turn.

There was some hesitation accompanied by the explanation that they wanted to reflect further on the appointment. Then they later took me completely aback by saying that they would like me to consider taking on the role!

Nothing was further from my mind. I had a full range of corporate and voluntary activities including chairing the Development Appeal for the Royal Academy of Engineering, which of itself was heavy lifting, and leading Young Offenders into Work.

However, after talking it over with Bill Wakeham, whom I had the highest regard for as Vice Chancellor – both as a leader and as a very talented academic – I agreed to serve a five-year term. The duties were not overly onerous except at the Summer graduation which stretched over a week or more with six ceremonies a day to accommodate more than 6,000 graduates.

Bill and I shared the majority of the ceremonies. We had great support in the latter years from the dedicated Pro-Chancellors in Dame Valerie Strachen (the excellent Chair of Council) and Sir David Cooksey, whom I had succeeded as senior Non-Executive Director and Chairman of the Court of the Bank of England. In my last year, Bill was succeeded as Vice Chancellor by Don Nutbeam, a former Southampton graduate who had spent time in Australian academic life. He has subsequently been succeeded by a former Deputy President of the Royal Academy of Engineering, Sir Chris

Snowdon, who is making his mark by building further success at this great institution.

At the Graduation ceremonies, we spoke with every graduate, clasping their hands and holding some interesting, albeit brief, conversational exchanges. One year, Bill reported that he had asked a young man what his ambitions were: 'It's to own a Porsche like yours, sir!" came the reply. My most moving experience was to see a guide dog for the blind accompanying a robed lady on to the platform with another female companion alongside. The robed lady was partially blind and deaf. She was about to receive an MSc in Psychology, if I recall correctly.

I was able to convey to her my admiration for her tremendous achievement. I also offered to graduate her beautiful Labrador guide dog and we all enjoyed the humour of that as we made a fuss of the dog. After the ceremony, I was disrobing while looking out on to the lawn when I saw the new graduate being photographed with her dog. I hastily put my Chancellor's robes back on and headed out to see her and ask if I could have a photograph taken with her. She happily agreed.

I found talking to this lady to be one of those truly inspirational moments in my life. When you realise the outstanding efforts and endeavours that some people undertake to achieve their goals, you can only be inspired. I keep that framed photograph in my office in London to remind me constantly both of that moving experience and to thank God for all the good things that as an individual I take for granted, in my health, vision and senses.

My stint as President of the Royal Academy permitted me to visit many of our universities and become so much better informed about their major research efforts and strengths. Without doubt, our universities are much more aligned than at any time in our history with industrial success for the UK and the part they can play in it. We need as industry to embrace and involve them more in our R&D efforts. They have so much to give.

Recognising the need to foster new spin-out companies from our universities and to develop new businesses based on commercialising research work, the Royal Academy of Engineering developed a very exciting and innovative approach, which we called the Enterprise Hub.

At the outset, The Royal Society was very keen that we put in funding alongside their own investment fund, to start investing in some early start-ups in science and engineering. We were grateful for the invitation, but we had little cash surplus after completing our new building. However, we realised that what we did have was a whole group of Fellows who had spun out companies or had built their own businesses from scratch.

A call for volunteers amongst our 1,500 Fellows produced about 100 with previous spin-out experience or who had established successful businesses, who were willing to act as mentors to young post-graduates who believed they had the potential to establish a new business from their research. Special facilities in the basement of Prince Philip House were established to facilitate mentors and researchers to meet and progress business and marketing plans, funding, and to provide technical expertise and general business advice.

We invited Ian Shott, a Fellow and successful investor and business developer, to oversee the Hub as chair of our Enterprise Committee. Ian has shown great drive and enthusiasm and the initiative has proved amazingly successful – well beyond our original hopes and expectations.

By June 2018, the Hub had 70 members, with some 46 fledgling companies already established and more in the pipeline. The companies employed 362 people in total and had attracted £64m in external investment. Each company is receiving free consultancy and advice from an experienced Fellow of the Academy. This initiative, still in its early days, goes with the grain of a developing and welcome trend in young engineers wanting to start their own business.

To maintain close links with our universities has been an important part of my business life and I look back with gratitude at the number of universities that have conferred on me Honorary Doctorates. These awards (now into double digits), without lodging a Thesis, are each one without doubt to be treasured and valued for the special linkages they create.

Professional institutions

It was a humbling moment to be nominated by my peers in 1996 to become President for a three-year term of my own professional institution, the Royal Institution of Naval Architects (RINA). I succeeded the great naval shipbuilder Peter Usher.

The RINA served me very well as a student. Not only did it offer the chance to win a number of awards, including the coveted Duke of Northumberland Prize, it also provided a forum to attend the delivery of learned papers together with presentations and discussions by some of the top professionals in our industry. Through this involvement, I got to know many people in the profession – but in my wildest dreams I never imagined that I would be elected President one day.

I subsequently had two papers published in the RINA Transactions: 'A Profile of British Shipbuilders (1979) and 'The Design and Build of BP SWOPS' (1988), the latter in partnership with the very experienced BP Project Director, Mark Wolveridge. We were awarded the RINA Silver Medal for the paper which we read in a number of joint RINA-Institute of Marine Engineers branches around the country.

Mark was a really outgoing, imaginative and creative character whose company I greatly enjoyed. When he was leading the large engineering team based in Aberdeen on the BP Magnus field development – his team grew restless and complained they had no social life. Could he not lay on "entertainment" at least once a month? He readily agreed, proposed a large dinner one Friday night and advised them all that "entertainment" would be laid on! A fine and hearty dinner was coming to a close when a certain type of music started up and was greeted by the team with loud, rhythmic clapping and cheering. Eventually the stage curtains parted – only to reveal a team of Northumbrian clog dancers!

At the RINA, with a new CEO in Trevor Blakeley (who was still serving more than 20 years later) we focussed on internationalising the Institution, making membership more accessible and relevant to young people, boosting the quality of our magazines and publicity, and generally promoting a higher profile for the Institution. We also elected, in each of my three years, distinguished and working Honorary Fellows with recognised international reputations: Lord Sterling, Chairman of P&O Group; Fred. Olsen, the Norwegian shipping and shipbuilding magnate who owned H&W and Corado Antonini, Chairman of Fincanteri and AWES.

We had memorable speeches from each of these global maritime leaders following the individual awards at our Annual Dinner. Often, we had interesting after dinner speakers including the actress-turned-MP Glenda Jackson when she had a spell as Shipping Minister. She was not wonderful company.

The motto of the Institution always had a special appeal to me: "Salum et Carinae Pignora Vitae", which, broadly translated, means: "The open sea and ships are the security of all life".

Lloyds Register

Another maritime body on which I served was the very historic Classification Society of Lloyds Register of Shipping (LR), which started life in a London coffee house in 1760. I served on its General Committee for many years and chaired for several years its Technical Committee which debated and approved all rule changes for the construct of ships and offshore structures.

Early in my design career, I had a six-month Ship Structural Research secondment to Lloyds Register, which is recognised the world over for its engineering prowess and technical integrity. This was a wonderful and enriching experience for a young man in his early twenties. I therefore felt especially happy in later life to put something back in the form of these voluntary roles at Lloyds Register. It was also particularly pleasing that LR under the chairmanship of David Moorhouse teamed up with the University of Southampton whilst I was Chancellor and Sir William Wakeham was Vice Chancellor. They ultimately moved from London on to the University Campus to create a unique Global Technology Centre under their then very active CEO, Richard Sadler.

Worshipful Company of Shipwrights

It was Derek Kimber, my chairman at Austin & Pickersgill, who encouraged me to apply to become a member of the Worshipful Company. I was elected a Freeman of the Shipwrights in 1977 and later obtained the Freedom of the City of London in order to become a full Liveryman of this ancient institution, whose origins date back more than 500 years.

Like most of the other livery companies, the Shipwrights was formed to ensure the accreditation of trained apprentices and tradesmen for its industry, shipbuilding, and associated industries. I served on its Charity Committee, Education Committee and Finance Committee before having the honour of being Prime Warden in 2000 – 2001 (unlike most other Livery Companies it had as a Permanent Master HRH the Duke of Edinburgh until 2012, when Prince Charles was installed).

The Millennium year 2000-2001 was a remarkable one to have had the privilege of leading the company. Apart from the raft of Charitable and Educational activities, the role positions you to see into the workings and governance of the City, insights to which you would not normally be exposed. We attended in that year some remarkable and memorable functions and celebrations.

I recall the Lord Mayor hosting a luncheon at Guildhall where Emma and I were seated on the same table as the Lord Mayor and the late Queen Mother who was then 100. She was greatly enjoying her lunch and her wine until the Bishop of London mistakenly picked up her wine glass. She was not going to let that pass, and said – in a humorous but firm tone: "'I think, Bishop, you will find that you have just taken my wine".

The Shipwrights is still one of the few Livery Companies that has diligently retained its original heritage. I always put it that no one can be elected unless they have 'salt water' running in their veins. You have to have a professional connection to the sea, be it as a ship-owner, having served in the RN, RFA or RNLI, as a yacht- or shipbuilder, ship repairer, a maritime lawyer, insurer or ship broker et cetera. At any dinner of the Livery you are sure to have an agreeable evening knowing you will share maritime connections with whoever you dine alongside.

Other professional institutions

I had the privilege to be President of the Smeatonians Society of Civil Engineers in 2010. The Smeatonians is the oldest Engineering Society in the UK and was formed in 1771 by John Smeaton and other pioneers of the Industrial Revolution, including James Watt. It meets several times a year and has an annual candle-lit dinner, some wonderful toasts, great discussion and debate on engineering topics of the day. Membership is confined to the election of some 50 distinguished engineers drawn from a wide range of engineering disciplines.

At Lattice and National Grid I spent time in support of the Institution of Gas Engineers and Managers (IGEM), speaking at many regional dinners and giving lectures. This included the Memorial lecture to the great Sir Denis Rooke, the founding father of the modern British gas industry. Indeed I was humbled when IGEM awarded me the first Sir Denis Rooke Gold medal established in his honour – which I will always cherish given the esteem in which I held this giant of an industrialist.

In connection with the gas industry, I also had served for a year as President of the Pipeline Industry Guild. The Guild involved a wide range of consultants and companies engaged in pipeline design, construction and maintenance. Again a valuable meeting place for all those engaged in this vital part of engineering systems which form a crucial role in every industry.

Trinity House

Trinity House is responsible for the buoyage, lighthouses and light-ships around our coastline in support of safe sea navigation. It was set up by Henry VIII in 1544 in a Forum not too dissimilar from a Livery Company. Today's Master is HRH the Princess Royal (Princess Anne), who took over from the Duke of Edinburgh after he had occupied the role for some 42 years.

I was fortunate to be in the presence of the Duke of Edinburgh at various events at the Royal Academy of Engineering as our Senior Fellow, and at Trinity House as an Elder Brother when he was the Master. A splendid stained glass window marking his unique service to Trinity House is in the Dining Room, and at its unveiling, at the end of the dinner in his presence, we saw someone who was genuinely taken by surprise in the extreme, but clearly was also very touched.

The Master Chairs the Court – equivalent to a Board which comprises the Elder Brethren. Younger Brethren, not always in age, have a similar position as Liverymen in a City Livery Company. The Court is supported by key committees to deal with what is a significant charitable involvement, pilot training and certification. A separate Lighthouse Board manages the Lighthouse/buoyage operations.

I was honoured to have been elected an Elder Brother and set amongst such distinguished colleagues and predecessors. Sir Winston Churchill was one of its most distinguished Elder Brothers. Once, President Charles De Gaulle, who enjoyed his military uniform and medals, visited Churchill, who was wearing the full uniform of an Elder Brother. De Gaulle was quite taken aback and asked Churchill why he was dressed up as a semi-retired naval officer. Churchill explained in French: "Je suis un frère ainé de la Trinité" ("I am an Elder Brother of the Trinity"). Thinking that Churchill was claiming membership of the Holy Trinity, the President replied: "Quelle belle situation!" ("What a beautiful situation").

Trinity House considers many important national issues of relevance to shipping. One particular and topical one is the impact of wind farms around our coast on safe shipping routes. The significant deviations involved for coastal shipping are quite material to the overall cost of a coastal voyage. It emerged that offshore licensing of wind farm sites takes little account of the impact on maritime transport.

Trinity House's most important task is ensuring all necessary navigational aids, from buoyage to lighthouses, are in place and maintained in order to deliver safe shipping routes around the UK, in co-operation with Irish Light and the Scottish Lighthouse Authority. Another important area is attending to safe navigation following ship collisions and groundings that need to be urgently buoyed appropriately. The depth of experience on the Court is very impressive, with the former Captain of the *QE2*, Captain Ian McNaught, in the role of Deputy Master.

21. LIFE, WORK, BALANCE

Wrestling with a business issue 24 hours in the day is not good for the human soul. We need to take a break; concentrate on something different and thereby get a new perspective on the issues you face.

I have been fortunate to have many interests outside of the day-to-day management role. I love literature, and recently voluntarily re-read a great many of the Classics that were mandatory at school, which made them less attractive then than they are today! Biographies are my favourite, from true sporting stars, statesmen and leaders in history to business leaders and individuals who have left their unique mark in history. With an open mind you learn from the experience of others.

I greatly enjoy watching sport – I particularly enjoyed watching our daughter, Fiona, in her university years as cox of the men's rowing eight at both Queen's University, Belfast and Trinity College, Dublin. One great sporting event that I thoroughly enjoyed was the excitement from an open top bus as we followed the annual Men's Eight rowing race between Trinity and University College, Dublin, rowed under the bridges of the Liffy with the particular coxing challenge this creates. On that occasion, Trinity won and Fiona and her crew were very happy at the outcome of this Irish equivalent of the Oxford-Cambridge Boat Race. In her last year in Trinity in 1997, she was selected as the Irish Cox and coxed the national team to victory at the

National (Ireland-Scotland-England-Wales) Universities Competitions on the International Rowing Lake in Nottingham.

Rugby internationals have to be at the top of my list of favourite live sports to watch, followed by soccer. I was fortunate to have been able to attend the 2011 World Cup Final in Auckland with Ray O'Rourke when New Zealand narrowly won against France. The 2015 World Cup in England was a truly wonderful sporting occasion, culminating in the great atmosphere of the New Zealand v Australia final. Following the Six Nations with visits to the Aviva Stadium in Dublin with close friends such as Ray O'Rourke or accompanying Nigel, Fee and the grandsons creates many special memories.

One of my main recreational hobbies has been sailing, which I came to in a roundabout sort of way. It all started when I was running Harland & Wolff and our son Graham was in his teenage years. We began to play golf together on Mahee Island, just a few islands north of where we lived on Sketrick Island in Strangford Lough in Northern Ireland, a beautiful location which underlined for me the quotation from Mark Twain "that golf was a good walk spoiled"!

We would play most Saturday afternoons when I wasn't travelling, along with the Harland & Wolff Sales and Marketing Director Ken Ruddock and his son Gordon. As time went on, Graham became much better than me which I was pleased about – but equally, I was coming off the course more frustrated than when I went on. When he left for Manchester University, I decided golf was not for me.

Despite making my career in shipbuilding and spending time on the sea on ships, I had not really considered sailing as a pastime. Now I made up my mind to take it up with enthusiasm. This was partly because we were living on Sketrick Island with a slipway to Strangford Lough and yacht moorings off the shoreline, and partly on the basis that if I pointed a boat in a given direction – unlike one of my golf club shots – it was likely to respond correctly.

I had some practical sailing lessons in Strangford Lough, which is a challenging area to sail in even when you are experienced. Uffa Fox, the famous racing yachtsman and yacht designer of the Flying

15, described Strangford Lough as one of the best sailing grounds in the world. For me as a novice, it was exacting but also exhilarating. It is said that there are 365 islands in the Lough, but a great number are only visible at half tide or below! The full tidal range of four-plus metres applies, with strong currents around the larger islands and particularly strong ones in the narrows: up to seven knots in the entrance to and from the Irish Sea.

Tidal knowledge is a prerequisite for sailing in the beauty of Strangford, which is now classed as an Area of Special Scientific Interest. Navigation too is critical to avoid the pitfalls of going aground on one of the unseen "pladdies", as these submerged islands are known. Some are marked by sticks which in a tough winter storm can be removed or their position distorted.

I took night classes in Carickfergus sailing school to Yachtmaster theory standard and clocked in the miles sailing with Judge Drew Donaldson, a neighbour in White Rock, or with Brian Law, who was another neighbour for a number of years on Sketrick. Both were very experienced sailors. Indeed, Brian held the speed record for some years for circuiting Ireland in a catamaran. Drew was keen to sail for about 10 days every summer, and for him as a Judge in Northern Ireland it was a great relief not to have security accompany you day and night. Inevitably from Strangford, it was the West Coast of Scotland which we explored. It is an area which Drew knew well and he also enjoyed cooking whilst cruising. This suited me on board my own boat!

My first boat was a Dutch-built Contest 29-ft *Queen of Mourne* which I bought from a neighbour, Noel Lindsey, on Sketrick Island. She was a quality build which held her price well on resale. I then had the opportunity to buy what for me was a dream boat – a lightly-used Halberg Rassy 38 which had originally been ordered by Fred. Olsen and later owned by one of his directors. She was a wonderful sea-keeping heavy-weather boat and ideal for sailing in the Irish Sea and the West Coast of Scotland.

I owned her for about five years, including two years after leaving Harland & Wolff in 1993 to join Babcock International. I then sold her and with the cash added to my savings, we intended to buy a holiday cottage on an ideal waterfront in Devon or Cornwall. Living as we were then in Amersham, Buckinghamshire, we were too far from the sea to get good use from a boat – despite being encouraged by friends to get a mooring in one of the river creeks in Southampton Water. For me, sailing there is too close to driving around Piccadilly Circus in London in dense traffic.

Moreover Emma – whilst competent on a boat – was not at all keen on sailing. My sailing was therefore with male colleagues or with Graham and Fiona and their friends from university. We ended up using any spare weekends, which were few given the challenge of turning around Babcock, to explore some of the South West's most attractive estuaries with a South West Yachting pilot guide to focus on ideal locations.

One weekend we came and stayed in Newton Ferrers on the River Yealm – the first river to the East of Plymouth Sound. We fell in love with the place after walking the path running alongside the creek separating Newton Ferrers from Noss Mayo. It took us probably 18 months to locate and buy a home – and not the cottage we set out to buy. In 1997, cottages were often sold as soon as they came on the market.

We bought Kemendine, a late-70s house beautifully sited along the front of the Yealm with a waterfront partial quay. Over the years we have extended, refurbished it and built a complete new quay with adequate boat stores and other facilities which are ideal for the sailor. As I stepped down from being Chairman and Chief Executive at Babcock International, and decided to concentrate on my Non-Executive Director portfolio, we sold up in Amersham and moved full-time to Devon. Whilst Emma had particular pangs leaving Tinkers Hall, which really was a character property, with its original open fire-side bread oven and original oak beams, we have never regretted the move.

The move took me back to owning a boat again and I bought *Moon Tiger*, a 29-footer Swedish Hallberg Rassy, to explore the South West coast and estuaries. Hallberg Rassy, which were truly quality boats with much hand-finished woodwork, has now moved to more industrialised production methods and in the process I think has lost some of that original quality finish of my 1982 built Halberg Rassy 38 that endeared them to so many sailors. They are built on the Island of Orust, just about an hour's drive North West of Gothenburg.

On the same island over the years they produced the famous brands of yachts, Najad, Swede Yachts and Malo. Malo was a smaller family-run boat builder but the quality was similar to the original Halberg Rassy. I ordered a new Malo 39 *Parabola* from the UK agent Nordic Marine in 1999. Olle Anderson owned the Nordic agency in Poole with his wife Donna, and he ran a special business. I can say that he was one of the most honourable men I have ever done business with. Any problem was dealt with promptly and as a customer you always felt good about and loyal to this high-quality brand.

I visited the yard at Orust with all the family to see *Parabola'* in build, which was a great experience. We again visited six years later in 2005 for the construction of our next boat, a Malo 46. I named her *Shimna* after the river in Co. Down that runs through the valley where I was born. It enters the sea at Newcastle after transcending one of the most beautiful public parks in Ireland, Tollymore.

This was originally owned by Lord Roden before he handed it over to the N.I. Government. I can well remember as a boy the Roden family castle in the park being demolished after Tollymore was handed over. Watching an era end must have been an emotional time for the Roden family. Today as in the past, there is an amazingly peaceful atmosphere just walking among the beauty of the park, with its great forestation and shrubbery towered over by the stunning majesty of the Mourne Mountains. At one location there is a huge granite stone with the words: 'Look around and behold the beauty of Him who made it all'.

Sailing has become much more than a mere hobby. As I said, I believe that every senior business person needs an outlet which takes them away from the often intense pressures of working life and the demands of our stakeholders, and for me, sailing has more than filled that requirement. Not just because of the activity itself, absorbing as it is, but for the close community of crew members that have accompanied me, be they family or friends from business.

I have continued to sail regularly over the years, fitting in short stints for weekends to Fowey, Salcombe or Dartmouth and making time for longer voyages of two weeks or more, taking in the West Coast of Scotland, the Clyde, other parts of Northern Ireland, South West Ireland and the Channel Islands. The estuaries of Devon and Cornwall are one of my favourite destinations, along with the Isles of Scilly.

I have a great crew which in recent years has included Sir Jonathon Band (former First Sea Lord). Jonathon has been a special friend for many years, since well before he became First Sea Lord. He has great leadership characteristics and communication skills, as well as being a seasoned commander of a range of naval vessels including aircraft carriers. It was a particular joy to me that he was elected by the Carnival Corporation and PLC Boards as a Non-Executive Director from the UK, following Baroness Sarah Hogg completing her term. He has been an outstanding NXD, in particular as a highly effective member of our HESS committee to which he has brought his extensive Ship Operation and Safety Management dimension, complimenting other skills around the table. Jonathon has succeeded me in 2017 as Chairman of the Group's HESS Committee (Health, Environment, Safety, Security) after a 10-year stint.

Murray Easton is also a regular crew member. He ran the Rosyth Dockyard for me after we bought it whilst I was at Babcock International. Other regulars are Robert Woods, whom I was privileged to have as my CEO while Chairman of P&O, my son Graham when he comes back from his home in the USA, my son-in-law Nigel, who is an engineer and a very competent sailor, and his father Brian Curry (a former Westland Engineer) and Dr Peter Brown, a retired Ear, Nose and Throat specialist who hails from N.I. and who has retired to Newton Ferrers. Whilst it doesn't happen often, a weekend sail to Fowey with Nigel in particular is very rewarding and keeps me youthful!

We have great fun on these trips and we take no unnecessary risks. We plan carefully and ensure high standards of safety. We can sit on board at the end of a cruising day and regale ourselves with recollection of events planned and unplanned that have absorbed our physical and mental powers ... ... like the anchor that dragged in the Scilly Isles, the outboard that failed to start when it was desperately needed close to midnight when we were still ashore, and the dinghy tender allegedly tied on safe at the stern in Castletownend (South West Ireland) that went walkabout during the night – we sighted it underneath a disused wooden wharf on a rising tide that was sure to lock it in: trying to raise someone from one of the neighbouring yachts on a Sunday morning in the South West of Ireland to no avail, leading to the intervention of the Coastguard and the launching of the fast lifeboat rib with two heavyweight locals on board. They jumped up and down on the dingy below the wharf against a rising tide but finally had to deflate it to get it released. I offered these wonderful volunteers a gratuity which they said they could not take but they could accept a donation to the local lifeboat station. The RNLI is a wonderful organisation. I was privileged to have served on its Council for about a decade, and I salute all those who render great voluntary service in it. We were relieved to get our dingy back – a necessity for cruising in an area with limited marinas.

You also run across great local characters in small estuaries in the West Coast of Ireland and Scotland. It was in Glengariff at the top of Bantry Bay – a beautiful village with tropical gardens blessed by the Gulf Stream that a local resident joined us as we ate an evening meal outside a pub. The pub also collected your mooring fee for the night in an honesty biscuit tin box with the receipt written on a yellow memo sticker.

This chap was a very interesting guy who, seeing our sailing gear, recounted some of his journeys around the world. He had earned and saved money to return home and start a business. We asked him about the make-up of the population – there were some that went off like him but didn't come back, and others that did return. There were those in tourism and fishing and odd jobs. Then there were the retired people, some of them well-off who came mainly from Dublin. "Do they live in the range of large houses we see around the estuary we enquired and would we recognise any of the names?" we asked him.

"Ah, now you're talking – would you know who lives in that big white house yonder?" We had no idea. "None other than Maureen O'Hara – she's 92 and nothing moves in this Parish without her authority."

I almost fell off my seat on the news, as I had wrongly assumed that the famous film star had passed on. She was the feisty, red-headed actress that played opposite John Wayne in my favourite film of all time – *The Quiet Man* – which was mainly filmed in the village of Conn, not far from where we were sitting that night in Glengariff.

There are so many happy experiences that one can recall, in good weather and bad, from sailing in the company of great and competent friends. The planning of cruises, studying the tides, calculating tidal gates is a wonderful hobby that clears the mind on a winter's evening.

Young people have probably got a point: 'Get a Life' is their refrain when they observe the long and what they consider as the boring hours put in at work by some of their friends or parents. Sailing has also enabled me to meet and converse with people I would not otherwise have met. This has been particularly true through my membership of a number of yacht clubs – Royal Ulster, Royal Thames and The Yealm Yacht Club in Devon. My election as a member of the Royal Yacht Squadron in 2012 was something that gave me a great deal of pleasure, being able to sail *Shimna* with a White Ensign over her stern and the RYS pennant at the top of the mast is an honour.

The sea provides the wider family with other great pleasures. One pastime we greatly enjoy is cruising in today's modern ships. Being able to see the world, travelling from destination to destination with no airports to transit and no suitcases to pack or unpack at each hotel. I find this a luxury after the amount of business travel I have done over the years. It is also a very cost-competitive holiday, in 4-6 Star comfort, depending on your choice of brand with all meals included and a range of entertainment laid on.

From Southampton with P&O, Cunard or Princess to Scandinavia, the Baltics and St Petersburg, the Mediterranean or the Canary Islands is one of the easiest and most relaxing ways to travel. Flying to other locations to take in Alaska, Asia, South America, New Zealand, Australia and China has been all part of our rich cruising experiences. We have also travelled with Seabourne – in my opinion the world's best cruise line – and Holland America and Princess, all of the above being Carnival Group brands. Our grandsons, who have often accompanied us on cruises along with their other grandparents, Brian and Jean Curry, have greatly enjoyed on-board activities including drama classes and many other activities. The travel, meeting new people, seeing new countries and cities has added real value to their education.

Then there is fishing. Taking my two eldest grandsons Jack and Charlie fishing off Newton Ferrers and see both of them catch their first fish in 2012, when they were aged nine and seven, was a moment that will be with me always. The excitement and joy on the faces of those young boys brought me untold happiness. I hope I can repeat that fishing trip for the two youngest grandsons – Alfie, aged seven in 2018, and Arthur aged five – in another year or so.

We are better executives and better chairmen when we get that balance right between leisure time and the hours of work which you must fit in with vigour, drive and enthusiasm. Thinking time is one of the most important, yet scarcest commodities in our corporate life of around 16-hour days. It's a critical component which can also be an integral part of leisure time as the mind gently turns over some options.

22. BUILDING EFFECTIVE BOARDS: SUCCESSION, GOVERNANCE AND DIVERSITY

Effective Boards are the main bulwark against the destruction of shareholder value and company reputation. Surprisingly in my experience, the effectiveness of a Board and its composition remains one of the least discussed topics with shareholders on a range of continents.

As Chairman, I take considerable care and derive great satisfaction from building quality Boards which create a culture of professional openness, transparency and respect to challenge. You have to have that open challenge from the Non-Executive Directors to the Executive Directors and yet in turn they, the Non-Executives, need to give full support to management when they believe proposed actions are in the best interest of shareholders. You can get such wise collective advice and steerage from a highly professional Board team. As a Chairman working with the Company Secretary and General Counsel, I endeavour to seek constant improvement in all our Board management and administrative processes with the aim of keeping at the forefront of best boardroom practice.

The effectiveness of a Board starts with its composition and the open and transparent relationship of the CEO with the Board. This, together with the breadth of experience and range of skill sets of the

Non-Executive Directors (including a number of NXDs with domain knowledge), plus the leadership skills and experience of the Chairman are all crucial ingredients for good Governance and have a major impact on the culture of the boardroom. As a Chairman, I always aim to secure a broad mix of skills and relevant experience which can deal with any issue that might walk through the boardroom door.

I would challenge the view that every Board member needs to know everything. It isn't necessary or possible – even though, in the financial services sector these days, this is increasingly the expectation. But if you are a scrum-half, you don't try to play like a prop or a lock – and the same is true in the boardroom. The value of a board is its collective expertise. We all need to be reminded that, in the words of the Chinese proverb: "None of us are as smart as all of us". It is the combined strength, competence and summation of experience and range of skills that deliver Board effectiveness.

The most important job that a Chairman must manage is that of Chief Executive succession. As corporate history demonstrates all too clearly, the wrong choice of CEO can be at best disruptive and at worst disastrous. In this context, a fundamental requirement is that the Board as a whole must have deep involvement in, and take ownership of, the corporate strategy. Only if this happens can the Board be best placed to choose the right CEO to lead the business through the cycle that the company will be engaged in. I comment further on this later.

A secondary but important issue is for each member of the Board to have a clear and aligned understanding of what the key roles of the Board are. As I see them, those roles are as follows. They must and do take account of the need to have a range of benchmarks against which you can measure your performance in Board evaluations.

Role of the Group Board

As set out to our Non-Executive Directors by the Chairman:

Tone from the top

The "Tone from the top" is driven by the integrity, honesty and professionalism of each of us as Board Members. The Board must set the drumbeat for the behavioural expectations of directors and management. Each of us must consistently live out the company's values in our interface with all our stakeholders.

Strategy

The Board must own the approved strategy, formulated by the CEO. This should be robustly debated and stress-tested. The strategy should aim for technical excellence, long-term sustainability and profitable growth whilst balancing the interest of shareholders and our other stakeholders. The Board must empower the CEO and the Executive to execute the strategy and hold them accountable for its delivery.

Management and compliance

The Board must ensure the highest standards of governance are embedded in the management of the company, whilst ensuring full compliance with the laws and regulatory processes wherever you operate.

Boardroom culture

To build a culture of mutual trust and integrity, supportive of the CEO and Executive Management. NXD-Management engagement should be based on a transparent and open relationship whilst respecting the right of robust challenge. The Board via its Audit Committee should be assured that a strong financial control culture is in place, both at the centre and in the operating divisions/subsidiaries.

Boardroom and people

The Chairman should take the lead, with the Nominations Committee, in ensuring that the Board is comprised of the right mix of skills, relevant domain knowledge, diversity and broad-based experience to support the creation of shareholder value and deal with the range of challenges that are likely to walk through the boardroom door.

Health, Safety and Environment

Through the Sustainability Committee, the Board should put leading-edge practices in place to manage successfully the health and safety of our employees, contractors and the public, our environmental commitments and our role as a responsible corporate citizen wherever we operate.

Succession and development

The Board should ensure that a professional Talent Management and Development system is in place for senior management and throughout the organisation. In particular, it should identify potential internal CEO successors and understand their development plans. If succession options are not strong, it should highlight early the need for an external, confidential 'monitoring search' of potential external successors.

Risk Management oversight

To understand through debate and challenge the major risks facing the company and the mitigation measures in place. Reputation is one of the key considerations as part of prioritising those risks. The Audit and Sustainability committees play the most direct role here. To ascertain the status and encourage the application of Risk Management processes as a management tool throughout the business. Business leaders in their presentations to the Board should highlight how they are applying Risk Management as a live management tool. The Board and the CEO should be positioned to be decisive in a crisis. Increasingly, a Sustainability Committee will also evaluate the operational risks undertaken in the normal course of business, and provide their views to the Audit Committee.

The Role of the Non-Executive Director (NXD)

To go from CEO to Chairman without extensive experience as a Non-Executive Director, must be very challenging. I would say that learning to be an effective NXD is a pre-requisite to being an effective Chairman. Rightly, it is now fairly common practice for a Board to encourage its CEO to take an NXD position with another company so that he or she can gain experience of the Non-Executive's role.

Learning to be an effective NXD takes time, counselling and good advice. The transition from Executive to Non-Executive is not always smooth and uneventful. You have to work at the different style of approach that is necessary.

In the boardroom, both Non-Executive and Executive Directors share equal responsibilities under Company Law. However, while NXDs occupy some common ground with the Executive Directors, there are also considerable differences.

The effective Non-Executive above all:
- is an influencer of out turns in Board room debate/decisions; this is one of my acid tests for a NXD's performance;
- has the ability to put their finger on key issues;
- has real focus on shareholder value and sees the total

shareholder values picture and therefore opposes risky investments which could destroy value;

- is listened to when he/she speaks;
- leaves their ego at home. I have once or twice seen the arrogant "know-all" NXD at their first Board meeting press the
self-destruct button through lecturing the Management and
scathing comments;
- takes a keen interest in a wide raft of areas and shows
continuing interest in learning: spends time with Executive
Directors, learning the business;
- reads the Board papers thoroughly and avoids superfluous
questions: nothing upsets me more than an NXD who comes
unprepared;
- is generally supportive of the Executive's proposals but is
courageous and independently minded to challenge and if
necessary oppose, when they can't get comfortable with the
value impact on the business.
- wants to do things correctly;
- supports well-developed investments that underpin strategy;
- leverages his/her skill-sets and experience to add value.

A very helpful development ground is to chair one of the Board
committees. There is usually good opportunity to do this and each
of the main committees –Sustainability, covering Health & Safety,
Environmental and Operational risks; Remuneration – now a
very demanding role; and Audit, including Risk Management and
Ethics Oversight – provides significant experience of areas which the
Chairman must know well. Remuneration, for example, will give you
exposure to the major investors who, these days, expect to be consulted
about executive pay and benefit issues. In addition, transiting to the
SID role will position you well to gain further boardroom experience
on your journey to a Chairman role.

With luck and good judgment, you will be serving under an able
chairman and you can learn from him or her. Certainly I have been

fortunate over 30 years as a NXD on a range of Boards to have sat with some outstanding Chairmen (and some who weren't so good!) who taught me a great deal about the role.

In summary: serving a quality apprenticeship as an NXD, chairing a Board committee, and serving as a SID and learning from good chairmen are all pre-requisites to ultimately being an effective Non-Executive, positioned to transit to an authoritative and successful Chairman.

Non-Executive Directors' engagement

The Non-Executive Directors should feel free regularly to communicate their individual views and concerns to the Chairman, and vice versa. The NXDs should be encouraged to have dialogue with the CEO and the Executive Management and to visit any of the operations in order to build up their knowledge of the business. They should participate in an annual assessment of CEO performance. The CEO will also participate, alongside the NXDs, in annually reviewing the Chairman's performance, led by the senior NXD.

Board service

The appointment duration for NXDs in the UK involves three-year terms with nine years seen as the maximum total period of service as stipulated by the UK Combined Code on Corporate Governance. This has merits but also drawbacks, since it assumes this is a guarantee of independence, which isn't necessarily the case. In fact, on FTSE 100 Boards in 2017, 69 men and 15 women had served more than nine years, with male tenure ranging from 0 to 53 years!

The positive aspect of the triennial reappointment process is that it provides a phased review of the competence of each director and their suitability for re-election, because each director's three-year term generally ends on a different date from that of their colleagues. The opportunity to refresh the Board is therefore a natural and evolutionary succession planning event, something which clearly has merits. However, independence in my view is not dictated solely by the length of service but predominantly by the character and professionalism of the individual concerned.

I sit on the Carnival Corporation and plc boards where the Senior Independent Director, Stu Subotnick, has served for some 30 years. He is therefore somewhat of an outlaw in today's UK Boardroom Governance environment. Yet Stu is an outstanding example of NXD best practice, consistently demonstrating independence and facing up to any proposal from management with which he is not personally comfortable. I value him very highly as a Board colleague. We both share similar business and governance views. Both of us endeavour to add value, partly by challenging management proposals in a professional and objective way that is not motivated by personal prejudices, or indeed personal views of the competence of the individual executives who may be tabling them. As our ultimate guiding star, we always ask ourselves: is this proposal in the overall interests and well-being of the company and its shareholders? As an independent director you must always strike the balance between shareholder and other stakeholder interests.

Governance

Boardroom Governance has come a long way in the UK from the original Cadbury Report of 1992, where the big emphasis was specifically the separation of the roles of Chairman and the CEO. At the time, it was common practice for people to combine the two roles so that you had a plethora of executive chairmen, which in most cases was not conducive to good governance or boardroom management. Splitting the role to a Non-Executive Chairman and the Chief Executive was heavily debated when first proposed but is now virtually the norm in the UK. Today, I believe, UK Governance represents the highest standards to be found in the corporate world and I am heavily committed to it.

In the pre-Cadbury era, a significant number of FTSE 150 companies had combined Chairman/CEOs. However by 2016 the number had reduced to just two. Even in the US, which has been far more traditional in continuing to favour a single Chairman/CEO, the S&P 500 companies moved from 67% with a single Chairman/CEO 10 years ago to 52% in 2016, according to the annual Board Index compiled by the head-hunter Spencer Stuart. So the trend is growing in the US and I believe will accelerate during the next decade.

The Roles of the Chairman and the CEO

I first prepared the following template of the differing responsibilities of the Chairman and the CEO many years ago. It is still, I believe, very relevant today.

Boards in the UK are expected in line with the Combined Code to approve such a statement of the respective roles to ensure clarity and the avoidance of the Chairman seeking to be 'Executive'.

Responsibilities of the Chairman and Group Chief Executive

The Combined Code requires that the division of responsibilities between the Chairman and Chief Executive should be clearly established, set out in writing and agreed by the board:

The following template is one I have used to define the respective roles:

CHAIRMAN	GROUP CHIEF EXECUTIVE
MANAGES THE BOARD	MANAGES THE COMPANY
• Board leadership, composition and succession planning • Governance • Advise, counsel and be a confidant to the Group Chief Executive • Act as the bridge between the Group Chief Executive and the Board • Quality of resource base • Corporate values and corporate citizenship • Take on ambassadorial assignments for Board/Group Chief Executive • Available for shareholders • Lead Defence Committee	• Executive leadership • Formulate corporate vision, strategy and business plans • Organisational concept, structure and appointments • Key objectives and performance review • Corporate management processes and systems • Acquisitions and business development • Corporate and internal communications • Employee relations • Leading sector and commercial relationships • Oversight of regulatory interface • Shareholder relations
SHARED	
• Major acquisitions • Defence situations • City and media relations • Top external contacts and representation, government relations • Major shareholder issues • Embedding the values by which we operate	

The Higgs Report in 2003 on the role and importance of NXDs produced what I also believe to be sound guidance on the role of Chairman, including the basic responsibilities of the post.

As Higgs put it, the Chairman is pivotal in creating the conditions for overall Board and individual director effectiveness.

Specifically, it is the responsibility of the Chairman to:
- demonstrate ethical leadership
- set the Board Agenda. The Agenda should primarily be focussed on strategy, performance, value creation and accountability, and ensuring that issues relevant to these areas are reserved for Board decision
- ensure timely flow of high quality supporting information, and manage that information effectively – information is the lifeblood of the Board, but I've received Board packs over 700 pages long, which is of course just far too much;
- make certain that the Board determines the nature, and extent, of the significant risks the company is willing to embrace in the implementation of its strategy, and that there are no "no go" areas which prevent directors from operating effective oversight in this area
- regularly consider succession planning and the composition of the Board
- make certain that the Board has effective decision making processes and applies sufficient challenge to major proposals;
- ensure the Board's committees are properly structured with appropriate terms of reference
- encourage all Board members to engage in board and committee meetings by drawing on their skills, experience, knowledge and, where appropriate, independence
- foster relationships founded on mutual respect and open communication – both in and outside the boardroom – between the Non-Executive Directors and the executive team
- develop productive working relationships with all executive

directors, and the Chief Executive in particular, providing support and advice while respecting executive responsibility: as a CEO, I always valued a strong, professional Chairman who could give me strength and support – I didn't want a timid non-influencer of events. You want a relationship where Chairman and CEO feel able to walk in and out of each other's offices for informal chats

- consult with the senior independent director on Board matters in accordance with the Code
- take lead on issues of director development, including through induction programmes for new directors and regular reviews with all directors
- act on the results of Board evaluation
- review and consider own development needs, including people and other skills
- ensure effective communication with shareholders and other stakeholders and, in particular, that all directors are made aware of the views of those who provide the company's capital.

What are the worst traits in a Chairman?

- Can't let go of the operational levers or the Executive authority that goes with them.
- Propensity to give Executive commands as he/she tramps around the Parish ("confusion" at best, "disaster" in practice)
- Wants high personal profile in the media – regardless of its value to the company.
- Too dominant – too dictatorial – too arrogant
- Does 15 rounds with the Executive Directors.
- Poor listener – doesn't harness the collective experience and wisdom of the Board and the NXDs.
- Burns up all the O^2 in the boardroom

- Creates a dysfunctional relationship with CEO.

Of all these faults, probably the most dangerous is arrogance or conceit (which is also the greatest negative in the character of a CEO).

Back to best Chairman practice: in the great class of Chairmen, I'd put:

- the late Lord (Bob) Haslam, Chairman British Coal (I served as an NXD under his Chairmanship for seven years) and British Steel Corporation, Tate & Lyle, and Deputy Chairman of ICI – low profile but a great influencer. In nationalised industry, he gave the Executive 'Air Cover' from Government/Civil Service to allow them the space to perform.
- Sir David Lees, Chairman GKN (I served 10 years under his chairmanship), David was unusual by today's standards because he moved up from CEO of GKN to Chairman. However, his superb emphasis on good governance and sound administration drove the business through performance goals and unemotional Portfolio Management
- Sir Richard (Dick) Giordano (three years) – a very dominant personality who appreciated strong NEDs and used them to force through the break-up of British Gas into Centrica, BG and Lattice – which ultimately merged with National Grid to form National Grid Transco. These corporate moves created outstanding shareholder value.

All of them chose their NXDs carefully to give a blend of skill-sets, experience and, yes, diversity. They marshalled their NXDs well, consulted well and independently strove for transparency. Leadership of the Board is important in support of the CEO's leadership and management of the company.

Unlocking the effectiveness of the whole Board involves a number of elements and techniques:

- first, there must be something there to unlock – hence the importance of creating a well-balanced Board in composition/skill/experience/wisdom

- build a unified Board
- have relaxing times together, particularly through Board dinners
- holds a number of dinners a year for the Board, and at least one or two a year that the Executive Committee attends. This allows social time with that important next layer of management. There should also be one dinner which the CEO attends with the Chairman and NXDs, where the performance of the Executive and succession and development issues are discussed. Not enough Boards meet informally outside the Boardroom – pre-Board dinners are a simple way to ensure that they do. In a less formal setting than a Board meeting, you get to hear what your Board colleagues are really thinking. And having debated and slept on the really big issues, you'll find a 10,000-foot high challenge has a way of reducing to 1500 feet by the time you get to the Boardroom the next day
- Prior to a Board dinner, don't always be in a great hurry to sit down: if there is good buzz, then encourage circulation and let the pre-dinner socialising continue. After you sit down but before starting to eat, if necessary have a presentation on a tough topic. Over the main course, hold an informal discussion, a strategic knock-about which allows directors to "ventilate"
- Between Board meetings, take regular soundings of NXD views on any important issues
- Ensure the Board is periodically refreshed
- Provide advice in advance to the Executive Committee through the Board's 12-month "rolling-forward" Agenda
- Make full use of Board committees
- Use appointment of Chairman of Committees as a development ground for NXDs

- Get out of the office periodically for Board visits to an operation. Allow at least 1–2 days each year for a thorough review of Strategy – but weave strategic debate into most Board meetings.

Future trends for the Chairman's role

As I look ahead, I anticipate a number of developments in the Chairman's role which will profoundly affect Board agendas:

- A continued move to separate the role of CEO and Chairman in those countries – notably the US – where separation is not yet common practice
- Further increases in shareholder activism, which is increasingly widespread in all manner of corporate situations ranging from underperformance to M&A and Executive Remuneration. In 2017 alone, we saw this with the takeover approaches to Akzo Nobel and Atkins and the break-up pressure on BHP
- The Chairman will be increasingly pressurised to make changes where the shareholders see weak governance or a poor blend of skills on the Board, caused by insufficient weight/stature/diversity, including ethnic diversity, of NXDs
- Increased pressure on the Chairman to act will also come from concerns about NXD independence, Audit fees, remuneration not linked to performance or where confidence in the CEO (ie Management) or strategy is low
- Heightened pressure group activity, be it related to environmental or animal rights or other issues
- Further legislation on Health & Safety, corporate manslaughter and other areas of corporate activity.

Looking out 10 years, I foresee that the Unitary Board with separate Chairman – CEO and increasing role for Non-Executive Directors will be the model that survives, along with increasing pressure on transparency for investors and all stakeholders.

As always, it will be critical for the Chairman, as leader of the Board, to ensure that the right values are embedded and the expectations of the behaviours of our people are clear to all, regardless of where we operate. The tone from the top of the company is critical to our reputation and licence to operate.

As an individual, the Chairman will have to decide how his/her optimal portfolio should look; he/she will need to retain currency, continue to learn and have high impact and be prepared to give the time it takes to perform to the maximum – particularly if a crisis arises. You cannot answer the question of "over-boarding" without recognising:

- the breadth of experience and 'time served' in previous roles as Non-Executive Director or Chairman. Boards need to ask of their Chair: Is he/she seasoned?
- the competence and productivity of the individual. Boards need to know if their Chair is someone who likes to play golf twice a week or whether his/her five-plus working days are available to the companies with which they are involved. It is also a function of the productivity of the individual – their effectiveness at administration and ability to absorb and dissect complexity. In today's Boardroom, financial and numeracy skills are assumed in the Chair of a large FTSE company.

Delineating the Chairman's role in relation to the CEO's will continue to be vital. Lack of understanding by either or both parties of their respective responsibilities is a recipe for corporate misgovernance and management under-performance.

Very importantly, the CEO should never surprise the Chairman! Out-of-the-blue shocks shouldn't happen if the CEO and Chairman have established the right relationship of regular and mutual communication.

Change from CEO to Chairman

The vast majority of future chairmen will likely be former Chief Executives. With that in mind, I offer these thoughts on how you can best equip yourself for the change of role from CEO to non-executive Chairman.

One point worth making up front, because of how the practice has changed over my career from being a rarity to becoming the norm, is that most new chairmen, at least in British companies, will assume the role in a company or, in some cases, in an industry which is unfamiliar to them. Certainly, very few will move up to take the chair in their current company.

How we do strategy – the cycle

This transition used to take place quite often but is now frowned upon by UK investors because – quite rightly in my opinion – it is not good governance and militates against strong executive leadership. Except in special circumstances, such a move from CEO or CFO to Chairman within the same company is fraught with unnecessary challenges and difficulties. Unless you are very disciplined, unemotional and capable of detachment from your previous role and what you have created, I doubt if your successor as CEO will ever have free rein or unbiased advice.

So as the new Chairman, you will find yourself in an unfamiliar company or industry and in a role which demands very different skills from those which make a chief executive successful. As in all such transitions, a solid apprenticeship and proper career development is in most cases a pre-requisite.

The role of Chairman of a UK plc is increasingly demanding because of the exponential growth in recent years of corporate governance and compliance as priority issues. If things go wrong you are in the firing line – from 21st century UK corporate history, the differing examples of the electronics group Marconi, the engineer Mayflower, the British-Dutch oil giant Shell with the mis-statement of its data on reserves, BP and the Gulf of Mexico oil spill, and Tesco's accountancy treatment all bring that home very vividly.

How we do strategy

The Board is the owner of the company's strategy. The simple process cycle is that management, led by the CEO, formulate strategy. The Board's role is to debate it and robustly stress test it. The Board may finally require amendments, as it seeks to balance the interest of shareholders and other stakeholders. When the Board approves the strategy it empowers the CEO and Management to execute it. The Board then holds the CEO accountable for its delivery.

This simple cycle has not always been practised in some boardrooms that I've served in. You may find the Chairman considers himself to be in charge of strategy or the CEO expects the Board to nod through what he wants to do. This is one of the most important collective roles that the Board performs. 'All of us are smarter than any of us'. In today's complex world it is the strength of the combined skill sets and the embedded wisdom of the Board that is so essential to capture.

The Board – reputation and accountability

The quality, breadth of skill-set and experience of those who serve in the Boardroom is the critical bulwark against the destruction of shareholder value and corporate reputation – creation of value not only being related to good reputation, but dependent on it.

However, in all except the smallest companies, there will be a multitude of actions that the company, acting through its employees, will be undertaking for which the directors are ultimately responsible but over which they have no direct view or control. As a Chairman with my Board members, we need to be able to count on our management and employees to act in a way that is not just right for compliance reasons, but because it is the right thing to do. Indeed, Anglo American entitled the 2016 review of its Code of Conduct: 'Choose to do the Right Thing'.

The separation of powers at the apex of the company is a key factor in ensuring that a proper culture of accountability permeates the organisation. There must be a real and effective separation, with a chairman and chief executive who understand each other's roles and responsibilities, work well together but challenge each other where necessary and ensure that neither they, nor anyone else, has undue power and influence over the organisation. Ensuring that this is the case is one of the chairman's most important duties.

Clearly, we all need to be wary of hubris. Many companies with deep traditions and good standing have been caught out by examples of individual or systemic behaviour which conflict with their stated values. The Board of Directors is "accountable" to its shareholders and other stakeholders for the actions that the company takes, or fails to take, in fulfilling the purposes for which it was established.

To achieve thorough accountability, Directors must decide which matters they will reserve to themselves for consideration and decision, which they will delegate to Board committees, and which they will delegate to the Chief Executive and his or her Executive, who will then devolve some matters to specialists in technical areas. I believe that if all these delegations are clear in terms of their scope and limitations, accompanied by a highly professional internal audit, then there is less likelihood of the company experiencing the type of issues which surface in the media, and which can severely impact corporate reputation.

Executive search

Executive Search consultants – generally known as head-hunting companies – can play an important advisory role in facilitating good Board governance.

Over the years, I have got to know and work with a range of head-hunters on recruitment, Board evaluation and Executive assessment to define development needs.

Over the last few years, I have had the privilege to chair the Advisory Board of Spencer Stuart, one of the world's leading Executive Search companies. More recently, I was invited to join the practice as a senior adviser, which I was honoured to do.

It has been a rewarding experience to get behind the scenes of this global business, whose highly competent International Chairman Edward Speed is based in the UK. A group led by Edward, along with an impressive team of UK Board consultant partners, together with the highly regarded Katherine Moos representing boardroom search in Europe, and five Non-Executive Director colleagues drawn from a range of UK business leaders, meets three times a year. We discuss corporate issues of the day, recent governance changes and the latest challenges facing company Chairmen and CEOs, and how to improve Executive Search, development assessment and other similar questions – all of which leads to rich debate and fresh ideas.

Board diversity

Over the years, I've served on a number of Government committees and had to decline invitations to work or lead on others. One committee I did feel it was important to join was 'Women on Boards', set up by Vince Cable when he was BIS Secretary in the Coalition Government, under the chairmanship of Lord (Mervyn) Davies. I gladly accepted the invitation to become a member.

This is an area I've championed consistently. National Grid, Mondi, Anglo American and many of the other companies where I have served have and continue to benefit from talented women being in the boardroom. They change the dynamics of the all-male Board and often view issues from a different perspective. Thankfully, they have the ability to disrupt male group think!

I was and remain opposed to quotas – as do all experienced professional women I meet. The voluntary code we put in place in the Davies Report which set an aspirational target for FTSE Boards to ensure that by 2015, 25% of their directors would be women was, I believe, a good one. Even better, it was achieved without the imposition of a quota system.

There is a safe speed for the convoy here to enable companies to discover the true worth of women's contribution in the boardroom. That approach rather than imposition will get us where we want and should be. Head-hunters and companies need to do a better job in mining new seams of talented women who can add real value to our Boards. This and other actions, as proposed by Sir Philip Hampton and the late Dame Helen Alexander's Review, to promote more women into executive roles are necessary to enrich the pool of choice.

The Executive pipeline

The challenge for corporates remains how to bring more women through to the Executive Committee and into Senior Executive roles in a company. We have a lot of talented women originally from, for example, graduate entry, particularly among those who are now in their early 30s. The Hampton-Alexander Review studied this critical issue and set a target for FTSE 100 companies that women should account for 33% of the top two layers of management below Board level by 2020.

This is an area where corporates have to think out of the box. They need to create the opportunity for women either to take a break in the early years as a mother, or provide them with adequate support to enable them to continue working after childbirth, knowing their children are being properly taken care of. I realise now that there is a growing number of fathers who are taking care of the children while their wives pursue their careers, but the continuing dearth of female executives across the corporate spectrum highlights the need for measures such as the ones I've discussed.

Corporates can also do better in providing the right career re-entry potential for women when their children reach an age where less direct parental support is required, and I for one Chairman have yet to be associated with the optimum model.

Corporates need to get their heads around these alternatives if we are to have the benefit of talented women contributing at Executive Committee and Board level to enhance a company's well being. Bold actions are needed in most corporates and in the head-hunting firms to bring this about.

Ethnic diversity on Boards

Increasing female Board representation is a major part, but only a part, of an even broader and bigger issue: the need for British companies to increase inclusiveness and the diversity of their senior talent, both executive and non-executive, to add value to a Board and enrich its capability. Diversity of thought and culture enrich the board debate. It's not just that directors with different backgrounds think differently – they impact the way everyone around the table thinks too. In 2016, my long-standing concern about this issue of diversity led me to accept the invitation to chair a Review for Government on the ethnic diversity of UK Boards.

The origin of the Review was an announcement in September 2014 by the UK's Financial Reporting Council, the governance body for UK-listed companies, that it would consider adopting new provisions in its corporate code, requiring companies to report regularly on the state of their ethno-cultural diversity.

This prompted calls by politicians – notably Vince (later Sir Vince) Cable, the Coalition's Business Secretary – for UK companies to increase Board diversity. Before the general election the following year, Sir Vince and I discussed the issue and he asked me to talk to business leaders in order to develop the Davies Review's work into the broader field of Board diversity. Continuity was assured when Sajid Javid, Sir Vince's successor as Business Secretary in the new Conservative Government, invited me to conduct an official Review.

I was delighted to accept the commission, which provided a Board-level complement to a parallel inquiry led by Baroness Ruby MacGregor-Smith into ways to improve the progress made by members of minority ethnic groups in the general labour market.

We established an excellent committee, whose members included my co-Chair David Tyler, Chair of Sainsbury's, Trevor Phillips, former Chairman of the Commission for Racial Equality, Amy Winepress, a Director of EY which generously supported the initiative financially, and Tom Shropshire, a partner in Linklaters. Linklaters also generously contributed financial support to get the final report published. As a group, all of the committee members brought enormous experience and insight into all the issues involved.

Embarrisingly the Government referred to the report as the Parker Review. We gave it a strapline sub-title: 'Beyond One by '21', to capture the first of our recommendations – that each FTSE 100 Board should have, at the very least, one director of colour by 2021. For FTSE 250s, we set the same target by 2024.

These objectives and the other recommendations were driven by the simple fact that the boardrooms of Britain's leading public companies do not currently reflect the ethnic diversity of either the UK population, or the stakeholders they seek to engage and represent. In 2016, UK citizen directors of colour represented only about 1.5%

of the total company director population, even though 14% of the UK population was a 'person of colour'. By 2030, this proportion is expected to be closer to 20%.

These figures alone point, not only to the customer base of many companies changing significantly, but also to the changing core of talent that will be needed to occupy Senior Executive positions and possess the skill and experience to compete for non-executive and executive boardroom seats.

In all, 53 of the FTSE 100 did not have any directors of colour – and the under-representation was actually much worse, because a mere seven companies accounted for over 40% of the total, five of whom had headquarters historically located outside the UK. Only nine people of colour were chairs or CEOs.

Or, to consider the problem from another angle: more than three-quarters of the FTSE 100 companies' revenue comes from overseas – yet of the 1,087 director positions in the 100 at the time of our report, only 8% were held by people of colour. Whichever way you look at it, Boards are unrepresentative of their workforce and their customers.

We identified the significant benefits, both internal and external, that would result from an improved ethnic mix. These range from enhanced Board capability and the avoidance of "Group-think" to increased brand value, higher-quality recruitment and better supply chain management. We stated that "now is the time to begin making changes that will ... better prepare UK companies to continue to be global leaders in business over the longer term."

Personally, I believe it is critical for the successful future of British companies that they meet the targets we recommended. The alternative would be to sow the seeds of relative decline against our international competitors. And the commitment has to come from the very top: as we said, without the leadership of Chairs, Boards and executives, "UK companies will not attract, develop and retain the best talent."

23. MANAGING SUCCESSION: CHAIRMAN AND CHIEF EXECUTIVE

Chairman succession

Someone once said that the Chairman is 'a unique commodity of one'!

Perhaps not surprisingly therefore, the Chairman's succession plan is the least openly-discussed topic that I have experienced in most of my boardroom experience.

The Chairman is not subject to the UK's three-, six-, and nine-year review periods and the appointment process that applies to the other Non-Executive Directors.

The timing of a Chairman's departure is therefore something of a subjective or informal issue. On occasions, I have experienced the pressure from Non-Executives to remain in post as Chairman even when I have served what I believe to be an appropriate term. Conversely, I have seen instances when the Chairman has been hanging on in there against the will of some on the Board. This is an unwelcome and unhealthy corporate situation.

In the case of the Chairman – just as with the CEO – a fresh pair of eyes and different skill-set and experience can bring added value, depending where the company is in its cycle of transformation, consolidation or expansion.

The timing of a Chairman's departure is influenced by the need for continuity at the top of the company, and should be decided with particular regard to the timing of the CEO's departure. No Chairman should leave at the same time or within at least a year of the CEO. The Chairman must oversee the CEO recruitment process and probably overlap with the new CEO for a minimum of, say, 18-24 months.

The Chairman has a duty to ensure that the new CEO is well settled into the role, as it's the most important transition he/she will execute with the Nominations Committee and the Board. A retiring Chairman should therefore depart well before a new CEO appointment process is launched, in order to give the new Chairman adequate time in post to access the requirements and the skill-set and experience of the next CEO well before the process starts.

It is also important that a Chairman leaves at a time when a few new NXDs are required over the next two years. This provides the opportunity for the new Chairman to move early to be involved in the selection of new NXDs to start his 'refreshment cycle' of Board replacements.

In terms of the actual process, the key figure in the identification and appointment of a new Chairman is the Senior Independent Director, otherwise known as the SID.

The position of SID was created in a formal way by the Higgs Report on Governance. Initially, it was viewed with a degree of suspicion by some Chairman and NXDs as undermining the Chairman's role in particular. Some NXDs did not like the fact that one of them was more important than themselves. However, I have always seen the logic in shareholders having a nominated person on the Board whom they can formally approach if they have issues which they cannot feasibly address to the Chairman or the CEO. In addition, it is very helpful for the NXDs to have someone to turn to if they lose confidence in the leadership or style of the Chairman, or indeed if they feel that certain issues are not being addressed.

The SID also provides the Board with a leader for the NXDs in evaluating the performance of the Chairman and in providing important feedback on style and on areas where they would like more focus. For me as Chairman, the SID is a valued sounding-board with whom I can discuss many issues where I am seeking a second opinion before progressing.

SID to Chairman

Creation of the SID role has also facilitated the progression of NXDs to become chairmen, not necessarily in the same company but in others. According to the latest statistics, a high percentage of Chairman appointments are now being filled by men and women who have served as SIDs, mainly in another company. In 2014, 56 of the Chairmen of FTSE 100 companies were previously SIDs. This is not surprising, given the pyramid of boardroom development that now exists from NXD, via Committee Chair or membership, to SID.

Providing that the SID is not putting their hand up to be considered for the role of Chairman in the same company – not a totally unusual situation – the SID is automatically in charge of the selection process for the next Chairman.

Other than responding to questions posed or opinions sought by the SID, the outgoing Chairman is not involved. The process is for the SID and the Nominations Committee to manage.

They may co-opt other NXDs to assist with shortlisting and interviews in advance of making recommendations to the Board as a whole. If the SID is a candidate, he/she must withdraw from managing the process and another NXD must be appointed to lead it. In that event, it is the job of the existing Chairman to ensure that an independent process is put in place. The Chairman then steps back and does not participate further.

The CEO must be involved in the process, particularly if he/she has a number of years of service ahead of them. The chemistry between a company's Chairman and CEO is vital. Respect for the Chairman and his/her credentials by the CEO are important ingredients for a successful combination at the top of the company.

The SID will manage the involvement of the CEO in the selection process. This entails something of a balancing act by the SID, who needs to ensure, on behalf of the NXDs, that the Board's final decision is taken independently of the CEO. So, while involving the CEO in a meaningful way, the SID must also ensure that the CEO has no ultimate veto over the selection. A way to achieve this is to invite the CEO to sift the shortlist of candidates once the SID and the Nominations Committee have drawn this up, so that the CEO can make it clear early on if he finds any candidate "not acceptable". The SID can then arrange for the CEO to interview the final two candidates and make his/her views known to the NXDs.

I cannot overstate the importance of involving the CEO in the selection as far as you can without infringing NXD independence. The new Chairman/CEO relationship needs to develop in order to ensure that the CEO can regard him/her as a confidant, a sounding-board, a bridge with the Board. Although their formal roles can inevitably throw up some grey areas of responsibility, these should never turn out to be an issue for tension – as long as both have a mutually respectful relationship. This underlines the need for both to ensure they leave their egos at home and put the well-being of the company and its relationships with its key stakeholders first. The Chairman/CEO relationship is very visible to the executive team and to the whole company. It is certainly a visible ingredient in the tone set by the top of the company.

The Chairman must be 100% supportive of the CEO until the day, should it come, when he/she loses confidence in the executive leadership. At the time of sensing this, the Chairman must talk confidentially with the SID and then, at a time you both decide, also with the other NXDs.

Over time a good SID will build a close relationship with the Chairman which enables mutual dialogue on the topic of the CEO, and which allows the SID to share the Chairman's thinking with the Nominations Committee. That arm's length sharing can on occasions cause turbulence amongst the NXDs if they hold personal views that may differ from those of the SID about the effectiveness of either the Chairman or the CEO. Collectively, they should always be mindful of the need both for stability at the top of the Company and for supporting a positive relationship between the Chairman and the CEO.

Chief Executive succession

Succession for the CEO and key executives is a critical part of the Board's responsibilities. In particular it is critical, for CEO succession, to have a clear view as to the realistic potential of internal candidates, within the likely timescale of the CEO's corporate life span.

Today, few CEOs of FTSE companies serve more than seven years and the average by 2014 was just around five years. If a CEO remains beyond that, the Board has to be reassured that the commitment, energy, enthusiasm and support for leadership development and so on remains fully in place. Where uncertainty about the readiness of the internal candidates exists or there is a clear view that no suitable internal successor is available, then the Board has a duty to ensure a smooth transition by starting to look outside the company.

A very practical way ahead is to recruit a trusted head-hunter to undertake desk research to identify the people out there who could fulfil the criteria that the Non-Executives in the Nominations Committee will have already defined. Such an exercise can be conducted on a totally confidential basis with no approaches to any candidates. It can also extend over, say, an 18-month period prior to the incumbent CEO's departure. And it can be regularly updated based on in-house head-hunter intelligence gathering.

The great benefit of such an approach is that you build up a detailed profile of the best-fit candidates so that when the departure date of the CEO is announced, you can commence approaches and get interviews underway within a week. The best-fit candidate was agreed by the Board of Anglo American within eight weeks of dropping the flag with the head-hunter for interviews to commence. After sorting out contracts, extraction dates from his current employer and other matters, a Stock Exchange announcement on the appointment was made in an overall cycle of 11 weeks.

Speed is of the essence to avoid a leadership vacuum and the desta-bilisation of top managers. To counter this, in such handover situations the Chairman should be even more visible than usual. This is the most important job you do as the Chairman in managing the process to choose, with your NXDs, the right leader for the cycle in which the company finds itself. It is important to communicate with the outgoing CEO and the Executive team the likely timing of the appointment. Indeed, explaining openly to your Executives – some of whom have probably put their "hats in the ring" – the reasons for choosing the new CEO, and the characteristics and experience that he/she will bring, is most important. So is seeking their continued commitment and their support for the new CEO, in order to avoid potential talent leakage, which is a heightened risk during this corpo-rate change period.

The succession date of a CEO changeover is often anticipated by the whole of the executive team – whether it be the approach of the CEO's known retirement age or the fact that he/she has been CEO for well beyond, say, seven years; or because of an earlier announce-ment which stated that the CEO would serve until a certain date.

Where such a date is visible, it is a "line in the sand" and should not be varied even under pressure from the incumbent CEO if he/she changes their mind and decides that they would like to do another two or three years.

I know of one such situation at a FTSE 100 company: the date at which the CEO was to leave was well publicised – but at the last minute, the CEO persuaded the Chairman that he should do another three years and was granted a contract extension to that effect. There were three executives inside the company who could have thrown their hat into the ring to succeed. Some members of the Board questioned the wisdom of this contract extension, on the grounds that it could cause some of the three top executives to leave. The Board was assured that the CEO had talked to them all and all were supportive. Nevertheless, all three left within a year.

The Chairman misread the situation: he allowed his relationship with the CEO to prevail over the best long-term interests of the company. It was difficult for him – the company had benefited over the years from the constructive relationship he had struck up with the CEO. But he should have used the robustness of their relationship to explain, gently but firmly, to the CEO why it was time for him to move on. Instead, he made the wrong call. The Chairman disregarded one of the fundamental laws of Boardroom life: that, just as the Chairmanship and the Non-Executive team need refreshment at the right time, so too does the leadership in the shape of the CEO.

24. BUSINESS AND GOVERNMENT IN BRITAIN: THE DAMAGING DIVIDE

I have always believed that a close relationship between Business and Government is essential if a country is to achieve sustained economic growth for the benefit of its people. Unfortunately, the UK has not always achieved that relationship – in fact, it has been a hole in the heart of British industry for much of my working lifetime. As a result, this country has lacked the kind of informed, modern industrial policy which a wealth of other nations, both developed and developing, take for granted.

Nonetheless, I have consistently sought to improve the relationship when I have had the opportunity to do so – and in recent years, I have been fortunate to have been in several positions where I could try to influence the policy-makers' approach to industry.

Just prior to Gordon Brown's appointment as Prime Minister in 2007, he sounded me out about my willingness to come into government as a minister operating from the House of Lords. I had known Gordon a long time – I first met him in the 1990s when I was Chairman of Babcock and he was shadow Chancellor of the Exchequer and constituency MP for the Rosyth naval yard which we were operating for the Ministry of Defence.

I greatly respected Gordon and his integrity. However, I told him that with my range of commitments to a number of companies, I could not cut loose from them without serious disruption. Furthermore, I was not convinced that businessmen make great ministers in that they are not acquainted sufficiently with the ways of Whitehall and how to get things done.

The roles of Business and Government are so different. This was my honest assessment and I therefore had to say no. At the same time, I made it clear that I wanted to support him as Prime Minister and the country at what was a challenging time.

He had a concept for getting a team of businessmen together as an advisory group. This was at an early stage and he asked me about it: did I think top businessmen and women would respond to an invitation from a Labour PM? I said undoubtedly, yes they will. A number were like me – not linked to any Party but wanting to see the country, as well as their companies, successful. I was sure that they would respond to a personal invitation from the Prime Minister to serve in an advisory group – but I said he would need to ensure they were genuinely involved.

Gordon asked me to think about the idea further and to give my views on the mix of people we would need. This I did, both in terms of optimal structure and the range of company leaders that might be considered to provide a good cross-section. I had a discussion along these lines with Sir Gus O'Donnell, then the Cabinet Secretary, prior to the Business Council being formed.

It was a valuable forum but the Council got too big – which meant those who talk burned up too much oxygen around the Cabinet table where we met. Having said that, Gordon, as the Prime Minister, the Chancellor Alistair Darling, the Business Secretary Lord Mandelson and other ministers attended very regularly and big topics were indeed discussed, work commissioned and decisions made.

Because of my P&O/DP World experience with the London Gateway port, and other long approval delays for major projects at National Grid, during my time as a member of the Council I pursued the issue of expediting major infrastructure projects. We desperately needed to depoliticise and speed up the tortuous and

labyrinthine planning process because it had made the UK internationally uncompetitive.

Out of this was born in the dying days of the Brown administration an independent national planning commission that would
have been a one-stop-shop for inward or domestic investment for
major infrastructure that was judged to be in the national interest.
The PM's Council did useful work with input from the consultancy
McKinsey and National Grid, including looking around the world
at countries with the most effective infrastructure planning arrangements. We found that Singapore provided the best model and so we
recommended the establishment of a commission on similar lines.

The Government moved fast: a National Planning Commission,
to end the uncompetitive UK planning cycle times for infrastructure
critical to the national interest, was being set up prior to the 2010
general election. However, even as the post of CEO was being adver-
tised for the new commission, the 2010 general election was upon us.

Not for the first time, politics disrupted a much-needed industrial reform. The new Chancellor George Osborne considered the
Infrastructure Commission a quango – and Conservative Manifesto
policy was for a "bonfire of quangos". I had suggested to him at a
business lunch just before the 2010 election, that he should protect
the Commission and depoliticise major infrastructure planning, but
he insisted: "No, a Secretary of State must sign off major planning
approvals – and this Commission is a quango and has to go."

So the Commission was chopped – only to be resurrected five
years later at the start of the new Conservative administration after
the 2015 general election. Clearly, the Chancellor eventually realised that the politicisation of major planning decisions is not in the
interests of the country.

More important even than infrastructure policy was the country's
need for a modern industrial strategy. In this context, important
work was done, working with my colleagues at the Royal Academy
of Engineering, during my presidency from 2011 to 2014.

Royal Academy of Engineering

The Royal Academy (RAEng) was formed in 1977, and over the ensuing period it has become a leading light in Britain's industrial and economic life. It was established by a group of Britain's top engineers under the inspiring leadership of the Duke of Edinburgh who in 2017 remained our Senior Fellow.

I had very constructive dealings and many challenging conversations with the Duke when I was President of the RAEng. I would, on occasions, meet with him in his study at Buckingham Palace, along with our esteemed CEO on the Academy Philip Greenish, to discuss a range of special occasions at the Academy. Without his drive and enthusiasm, the Academy would not exist today as the influential forum for the country's top engineering professionals.

The Academy consists of 1,600 of the country's leading engineers across all engineering disciplines, with about 45% from academia and the balance from industry and consultancy. I was elected in 1983 as one of the youngest RAEng Fellows at that time.

It was a very humbling experience to be in the presence of the country's leading engineers, covering every discipline. In fact, I was in awe of the stature of the first four Presidents – Lord Hinton, Lord Caldecott (Former Chairman of Delta Metals) Sir Denis Rooke (Chairman and CEO of British Gas) and Sir William Barlow (Chairman Post Office, the electrical cable group BICC and other firms). It certainly never occurred to me on my election that one day I would be seen as worthy to become the President of such a distinguished Academy.

The aim of the RAEng from the outset was to establish a strong, unified voice for engineering across all disciplines. Prior to its creation the profession's voice was fragmented, given that we have institutions which do a great job within their specialist discipline: Chemical Engineers, Electrical, Mechanical and so on. Distinguished and valued though these institutions are, the fragmentation also meant division – there was no single entity to project the value and importance of engineering as a holistic profession in the nation's life at the highest level of Government.

This was particularly important for Britain, where – unlike almost any other major industrial country I can name – engineering has historically never been respected in the way that other professions, such as medical and legal, have been esteemed. It is a cliché, but unfortunately one which has more than a measure of truth, that to many British people an engineer is someone in blue overalls carrying a spanner. Since engineering is a crucial driver of national economic growth and prosperity, this preconception has undoubtedly disadvantaged the UK for many decades, if not centuries.

The Academy is therefore a body of unique expertise from which Government can take soundings and seek opinions on major engineering issues confronting the country, given that the Academy can coordinate inputs from the 35 different engineering institutions that exist in the UK today. Mergers between institutions are the hardest act to bring off, as I know very well – when I was President of the Royal Institution of Naval Architects in the 1990s, I tried (and failed) to merge it with the Institute of Marine Engineers. I believe that it would have strategically been the right thing to do for both sets of members, but resistance to such combinations often comes from the full-time administrators and managers, as it did on that occasion.

My tenure as President coincided with the start and early evolution of an absolutely critical debate about Britain's economic and industrial future, a debate triggered by the consequences of the 2008 financial crisis.

This was such a fundamental period – a time when industrial strategy moved from the fringes of political debate, where it had languished for more than 30 years, back to the centre where, I would argue, it belongs. Because of the Presidency, I found myself in a position with the Academy to play a formative role with a range of colleagues from academia and industry in establishing this change of emphasis.

During 2006 Lord (Alec) Broers then a very committed President of the RAEng invited me to lunch. I greatly admired Alex particularly for his leadership at Cambridge as Vice Chancellor and in the House of Lords for his advocacy of the importance of engineering and technology in society. He deployed his charming style on me that day by persuading me to take on the Chair of the Academy Development Board which was focussed on a major fundraising campaign which lasted four years, to raise the funding for our newly refurbished home – the "forum for engineering" in Carlton House Terrace, near Trafalgar Square. The many names of companies and individuals on the donation board in the building's foyer tells the full story of their generosity. One anonymous donor provided the foundation for the funding, and I must acknowledge the great generosity and passion for engineering shown by this industrial leader, along with those from many other companies, public and private, plus generous personal contributions.

We named our new building Prince Philip House, in honour of our Senior Fellow, at a very happy ceremony where the Duke of Edinburgh made a moving speech of his early involvement in establishing the Academy and we jointly unveiled a fine triptych portrait of himself. We were rather anxious about his reaction to this painting, but he did not seem disappointed!

The naming ceremony occurred following my election as President in 2011, following on from recent Past Presidents Sir David Davies (Vice Chancellor Loughborough), Lord Broers (former Vice Chancellor of Cambridge University), and Lord Browne (former CEO of BP). My three-year term was demanding, but very rewarding. Above all, it was a privilege to work and meet with so many exceptional people.

As RAEng President, I was an ex officio member of the Prime Minister's Committee of Science and Technology (CST) along with the Presidents of the three other major Academies: the British Academy (Lord Nicholas Stern), the Academy of Medical Sciences (Sir John Tooke) and the Royal Society (RS), whose president was Sir Paul Nurse.

I had a huge admiration for, and formed a continuing friendship with Sir Paul, the Nobel Prize-winning scientist. He is now the leader of the new Crick Research Institute – built by Laing O'Rourke – which he will establish as a world leader. He and I together ensured, with our respective CEOs, that a positive relationship existed between the RAEng and the RSoc. We shared many areas of fruitful cooperation on huge topics such as the safety of fracking in the UK.

The Committee of Science and Technology was led by Sir Mark Walport, the Government's Chief Scientist, who succeeded Sir John Beddington – both of them outstanding men. Many important issues are discussed there and the Royal Academy of Engineering is always in standby mode to provide independent engineering and technology advice. The Committee, for example, commissioned and subsequently requested our assistance on a report on data mining as a growth business stream and the potential for Britain to expand its role in this area. The working group involved was chaired by one of our very able Fellows, Dr Mike Lynch, who founded the software business Autonomy. In addition, the Academy did a considerable amount of independent research into security of the UK's energy supply, which I touch on later.

During my time as President, I also chaired the selection committee process for the new form of the Duke of Edinburgh Commonwealth Conference. It involved selecting 100 potential leaders from many walks of life from former or current Commonwealth countries. The first of the new-form Conference started with a reception at St James Palace in 2013 attended by the Duke of Edinburgh and HRH Princess Anne. The programme for the 100 chosen leaders visited corporates and Government departments in England, South Africa and Mumbai. It was a huge and unique development opportunity for all those who were selected to attend.

With all these different activities, I certainly was not short of duties as President. But my colleagues and I had no doubt that our greatest responsibility was to play the most influential role that we could in shaping the revitalised debate about engineering, industry and a 21st century industrial strategy.

The problem of decline in engineering and industry

To appreciate the full significance of this sea-change in political attitudes, I need to take you back to the 1970s when the seeds of the very damaging marginalisation of British engineering and industry were sown. UK industry had a bad time and a bad press in that decade, and by the end of it, industry was widely seen as poorly-managed, bloated, uncompetitive, driven by industrial disputes and in need of significant reform.

There were, of course, many exceptions but the perception was in large part true. UK industry had also suffered from political interference and the wrong sort of political intervention. Not surprisingly therefore, the free market revolution of the 1980s was accompanied by a strategic shift from manufacturing and extractive industries – which were widely, but misguidedly, viewed as "sunset" sectors – towards a thrusting new, "sunrise" services sector, largely focussed on financial services and later the dotcom bubble.

Over the next three decades of growth in the UK, the very notion of industrial policy seemed like a relic of a different age. It carried connotations of the political intervention that had propped up ailing state-owned companies, or so-called "national champions". Beyond that, there was serious talk that the UK had in fact become a post-industrial or "knowledge" economy – as if there was no knowledge in engineering or industrial activity.

The 2008 financial crisis, which I witnessed at such close hand through my role at the Bank of England, triggered a rethink by many people in influential and decision-making positions about the composition of Britain's economy. There was a growing realisation that over the quarter-century prior to the crisis, we had become overly dependent on the financial services industry for growth while neglecting our engineering and manufacturing industries and the services they generate Furthermore the contribution to the economy from the North Sea oil and gas bonanza had peaked and was in decline. There was now a growing debate about the need to "re-balance" the economy by growing the non-financial sectors.

For the first time in decades, parties of every political hue now committed themselves to a sustainable recovery based more on production and less on consumption, and on engineered products and services fuelled by the strong science and engineering base in our universities.

The re-balancing challenge was exacerbated by the economic situation at the time I became President. Britain was still in the grip of recession, because of the Eurozone crisis that had erupted in 2010. The financial services sector remained on its knees, as it had been since the 2008 meltdown. Construction and manufacturing were also in the doldrums.

As an Academy, we knew that there was still excellent engineering going on in companies around the UK, along with continuing outstanding innovation in our universities. But while many people expressed the will to revive UK industry, after 25 years of detachment from the key issues, few policy-makers and opinion-formers were well versed in the ways to do it. Moreover, no-one went so far as to advocate a modern industrial strategy to lock in a long-term policy framework which could build a new industrial future for the UK. There was a clear danger that, in the absence of such a strategy, well-meaning but uncoordinated initiatives to boost industry could have negligible or even negative effects in the longer term.

I felt strongly not only that what the UK needed was a modern industrial strategy to provide a vision for where we should be heading – focussing on key sectors with leading technology and capacity for growth – but that the Academy should make the promotion of this vision its top influencing priority. We knew that, in some quarters, this would be a very unpopular proposition. We also recognised that some very influential people would deride our proposal as a throwback to the bad old days of Government trying to "pick winners".

But I also knew that, even if we were a lone voice in the wilderness, the Academy had a duty to press the case home. We took the decision to communicate our vision boldly and broadly. At first we were ignored, even criticised as politically naïve and backward-looking. But we demonstrated one of the critical attributes of leadership: resilience. We worked at promoting our case, persistently articulating the vision of what a modern industrial strategy should look like and what it could achieve for UK plc.

To raise public consciousness, both of the need for an industrial strategy and of the Academy's authority in promoting it, I gave a series of national media interviews during 2012 in which I set out what we thought was an appropriate policy framework. This kind of advocacy was an area where the Academy could be immensely powerful, so long as it chose its areas of influence carefully and spoke from a clearly communicated position of strength. By pointing to the expertise of our leading members in academia and industry, as well as my own wide-ranging industrial experience, we were able to establish ourselves early on in the forefront of the debate.

We were careful not to fall into the traps of the past by being overly specific and prescriptive – so we made it clearly understood that we were talking about industry in its broadest sense, from research through manufacturing to services.

It was helpful that the concept of a modern industrial strategy did not have a natural home in government, because this meant we had free rein to define afresh what an industrial strategy could be – rather than having to work within an existing framework.

A first principle was, and remains, that we need increasingly to live off our intellectual horse power. For me, industrial activity embraces research, applied science, design and innovation in product and systems, design of new services in computing, international consultancy. The design of new, advanced and lean manufacturing plants and the support services that flow from this range of industrial activity.

We also had to win recognition that the concept of industrial strategy needs to be nourished both across changes in Government, and through continuing dialogue within the Sectors between companies, universities and relevant Government departments that can influence and align policy.

That is evident in Germany, Europe's most successful industrial nation. I understand that Angela Merkel was once asked about the German Government's industrial policy – "I expect my ministers and the Administration to tilt policy in favour of industrial activity," she said immediately.

It was interesting to talk with Lord Mandelson, the former Business Secretary in the latter years of the Labour government of 2005-2010, on the issue of Government involvement within the industrial framework. He had returned from his stint as a European Commissioner and clearly saw how industrial policy was done in Europe, and in particular how German industrial supremacy was the bedrock of their European success. He introduced "industrial activism". I fully supported his efforts and in his call "for engineering – not financial engineering!"

We had to bring everyone – decision-takers, policy-makers, opinion-formers – along with us. All these concerned parties – politicians, officials, representative bodies like the Confederation of British Industry, and the UK media – were having to re-orientate themselves after all the years of focussing on services. We achieved our aim through valuable workshops with a group of creative and knowledgeable Fellows drawn from industry, leaders spun out of successful companies and academia.

Specifically, in late 2012 under the Academy's aegis, I chaired a round table of senior engineers and business people including the 'very experienced' plc Chairman Sir Roger Carr, then President of the Confederation of British Industry, and other CBI representatives who with the Academy staff collated our views on a modern industrial strategy. We also fed them into the review of Britain's industrial capacity and competitiveness that the Prime Minister had set up and which was led by Lord Heseltine, the former President of the Board of Trade (head of the Department for Business) in John Major's 1992-7 Conservative Government. Lord Heseltine responded by discussing the issues with a group of our Fellows. His report, entitled 'No Stone Unturned in Pursuit of Growth, laid down important principles and action points for Government policy.

As a result of these consultations, we defined what we thought were the six key elements of a successful modern industrial policy:

- clear signals from the top of government that industrial activity was critical to the future of the economy – this we believed was also important to young people contemplating their career choices;
- research and innovation to support new ideas;
- recognition of the importance of large companies: we envisaged that the UK's big flagship companies, the sector champions, would act as traction engines to pull through all the pillars of competitiveness they needed while bringing, in their train, an empowered supply chain of Small and Medium-Sized Enterprises (SMEs);
- the need to grow new companies, including in emerging sectors;
- stability and alignment of policy across government departments;
- a robust skills base: Academy research revealed that Britain needed an extra 40,000 graduates a year in science, engineering, technology and maths just to replenish its skills base, let alone to build future industries.

In the corporate world, strategy is pretty straightforward – at its simplest, it provides coherent signals from the boardroom for the alignment of the technical and commercial direction of the business. You then gear up your organisation to pull through the right leadership, skills, optimal financing, the R&D required and the other critical components of the business plan.

What we were advocating was simply an application of those core principles to the business of government and its role in formulating a modern industrial strategy. In practice, this meant identifying the areas likely to drive the UK economy in 25 years' time – choosing sectors, not particular companies.

Nothing could be taken for granted over these timescales, but it seemed sensible to look at sectors in growth markets with high technology export prospects, globally competitive UK companies and robust supply chains, and then say that these are likely to be future core strengths. Once the priority areas were identified, this would create a pull for other inputs into growth – from R&D programmes to skills training initiatives. It would also provide a long-term context within which difficult political decisions around the future of individual companies or industrial sectors could be framed.

It was a proposition whose time had come. Gradually, the strength of the proposition revealed itself and began to gain traction. The policy mantra has shifted radically from "the UK should not be picking winners" to a sensible recognition that, to compete internationally, we must work with the grain of our industrial strengths and harness companies, academia and Government in the essential conversations.

Happily, our initiatives met a positive response from the Conservative-Liberal Democrat administration and from a highly-competent Business Department Permanent Secretary in Sir Martin Donnelly. The most important industrial sectors were identified, reflecting where the UK was already strong and where there were excellent future growth prospects in advanced technology businesses. These included:

- Aerospace and Aero Engineering
- Construction
- Automobile
- Pharmaceutical
- Other.

One vital element was to ensure that departments across Government had aligned policies in support of such a strategy to ensure, inter alia:

- education and training policy which meets future skill needs;
- stable tax policies and incentives that encourage long-term investment;
- the Bank of England's low interest rate policy. Inflation-targeting enhances inward investment.

The Coalition strategy paved the way for real progress and important dialogue between industry, academia and Government. Such a strategic framework also brought about important policy alignment across Government departments. The key point was the sectoral approach and Vince Cable, the Liberal Democrat who was Secretary of State for Business, deserves congratulations for having taken this on board – as of course does the Government as a whole.

Alongside the sectoral strategies, the Government also announced a near-£6 billion investment over five years in science capital, to be deployed in areas of strategic value to the UK. It also created a network of national "Catapult" centres focussed on different sectors and located in different parts of the country to act as an interface between academia, industry and Government.

The national strategy we advocated could not just focus on core industries, important as those were and continue to be. It also had to map out the development of the critical enabling technologies that provide the edge in a host of known, and as yet unknown, applications including emerging sectors.

This is not easy and the UK Government – as would any government – found it more challenging to identify, let alone create a dialogue with, these newer sectors and those that were less well structured. Building new industries from emerging technologies requires a different set of values from dealing with established growth sectors: flexibility, responsiveness and the ability to seize unpredictable and unpredicted opportunities where they present themselves.

The UK addressed this challenge by developing a number of bottom-up initiatives to build up strength in emerging technologies which complemented and enhanced the top-down industrial strategy. The then-Science Minister, David Willetts, focussed on "eight great technologies" that are seen as key areas for future development:

- big data and energy-efficient computing;
- space;
- robotics and autonomous systems;

- synthetic biology;
- regenerative medicine;
- agri-science;
- advanced materials and nanotechnology;
- energy and its storage.

Quantum technologies were later added to this list. Interestingly, I presented this list at a huge International Engineering Symposium hosted by the Chinese Academy of Engineering and involving the American and Royal Academies of Engineering and it overlapped closely with the seven strategic emerging industries identified in China's 12th Five-Year Plan.

The commitment of the Chinese President to Industrial Research and activity was well underlined as this event came to an end, by his giving the final address to the conference in the Great Hall of the People. However, prior to that speech, he invited each of the international speakers to meet with him in an anteroom, greeting us personally. He spoke via an interpreter about the importance of engineering and technology to China's future. At the end of this conversation, he explained that both he and his deputy were graduates in Chemical Engineering but, "… we subsequently went wrong and went into politics!"

In my own continuing discussions with the UK Government and the media, I constantly focussed on promoting the modern industry strategy, including the need for infrastructure renewal accompanied by the one-stop shop and a National Planning Commission independent of political sign-off.

Not everything went smoothly. Gordon Brown's National Planning Commission got caught up in the unintended consequences of the new Coalition Government's "bonfire of the quangos". Like many such broad-brush policies of newly-elected governments, this one swept the baby out with the bathwater: the new Government axed the Commission.

Some quangos are very necessary in order to put distance between the issues, the politicians and their constituents. And there are some projects critical to the nation's competitiveness that should not be politicised: key infrastructure is one of them. At least an infrastructure central body in the Treasury survived to take a holistic view to which the Royal Academy of Engineering provides key input.

Partly overlapping with infrastructure, energy policy was another critical issue facing the new Government. The RAEng contributed significantly to the debate about how to renew Britain's energy infrastructure to reconcile the conflicting imperatives of climate control policy, security of supply and affordability. We published a succession of independent reports, including one on Shale Gas Operations (in conjunction with the Royal Society with whom the Academy has a growing and important relationship). Other wide-ranging RAEng studies on this crucial subject focussed on security of energy supply, offshore wind energy and Britain's engineering skills needs. These were either specifically requested by, or formed the basis of debate with the Government of the day.

Our work to promote engineers and engineering took several different forms. We established an Enterprise Hub which involves about 100 of our experienced Fellows in devoting at least one day a month to free mentoring and providing advice to young engineers, entrepreneurs and start-up teams. They provide technical expertise, advise on business planning, point the way to funding resources and dispense general business advice.

Alongside all this work by the RAEng, I saw it as an important part of my personal role to communicate through media interviews, public speeches and other events the importance of engineering in society. Britain lost sight of that for far too long.

To accelerate the process of re-establishing the importance of engineering in the public mind, we needed an initiative to act as both catalyst and symbol. Government got behind the process with Lord Browne and, as a result, in 2013 the Queen Elizabeth Prize for Engineering was introduced. This is a £1 million biennial global prize which is funded entirely by the private sector. It is awarded to between one and five engineers who have developed a breakthrough which benefits all of humanity. Engineering is a global, not a parochial discipline.

At the first announcement of the Prize, the Prime Minister David Cameron, the leader of the Labour Party Ed Milliband and the Deputy Prime Minister Nick Clegg all appeared at London's Science Museum. The Prize programme is managed by the Academy and its first Director was the talented Anji Hunter, who worked with us at Anglo American from where I enticed her to take on the role at the RAEng. She also had the advantage of having worked at BP with Lord Browne, who has done a sterling job as Chairman of the QE Prize Trust.

I accompanied HRH Princess Anne when she announced the Prize winners at the Academy. Following the Prize announcement, there is a ceremony and reception at Buckingham Palace hosted by HM The Queen. The first of these was an event that will long live in the memory as Lord Browne accompanied Her Majesty in presenting the first QE Prize in Engineering.

Sir William Wakeham played an important role in promoting the QE Prize across the world, and I was delighted that he was elected as RAEng Senior Vice President and my Deputy. He is a hardworking and wise councillor who has contributed much to the Academy, to academia and to research. He carried out a very important and far-reaching review of the Academy's governance.

I want to acknowledge the enormous support for the Academy from the Duke of Edinburgh and, in my period as President, the outstanding contribution from HRH Princess Anne to the development of science and engineering. Underpinning all our efforts, the team at the Academy led by our CEO Philip Greenish, was of a very high calibre with an outstanding work rate. It is very gratifying that an internal successor to Philip, who retired at the end of 2017, is Dr Hayaatun Sillem, a very competent and talented lady who has a great deal of experience dealing with Government. There is a long way to go, but the Academy has made great strides considering that we started so far behind our international peers.

We also tried to ensure that Government ministers understood the need to have joined-up, cross-departmental policies in support of a modern industrial strategy. Lack of such synchronisation has been a fundamental flaw in our approach to industry for many decades, following on from the conscious disregard for such a strategy. Not only does a well-articulated strategy pull in other investments and inputs, it also has a secondary, and more wide-ranging policy effect because it forces Government to understand the broader impacts of its own policy as a system.

Each new policy potentially has an impact elsewhere. Having an industrial strategy in place compels Government to understand and stress-test all likely consequences of policy decisions, including unintended ones, from all departments. This is a familiar concept to the engineering community, where systems-thinking is a core competency. But it is more of a challenge for policy-makers.

A classic case in point relates to the mass conversion of polytechnics to universities in the 1990s. Polytechnics used to provide a quality education, preparing people for work and, importantly, producing skilled technicians. In doing so, they served the UK's industrial base, and our young people, very well. It is true that, over the last 25 years, many polytechnics have become fine universities – but, over the same period, that critical mass of professional, technician and vocational learning has been lost. Another, more recent example of new policy producing unforeseen consequences is the impact of new visa restrictions on talented people who want to study, undertake research and work in the UK.

Embedding a joined-up approach in the UK political system is not an overnight job. In many other nations, not only Germany, policy is tilted in favour of the industrial base. They cherish and nurture their flagship sectors, and that produces a real competitive advantage. Historically, the UK has not started from this point and now it has to re-orientate fundamentally. We simply cannot afford to put ourselves at a disadvantage in the increasingly global marketplace.

We face other major challenges too. While UK Government is doing much more to embed engineering expertise in its decision-making process, including through a network of Chief Scientific Advisers in each Whitehall department, the lack of engineering and technology skills among UK politicians remains a real concern.

This Westminster knowledge gap reflects a national shortfall in high-level engineering skills which poses the biggest single threat to our country's future competitiveness, growth and prosperity.

Such high-level Government backing for a modern industrial strategy sends a message to society and particularly to families: it says that industrial activity in all its forms is important and provides a rewarding career choice for our young people.

We badly need such signals if we are to make up the ground we have lost over the past decades. One manifestation of how we are running behind is our chronic shortage of engineers. This is a Europe-wide problem – in 2016-17, Airbus was probably short of 2,000-3,000 professional engineers – but it is most acute in the UK. Just consider how much emphasis the newly developed giants such as China and India place on technology and engineering. This is something I saw at first hand when, during my RAE presidency, I was invited to visit Beijing and talk with many of China's leading politicians, business people and academics. They took for granted the paramount importance of technological skills in driving growth.

Building a modern skills base

In 2017, the UK engineering sector employed more than 5.7 million people, but at least 1.28 million new professionals and technicians will be needed by 2020 to work in the science, tech and engineering sectors. According to analysis carried out by the Academy, the UK needs an extra 40,000 graduates a year in the STEM subjects – Science, Technology, Engineering and Maths – just to replenish the current skills base, let alone build future industries.

We have to work from the grassroots up to promote STEM subjects, and the engineering profession and industry are running many good schemes to inspire and engage young people both in and outside their schools.

But I fear that all the work is not delivering at the pace and scale we need to enable future growth. Some very serious voices across the UK engineering industry are telling us that the lack of skills is already a brake on their business.

There are some structural issues that we must address. Across the different UK administrations, around 40% of students do not achieve the necessary maths grades to progress with subjects that lead to engineering. Beyond the compulsory education age of 16, the number of students choosing qualifications that lead to careers in engineering plummets. The reasons for this are many and complex, including poor perceptions and attitudes towards engineering, the perceived difficulty of the subjects needed for engineering, the lack of specialist teachers, particularly in physics, and the pressures of school performance tables.

During my presidency and that of my successor, Dame Ann Dowling, Head of Engineering at Cambridge University, the Academy has worked with partners across the profession to address critical issues around the curriculum and other aspects of education and skills policy. We have built a real profile on these critical matters and I must thank Professor Helen Atkinson, past president of the Engineering Professors' Council, for so successfully leading and chairing the important work of our education and training committee.

This work will be increasingly vital if the UK's industrial strategy is to be successful, because we will need to raise our game across the gamut of engineering developments.

At apprentice level, we must make a much bigger push for high-quality apprenticeships and other vocational pathways to engineering careers. As a former student apprentice naval architect, I know the benefits that flexible, comprehensive apprenticeships bring, and to enable shop-floor apprentices with the aptitude to progress through to university – all essential to increase the supply of engineering technicians and graduates.

The figures for engineering higher education are also a cause for concern. The number of UK-domiciled students who achieved engineering and technology degrees has virtually remained static over the last 11 years, from 12,900 students in 2004 to 13,775 in 2014.

The changes to student fees have not helped with the provision of expensive-to-teach courses such as engineering: the pre-92 universities' courses are oversubscribed but we know that the post-92 universities are finding it hard to make a business case for expansion of engineering places. So, if the situation remains unchanged, even if we succeed in attracting more young people into an engineering career, there will not be the university places to teach them. Only Government can fix this problem, but the profession and industry must be vocal in making the case.

Financial pressures on degree course provision are being further increased by the fact that many engineering MSc courses are entirely dependent on non-EU international students for their continued existence – yet the current mood music around immigration and the loss of the opportunity to undertake two years' post-study work in the UK means that some, especially from the Indian sub-continent, are staying away.

Another even more fundamental concern lies in the number of doctoral engineering students available to UK industry. In 2016/17, UK-domiciled students obtained only 53% of engineering doctorates in Britain: this amounts to a real shortfall for the industry in this country.

Do we need to import high-quality science, engineering and technology people from abroad in order to plug our skills hole? The question raises complex issues which have been made even harder by Britain's 2016 Referendum decision to leave the European Union. The fact is that migrant engineering workers are needed in the short term, but it is equally important that we act now to increase the size of the home-grown skilled science, technology and engineering workforce.

Part of the solution is to increase diversity in engineering – on 2016 figures, only nine per cent of the professional engineering workforce were women, the lowest percentage in the EU. And although ethnic minorities made up almost a quarter of first degree qualifiers, according to the most recent Labour Force Survey, they comprise only six per cent of those working in engineering.

The Academy, together with the Royal Society, continues to lead a major drive to promote diversity across the engineering and science professions, including through the identification and promotion of role models to fire the enthusiasm of younger people. The lack of senior female and ethnic minority executives means that this is a long-term effort, but it is absolutely crucial for the UK's future success.

Innovation poses a huge challenge. We have strong academic research in the UK, but translating it into successful innovation does not happen automatically. On a European basis, our innovation performance is only average – we lag behind Germany, Denmark, Finland and Sweden. There is a pressing need to address this problem.

Innovation comes from creative interactions between science, engineering and business. That requires communication between academia, businesses and Government so that each can contribute to the process; access to finance, because there needs to be better ways for the public sector to fill the gap where it is not possible to attract private sector investment in early-stage ventures; and scale –: we need a critical mass of companies in order to compete in a particular sector.

It is critically important for an industrial strategy to have success in the long term that it must not flounder on the election of a new Government. Unfortunately, this approach appeared to stumble on the election of the new Conservative Government in 2015, when Sajid Javid became Business, Innovation and Skills Secretary and was more lukewarm than his predecessor to the concept of industrial strategy. It was therefore truly encouraging to see BIS renamed Business, Energy and Industrial Strategy by our new Prime Minister Theresa May in 2016. Considering the political and media opposition and scepticism at the time we set up our round table debate at the RAE in 2012, I never dreamed that within five years, a Government department would actually embrace the words 'industrial strategy'!

The Government's conduct of the Brexit negotiations is a different matter. I was not impressed by the post-2017 General Election lack of Cabinet alignment in dealing with the most critical issue to face our country since World War II.

Alignment on the priority drivers for the health of our economy and jobs for our communities should have dominated our approach. Instead, the Cabinet debate had all the negative characteristics which permeated the rhetoric in the vote to leave.

This was often driven by personal political ambitions, laced with untruths and sugar-coated statements about the future that had no connectivity with reality – well illustrated by the lies on the 'Red Bus'. The vote of Yes or No for remaining in Europe was flawed. The majority of voters did not have a clue as to the complexity of the issues surrounding withdrawal that have emerged and, as a result, they did not know the risks to jobs, careers or their children's future by the upheaval of withdrawing from the largest single market in the world. It will take years to negotiate new trade deals to substitute for this loss.

Let us hope for no more imperfect referenda. It is worth noting that in corporate life, if an issue to vote on could radically change the nature of the company – for example, a large acquisition or a split-up of the Group – then a 75% voting majority by shareholders is necessary to carry the day. The 50% threshold of the EU referendum was yet an additional flaw in a very imperfect mechanism on such a major issue of change for our country.

Most businessmen who have negotiated for major export business around the world over the years were flabbergasted by the amateur approach by a number of ministers, airing their negotiating positions in public. Keep your powder dry, get your target objectives in priority order, sort out what will be good for the country's economic well-being rather than rigid doctrines of right or left, or hard or soft. Collective Cabinet alignment should take precedence over personal political positioning, and there has to be a degree of flexibility by definition in negotiation, and always a backstop plan if you cannot achieve your target objectives.

Outcomes

As a businessman who has done business for some 50 years around the world, and bought and sold companies from and to various geographic locations, I am enthusiastic about what's commercially good for our country.

I am enthusiastically supportive of British companies having:

- the freedom of movement of highly-skilled personnel and experienced professionals around the world. Take professional engineers as an example: given the age profile of Britain's engineers and the increasing demand for their skills, our universities cannot satisfy the requirement;
- the freedom to trade across borders with minimum or no tariffs;
- The freedom for UK companies to buy and sell businesses in the international market, across borders, without artificial barriers.

Protectionism diminishes international trade growth and, as such, impacts on the health and growth prospects of our companies. About 75% of the sales in FTSE 100 companies is generated overseas. The value of strong companies in our economy and the importance of our ability to attract foreign inward investment to fuel growth does not appear to be well understood in our society or amongst many of our MPs. Many of our large companies – both private and quoted – are like massive economic traction engines towing long supply chains of Small and Medium-Sized Enterprises (SMEs).

The UK private sector employs some 27 million people, and accounts for 83% of employee average weekly earnings. By contrast, the public sector employs 5.5 million. In 2017/18, the UK's private sector businesses contributed 27% of all taxes collected by HM Treasury. This amounted to £186 billion, almost the same amount as that deployed on Health and Education spending combined. In addition, the tax and National Insurance contribution by private sector employees was a further £208 billion. Thus, the total of business and private sector employee tax receipts of £394 billion was equivalent to about 57% of the Treasury's annual total tax take. Without these contributions, we could not sustain our Health Service, build and expand our schools and universities, or provide national defence and homeland security.

Such economic well-being could not be taken for granted if we were not generating profitable prosperity – the alternative is the economy of Venezuela and the hardship that has brought to its citizens.

Government has the responsibility to develop over-arching strategic composites to ensure economic well-being beyond narrow party, department or personal agendas. I fear this is what has been lost by our political parties in the wake of the Brexit referendum, and its neglect will cost us dearly.

25. IN CONCLUSION: ENGINEERING AND LEADERSHIP

The Duke of Edinburgh, interviewed by Lord Browne on BBC Radio in 2016 at the age of 95, was asked about the importance of engineering. He declared: "Everything that wasn't invented by God was invented by an engineer."

Engineering is ubiquitous – so much so that society takes it for granted. Engineers are problem-solvers; we are creative, we are analysts, we are innovative, we are designers, we are not publicity-seekers – but, in certain circumstances we need to deploy a higher profile in promoting the value of engineering to society.

I look back with a degree of wonderment at all the great experiences and opportunities that have opened up during my industrial journey. As a younger engineer, I could not have dreamed that this would happen. My life has been enriched, not only by all the challenges – some of them fairly daunting at the time – but by the great people I've worked with, known and learned from over the years. I'm also glad to say that I'm still learning!

On 15 November 2016, I had the opportunity to review my engineering journey in the illustrious surroundings of Trinity College, Dublin. I had been invited (by the Provist Professor Patrick Prendergast) to address the School of Engineering on its 175th Anniversary – it was formally opened on 15 November, 1841 – 175 years ago on that day!

It was a great honour to stand in the place of Professor Henry Lloyd, who had primary responsibility for establishing the School at the culmination of the Industrial Revolution. His inaugural address communicated views and values which I share, and which are as relevant today as they were that day in November 1841. He told his students: "The profession which you have adopted, whose duties were not long since limited to the constructions and care of engines, has now risen to take its rank among the first of the liberal professions.

"In a country like ours, where public works of such magnitude are ever in progress, the interests committed to its keeping are numerous and weighty; and the knowledge demanded of it proportionally varied and extensive. It is your part, then, to try to profit by the opportunities thrown open to you … The path which is to conduct you to the goal of your profession is an interesting and attractive one; and the career which afterwards expands before you is one in which you may serve your country nobly, and earn for yourselves an honourable independence, and an honourable fame."

As I said – very relevant today, when we as a country are rediscovering the importance of engineering to our society and our economy. In only one respect do I find Professor Lloyd somewhat at odds with prevailing sentiment in Britain today: it is probably not the case that engineering stands among the first of the liberal professions. That is partly due to the prevailing neglect of engineering in the 25-30 years before the 2008 financial crisis, and partly to the fact that we as a profession often fail to ignite the beacon of excitement about engineering that deserves to burn much brighter in society, and which should burn particularly bright for our young people. When we do so – and that effort is now under way – engineering will recapture the high standing that it enjoyed when Professor Lloyd was speaking.

I would underscore that the opportunities now thrown open to young engineers have never been more exciting – not even in 1841 – and their "potential to expand before you" is very real today. Just take a glimpse at the advances in modern surgery enabled by the close research collaboration between surgeons and engineers on: robotic surgery; stent design; intelligent artificial legs; tools and equipment to avoid major surgical impact et cetera.

I could mention the transformation of productivity taking place in many industrial sectors through the application of digital engineering. It has had a huge impact on product development timescales and cycle times in manufacturing and modern construction businesses. We are in the foothills of the transformation potential that these digital approaches can deliver. So many other sectors and new developments await the young engineer as I am certain it will be filled with new excitement and unknown opportunities for your career path.

My own career certainly bears out Professor Lloyd's words. To take one specific example – when as a student naval architect in 1961 at H&W I mentioned earlier that I was given a modest role in charge of the Deck Covering Plan for SS *Canberra*, I would never have expected, in my wildest dreams, that more than 40 years later I would be appointed chairman of Canberra's owner, P&O.

On a larger and broader scale, I could never have conceived that my training and qualification as an engineer would eventually take me on a journey to industrial leadership. The application of the engineering sciences has been the life-blood of all the companies in which I have served. Except for the Bank of England, I have never joined a Board where engineering was not within that company's heartland.

For me, it was a natural progression, born out of the disciplines I learned as an engineer – both technical and, more importantly still, those related to working with and managing people. Ultimately, while technology is of course vital, it is great human talent that makes great companies. A successful industrial leader must always remember and recognise that.

I regard it as a great honour and a privilege to be chosen to lead – to lead teams, departments, companies, voluntary organisations; to develop them and to get the best out of them. It took me some time on my journey to appreciate fully the extent to which you, the leader, can really influence and shape the future. No leader should ever under-estimate the power he or she has to change things for the better, and always leave things better than you found them.

Young people, "Take the journey." I would happily do it again.

ACKNOWLEDGMENTS

To all those great people who have been with me and supported me on different stages of the journey.

I acknowledge them all with gratitude.

I also want to record my appreciation to Andrew Lorenz who brought his professional skills as a former Business Editor to bear and ultimately encouraged me to publish.

My thanks also to the highly collaborative way in which the publishing team at Endeavour Media worked with us.

INDEX